Readings in Latin American History
Volume II: Since 1810

Readings in
Latin American History

Volume II: Since 1810

Selected Articles from the
Hispanic American Historical Review

EDITED BY

LEWIS HANKE

THOMAS Y. CROWELL COMPANY
Established 1834 New York

Dedicated
to
the authors, editors, proofreaders, and
secretaries whose labors prepare
The Hispanic American Historical Review
and to
the enlightened institution
that makes its publication possible
Duke University Press

PREFACE

This two-volume anthology consists of selected articles from the *Hispanic American Historical Review* which, by their lively scholarship and range of subject matter, are intended to attract the interest of students, primarily undergraduates, taking general courses on Latin America with the Columbus-to-Castro sweep.

Every anthologist, including this one, learns to accept the inevitable fact that, to keep his collection of reasonable size he must omit many valuable pieces which he would like to include. In order to convey something of the quality, flavor, and variety of the *HAHR*, I have chosen for each volume articles which, throughout the nearly fifty years of the *Review*, have made permanent contributions on significant topics, sometimes embodying new approaches to the study of Latin American history, and in general representing a balance between the work of veteran historians and younger scholars in the field. The text of each article appears in its entirety, minus the footnotes but with a brief introductory note to identify the author and to suggest the relation of his article to the relevant literature on the topic he treats.

The *HAHR* itself has not been used intensively by undergraduates, partly because librarians naturally cherish professional journals and attempt to protect them from damage or loss. Thus there is need for an easily accessible anthology which will bring students face to face with some of the valuable material the *Review* has published. At the end of most of the selections a list is given of other relevant articles, at times with descriptive notes that have been taken, with the permission of Duke University Press, from the two guides to the *Review*. In this way readers of this anthology will have access to a considerable part of the total contents of the *Review*. In addition, at the end of each volume a list appears of a number of important bibliographical articles published in recent numbers of the *Review*, which will be especially useful to students preparing term papers or special reports.

Many persons and institutions have built and sustained the *Review*, fulfilling President Woodrow Wilson's hope, expressed in his letter printed in the first issue, that the new *Review* would lead "to very important results both for scholarship and for the increase of cordial feeling throughout the Americas." One institution, Duke University, deserves special mention, because it assumed in 1926 the responsibility for publication of the *Review* by the Duke University Press. This generous support has enabled the *HAHR* to survive financially. Its quality, however, depends and will continue to depend upon its editors and its contributors. One may with reason hope that some of these will surely be found in the future among readers of this anthology.

The introductory notes for the individual articles were prepared in Santiago, Chile, where I was able to use the excellent collection of the *Review* in the Sociedad Chilena de Historia y Geografía, thanks to the kindness of my long-time colleague Dr. Ricardo Donoso, whose valuable aid is hereby gratefully acknowledged.

LEWIS HANKE

New York City
February, 1966

CONTENTS

CHAPTER FOUR

SPANISH SOUTH AMERICA

CHAPTER FIVE

BRAZIL

REVOLUTIONARY PERIOD

1. Economic and Social Aspects
of the Era of Spanish-American Independence

CHARLES C. GRIFFIN

The shadow of the "Great Liberator" Simón Bolívar and the heroic interpretation of the wars for Spanish American independence long dominated historians who wrote on the turbulent period 1810–1826. Professor Griffin of Vassar College, a veteran in the field and former managing editor of the *HAHR*, breaks with this tradition in the present article and provides ideas and information on which he bases the story of the basic changes in society during the wars of independence from Spain.

The revolutions which brought about the establishment of independent governments in America differed in marked degree from the classic revolutions of modern Europe—the French and the Russian—in that their primary effect was to throw off the authority of a transatlantic empire rather than to bring about a drastic reconstruction of society. In the case of the United States, however, it has long been recognized that the revolutionary struggle did not confine itself to the political sphere, i.e., to independence and the establishment of a new federal government. Almost a generation ago the late J. Franklin Jameson published his essays on *The American Revolution Considered as a Social Movement* in which he suggested relations between the revolution and the manifold changes of the era, some already recognized, and others destined to be more fully charted by a subsequent generation of scholars. Because many of these changes were not the result of conscious revolutionary planning, but came about under the stimulus of new conditions created during and after the revolution, they had not earlier been sufficiently closely related to the revolution and to each other.

It is possible that the time may be ripe for a similar shift in emphasis in the interpretation of the revolutions for independence in Spanish America. It was natural that these movements, as starting points for new national traditions, should have been regarded at first as epic conflicts. Heroism and leadership were the main themes. When this was not enough, diplo-

From Volume XXIX (1949), pages 170–187.

matic and constitutional history were emphasized, in consonance with the popularity of such studies in nineteenth-century European historiography. Interest in political change led eventually to the study of political theories in relation to the revolutions and hence to the broader field of the history of thought. On the one hand, the background of the revolutions has been clarified by studies of the impact of the Enlightenment on Latin America; on the other, changes closely related to the triumph of new ideologies have been charted. Of these, the new status of church-state relations and the abolition of slavery can be mentioned as examples. Until fairly recently, however, the study of economic and social history has been directed primarily to the antecedents of the revolutions rather than to the developments of the era itself.

There is, however, a large body of literature dealing with the socio-economic history of the revolutionary period proper. With minor exceptions, however, it is scattered through works on local history, sociological treatises, and books dealing with particular aspects of the history of individual countries. Except for travelers' accounts, the sources for such study have not as yet been classified, calendared, and made easily available. The use of such materials is laborious and general interpretation of the revolutionary era has been only slightly affected by their exploitation. Since 1935, we have had a general guide to the current historiography of Latin America in the *Handbook of Latin American Studies*. A survey of the sections of this bibliography which relate to the period of the movement for independence indicates the fragmentary character of material published on social and economic aspects of the era. A number of articles and books have appeared on the commerce of various regions, but publications on other economic themes have been scant. In the aggregate, less than a dozen titles can be cited which deal with agriculture, industry, finance, and labor for this period, though a larger number touch incidentally on these topics. Somewhat more attention has been given to cultural subjects such as journalism, education, and religion.

It may be worth while to mention, briefly, a few of the recent contributions which provide new social and economic interpretations. Rodolfo Puiggros, for Argentina, and Carlos Irazábal, for Venezuela, have studied the independence movement from a Marxist viewpoint, and have provided food for thought, even for those who may reject their general premises. More recently, an objective economic analysis of developments in Argentina has been presented in Miron Burgin's *Economic Aspects of Argentine Federalism, 1820–1852*. Though this study centers its attention on the era dominated by Rosas, its early chapters provide a clearer view of the economics of the revolution in Argentina than any previously written. Cline's work on Yucatan in the early nineteenth century, though as yet only partly published, throws a searching light on problems of regional economy.

Stimulating interpretations of social aspects of the independence movement come from the pen of the noted Aprista writer, Luis Alberto Sánchez and from that of Rufino Blanco Fombona, the celebrated Venezuelan man of letters. Both contribute to a better understanding of the part played by various social elements in the revolution.

Undoubtedly, much more needs to be done in both regional and topical analysis before a really sound general interpretation can be achieved. This paper may serve, however, as a basis for discussion and may encourage further study of the field.

The presentation of a general view, however exploratory, is complicated by regional diversity in the character and course of the independence movement in its various centers. Differences in geography, in population, in tradition, as well as in the duration and intensity of military operations must be considered, together with variations in the extent of contact with Europe and the United States. These differentiating factors modified certain general tendencies: the destructive force of war, and the stimulation produced by free intercourse with foreign countries.

The immediate economic consequence of revolution, except in a few favored areas, was disaster. The prosperity of the later colonial economy of Spanish America was shattered by warfare which was everywhere waged with little regard for the rights of private property and the lives of noncombatants. It is only possible to suggest here the terrible destruction suffered by many regions. This reached its maximum in Venezuela, where both the human and the livestock population declined, the latter by more than one-half between 1810 and 1830. Almost as severe were the losses in the Banda Oriental and in certain parts of the Viceroyalty of New Spain. New Granada and Chile represent areas which were less continuously theatres of military action, and with a consequently lighter incidence of destruction. The extreme horrors of the *guerra a muerte* in Venezuela and the slaughter in Mexico during the early stages of revolution were not often matched in scale elsewhere, but, even where loss of life was less severe, interruption of normal economic life was serious. People were uprooted from their homes in various ways. Men were recruited, often by force, for the rival armies. Even when they escaped death they frequently never returned, taking up life again elsewhere. There were also many examples of emigration on a substantial scale. These dislocations of population had unfavorable results for agriculture and mining, removing the necessary labor force, and on business in general owing to the flight of capital along with its owners.

The interruption of normal lines of trade and communication also had serious adverse effects. Northwest Argentina suffered from the halting of trade with Peru. Montevideo, while in hands hostile to Buenos Aires, lost part of its commercial function. Guerrilla warfare in New Spain at times disrupted internal communications except by armed convoys. Wartime financial exactions, ranging from confiscation to forced loans, appropriation of goods for the use of the rival armies, forced acceptance of depreciated currency, and high and arbitrary taxation brought ruin to many. Cattle-raising countries like the Banda Oriental and the Venezuelan hinterland suffered from wholesale robbery and expropriation of the livestock on which the economy of these regions was based. Mining regions were paralyzed by flooding of the workings and destruction of equipment.

It is impossible to measure exactly the total effect of these varied consequences of war, but it is probably safe to say that from 1810 to 1820 Buenos Aires and Peru, the stronghold of the rival forces in South America, were least affected. Regions like Paraguay and, to a lesser extent, Central America suffered from isolation but were little damaged. Chile, New Granada, and Mexico underwent severe destruction at times, but were not equally affected throughout the decade. On the other hand, Venezuela and Uruguay saw no real peace during the period and their normal economic activities were totally upset.

In the second decade of revolution theatres of military operations shifted. Warfare on a large scale was over in Mexico by 1821, and in Colombia after 1822. Fighting in Chile ceased, except for guerrilla warfare in the far south. On the other hand, Peru, which had previously escaped, became the center of the fighting. Though devastation here was not so widespread nor long continued as in some other areas, the burden of supporting large armies (patriot and royalist) in the field for several years was a heavy one. The duration of military activity in what is now Ecuador was briefer, but this region gave a good deal of support to the later Peruvian campaigns. For the war as a whole, therefore, only the province of Buenos Aires and its immediate neighbors to the north and west were able to escape the direct scourge of war. Even here there were intermittent skirmishes between patriot factions especially after the year 1820.

The upheaval caused by war was not limited to destruction of life and property and the disorganization of business; it also brought changes in society which were not envisaged by the creole aristocrats and intellectuals who headed the revolts of the *cabildos* in 1809 and 1810. Except in Mexico, the revolutions had begun with efforts to dislodge the peninsular bureaucracy without otherwise changing relations among classes, but war unleashed forces that these early revolutionists were unable to harness. Race and class antagonisms flared up which could only be brought under control by the exaltation of nationalism and a parallel minimizing of class distinctions. Without any general upset in these relations, there was a blurring of lines. None of the new independent governments recognized legal disabilities for *pardos* or *mestizos*. In Mexico, the clergy no longer kept the elaborate records of caste as a part of their parochial registers.

The "career open to talents" seems to have been the rule. A *mestizo* general might rise to the presidency of his country; a *mulato* colonel might become a large landowner. This does not mean that an equalitarian society grew out of the wars, but it does indicate that the wars brought new blood into the ruling class and simplified the social distinctions in lower strata of the population.

The annals of revolution in Mexico and Colombia are well sprinkled with the names of prominent military officers with Indian or Negro blood in their veins, or both. Piar and Padilla in Colombia were conspicuous examples. In Mexico, Guerrero and Morelos reached even higher renown. In the lower ranks officers with similar racial antecedents were numerous. In Peru and Bolivia *mestizos* also held high military rank. Santa Cruz, who became president of the latter republic, was the son of an Indian woman and a Spaniard. In the naval service of Colombia a number of *mulatos* held commissions. The large percentage of color in the ranks of Bolívar's officers was frequently commented on by the race-conscious European officers who served in Colombia.

The tendency toward greater racial tolerance was not unchecked. White creole fear accounts in part for the severe treatment meted out to such officers as Piar and Padilla. Their insubordination might well have been condoned if it had not been for their race. If there had not been great gains for the mixed bloods, such severity as that which led to the execution of both, in spite of the brilliant military services they had rendered to the cause of independence, might not have been considered necessary.

In Río de la Plata and in Chile there do not seem to have been instances of high military commanders of recognized mixed blood. We can cite, however, the cases of politicians and journalists like Vicente Kanki Pazos (an Indian from Upper Peru) and the meteoric career of Bernardo Monteagudo (a *mulato* from Tucumán). The strength of the creole element in the population in the Viceroyalty of Buenos Aires, except in the north, and the fact that it was not heavily depleted by the wars may be one explanation for the less conspicuous place of the *mestizo* in military leadership. The relatively stable agrarian economy of Chile with its strong personal ties between landowner and *inquilino* provided fewer opportunities for social change than the more elaborately stratified population of Peru, Colombia, and Mexico. In these southern regions, however, the revolution brought increasing fluidity among economic groups. "Self-made men," among them many foreigners, began to make themselves increasingly evident, beginning the process which was to ease their way into the upper social ranks of *estancieros* and merchants. This tendency was stimulated by the procedure followed by many governments in paying off officers and men with land confiscated from royalists or from the public domain. Land had been for so long a badge of social position that it proved impossible to discriminate for more than a generation against the owner of a large estate.

Another series of important social and economic changes grew out of the increasing contact with foreign lands during the course of the wars of independence. In this respect local differences are also notable. Buenos Aires, without question, developed a new economy based on foreign trade earlier than any other Spanish-American country. The accumulated demand for free trade during the later years of the viceroyalty had paved the way and the absence of Spanish power to interfere, after 1810, gave the development free rein. This ushered in the cattle boom which was to fix the character of the Argentine economy for generations. It led to expansion on the Indian frontier and to the rapid growth of the city of Buenos Aires, as population flowed in to serve the needs of an expanded commerce. Small shops and factories on a handicraft basis multiplied and the accumulation of wealth created new luxury trades. On the other hand, as Burgin has shown, free trade brought depression to Cuyo and to the northern provinces from Tucumán to Jujuy, which lost much of their market for home manufactures to foreign competition.

In Chile, with interruptions due to the wars, similar changes can be seen. Free trade meant a larger market for the grain and other food surpluses which before the revolution had been shipped almost exclusively to Peru. Valparaíso became a port of call for ships bound to the Orient and for the northwest coast of America. The export of Chilean silver and copper increased under the pressure of need to balance imported manufactures. By 1825 a number of English mining experts were planning developments in the Coquimbo region. Chilean naval activity stimulated the work of shipyards and attracted both business men and laborers to the port city, which soon lost its sleepy colonial aspect. Free trade, however, had a less violently stimulating effect on the economy of Chile than in Río de la Plata. The immediately available resources of Chile were less vast, and depended, for expanded exploitation, on growth of population and on a long-range development of mining equipment and transportation which could not be carried through at once.

The ports of Peru and Colombia were opened to world trade at a later time and these republics were less favorably situated than those of the far south from a commercial point of view. Trade did not develop here on a healthy basis. In Peru it began with a hectic wartime flush, with government purchases of munitions of war and naval stores and even of food (including flour from the United States), and with considerable speculative purchases of luxury goods. This drained the country of its currency and saddled it with large commercial and governmental debts. The economic situation was still further complicated by a heavy flight of capital which took the form of specie exports in British and American warships. Silver mining did not recover quickly from wartime interruption and nitrates and guano had not yet appeared on the scene to provide a temporary solution to the balance of payments problem. At the same time, the domestic production of coarse textiles in Peru was largely displaced by foreign goods and did not recover after the war.

Free trade in Venezuela began, except for the brief interlude of the first republic in 1810–1811, with operations which bear little resemblance to regular business. Private ownership of the livestock of the Orinoco valley was largely disregarded, and after Bolívar established himself at Angostura, the livestock resources of the region were swept up by his agents and shipped to the West Indies to pay for the war supplies sold on credit at high prices by British, Dutch, and American merchants. There was no expansion of the agriculture of the coastal area of Venezuela during the period under review. It continued to seek an outlet in the *colonias extrangeras* in the Caribbean, as it had under Spanish rule, though it was now a legal trade. Privileged products like Barinas tobacco and the cacao of Caracas lost the protected markets of later colonial times and production declined. New Granada's economic recovery was also slow. There was a flurry of imports, chiefly for government account, from 1822 to 1825, financed by the loans floated in London. Apart from these years, foreign trade grew much more slowly than in Buenos Aires or Chile. Only in Guayaquil, in the southern part of Colombia, did a business boom develop. This was based on the export of lumber, rice, and cacao and the exploitation of the favored situation of this port.

In Mexico free trade did not actually begin until 1823. Until that time, all but a trickle of irregular trade had continued to follow traditional colonial channels to Spain and Cuba. When commerce with Spain was suspended, great difficulty arose owing to the disappearance of Spanish commercial capital at Veracruz. It was to take time to build up a new system of credit depending on agents of European manufacturers, established at Mexico City. In spite of English interest in Mexican mining, production of the precious metals, which accounted for most of Mexico's export surplus, did not wholly recover in the period before 1830.

The foregoing would appear to indicate some correlation between commercial progress and a lesser degree of severity in military operations in the different regions mentioned. This factor, however, cannot have been decisive. The extent to which free trade brought economic revolution also depended on the existence of resources in demand in the world markets and on adequate transportation facilities for bringing these to the seaports. Obviously, Buenos Aires, with its easily traversed *pampa*, and Chile, with production located never very far from the sea, had a great advantage over Peru, Colombia, and Mexico.

That the statesmen and politicians of Spanish America recognized the vital importance of transportation at this time is evident in the many efforts to develop steam navigation on South American rivers during the revolution. Plans were put forward involving the Orinoco, the Magdalena, the Atrato, and the Paraná. Several concessions were granted to foreigners, but none brought significant results until a later time. Interest in road construction in Ecuador, Mexico, and Colombia also failed to bring results in view of government financial embarrassments.

The rate and extent of trade expansion varied considerably from region to region, but the direction of change was the same. All the new republics headed toward a broader production of resources demanded by the world market and became increasingly intimately linked with the expanding economy of the nineteenth century, centered on and directed

by Great Britain. This trade expansion brought other economic developments in its wake. Taxation shifted from the complex system of colonial
days, with its multiple excises, monopoly franchises, and sales taxes, toward
reliance on the customs duties on imports as the all-important source of
revenue. Consumption of imported goods tended to outrun the ability
of exports to balance them, leading to the negotiation of foreign loans
on highly disadvantageous terms. Buenos Aires, Chile, Peru, Mexico, and
Colombia all experienced the beginnings of their troubles with foreign
creditors during this epoch. The too rapid expansion of imports may have
been one cause of the financial crises which contributed to widespread
political instability after the establishment of independence.

Along with the economic liberalism, of which the removal of trade
barriers was concrete evidence, there developed a broader liberalism which
also influenced society. The story of the abolition of slavery has often
been told and need not be repeated here. It should be remembered, however, that outright abolition in some countries and gradual emancipation
in others had reduced slavery to insignificant proportions in republican
Spanish America before 1830. This was, of course, preceded by the manumission of slaves on a considerable scale in the course of the revolutionary
wars. Freedmen formed part of San Martín's liberating forces that fought
at Chacabuco and of the army of Sucre that completed the liberation of
Peru at Ayacucho.

The Indians fared less well in this era. In spite of frequent references
to their ancient woes in propaganda directed against the Spanish regime,
the achievement of independence meant little to the native race. Though
frequently involved in revolutionary fighting, Indians never wholeheart-
edly sided with either party in the struggle. In southern Chile they were
active as royalist guerrillas. In Mexico they fought and bled with Hidalgo.
In Peru and Colombia they fought on both sides, either because they were
forced to do so, or because they followed some leader who had a personal
reason for taking sides. The lapse of colonial protective legislation exposed
them to exploitation under the increasingly individualistic republican legal
codes and the war of independence ruined many of the missions which had
preserved their existence, even if they did not succeed in fitting them for
the competitive society they now had to face.

Perhaps the most marked social change of the era was the growth of
the rift between the society of the seaports and capitals, on the one hand,
and rural and provincial society, on the other. At the seats of government
and in the ports upper and middle classes began to be affected by the
streams of foreigners (diplomats, visiting scholars, pedagogues, merchants,
soldiers and sailors) which began to appear on the scene. Fashions began
to ape the styles of London and Paris; new sports and pastimes replaced
colonial recreations; even habits of food and drink changed. Provincial
cities were but little affected by these newfangled notions and the countryside was largely unconscious of them. Thus, the wider, European outlook

of the elite in almost every country began to show itself in minor ways long before it was enshrined in law, educational institutions, and in the arts.

The hypothesis suggested by the foregoing remarks may be summarized as follows: the revolutionary wars which led to independence were a profound shock to the society and to the economic life of the Spanish colonies. Wartime destruction left many countries less able to maintain traditional ways and opened the way for new developments. Ensuing changes were brought about, first of all, by the expansion of foreign trade, which, in turn, had repercussions on the whole economic and social structure. Nevertheless, only the beginnings of a basic transformation took place and there were many ways in which colonial attitudes and institutions carried over into the life of republican Spanish America. Liberal ideas, however, used at first to buttress the rising power of landowners and business men, weakened paternalistic aspects of colonialism.

The Río de la Plata region was most deeply changed by the revolution. Throughout the continent, too, the greater cities and the ports were more affected by the new than were the provinces and the countryside. There emerged, therefore, no single clearly identifiable pattern of change, and developments noted were not so much revolutionary as they were examples of an accelerated tempo of evolutionary transformation.

Other Articles of Interest

Humphreys, R. A. "The Historiography of Spanish American Revolutions." XXXVI (1956), 81–93.

King, James F. "A Royalist View of the Colored Castes in the Venezuelan War of Independence." XXXIII (1953), 526–537.
A document from the Archivo General de Indias, Audiencia de Caracas, Leg. 109, expressing the views of the acting Captain-General of Venezuela in 1815 on ways to reconcile the colored *castas* to the royalist cause.

————. "The Colored Castes and the American Representation in the Cortes of Cadiz." XXXIII (1953), 33–64.
The General and Extraordinary Cortes of the Spanish Nation, convening first in 1810, forbade equal representation to the colored castes of America, denying their citizenship and excluding them from the electoral count. The Cortes thus sought to prevent American control. The American representatives' sympathy for the castes depended mainly on the desire for larger representation. This act of the Cortes more than any other stimulated American resistance and enabled American leaders to appeal to colored elements of the population with charges of racial discrimination.

Schmitt, Karl M. "The Clergy and the Independence of New Spain." XXXIV (1954), 289–312.

The upper clergy in New Spain were for the most part consistent in their opposition to "liberalism," even to the point of separating a conservative-controlled Mexico from a liberal-governed Spain in 1820. Of the lower clergy, who formed the only educated group possessing a close connection with the masses, an important segment joined the insurrections and led the mass uprising of the early period. Many others of the lower clergy remained loyal to Spain without playing an important intellectual or military role. The majority of the lower clergy were probably neutral, and thousands were never called upon to take any stand at all.

2. The Creation and Control of a Caudillo

ROGER M. HAIGH

Caudillo is a term used frequently in Latin American studies, and too often this kind of military leader is dismissed "as an autocratic expression of some flaw in Latin American character." Professor Haigh of the University of Utah refers to the above misleading generalization before he proceeds to analyze the rule of Martín Güemes, who controlled the northwestern Argentine province of Salta from 1815 to 1821. This article shows that Güemes was so dependent on the support of his kinfolk that when he broke with the leaders of his family his own career was destroyed. This article suggests that no one formula may be applied to caudillos and that they must be examined individually in the light of their times, their spheres of influence, and their personalities.

After fifty years of rather blasé tolerance from United States society, Latin American specialists in every realm of endeavor are being called upon to answer complex questions about their area of interest. As a result a great deal of material has been amassed to provide some guide-lines to answering these problems.

Probably the plea which appears most frequently is one for understanding between two cultures with very different systems of values, governments, and peoples. This plea has produced a marked emphasis on the differences of the two cultures and a phenomenon that many scholars feel is unique to Latin America.

One of these features that has received some scholarly attention is

From Volume XLIV (1964), pages 481–490.

the phenomenon of caudillismo. The term caudillo means simply military leader. It has assumed a rather derogatory meaning chiefly through association of the term with such individuals as Francia, Rosas, Villa, Gómez, Franco, and more recently, Fidel Castro. As a result of such association, studies of the caudillo as a type tend to dismiss him as an autocratic expression of some flaw in the Latin American character, and to classify caudillos as among the unfortunate features of Latin society.

One of the earliest caudillos was Martín Güemes. He was active in the war for independence in Argentina and ruled the northwestern province of Salta from 1815 to 1821. During his tenure in office the province repulsed several Spanish attempts at penetration. As a result of his seemingly arbitrary actions, the terms caudillo, despot, and tyrant are frequently used in historical treatments of his career.

Martín Güemes was born in Salta in 1785. His father was the royal treasurer of the province, and his mother was a member of the prominent Goyechea family in neighboring Jujuy. He was one of nine children, and the subsequent marriages of his brothers and sisters were to aid him in his career. His father died in 1807, and his mother remarried into the Tineo family, thus establishing more connections of importance.

Güemes was educated in Salta; at fourteen he enlisted in the cadets and began a lifelong military career. He served in Salta until 1805, when his unit was transferred to Buenos Aires. While there he participated in the resistance to the English invasions as an aide to Santiago Liniers. In 1807 Güemes returned to Salta because of the death of his father. He remained in Salta until the break with Spain in 1810, when he was incorporated into the garrison in Salta with the rank of lieutenant.

His first command was an observation expedition into royalist Upper Peru. As a result of the expedition's success he was promoted to capitán. His subsequent military career included services with Balcarce in Upper Peru in 1811, attachment to the General Staff in Buenos Aires, and participation in the siege of Montevideo. In 1814 Güemes returned to the area of Salta wtih a military expedition to reinforce Belgrano at Tucumán. José de San Martín replaced Belgrano in 1814, and he commissioned Güemes to take charge of the defenses of Salta. Upon arrival in Salta he found a defensive campaign under way under the leadership of local estancieros. Commander of these groups was Pedro José Saravia, Güemes' uncle. Güemes assumed control and soon expelled the Spaniards from the province.

After securing the province of Salta, Güemes accompanied Rondeau on the invasion of Upper Peru in 1814. He fought in the battle of Puesto del Marqués, and returned to Salta in 1815. In May he was elected governor. Until this occasion his career had been completely devoted to military affairs. From 1815 to 1821 his career acquired characteristics commonly associated with caudillos, and he took actions that resulted in his being branded as a tyrant. The purpose of this paper is to indicate that Güemes was not a tyrant at all, but was created and controlled by a much older, more stable structure of power which held political, economic, and military control of the province.

Salta was situated on a trade break in the route from Buenos Aires to Lima, until 1776 the capital of the viceroyalty. At Salta all goods had to be transferred from carts to mules in order to cross the Andes. The salteños prospered from the trade passing through the city and enjoyed a virtual monopoly on the sale of mules to the caravans moving toward Peru. As a result of the profits in mules the land around the city was used as grazing land for these animals. This land was owned by several creole families who controlled most of the wealth of the province. During the colonial period these families demonstrated their power by domination of the cabildo, their mention in the records of the viceroy, and the frequent marriages with ranking Spanish officials.

The break with Spain in 1810, by eliminating Spanish officials, greatly augmented the power of the families. From 1810 to 1821 this family structure provided the basic source of strength that enabled Salta to repulse seven invasions and to earn the title "Bulwark of the North."

In an effort to determine the composition of the family structure, a search of the documents of the independence era and the colonial period revealed frequent references to several powerful families, specifically the Figueroas, Cornejos, Saravias, and Toledos. Further research into the nature of these families revealed that they controlled most of the wealth of the province and were directly related to those who controlled the remainder. These relationships were the result of a multiplicity of kinship connections, a network of families that made up the socio-economic elite of the province. The connections in kinship were strengthened by similar ethnic backgrounds, mutual economic interests, and a common, isolated locale. The family structure of Salta thus represented the combination of several types of informal group solidarities, connected intimately by repeated ties of kinship. The core of this kinship elite was composed of the families of Cornejo, Figueroa, Saravia, and Toledo.

In dealing with kinship, the uniqueness of the institution of the family is immediately apparent. The Spanish family was unusually strong due to its position, not only in custom but in both secular and religious codes. The family was formalized in law by a very detailed body of regulations governing various manifestations of family life. Among these were codes governing the dowry, entailed estates, primogeniture, and the care of adopted and orphaned children. These regulations gave the Spanish family a basic foundation in legal responsibility. The Church also gave the family additional strength. Marriage was sanctified and protected through the sacraments of the Church, and the family itself was recognized through the administration of sacraments concerning the children. This legal and religious background of the Spanish family gave it an uncommon solidarity.

The position of the family in Salta was further strengthened by local conditions. Among the most apparent of these were the relative inaccessibility of the province, the concentration of families in the isolated valleys of the province, and the difficulty of transportation and communication in the early years of the nineteenth century. These factors tended to limit the scope and contacts of the salteños with areas outside the province and produced a multiplicity of internal connections in socio-economic affairs, and restricted external relationships.

Finally and most importantly was the size of the province. The city was inhabited by nearly 7,000 people. The province held about five times that number. This relatively small population, coupled with a rather stable growth rate, could in a few generations of intermarriages, produce a province of relatives. This extended family would have its leaders, who generally came from the elite and its affiliated families.

Economically, the four main families were estancieros, and among them they controlled most of the land in the vicinity of Salta. The first evidence of the economic strength of this group came in 1778, when the Figueroas, the Cornejos, and the Toledos were three of five donors who provided basic funds for the establishment of a royal treasury in Salta. From 1810 to 1815 the economic power of this group was demonstrated by its support of the armies of Buenos Aires in the various invasions of Upper Peru. In 1810, for example, the Figueroas donated 22,000 silver pesos to Balcarce's army; in 1812, the Saravias gave 5,000 cattle; the Cornejos also gave livestock and equipped a unit of 1,000 men to serve in the porteño force; and the Toledos supplied over 1,300 horses to the armies preparing to invade Upper Peru. For support of this kind, Feliciano Antonio Chiclana, the first representative of the junta of Buenos Aires to Salta, consistently lauded these families for rendering invaluable service to the cause of independence.

Militarily the strength of the families can best be explained by a consideration of the corporate nature of the estancia. Within the bounds of this institution the landowner was the patrón of all who lived on his land. In Salta the gaucho had acquired a sedentary position on the large ranches, working as did the cowboy in the American West. When the estancia was threatened, members of the patrón's family led the gauchos in its defense. In this manner the Cornejos managed to put in the field about 1,000 men, the Figueroas about 500, and the Saravias about 600. Together with similar units under the leadership of affiliated families, the forces of the kinship elite were consistently the bulk of the troops that defended Salta.

The union of the economic and military strength of these families was formed by a vast web of kinship connections. The Toledos and the Figueroas were related by the marriage of María de Toledo to Antonio de Figueroa. This connection between the Figueroas and the Toledos is indicative of the interconnections among the kinship elite and the other wealthy families of the region. The Figueroas and the Cornejos intermarried six times in two generations, and the Saravias and the Cornejos twice. The frequency of unions produced a superfamily which in two generations established marriages with 36 other leading families of the area. If the average size of a family is assumed to be about 50 members, the kinship elite and affiliated families would total about 2,000 people or about 5 per cent of the population of the province of Salta. This network was the structure that controlled not only the socio-economic life of the province but the caudillo Martín Güemes as well.

The political power of the structure can best be measured by the representation of the family group in the bodies of government, in the cabildo and the provincial assemblies. The cabildo or town council was the principal organ of politics; the provincial assemblies were called only for special problems.

Prior to the accession of Güemes to the governorship, the power of the cabildo in provincial affairs was checked only by a representative of the junta of Buenos Aires. This representative held the position of governor of the province and presided at the meetings of the cabildo. During the period 1810 to 1815, 37 different individuals held seats on the cabildo. Of this number 30 were either members of the four leading families or directly related to them. Such heavy representation gave the kinship elite an effective majority of the members of every cabildo in this period.

In May of 1815 Martín Güemes returned to Salta from Rondeau's forces in Upper Peru, and on his arrival the cabildo elected him governor. Historians have usually concerned themselves with the legality of the election and the rupture of control by Buenos Aires. The question as to why Güemes was elected has been dismissed by referring to his military reputation and his popularity with the masses. While these factors no doubt had some part in his selection, they fail to give a complete answer. He was not the only salteño with an admirable military reputation, for the province had been a battlefield since 1812; his popularity with the masses was limited to the gauchos living in the less-civilized regions of the province, and they had no political influence at all. More important than his military abilities and his mass appeal was his position in the kinship elite.

Eight men made up the cabildo of Salta in May of 1815. Seven of these were relatives of Martín Güemes, the most apparent being his brother, Juan Manuel Güemes. The connection of Güemes to the kinship elite was direct; his sister Francisca was married to Fructuosa Figueroa y Toledo; his maternal uncle, Lorenzo, was married to María Ignacia Cornejo; his paternal aunt, Barbara Tineo, was married to Pedro José Saravia. These ties of kinship relate Martín to the four leading families of the area. His accession to the position formerly held by the representative of Buenos Aires was not usurpation of power but elimination of the only check to the power of the kinship elite of Salta by replacing a stranger with a member of the ruling coterie of families.

Güemes governed the province of Salta during a period of chaos in Argentine history. What semblance of national unity that had existed prior to 1815 collapsed with the rupture between José de San Martín and the central government under Carlos Alvear. From 1816 to 1818 the country was tied together by the Congress of Tucumán. Between 1818 and 1820 all unity disappeared, and authority was limited to the confines of individual provinces or even individual towns.

Salta had very little contact with the problems of nationhood during the Güemes administration, as the basic preoccupation continued to be survival from the Spanish power in Upper Peru. During the six-year period the province faced and repulsed four Spanish invasions in 1817, 1819, 1820, and 1821. As governor of the province Güemes' basic concern was the defense of the area, and here he proved himself an able military commander.

The authority and power wielded by Güemes was relative to the amount of support given him by the family structure. In most matters that confronted the province, the families gave Güemes unqualified support. On such occasions he had the appearance of a leader possessing tremendous power. As long as his interest coincided with that of the group he shared its power and it benefited from his exercise of authority. Examples of this were the Spanish invasions, the attempt of Rondeau to requisition 1,000 rifles from Salta that Güemes considered vital to Salta's defense, and his attempts to purge salteño society of Spanish sympathizers. On these issues the family structure backed him and the projects were carried out.

Politically the kinship elite continued to dominate the province. With the exception of 1820 the cabildo of Salta was controlled by an effective majority of members of the family structure. That year a provincial assembly was established to handle provincial affairs, and the family group dominated it. Nine of the assembly's fifteen members were affiliated with the kinship elite. Its political power thus remained essentially the same during the Güemes administration as it had been prior to his taking office. The only difference was that the governor was also a member of the structure rather than a representative of Buenos Aires.

The relative military power of the families decreased somewhat between 1815 and 1821. While the ranchers still maintained command of their units, Güemes regularized the urban militia, reorganized the defenses, and created new units under professional commanders. In 1817, nevertheless, at the height of Güemes' power, after the successful expulsion of La Serna's invasion, the kinship elite held field command of four of the six divisions of gauchos, and its members occupied such key positions as Chief of Staff and Commander of the Frontier.

To measure the relative power of Güemes and the group of which he was a member, it is necessary to consider areas of disagreement between him and the kinship elite. Between 1815 and his death in 1821 there were only three serious issues of conflict between them. These were a primitive land reform program in 1817, a tax reform program in 1820, and war with the neighboring province of Tucumán in 1821. Güemes supported all three but the kinship elite was either adamantly opposed to them or unenthusiastic.

All three were the result of a basic difference in the ambitions of Güemes and those of the kinship elite. Güemes was primarily interested in the defeat of the Spaniards, secondarily in the welfare of the province. The kinship elite was interested in its own welfare and that of the province first, and defeat of the Spanish ranked a poor second.

In 1817 Güemes attempted to reward the gauchos of Salta by absolving those who had fought against La Serna's army from paying rent to the ranchers who owned the land. The ranchers, including most of the kinship elite, opposed this assault on their property, and the gauchos' devotion to their patrones was seemingly stronger than their desire for rent-free land, for they refused to take advantage of the law. Güemes dropped the idea.

In 1820 San Martín urged Güemes to mount an offensive against Upper Peru. To support this military objective Güemes proposed to the provincial assembly that a system of regular taxation be adopted to guarantee him a dependable source of revenue. His proposal included taxes that would be levied on the kinship elite. The proposal was voted down and the burden of taxation was placed on interests essentially alien to the kinship elite. These were the Church, small businesses, and the urban citizenry.

In 1821 Güemes' preoccupation with the invasion of Upper Peru provoked the war with Tucumán. Civil war had broken out between Tucumán and Santiago del Estero to the south of Salta. This struggle prevented Güemes from obtaining from the other provinces military supplies which had been promised. Without this support his projected invasion of Upper Peru was hopeless. Rather than give up this project, Güemes asked the provincial assembly for permission to invade Tucumán and re-open his supply route. The kinship elite, by a vote of eleven to nine, gave its approval. The situation was changed rather suddenly when the salteño force was defeated by Tucumán, and the royalists began a new invasion of the province from the north. The province now faced hostilities from the Spanish to the north and from Tucumán to the south. Güemes left Salta to take command of the units facing the Spanish, and left the kinship elite in control of the cabildo. On May 21, 1821, the cabildo voted to depose Güemes and to make peace with Tucumán. This action initiated a short struggle between Güemes and the family structure that ended in his death.

The cabildo appointed Saturnino Saravia governor and José Antonio Cornejo military commander of the province. Güemes heard of this action and on May 31 he returned to the city with a force of 600 men to assume control. Seven days later a royalist force of several hundred men entered Salta in the evening and fatally wounded Martín Güemes.

After the death of Güemes a reunion of interests was accomplished. The war with Tucumán came to an end, and the forces of the kinship elite, under José Antonio Cornejo, Apolinar Saravia, and Luís Burla joined the forces of Güemes; by mid-July they had forced the royalists out of the province. Saturnino Saravia and José Antonio Cornejo, both members of the kinship elite, controlled political and military affairs respectively.

Some rather curious circumstances surrounding the death of Güemes suggest that the royalists were aided by local forces. The first incongruity was that an enemy force of such size could enter Salta without being observed. This contrasts sharply with previous salterño surveillance of royalist movements. The second curious feature was the reaction of Güemes to the trap, for he immediately assumed that it was an internal movement. There is, finally, some evidence that the royalists were assisted in their entrance into Salta by gaucho leaders such as Pedro Zavala and Ángel M. Zerda. Güemes was certainly killed by royalist troops, but it is doubtful that his death was necessarily the result of a chance encounter. The abrupt end of the power struggle between Güemes and the kinship elite may have been no accident.

In summing up the relationship of Güemes to the kinship elite, the continued domination of the family structure is apparent. He was selected by it and was successful only when he enjoyed its support. On points of discord between Güemes and his supporting group he was either defeated or forced to compromise his position. Güemes was dead within a week after the final break ensued, and the family structure immediately assumed complete control of the province. It appears that Güemes was more an instrument of the kinship elite than the tyrant of Salta.

It is not suggested that what has been learned of the kinship elite and the structure of power of nineteenth-century Salta is wholly applicable to Latin American caudillos in other areas and other eras. It does seem, however, that a similar approach to the question of caudillo power might, at least in certain cases, be more fruitful than the approaches thus far employed. It is in this regard that the present study may prove to have wider validity.

Other Articles of Interest

Chapman, Charles E. "The Age of the Caudillos: A Chapter in Hispanic American History." XII (1932), 281–300.

"The leader, which meant the caudillo, was party, flag, principle, and objective, all in his own person." The term is as old as *cacique* among the Indians. In the colonial period the caudillo was usually a local figure, but he assumed national stature with revolutions. He appeared in every country, for among the peoples of South America, with their race problems and their excessive illiteracy, the rule of the picturesque caudillo, with many sycophants, was inevitable.

———. "List of Books Referring to Caudillos in Hispanic America. XIII (1933), 143–146.

GENERAL

3. Colonial Institutions and Contemporary Latin America:

A. Political and Economic Life

WOODROW BORAH

The intense interest in the economic and social ferment of Latin America today has tended to diminish interest in the history of the long centuries when Portugal and Spain ruled their immense dominions in America. The following group of papers demonstrate the need to keep in mind the intimate relation between the past and the present. They also prove the value of a sophisticated conversation, in this case at one of the annual sessions of the American Historical Association, between such thoughtful historians as Professors Borah (University of California, Berkeley), Gibson (University of Michigan), and Potash (University of Massachusetts).

Our subject is Colonial Institutions and Contemporary Latin America: my portion is political and economic life. Both subject and portion are vast and attractive but fearfully complex. As we all know, Latin America is a continent and a half, by no means of uniform heritage and with regions of considerable cultural diversity. Furthermore, these regions are undergoing change which moves at differential rates and may not even be in the same direction. There are, in addition, ambiguities and assumptions within the topic itself that require at least mention. Within this context, what is an institution? One can accept at once the statement that it is an organized society, or a form of social organization, or an established practice or custom. But is it also an attitude or a complex of attitudes that constitute a way of looking at life and organizing life? I think that this too must fall within our definition. Next, the subject would seem to contain the idea of survival. Is that term to mean that a colonial institution continues to the present day in demonstrably uninterrupted continuity and value? Here the lapse of old needs and the appearance of new ones obviously have meant in many instances extinction but in many others change in function and value so that one must examine the degree of alteration.

From Volume XLIII (1963), pages 371-394.

Again, the topic, it seems to me, carries within it a conception of divisions of time and nature of change, which may be summarized as follows: There was a colonial period which began some time after 1492 with the European incursion and came to a close about 1825 when most of Latin America became politically independent of Europe. During the colonial period a fairly uniform pattern of life developed or was implanted. This has remained as a relatively rigid mold that has broken down more or less gradually in the period of independent states. The latter period is frequently called national on the theory that the states contain nations or will do so in time. This kind of division is characteristic of our textbooks. It has the blessing of many of our own members, and carries with it some interesting analogies to the conception of mega-evolution in the sciences. In comment, let me suggest that one can hold with equally good reason that the colonial period has not yet ended. Today's program with equal logic and identical wording of topic could deal with the institutions that work to keep Latin America impoverished and subservient to other regions. However, since the intention of the Program Committee is clear, I shall accept the definition that colonial means whatever existed in Latin America in 1825, without reference to questions of dependence. Even within those terms, the lapse of time between the coming of Columbus and the achievement of formal political independence for most of Latin America is greater than that since 1825 to our day. Despite the steady acceleration in human history of rate of change, it is unlikely that so long a period of time meant merely an initial explosive contact and then the firm setting of a mold. What is called the colonial period contained fairly steady change even after the first century of European domination. The eighteenth century particularly was one of especially great change, both directed and unplanned, with profound effects upon popular life as well as government. Indeed, I personally should be inclined to hold that the inter-semester pause in the school year, which underlies much of this search for periods, falls better at the middle of the eighteenth century. For, in many ways, the history of Latin America since perhaps 1760 has been the implantation and working out of the ideas of the Enlightenment in administration, religious life, and the application of rational ideas to such matters as economic improvement. In consequence, if we consider colonial anything that appeared in Latin America prior to 1825, however few years earlier, the number and importance of survivals we shall find will be very much greater. Lastly, let me point out that the formulation of the topic and the conception of the nature of the colonial period implicit in it have the virtue of ignoring the problem of origins, that is whether an institution or trait is Indian or European, some blend of the two, or a new development within new needs. We may thus declare irrelevant a particularly thorny set of questions. Now that I have stated some of my caveats, let me embark upon what must be at best a partial and inadequate catalogue.

In the field of government and administration, perhaps a broader term than political life, even the casual visitor to Latin America is struck by the survival of institutions and features that are patently colonial. The systematic codes of laws clearly derive from the French Revolution and through it from Roman precedent rather than from the codifications of the Iberian monarchs, but behind that logical renewal and revision lie older peninsular and American content and notarial and administrative forms. In most of Latin America notaries continue to draw up legal instruments and serve as witnesses of integrity and credibility; except for the dates and circumstances, their documents are couched in the same form and language as those of their sixteenth century predecessors. Court procedures and writs, in many instances such, notably, as the famous Mexican writ of amparo, represent modifications and adaptations of colonial and earlier peninsular practice. The very form of administration is inherited from colonial times in a characteristic Latin American phenomenon to which William Whyte has applied the term external administration. The person needing a document or permit must himself coordinate the operations of the various agencies, and even of the people within an agency which must pass upon the issuance of a permit, or authorization or even collection of a tax. The client himself moves his papers from desk to desk and from office to office. He himself arranges to reconcile the conflicts which arise from contradictory hours or severely limited periods of service set by unconcerned agencies. The idea is virtually unknown of a systematic organization of procedure in which the government itself sees that once the application is filed, all steps follow automatically as a coordinated responsibility of its employees. Correspondingly, fees, tips, or bribes for coordinating and expediting functions became an indispensable lubricant.

Latin American government in general is characterized further by a series of survivals which may be grouped under the term centralization. Whatever the legal fiction of local autonomy, the province captures power and revenue from its local units, and the national government in turn strips states and provinces of sustenance and vigor. The extremities are left to a rachitic and penurious existence, in which they are forced to apply to higher authority for assistance in so local and elementary a matter as the repair of a town pump. This destruction of local vigor is clearly not an inheritance from the sixteenth or seventeenth century in Spanish America but rather derives from the great reforms of the eighteenth century. In Brazil it may go back to the reforms of the 1690's.

The phenomenon of centralization also embraces the characteristic vesting of power in the executive, converting legislative bodies into adulatory claques and depriving judicial bodies, to a degree that varies widely from region to region, of much of their independence. The effective appointive powers of the center, whatever the legal fictions, reach far down the lines of authority, just as the effective control of the Minister of the Interior extends to all territorial units and very often sets the results of elections. Paralleling and reinforcing this extension of centralized executive authority is the very real fear in lower or regional officials, of making a decision without knowng the mind of the higher official or of the center. In effect, whatever the constitutional provisions, the presidents have the royal power of former regimes but, perhaps because office is not hereditary and tenure is precarious, are somewhat less inclined to show the scrupulous royal respect for vested interests. Further, because of this absorption of all effective power by the executive, and by the supreme executive above all, much of the necessary dealings with government proceeds by personal interview and appeal, which may secure finally an order to enforce rights, or may guarantee that an inconvenient regulation will not be enforced. A number of us who have seen peasant delegations waiting for the President of Mexico in the presidential patio of the National Palace or in the antechambers of Los Pinos have been struck by the fact that we were watching the General Indian Court of New Spain functioning today rather much as it must have when Antonio de Mendoza gave it informal existence or Luis de Velasco II gave it formal structure. Personal intervention and wide use of dispensation, I should hasten to add, although colonial, may well be beneficial and give needed flexibility to an otherwise rigid and at times brutal administration.

Local administration in whatever function is left to it is characterized today very much by a colonial organization. Much of it is carried on through the *cargo* system. Unpaid or very poorly paid local officials work for the social prestige attached to their posts and the posts of local administration, official and customary, are organized in a progressively more responsible and prestigious order. A young man enters upon the lowest of these and works his way upward as a matter of community service and prestige, defraying community expenses out of his own resources. It is the translation to America of the *cursus honorum* of ancient Rome.

Unpaid or poorly paid officials, wide dispensing powers, and the need of each person to negotiate passage of his papers through the numerous official agencies and formalities have fostered survival and perhaps extension of yet another colonial phenomenon. We call it graft; Mexicans, the *mordida;* Brazilians, the *suco.* Virtually every country has its own term, but the phenomenon is really the survival of the characteristic system of the Middle Ages and Early Modern Period, and in many instances of our own time, by which the person who needs an official or legal service or document, pays for securing it. In other words, government service is financed directly through fees of some kind levied upon the person who requires the service. The mordida functions to a great extent as a means of supplementing painfully low salaries or providing payment where there are none through imposition of a moderate surcharge which in turn is earned by prompt and efficient or even extraordinary service. The custom has the vast advantage of enabling the private citizen to cut through bureaucratic detail and spare himself hours and even weeks of exasperation; it is probably as efficient and more accessible to the average man than our own proud invention of the expediter or troubleshooter. In yet another form the mordida functions like the colonial *composición*, payment to the state for dispensation from inconvenient law or conflicting right. It goes back to the vast extension of such practice in the seventeenth century as the impoverished Castilian Crown tried to meet the fiscal burdens of the Thirty Years' War. In its perhaps most unpleasant form, the mordida functions as graft or peculation, but again with ample colonial precedent. One may recognize the practice in accordance with which the viceroy brought an entourage of hungry followers and organized the colony for yield.

Finally, in this series of items relating to administration and political life, let me point to two fundamental features of Latin American society which have strong colonial roots. The first is *caudillismo* or *caciquismo*, the organization of political life in terms of congeries of leaders, each with his band of followers bound to him by personal interest, family, or regional association. The phenomenon is remarkably reminiscent of the Europe of the early Middle Ages, the Spain of the Reconquest, and the America of the Conquest. Since it is essentially social, I merely mention its existence. The second feature is the militarization of political life: the holding of civil office by military, the discharge of civil administration by military process, the predominant advantage of the military career as the means of political and economic advancement, and the special legal and de facto privileges of the military. The widespread nature of this militarization is most easily gauged by the extraordinary degree to which ordinary and unrelated civil administrative posts are held by military men. In its most extreme form such militarization becomes pretorianism: steady interference in political life by the armed services either as organized pressure groups or as participants in a series of coups-d'etat. Pretorianism can hardly be ascribed directly to colonial Hispanic America with its monarchs ruling by divine right, but the militarism which has fostered it is a colonial heritage and gives further point to my earlier comment that the centuries of European political domination witnessed continuing change. The governments of the earlier colonial period were singularly devoid of organized military establishments. For decades the only semblance of a regular army was the armed guards around the viceroys. When forces were needed, they were raised by calling for volunteers or by summoning the adult Spanish males to rally around the royal standard with whatever arms they could muster. Enforcement of law and the royal will was secured far more through the persuasion of the Church, just as royal administration relied relatively heavily upon advisers and administrators recruited from the clergy. Until the accession of the Bourbon dynasty in Spain, and the regime of Pombal in Portugal, the only regular forces to come into being in Latin America were the army in Chile and the garrisons at some of the ports. It was the massive reorganization of colonial life in the eighteenth century that changed the pattern. Royal administration relied far less upon the Church and even came into serious public conflict with the Church through the expulsion of the Jesuits. The royal bureaucracy increasingly was recruited from soldiers until the practice of employing military for civil functions became common. Substantial army garrisons were built up, and finally Charles III in his dominions and Pombal in Brazil established an organized militia in the colonies with special privileges, legal, social, and economic. The preferred position gained by the military has been consolidated since. Some may demur that in the collapse of traditional authority in the past century, the armed forces would have become the core of effective authority whatever previous practice. I can only say that the practice was there.

Let me turn now to economic life. This is a field so vast in itself that I can do no more than point to some institutions and practices. Differential rates of change have been especially prominent here so that any generalizations at best apply only to parts of our continent and a half. I shall be brief primarily because, for an audience with your knowledge, I fear that I belabor the obvious.

We all know the role of Latin America as a supplier of foodstuffs and raw materials to the industrially more developed countries—colonial in the other possible sense, with concomitants of monoculture, excessive dependence upon world markets and prices, and unfavorable relations of raw to processed materials. In this meaning, despite recent industrialization, nearly a century and a half of independence have made Latin America more rather than less colonial. The point is easily established if we compare the impact upon it of the interruptions of international supply during the eighteenth century, with the shortages and dislocations of 1914–1919 or 1940–1946. Spain and Portugal never were able to achieve such integration in their economic systems.

But, let me return to the more conventional meaning of colonial. Much of the technology of the colonial period continues in use to the present day and tends to preserve with its use the associated practices and forms of organization of production in agriculture, manufacturing, household use, and labor. I need merely mention the Mediterranean plow, the coa, foot plow, and backstrap loom among others. Thus in many regions village life has changed little in the past two centuries and retains traditional land tenures, forms of labor, especially labor exchange among neighbors, and contributions to communal needs in production. In Mexico there has even been an attempt to return more fully to the colonial system of *ejidos* but with the hope of moving away from the old rather than toward it. Throughout most of Latin America, village distribution and even much distribution within the cities remain the colonial one of barrio, town, and regional markets in which the market is not merely the center of economic exchange but provides a welcome social diversion, and may indeed be associated further with the celebration of a saint's feast day. In many regions, barrios and towns still specialize in the production of one item which is then exchanged at the markets. In complement to this system, there continues to exist the *pulpería* or general store with its supply of goods on credit and absorption of village products. It fulfills a function of exploiter, patron, and friend that no supermarket can replace.

Alongside the villages there existed and yet exist the haciendas that were both units of production and means of stable investment in an age that had few other outlets for capital. They were an answer further to the Peninsular stress upon land and livestock—particularly cattle and horses —as the basis of social prestige, and blended well with the social relations of caudillismo with its emphasis upon patronage and service. The relations might be reinforced by debt peonage but were not necessarily oppressive, as indeed the colonial hacienda with its varied relations was not invariably an oppressive institution. It evoked much loyalty on both sides until the development of profitable urban and foreign markets for foodstuffs and special crops in the nineteenth century made possible a much sharper exploitation aimed at large commercial profit and further made possible the life of an absentee landlord in the capital city or abroad. Despite the upheavals of a century and a half, the hacienda is very much a feature of the economic landscape today. With increasing emphasis upon new techniques, expensive machinery, and large-scale production, the hacienda may well triumph over the village. The forms that have been employed to save the village are the cooperative and the collective, the former of restricted feasibility and attraction in Latin America, the latter in the end a new and more efficient hacienda under state ownership.

Capital accumulation in Latin America is obstructed or even prevented by an interesting complex of survivals. Their effectiveness was reinforced through the destruction, early in the nineteeth century, of the well-developed class of artisans with its manufactures, especally textiles and metal goods. They could not compete with the flood of cheap British wares that entered the various countries once the metropolitan commercial system ceased to operate and the new rulers hastened to adopt the latest fashion of economic liberalism. A class that might have furthered habits of saving was thus eliminated, not to be replaced until almost our day and in other ways. As part of this complex of customs and outlook that militate against capital accumulation, one may point to the entire Iberian system of values with its emphasis upon a fairly static investment in land and cattle. It is essentially a non-industrial, non-saving psyche, interested in conspicuous expenditure and usury, in fees, rents, and salary rather than commercial or industrial profits. Such remains the criollo system of values today and the search for government posts often described as *empleomanía*.

In the villages this system of values and customs is paralleled by another, characterized by conspicuous and levelling expenditure, that may go back to the Roman custom of placing municipal burdens upon the wealthy. The holders of municipal and local posts must provide the costs of service and celebration, most often from their own substance. The majordomo of a confraternity in Mexico, for example, will bankrupt himself and his family in order to make prestigious provision of food, drink, and fireworks for the year's feast. Even in Brazil, where the *festeiro* can manage to spread the cost and even make a profit, the village or district uses in one splurge what is hardly a surplus. What takes place in essence is the consumption of the only possible saving—I repeat it is hardly a surplus—and a steady destruction of any accumulated savings held by any family in the town lest that family emerge above the general level. A recent study in Chiapas has disclosed that in a number of villages most of the saving, especially that which goes into productive forms, is by Protestant families, which as a matter of religious conviction refuse to participate in the system of cargos or *mayordomías*. It is an interesting corroboration of Weber's thesis. Further corroboration may be found in the report that in many Mexican villages returned *braceros* have been made *mayordomos* and have been forced to spend the savings of their labor for the year's festival. They are deliberately prevented from using their savings for investment that might disturb egalitarian village society. Were the missionaries who brought to the New World the European sodalities and confraternities to be polled, they might well approve the twentieth century operation of their work, but obviously further movement of Latin American countries toward capital accumulation and economic improvement will require massive modification in this complex. The counterbalancing factor in this picture is that governmental plunder increasingly results, in part, in productive investment and must be rated, to some extent, as an effective form of capital accumulation.

I should make one final comment. I have sketched (most inadequately) matters as they exist in this year. Inevitably there is an urge to look ahead, for we deal with process that does not halt. We can be sure that the next year will be somewhat different and the situation ten years from now more different. That is as far as we can go with any assurance. We can not even be sure of the direction of change which might permit some prediction of the degree or type of survival, for our ideas are based really upon the first forms of the Industrial Revolution with its emphasis upon metals and fossil fuels and with its temporary superiority of the English-speaking peoples. I recall the confident prediction in the 1920's of one eminent man still alive that Latin America could never hope to have an industrial revolution because it then had no known large deposits of iron ore and coal. Let us by all means discuss survival to this year. Let us further try to scan the future if we will, but let us do so with a decent lack of assurance in our own powers of prophecy.

B. Social and Cultural Life

CHARLES GIBSON

In Latin American history a familiar observation concerning the colonial period relates to its duration. The Spanish and Portuguese empires persisted in America for more than three centuries, and this extended time span not infrequently evokes a grudging admiration for the administrative systems that sustained them. Whatever else we may say about the Hispanic empires, runs a familiar comment—and the implication is that we may say a great deal else, little of it complimentary—whatever else we may say about the Hispanic empires, we must grant that they persisted in America for these 300 years. Their persistence is a foil that may be set against the briefer accomplishments of rival empires as well as against internal Hispanic deficiencies, and it appears as a measurable indicator of strength.

But the admiration or awe or grudging respect that we may express with regard to the duration of Hispanic rule is likely to become something quite different when we contemplate colonial survivals thereafter. Independence enforces fresh perspectives. Our new vantage point is liberal, and what were indications of strength now become obstacles to progress. It is as if the colonial period somehow had its historic role to fulfill, while we accompany it in retrospect and give it our support, and as if with independence a new role is called for, with which we also sympathize. If the observer is off his guard, this transition in perspective may pass only as a form of objectivity, a proper historian's accommodation to the spirit of different ages, or an absence of bias. It means however that we confront with quite opposite attitudes two related historical topics: the colonial period itself on the one hand and the persisting colonial features of its aftermath on the other.

Like any historical period the colonial portion of Latin American history is most obviously defined by its chronological limits. But the chronological definition has the practical disadvantage that it affords us no scope for our discussion. In the chronological sense the colonial period came to an end in the early nineteenth century, and in this sense there can be no colonial institutions in modern Latin America, for a modern institution, precisely by being modern, escapes the definition of colonial. The difficulty is one that has been appreciated principally in the terminology of Latin American folk art, where the term colonial is recognized as inappropriate for styles that extend into the nineteenth and twentieth centuries.

In a wider and looser sense the colonial classification is not limited to the period prior to 1810. I judge that the "colonial economies" of modern Latin America are so called partly because they are more or less unchanged from the real colonial period, partly because they are subordinate to foreign controls after the manner of true colonial economies. There appears, in other words, a characteristic type that we recognize as colonial, and a colonial institution of this type may occupy by extension any of several historical periods. An institution may begin and end wholly within the colonial dates, without any direct perpetuation thereafter. Examples would be the classic conquests, or the society of the viceregal courts. An institution may begin in the colonial period, persist into the middle nineteenth century, and then disappear, never becoming part of modern Latin America. An example is native Peruvian tribute liability, which has a full colonial history, a nineteenth-century history to 1854, and no history, or no official history, thereafter. An institution may originate before the colonial period and persist into, through, or beyond it. Examples would be the Araucanian family or the Christian church, and though in particular contexts we may refer to such institutions as colonial they are clearly not colonial in their origin or, necessarily, with respect to their major influence. Finally an institution may be post-colonial and yet so similar to a truly colonial institution that allowance is easily made. Thus exports of meats and bananas are understood to be aspects of the "colonial economy" of modern Latin America, despite the fact that these products themselves were not colonial exports. To surround our topic with further problems of this introductory nature we may add that all these examples depend on simplifications of reality. Institutions do not simply originate, exist, and die. They continually change, and as they change the question for us becomes: Are they the same institutions or different ones?

This last point may be appreciated through an examination of nineteenth- and twentieth-century attitudes toward the Spanish conquests. Conquest is a theme of importance for the entire subsequent history of the conquered areas, and it has been earnestly debated in the post-colonial period. In some degree, at least, approval or disapproval of conquest depends upon approval or disapproval of the long-term effects of conquest. Thus conquest is an issue in the modern intellectual history of Latin America. But it has no nineteenth- or twentieth-century existence except as a subject of discussion or as a remote cause for post-colonial conditions. Important as they are such long connections may be held to be irrelevant to our topic for the reason that the relationship is one of cause and consequence rather than continuous existence. One can avoid the difficulty, possibly, by identifying certain intermediate consequences of conquest which persist from late colonial times to the present. I do not mean to involve us in a discussion of the effects of conquests, but only through this example to indicate that a colonial institution may be consequential without being continuous and that modern legacies of colonial institutions may appear in disguised forms. Thus the classic conquests are associated with their own time and place; but one might argue that something of the spirit of conquest remains in Latin America in modern dress.

Because the particularities of institutions change through time, it may be felt that our most convincing instances of continuity are better selected at less concrete levels of institutionalism than any of those so far mentioned. If we now eliminate political and economic, and concentrate (in accordance with our assignment) on social and cultural, themes, we may consider such standard Latin American traits as family cohesiveness, aristocratic concepts of privilege, intellectual conservatism, cultural exclusiveness, and others, all of which can still be identified, in one or another particular form, in modern Latin America. These appear not as institutions but as attitudes or principles that are expressed in institutions. They appear more viable, less changeable, than the institutions that express them because they occur at higher or more durable levels of abstraction. The truth is that it is impossible to think of anything social or cultural that has not been modified in some degree in Latin America since the colonial period. But it is also possible to see some of these changes as superficial adjustments that do not affect underlying uniformities, or as variations on constant themes.

We may take as our next example the institutions of Latin American education. Our argument here would be that the institutions themselves have undergone transformation in numerous ways, while some of the larger attitudes or principles that these institutions express have remained constant. Between the colonial universities and the national universities of the middle twentieth century there appear immense differences, in size, in number, in composition, in function, and in technique of operation. The modern university's political role and the power of its student groups have developed far beyond any comparable conditions of the colonial period. The state has replaced the church, or is in process of replacing the church, as the controlling force in education. But the university's concentration on special subjects (we think of law and medicine), the pedagogical emphasis on memory learning and dialectics rather than on empiricism, the limited libraries, the dilettantism, the "manipulation of concepts," the elite principle that denies primary and secondary schooling to large masses of the population—these appear in unbroken continuity from the colonial period.

Again what could be more modern, more post-colonial, in Latin America than its urban industrial society, its rapid-tempo business culture, its labor unions, and its twentieth-century political pressure groups? One might expect little by way of colonial connection here, for the institutions are modern and their ultimate historical origins lie outside Latin America entirely. Further one might be inclined to classify them in wholly political and economic categories and hence as more appropriate to Professor Borah's paper than to mine. But they have all had to adjust to the continuing social-cultural conditions of Latin America, and among others to the intimacy of family ties and the nepotistic tangle that is characteristic of Latin America at all periods. The family, which is the social institution *par excellence*, fixed fundamental forms of association in the colonial period and continues to do so in the twentieth century. "In Latin America culture," as Frank Tannenbaum has said, "business is part of the total scheme of things; it is part of the family, of the *compadre* system, of the friendships, of the Church. It is done among friends in a leisurely and understanding way." Traditional cultural concepts in other words—concepts of interpersonal relations, of honor, of ethics, of work—continue to impinge on political and economic events in Latin America, and to the extent that they do so they represent persistent social-cultural forces to which other areas of life must make adjustment.

There is an opposite and contrasting type of colonial survival in which a particular thing continues with relatively little change, while the surrounding circumstances are so modified as completely to alter its meaning and its import. The type is most clearly exemplified in the physical survivals of colonial buildings and of colonial documents and artifacts. Public buildings, originally erected in a genuinely colonial spirit, are put to uses not originally intended. I have frequently been struck, in studying the history of Latin American towns, by how commonly the *casas reales* of the colonial period survive to become the *juzgado* or the house of correction or the local jail in subsequent periods. Documents that once served a legal purpose are relegated to archives and serve only a historiographical purpose. Works of art that reflected living aspirations fail to find a response in new environments and become testimonies to a dead past. Objects that were used in homes become objects that are looked at in museums. Such fragmentary remnants of colonialism sometimes require support in the twentieth century in order to withstand the destructive forces of modernization, and committees for their defense are sometimes created to safeguard their preservations. As in Peru after the earthquake of 1950, the colonial remains must also compete with the pre-colonial remains, for as one was built upon the other both cannot be simultaneously exposed or maintained. The effort to reconstruct the fortifications in Havana harbor, the effort to prevent the paving of the cobblestones in Pátzcuaro, and the effort to save Taxco from neon lighting are examples of this protectionism, which is partly romantic and nostalgic in spirit and which incidentally allows our tourist brochures to speak of locations of quaint colonial charm.

My impression is however that relics deliberately retained—I am speaking here of secular relics, not of ecclesiastical—are less a part of the Latin American than of the Anglo American or western European scene. Latin America has nothing to compare with the impressive institutionalized antiquarianism of the British Museum or Williamsburg, Virginia. The

Latin American cultural heritage has not, in general, been perpetuated in this way—perhaps for the reason that it is already being perpetuated in other, more immediate ways. Preservation in museums is not consonant with the aristocratic, antidemocratic tradition. It is not consonant with the program either of liberalism or of conservatism, for it stands apart from both. To Latin American liberals the society and culture of the nineteenth and twentieth centuries seem insufficiently changed from the colonial period, and the need for preservation of any kind is denied. Conservatives seek to retain colonial forms, but as realities in their own social lives, not as objects in museums, and not because they are colonial but because they serve a living purpose.

Historical change in Latin America often strikes observers as change of a peculiarly uneven sort. If I may cite our brochure again the "unique contrasts between the old and the new" are features of contemporary Latin America frequently remarked upon by visitors. The colonial and the modern worlds are juxtaposed. The references here are to oxcarts, single-handed plows, draft animals, digging sticks, backstrap looms, handmade pottery, adobe walls, thatched roofs, jugs carried on the head, and the leisurely peace of community existence, especially as these may be observed in conjunction with television, airports, modern architecture, and twentieth-century symbols in general. I do not mean to suggest that such contrasts do not exist. But I think that they need further analysis. The contrasts are "unique" partly because the foreign visitor is unfamiliar with them in his own society, and he should not forget that the contrasting solutions of his own society may appear equally unique from other points of view. In our own country the persisting influence of Puritanism and the continuing depressed position of the Negro provide what might also be called "unique" contrasts to modernism, and they relate the United States more closely to its own colonial past than we are likely to realize or wish. What we mean by "unique contrasts," in short, may imply some imagined or false standard of uniformity, as if there were a proper way for a society to change.

We call Latin America an undeveloped, or underdeveloped, or less euphemistically a backward area, but we could not do so unless we regarded our own, or some other, area as developed and advanced. The concept of underdevelopment, stated in other terms, implies an insufficient change from the colonial period, and the programs for development, or for progress, in Latin America, seek to widen the historical gap. But the notions of development and underdevelopment ordinarily relate to the political and economic spheres that are not the subject of this paper. In modern commentaries on Latin America of all kinds, it seems to me, economic and political topics are receiving more attention, and cultural and social topics less. The programs for progress ordinarily look to the economic scene in the belief that if economic reorientation is accomplished, appropriate social and cultural change will follow. Social, and especially cultural, underdevelopment are less easy to measure than is economic underdevelopment, and from the point of view of those who speak in these terms social and cultural underdevelopment are less important. An economic deficiency can be "corrected" simply by a grant of funds, whereas for a social or cultural deficiency much more subtle methods are required. Though we may speak of an outmoded social structure in Latin America, lacking a middle class, we do not normally allow ourselves to speak of a Latin America that is underdeveloped in its cultural life. Even if made with the best intentions such an observation is likely to be construed as unfriendly. Besides, in remarks that all of us have heard, the charge of cultural underdevelopment is one that Latin Americans make against us, not we against them. It may be that Latin America is closer to its colonial past socially and culturally than it is politically and economically, but I think either proposition would be difficult to prove, and, as we have said, these categories are not so easily separated in Latin American life as in our own.

I agree with Pedro Carrasco, who says that change or continuity will receive different emphases according to whether we consider the structure, the form, or the function of a social institution. We may exemplify the observation with reference to any of the institutions that span the period from the colony to the present. Thus the small Latin American community displays a structure and a form quite similar to those of its colonial prototype. Its function has been modified by modern communication systems and access to the outside world. In the city, on the other hand, both structure and form have been subjected to new influences; function, by contrast, appears to have changed least. The modern class structure, to take another example, is essentially the colonial class structure, despite the evident facts that slavery has been abolished, mobility facilitated, and social differentiations, especially that between peninsulars and creoles, modulated. In form the class system is being inflated and modified by population increase. In function, which is a kind of guide to future structure and form, class plays a still vital, but perhaps a progressively less vital, role.

Change and continuity may be classified in other ways. Between rural and urban societies the degrees of survival from the colonial period to the present consistently differ. Rural society displays the lesser inclination to change. There exist parts of rural Latin America where time appears to stand still, where the material cultures and the society and psychology accompanying them appear almost unchanged in 150 years. By contrast the great Latin American cities resemble, at least externally, not their urban antecedents of the colonial period but the metropolitan types of the twentieth-century world at large. Oscar Lewis has pointed out, with regard to the "culture of poverty," that even the proletariat society, the slums, of a Latin American city, though specifically deriving from their Latin American past, are closly related to the phenomena of twentieth-century world urbanism. In any case even the most unobservant visitor responds to the contrasts between city and countryside. He is familiar with them at home too, but in Latin America the degrees of difference are exceptionally striking and the rural resistance to change exceptionally strong.

In the social structure of Latin America there occur similar differences. As in other parts of the world, but here with a particular Latin American intensity, the upper classes choose to retain what they already possess and to resist changes that would equalize peoples. In some instances the present possessors of large properties are the actual descendants of colonial possessors of large properties, and the continuity of inheritance is unbroken. Both the ancestor and his modern heir exemplify social conservatism. In terms of power and wealth and social attitudes it would perhaps be true to say that the upper classes have changed least since the colonial period and the lower and middle classes most, while the very lowest classes—the rural agriculturists, Indian groups, and "marginal" peoples outside the main society—have changed least of all. But the greatest force for change appears in the unprecedented demands voiced in the twentieth century by a whole middle portion of the society whose colonial counterpart was nonexistent, or, if existent, inarticulate. My point here is that the rate of historical change is modified, not simply as we move from city to country but as we move up or down the social scale.

Again it seems to me that our analysis of colonial survivals will vary according to whether we consider the question primarily from a modern, or primarily from a colonial, point of view. To historians of colonial Latin America it is likely that the present-day world will appear quite different from the colonial world and that the elements of change, rather than the elements of continuity, will dominate a first impression. To the observer more familiar with the modern world, on the other hand, the peculiarities of present-day Latin America, by way of contrast with non-Latin areas, will present themselves in a more forceful way and will receive explanation as ideosyncratic, historically derived, characteristics. The matter is not confined to first impressions but is an integral part of the large, complex question of the relation of the historian, or of any observer, to the subject being considered. The historian of the colonial period typically takes a particularistic view, examines the details of colonial life, recognizes the changes that occur within the colonial period itself, and is less likely to consider the broad attributes that distinguish the colonial from other periods or to accept the characterizations that are postulated by persons who know the subject in less detail. Viewed from a greater distance, on the other hand, the colonial period has a kind of massive unity, and traits can be ascribed to it with less concern for qualification. From this latter standpoint, the object of attention, or the puzzle, is the chaos of modern Latin America and not the chaos of colonial Latin America. It is modern Latin America that demands explanation, and colonial Latin America acquires a certain clarity simply by being removed and subordinated in the formulation of the problem. But if the colonial scene itself constitutes the problem, these roles are reversed.

I think that we should not allow the term "colonial" to suffer the fate that has overtaken the word "medieval" at the hands of careless users and writers of editorials. We should not allow "colonial" to be applied to everything that appears illiberal in Latin America or that is vaguely out of date. Colonial status was what the revolutions for independence were against, and it is perhaps natural that when independence failed to achieve its liberal goals the colonial legacy was blamed. It may be pointed out, on the other hand, that Latin American liberalism has its own colonial antecedents, limited as these may be, and that some of what is condemned as colonial survival in modern times is colonial only in one of the extended meanings indicated above. Again if we consider internal peace and absence of revolution as desiderata then the colonial period appears to this extent preferable to the national period and a favorable aspect of the heritage was rejected. Moreover not all colonial legacies conform to the modern liberal's pejorative typology. Mestization for example is an evident social phenomenon of the colonial period. It was colonial in its origin and had no pre-colonial history. It continued and expanded in the nineteenth and twentieth centuries, and it appears with vigor in the contemporary social scene. In the colonial period "mestizo" might be synonymous with bastard or vagrant or outcast. In the nineteenth century mestization was still ordinarily viewed as a defect in the Latin American character. But in various interpretations in more recent Latin American thinking, mestization provides a nationalistic ethos wholly compatible with the most advanced social aspirations. Mestization exemplifies a kind of colonial legacy in reverse, neglected or denounced in its early stages, exalted and proclaimed in its later.

We come then to the major point. I think that most persons are not primarily interested in colonial survivals by way of an historical exercise or an academic question. The fact is that again and again what are called colonial residues in modern Latin America are the objects of condemnation because they appear to be obstacles to change. If Latin America could truly escape from its colonial heritage, so the argument runs, the way would be cleared for Latin America to take its rightful place in the twentieth-century world. In a sense the proposition is undeniable. The principal inhibiting social legacy is the rigid class system, which neither the revolutions for independence nor any of the subsequent revolutions successfully destroyed, and which is only now being partially modified. The inhibiting cultural legacies relate primarily to education, for though the 50% literacy, more or less, of 1962, represents a marked change upon the colonial figure, still the other 50%, of illiteracy, is seen as a colonial heritage in need of correction. To historians it appears obvious that both the rigid class system and the aristocratic educational system may be traced to pre-colonial origins in the Old World, and that there is a sense in which it is gratuitous to speak of them as colonial rather than as pre-colonial or nineteenth-century. But in comparison with the urgency of the practical demand for improvement, such questions appear immaterial. Who but an historian would consider them at all?

C. *A Commentary on Two Papers*

ROBERT A. POTASH

The task of commenting on two such thoughtful and penetrating papers is a challenging one, for the areas of agreement among us are so broad as to limit the opportunity for meaningful observation. There are, however, a number of points, some minor, others of greater importance, which call for comment.

Let me begin by noting that both authors were particularly sensitive to the various connotations of the term "colonial." Professor Borah pointed out that today's program "with equal logic and identical wording of topic could deal with the institutions that work to keep Latin America impoverished and subservient to other regions." Professor Gibson, on the other hand, offered a plea that "colonial" should not be allowed to suffer the fate that has overtaken the word "medieval" in the hands of careless users or writers of editorials. This plea, I fear, will have little effect where it is most needed. The term "colonial" has been so closely related to the word "imperial" as to be rendered guilty by association and thus doomed to suffer the penalty of pejorative usage.

Turning now to Professor Borah's paper, we find our attention directed to various survivals of colonial administrative experience. Any of us who have had to deal with governmental agencies in Latin America, whether to extend a temporary visitor's permit so as to complete an archival search, or simply to withdraw an international package from the customs, immediately recognize the features of external administration to which he refers. Were they ever to disappear, I fear that our capacity as historians to appreciate something of the human realities of colonial life would be materially lessened.

Professor Borah proceeds to analyze for us the centralizing features that characterize much of contemporary Latin American government. Here I find myself a bit puzzled since there is no clear effort to differentiate the colonial survivals from the accretions of one hundred and fifty years of new experiences. The current subordination of provincial and local authority to the will of the center cannot be regarded simply as a survival of eighteenth-century Bourbon administrative reforms. To do so would be to underestimate the twentieth-century pressures that have augmented the powers of national governments everywhere in the world as well as in Latin America, and also to deprive of all meaning nineteenth-century experimentation in administrative organization. At the least we should bear in mind the discontinuity between the centralizing tendencies of the eighteenth century and those that prevail today. After all, in Mexico it was not until the Díaz regime that the central government effectively controlled local and provincial elections, and determined the appointment of the lowliest officials. In Argentina the national government, when it existed, had only imperfect control over the provinces until after the 1880's; and in Brazil, between 1890 and 1930 the states, or more accurately certain states, seemed to have had greater power and revenues than the national government. The centralized political systems that do in fact exist today in such countries as Argentina, Brazil, and Mexico, despite their federal constitutions, are not lineal descendants of eighteenth-century centralizing tendencies. Rather they are the product of conflict between those tendencies and regionalist forces—another and unmentioned colonial legacy—and of the new economic, social, and ideological demands that have reshaped political relationships within these states since about 1930.

As regards the preponderance of the executive power within contemporary political systems, I find myself in greater agreement with Professor Borah. The presidency does seem to embody and perpetuate the vast powers and broad personal authority exercised by colonial viceroys and captains-general. Here too, however, one must be wary of generalizing from the example of the Mexican president to his counterparts elsewhere. The prestige this official enjoys within the Mexican political system—especially his freedom from public criticism while in office—is a case in point. If this is a legacy from colonial times then the heirs to the viceregal tradition in the Río de la Plata have reason to complain about their inheritance.

In his examination of the basic features of political life Professor Borah quite properly directs our attention to the eighteenth-century origins of Latin American militarism. The creation of standing armies, the extension of the *fuero militar* to officers of the colonial militia, and the employment of military men in civil posts undoubtedly helped to pave the way for the militarization of political life after Independence. But whether one can link the political influence of Latin American armies today in any causal way to eighteenth-century developments is something else. Perhaps a case for this could be made in negative terms. The failure of the colonial political experience to prepare civilians for effective self-government permitted the assumption by military men of political power after Independence. Subsequently, whenever and wherever civilian groups have been able to achieve a broad consensus and have learned to fashion effective political parties, military influence on politics has receded. The resurgence of Argentine militarism on the one hand and the decline of Mexican militarism on the other in the years since 1930 give little support to any hypothesis based on colonial precedents.

Professor Gibson's paper offers the intriguing observation that "a colonial institution may be consequential without being continuous," and that "modern legacies of colonial institutions may appear in disguised forms." What he is suggesting, it would appear, is that changes in form and structure of institutions—indeed their very disappearance as far as law or practice is concerned—do not mean that the function performed by the institution has ceased or even that the ideas associated with it have lost their vitality.

One can make a case for the persistence of colonial institutions in disguised forms. The problem then becomes one of definition: does a contemporary social, economic, or political practice similar to one found in colonial times but performed in a different manner constitute a colonial legacy? Is it possible to disembody the spirit from the structure of a colonial institution, recognize it in its modern social garb and acclaim it as a survival? The difficulties involved are illustrated by practical examples.

It has been suggested—although by a political columnist rather than an historian, I hasten to add, that the *residencia* has been recreated in contemporary Argentina. The allusion is to the investigatory committees that are created each time that a government has been forcibly overthrown. These committees, appointed by the successor regime, have inquired into the use and abuse of public office by members of the prior administration; they have produced reports, often voluminous ones, and in some instances their recommendations have resulted in judicial proceedings. The fact that such committees were consistently created after the fall of Yrigoyen in 1930, Castillo in 1943, Perón in 1955, and Frondizi in 1962 suggests that we are indeed in the presence of an institution. But its function appears to be less the administrative one of elevating standards of official conduct or of maintaining royal control over remote officials that we associate with the residencia and more the political one of providing the public with proof that the ousted officials were in fact corrupt, as their opponents had charged, and that they deserved to be put out of office. Perhaps the chief resemblance between the residencia of colonial times and the modern Argentine institution is the failure of either to raise standards of public morality.

Now let me cite one other example where I think the spirit of a colonial institution is still at work. This is the *blanqueo de capitales* or whitewashing of taxable assets that occurs in Argentina—and possibly other countries as well. In Argentina in 1956 and again in 1962 delinquent taxpayers—those who had failed to file statements of assets subject to certain taxes—were invited to register those assets and pay the current tax with the inducement that all previous tax obligations on those assets would be forgiven. Some 15,000 took advantage of this offer in 1956; some 100,000 taxpayers presented themselves this past September and October. Now what we have here, I believe, is the revival of the *composición*. Just as Philip II's government, pressed for funds, was willing to update land titles and overlook past irregularities in return for present payments, so the Argentine government in its deperate search for funds whitewashes past tax irregularities and regularizes the status of those who will come in and make payment of current taxes.

Returning to Professor Gibson's paper, I find myself attracted to his assertion that the most convincing instances of continuity are found at what he calls the "less concrete levels of institutionalism." As one reflects on the examples he cites—the persistence of the aristocratic principle in the sphere of education, the role of nepotism and family ties in the varied aspects of urban society—it seems evident that it is not institutions in the usual sense of the word that have slowed and complicated the transformation of Latin America but the survival of a system of values. Professor Borah confirms this in his definition of institutions and in his discussion of the obstacles to capital accumulation.

Even where, as the result of evolving class structure, sharp changes have taken place in the formal aspects of institutional life, certain basic attitudes have shown a tremendous vitality. In education for example it appears that the new middle class has taken over elitist viewpoints once associated with the colonial aristocracy. Victor Alba has recently asserted that one characteristic of the new middle class in Latin America is that "although it advocates public education, it is in fact much more urgently interested in developing higher and professional education, though this preference is never frankly stated." Thus the addition of engineering and economics facilities in the universities alongside the traditional ones of law and medicine expands the avenues through which one can join the elite but does not resolve the problem of the illiterate mass.

If it is true then, as these two fine papers seem to suggest, that the value system erected in the colonial era has been more impervious to change than the structure of institutions, and if those concerned with promoting the rapid modernization of Latin America become increasingly aware that the process involves much more than directing capital flows or altering the terms of trade, then perhaps next year's program committee could perform a real service by organizing a session to take up where this one leaves off, a session that could perhaps be called "Colonial Values and Contemporary Latin America."

4. The Balance of Power
in Nineteenth-Century South America:
An Exploratory Essay

ROBERT N. BURR

Latin American historians, and others too, have rarely studied the relations of the Latin American nations with each other, but have tended to study the relations of a single country with the United States or some European power. Professor Burr of the University of California, Los Angeles, has broken new ground in the following essay, by analyzing the balance-of-power principle in the light of the conditions and interests of various nations.

Numerous articles, monographs and books have been written about the foreign relations of Latin America during the nineteenth and twentieth centuries. The bulk of this work has been concerned with the relations of the Great Powers with Latin America, or with the legal aspects of boundary disputes among the Latin American nations or with topics related to international cooperation. Relatively few of these writings have attempted to define the changing national interests of individual Latin American nations or to relate these interests to internal economic and social conditions. Few, if any, writers have sought to provide an integrated pattern for the relations of the Latin American nations among themselves. Both of these deficiencies might be lessened by an investigation into the operation of the balance-of-power principle in Latin America.

A balance of power may be defined as an equilibrium in power among a group of sovereign nations. Individual nations may follow a policy of maintaining a balance of power within a group to prevent any nation from becoming sufficiently strong to enforce its will upon the others or to threaten their independence. It would appear that a perfect balance of power has never for long existed within any group of nations. The desired equilibrium is continuously being disturbed by the uneven development in nations of such elements of national power as population, production, technology, armaments, and governmental and political stability. If a nation

From Volume XXXV (1955), pages 37–60.

somehow manages to attain power superiority in its group, it may attempt to perpetuate its hegemony by seeking to maintain a balance of power among the other members of the group. However, the normal tendency is for these less potent nations to set about restoring the balance of power.

A well defined concept of a balance of power among the Latin American nations did not exist when they emerged as independent states in the first quarter of the nineteenth century. Three basic conditions were necessary to the maturing of such a concept: first, that the nations of Latin America should have certain minimum essentials of sovereignty such as definite territorial limits and effective government; second, that their relations with each other should be subject to a minimum of non-Latin American influence; and third, that channels of communications and points of contact among the Latin American nations should be sufficiently well developed to make each nation aware that its interests could be affected by the activities of the others.

Many of the Latin American nations were slow to acquire the essential characteristics of sovereign nation-states. In the early years of their independence they had but a vague notion of what the territorial limits of their new nations should be. Some ideas concerning the territorial divisions of independent Latin America were more or less generally accepted, for instance, that Portuguese America would constitute a separate state and that the former centers of power in the Spanish empire, as represented by the viceregal capitals at Mexico City, Lima, Bogotá and Buenos Aires and the captaincies at Santiago de Chile and Caracas would become nuclei of independent sovereign nations. But disagreements arose over the status of the lesser administrative units of the former Spanish empire such as those which centered around Montevideo, Asunción, Chuquisaca and Quito. Should they become independent nations or should they be absorbed into older and more powerful centers? Because these lesser administrative units often had economic and strategic importance, because they were generally weak in terms of power and because they were often situated between two or more larger centers of power they became areas of contention among their larger neighbors. These areas were power vacuums into which more powerful nations tended to expand, but where they generally encountered resistance either of a local nature or from other powers with interests at stake.

Many Latin American nations were slow not only in acquiring their definite territorial limits but also in establishing stable government. It was only when a modicum of stability had been attained that a given nation could effectively defend itself from outside pressures and at the same time expand economically and territorially. And it might be noted that a small nation with political stability could hold a power position superior to that of a larger nation afflicted with internal disorders.

For the growth of a balance of power in Latin America it was necessary that the nations of the area be left free to adjust relationships among themselves with a minimum of interference from Europe or the United States. That condition was not to be fulfilled in the Caribbean region where British-United States rivalry and the eventual achievement of a dominant position by the latter combined with geographic factors to differentiate this area from the power system which developed in South America. Consequently, this paper will deal with South America. Nevertheless, two attributes of the Caribbean area should be cited: (1) that the inter-relations of the Central American states provided a classic example of the operation of the balance-of-power principle and (2) that the Caribbean area tended to be linked to the power system of South America by common opposition to European intervention, by a common interest in the development of Isthmian transit routes and by the fact that both Venezuela and Colombia were not only South American but also Caribbean powers.

South America, obviously, did not develop a balance-of-power system hermetically sealed off from the rest of the world. Sporadic outside interference in the affairs of the nations of South America was common during much of the nineteenth century but its effect proved neither as permanent nor as decisive as in the Caribbean region. Such outside interference as was felt in South America affected the power relationships of the nations of that area in at least two ways. In some cases it prompted international cooperation among them which tended, at least momentarily, to reduce their rivalries and lessen the importance of their power relationships. In other cases outside interference tended to strengthen nationalism and the affected nation's determination to become more powerful. But during most of the nineteenth century rivalries among the nations of Europe and between them and the United States protected South America from any decisive foreign interference and made possible the development of a system of power relationship in the area.

Adequate channels of communication and points of contact among the South American nations were also slow in developing. It was in areas already linked at the time of independence by communications—primarily waterways—that the idea of a balance of power first took root on a regional scale. As the century progessed and communications and contacts became more widespread these regional systems tended to interlock into a continental South American balance of power.

The earliest regional balance-of-power system in South America developed in the area dependent upon the Río de la Plata. There, before the revolutions for independence, Spanish-Portuguese rivalry over control of the Banda Oriental and the fluvial system emptying into the Plata had moved Spain to create a viceroyalty with its capital at Buenos Aires in order to contain Portuguese expansion. The leaders of the *porteño* independence movement planned to maintain this area intact, but their insistence that Buenos Aires should dominate the new nation aroused opposition among provincial leaders, including those in the Banda Oriental. Internal strife thus caused the fragmentation of the power structure which Spain had created to contain the Portuguese. In 1816 the relatively strong Portuguese monarchy, now resident in Brazil, took advantage of this situation to move troops into the Banda Oriental where they were to remain for more than a decade. The Buenos Aires government was so handicapped by domestic difficulties that it was unable to oppose Brazilian expansion until the return of a measure of stability following the *"año terrible"* of 1820. But then steps were taken to drive out the Portuguese. In 1823 an Argentine representative was sent to Rio de Janeiro to protest Brazil's annexation of Uruguay and he made it clear that the Banda Oriental was of supreme economic and strategic importance to his government. When Brazil failed to heed the Argentine protest a demand for war grew in Argentina. The government of Buenos Aires then made an unsuccessful attempt to obtain help from Simón Bolívar who was then at the peak of his power. This porteño gesture may be seen as an attempt to establish a balance of power in the Plata through a coalition of Spanish American powers against Brazil.

Argentina's failure to obtain aid from Bolívar forced it to carry on war against Brazil alone. British mediation helped bring this war to an end in 1828—in a manner unsatisfactory to the ambitions either of Brazil or of Argentina—and the peace treaty which resulted was the cornerstone of the future regional balance of power in the Río de la Plata area. Uruguay was now to become an independent nation. Any attempt by either large power to dominate Uruguay would henceforth threaten the equilibrium between them. Paraguay, commercially and culturally isolated under the Francia regime, was as yet scarcely a part of this regional power system.

The sense of a balance of power was slower in taking shape on South America's west coast. There, in the early 1820's, the need for cooperation against Spain and its potential allies had overshadowed questions of power relationships among nations which had hardly acquired form. Yet even in the various plans for Spanish American confederation which were being discussed at that time it was recognized that cooperation had to be based upon guarantees of the territorial integrity and independence of the co-operating nations. These proposed guarantees of the status quo were in a sense the recognition of a need for a balance of power among the new nations.

When the idea of Spanish American cooperation began to decline and when the influence of Bolívar waned, northern and western Spanish South America disintegrated into a number of impoverished and disorderly nations, no one of which was strong enough to dominate its neighbors. Neither Peru nor New Granada was able to effect the annexation of Guayaquil and the resolution of their rivalry lay in the establishment of a new nation, Ecuador, the independence of which was guaranteed by the formerly contending powers.

In the 1830's two nations on the west coast of South America succeeded in pulling themselves out of the prevailing disorder. Chile, under the guidance of Diego Portales, achieved relative political stability and was able to intensify its economic and commercial expansion. In Bolivia, Andrés Santa Cruz welded conflicting elements into a strong and orderly state with a sound economic base. Both Chile and Bolivia proceeded to turn their attention to Peru where intense, sometimes violent, political conflict had created a power vacuum. Chile sought to expand its commerce with Peru and to prevent the port of Callao from regaining the hegemony of the Pacific trade which it had enjoyed during the colonial period; the goal of Santa Cruz was the reconstruction of the old Viceroyalty of Peru. A crisis developed when he intervened in Peru in 1835 and established the Peru-Bolivian Confederation.

Farsighted Chileans feared that the power concentration represented by the Peru-Bolivian Confederation might stifle Chile's growing economy and that an attempt might even be made to bring Chile under control of the Confederation. The balance of power on the Pacific coast had been disturbed and the Chilean government reacted by declaring war. Among the reasons given for this action was that "General Santa Cruz . . . menaces the independence of the other South American republics."

Chile attempted to develop a counterpoise to the power of the Peru-Bolivian Confederation by bringing other South American republics into a coalition against this "common threat." When Argentina, duly encouraged by a Chilean agent, declared war on the Confederation it included among its reasons that "the increase of the power of Santa Cruz by means of the abuse of force upsets the balance of power for peace in the republics bordering on Peru and Bolivia." President Francisco Santander of New Granada was also concerned. ". . . We all see," Santander wrote, "that [Santa Cruz] is raising a great power . . . which if it were consolidated would be a power menacing to the peace of neighboring peoples. . . ." But Santander felt that Santa Cruz would not be able to consolidate this power and he counseled peace. The administration which succeeded Santander appears to have been more concerned. In the spring of 1838 it sent a diplomatic representative to Ecuador whose mission, according to the Chilean agent there, was " . . . to agree with Ecuador on measures for dealing with the power of Santa Cruz if, unfortunately, . . . [Chile's] undertaking fails."

It was in Chile, however, that we find the most clearly defined concept of a balance of power. In instructions to his agent in Ecuador the Chilean foreign minister wrote, "The security of the states of the South, founded on the equilibrium of their forces, is a base which we cannot abandon. . . ." And in another note he stated "This Republic is ever firm in its purpose of reestablishing the former political equilibrium of the South American States."

By 1838, when Santa Cruz had been defeated and Peru and Bolivia had been reestablished as independent nations, a balance of power on the Pacific coast had begun to assume form. Although Argentina had been brought temporarily into the balance-of-power system surrounding Bolivia, it had taken no effective part in the war because it was faced at the same time with French intervention in the Plata region. After the war Argentina was to concentrate on Platine affairs for the next thirty years. Because of Argentina's preoccupation with the Plata region and Bolivia's westward orientation there existed two relatively dissociated balance-of-power systems in South America.

On the Pacific coast the Chilean government emerged from the war against Santa Cruz strong and unified, with a sharpened sense of nationalism and in a position to expand and grow while its neighbors lapsed temporarily into internal disorder. Chile's efforts to maintain a balance of power were at first confined to preventing Peru and Bolivia from reuniting. However, as Chilean west coast commerce expanded and as a revived Peru began to challenge Chile's hegemony, the Chilean government began more and more to play the role of regulator of the balance of power on the Pacific.

It was in the late 1840's that Peru, made rich by its guano monopoly and stabilized politically by Ramón Castilla, attempted to use its increased power to regain leadership on the Pacific coast. One result of Peru's increasing power was its active sponsorship of the movement for Latin American cooperation; another was mounting friction with both Chile and New Granada. The evils of this friction were somewhat mitigated during the 1840's and 1850's by a series of threats—real and imagined—to the Pacific coast nations from the Flores expedition and expansionist sentiment in the United States. In the face of these outside threats considerations of the power relationships among the west coast countries were sometimes subordinated to the need for cooperation.

But the balance of power was not forgotten. This was clearly shown in the Treaty of Union and Confederation signed by the representatives of Bolivia, Chile, Colombia, Ecuador and Peru at the Lima Congress in 1848. Although the chief purpose of this treaty was to organize the signatory powers for common defense, Article 8 indicated that stable power relationships among the west coast powers were considered essential as a basis for cooperation. In this article they agreed that "if it is attempted to join two or more of the Confederated Republics into one single state or to divide into several states any of said Republics, or to detach from one in order to add to another of the same republics, or to a foreign power one or more ports, cities, or provinces, it will be necessary . . . that the Governments of the other Confederated Republics declare, expressly, that such change be not prejudicial to the interests and the security of the Confederation." The delegates to the Lima Congress had not forgotten Santa Cruz or the interest of both Peru and New Granada in Ecuador.

In fact, international rivalries in Ecuador during the early 1850's brought consideration of the balance of power clearly to the fore. In Ecuador a power vacuum had been created by the political disorder which overtook the country in 1850 and which was to last until Gabriel García

Moreno assumed power in the early 1860's. The situation which developed was far too complicated to describe here in any detail, but its main outlines bring into focus the role of Chile as the regulator of the Pacific coast balance of power. In early 1850 the Quito chancellery reported to that of New Granada that a revolution had broken out which aimed at separating Guayaquil from Ecuador and annexing it to Peru. The Ecuadorean foreign minister pointed out that this would be prejudicial not only to Ecuador but also to the maintenance of political equilibrium among the Spanish American states. The foreign minister of New Granada replied that "far from regarding such a plan with indifference, the Granadine government would look upon it with profound distrust and suspicion . . . as a precedent of lamentable consequences for the welfare and security of the states neighboring on Ecuador. . . ." If Guayaquil were annexed to Peru, New Granada would live up to its duty to maintain the territorial integrity of Ecuador.

At the same time that New Granada was interesting itself in the threat to Ecuador, so too was Chile. Foreign Minister Varas, apparently suspecting Peruvian complicity, asked his minister in Lima to investigate that country's role in encouraging the annexationist movement in Guayaquil. But then events took place which placed the Chilean administration in a dilemma. These events stemmed from the influence of the European revolutions of 1848 upon the west coast of South America. In Chile, agitation led by Francisco Bilbao resulted, early in 1851, in a revolution which although suppressed left the government of Chile fearful of the radical ideas which had inspired it. In New Granada and Ecuador the radicals had gained control and in 1851 began to carry out the democratic leveling and the anticlerical ideas which the Chilean government so profoundly distrusted. In Peru, however, conservative President José Rufino Echenique supported an expedition led by Juan José Flores which aimed at overthrowing the radical government of Ecuador and replacing it with a more conservative regime. The government of New Granada then threatened to declare war if Peru persisted in its support of the Flores expedition.

Chile, while not eager to see the extension of Peruvian influence, was equally averse to the extension of the radical concepts of New Granada. Some Chileans feared that a coalition of New Granada and Ecuador might resort to force to extend its radical principles to Peru and even to Bolivia. In an effort to prevent this the Chilean government adopted a variety of measures, including an implied threat that it would come to the aid of Peru in case that country were attacked. But Chile's basic policy in this dilemma was to play both ends against the middle in an effort to maintain the balance of power. This was made clear in instructions dated July, 1852, to Chile's agent in Peru. He was told that it was difficult to predict the course of the Ecuadorean question but that the objectives which should direct his efforts in all events were ". . . the peace of the continent; [and] the stability of the present order of things, with neither dismemberments nor annexations."

While a balance of power was taking form on the Pacific coast, the one already established in the Plata region was being disturbed. The first serious threat to the equilibrium based upon Uruguayan independence commenced in the late 1830's when Juan Manuel de Rosas, who had forged a strong government in Buenos Aires, sought to extend his power to revolution-torn Uruguay. Then, when Paraguay emerged from isolation following Francia's death and made its entrance into the Plata power system, Dictator Rosas' threatening posture made it appear that Argentina sought to dominate not only Uruguay but also Paraguay.

Brazil clearly recognized the implications of such an Argentine policy. As a Brazilian diplomat in Europe explained, in 1846, ". . . if the independence of the State of Montevideo, established by the Convention of August 27, 1828, was a condition or guarantee necessary; for the equilibrium between Brazil and the Argentine Confederation, the independence of the Republic of Paraguay also is evidently necessary to complete said equilibrium. The annexation of Paraguay to the [Argentine] Confederation would give to the latter, in addition to pride of conquest, an increase of territory and forces such that the equilibrium would cease to exist, and all of the sacrifices made by Brazil when it adhered to the independence of Montevideo would be entirely fruitless."

From the early 1840's the Brazilian government moved to contain Argentine expansion, and as the disorders of the Regency period were quelled following the ascension of Dom Pedro II, and as the Empire's economy began to flourish, Brazilian opposition to Argentina mounted. This opposition culminated in 1851 when Brazil united anti-Rosas forces in Argentina and Uruguay to form an alliance which succeeded in over-throwing the Rosas dictatorship by force in the following year.

With the fall of Rosas the balance tipped in the other direction. Argentina, split into two separate and rival jurisdictions during most of the period between 1852 and 1861, was too weak to play a dominant role in the Plata region and Brazil, with its relative power position thus strengthened, assumed hegemony.

Brazilian dominance and Argentine debility had consequences both outside and inside the Plata power system. They contributed to the development of closer contacts between the Plata and the Pacific coast systems. This was particularly true in two areas. One was the Amazon region, which began to arouse heightened interest in the 1850's. Brazil, freed from preoccupation with Platine affairs by Argentina's weakened condition, was able to focus its attention on the Amazon River system and its attempts to control its navigation in the 1850's brought it into greater contact and conflict with those west coast powers interested in the region. The other area of Platine-Pacific contact was Patagonia. Chile, strong and expanding, had already established a colony on the Straits of Magellan in the 1840's and in the next decade it broadened its claims to include Patagonia. Argentina had protested what it considered Chilean encroachments but, divided, weak and concentrating on Platine affairs, had been able to do no more than sign an agreement with Chile, in 1856, to arbitrate their territorial differences in the future.

Within the Plata area Brazil intervened frequently in the affairs of Uruguay, came into increasing conflict with Paraguay and attained its objectives in the Río de la Plata region through a series of treaties which guaranteed the independence of Uruguay and Paraguay, the free navigation of the fluvial system and the neutralization of the strategic island of Martín García. But two events, both of which were in part a reaction to Brazilian power, were to alter the situation of the Plata region. One was the union of Buenos Aires with the other provinces of Argentina in 1862 which resulted in a strengthened Argentina. The other was the creation of Paraguayan military might.

Paraguayan militarism, nurtured and driven on by ambitious Francisco Solano López, was to burst into the disastrous Paraguayan War. In 1864, when Brazil threatened to send troops into Uruguay to obtain satisfaction for certain claims, López issued a dramatic ultimatum. In it he stated that the occupation of Uruguay by Brazilian forces would be regarded ". . . as an attack upon the equilibrium of the states of the Plata which Paraguay considers as a guarantee of its peace, security and prosperity. . . ." When Brazil disregarded this ultimatum and sent its forces into Uruguay, López declared war. Argentina, where strong sentiment against Brazil prevailed in the provinces, at first determined to follow a neutral course. Argentina was soon forced into the war, however, when Paraguayan forces invaded and occupied the province of Corrientes in spite of President Mitre's previous denial of permission to López' troops to pass through Argentine territory in order to attack the Brazilians. In May, 1865, Argentina, Brazil and Uruguay, the latter with a new government friendly to Brazil, signed a Treaty of Triple Alliance which bound them to fight together to overthrow dictator López—he who claimed to be the defender of the equilibrium of the Plata.

Whether or not López was sincere in his appeal for the maintenance of the balance of power the mere fact that he issued his appeal serves to indicate the strength which the concept had by this time achieved. As Domingo F. Sarmiento explained, "The word *equilibrium* of the Río de la Plata has appeared in the first rank among the ostensible motives for the present [Paraguayan] war. As vicious as the present application may appear, no one will deny that it was born of . . . necessity when it is applied to the influence of Brazil. It will always exist between a state of nine million inhabitants and others of one, a half and a quarter million." Sarmiento's solution to the problem of Brazil's power was ". . . to form a federation of the three Spanish republics of the Plata. . . ." He realized, however, that the creation of such a federation would produce continental complications. "The Republics of the Pacific," he predicted, "above all Chile, would offer great resistance, in virtue of the prevalent idea of the equilibrium of political nullities with Republics of one or two million inhabitants incapable of defending themselves against foreign aggression. . . . Crying against imperial preponderance they will [nevertheless] be opposed to the Republic in the Río de la Plata acquiring robustness, the only effective counterweight to that preponderance."

Brazilian preponderance in the Plata area also troubled another Argentinian, Juan B. Alberdi, who considered the Paraguayan War as one more manifestation of Brazilian imperialism. Alberdi's approach to the threat of an imperialist Brazil was to have the Argentine provinces and the Spanish American nations of the Pacific coast form an alliance. "The permanent aim of this league," Alberdi stated, "will be that of containing the annexationist efforts of the Brazilian Empire . . . in defense of the equilibrium which protects the Republics of Spanish American nationality."

While the Paraguayan War was in the making, the powers of the west coast had become involved in difficulties with Spain after Spanish naval forces had seized the Chincha Islands from Peru in the spring of 1864. These difficulties led to the outbreak of war a few months after the powers of the Plata region had signed the Treaty of Triple Alliance against Paraguay. To provide for cooperation in waging war against Spain, a quadruple alliance was formed by Chile, Peru, Ecuador and Bolivia in late 1865 and early 1866. The simultaneous prosecution of these two distinct wars, one against an American nation and the other against a foreign power was, paradoxically, to focus the attention of the west coast nations on the Plata, to bring increasing contact between the governments of the two areas and to point up the fact that the interests of the nations of these two areas were inter-related. Thus a basis was laid for the later fusion of the power systems of the Plata and the Pacific into a continental balance of power.

The attention of the Pacific coast powers to the Plata area was initially attracted by their wish to obtain Platine cooperation in their war against Spain. Argentina, Brazil and Uruguay had, however, little interest in joining an alliance against Spain while they were involved in their own war and the Pacific coast countries therefore tried to end the Paraguayan War through mediation. When such efforts failed and Argentina, Brazil and Uruguay persisted in their refusal to cooperate against Spain, a spirit of recrimination and ill feeling arose between the two regions.

Bad feeling was increased by the revelation of hitherto secret clauses in the Treaty of Triple Alliance—clauses which provided for the partial dismemberment of Paraguay and for the imposition of limitations upon its sovereignty. All of the nations of the west coast seemed to feel that Paraguay's dismemberment would disturb the status quo in the continent and all of them protested. The government of Peru told the Triple Alliance that ". . . to make an American Poland of Paraguay would be a scandal which Americans could not witness without being covered with shame."

The Peruvian envoy to the Plata region protested to the Argentine foreign minister that ". . . the treaty of alliance against Paraguay seems to demonstrate that the final aim of the war . . . is no other than that of carrying out overt attacks against the Law of Nations which would be at the same time a threat to the continental equilibrium and an injury to the principles which constitute the Public Law of the American States. . . ." Colombia's foreign minister, in his report to Congress of 1868 claimed that, ". . . The dearest interests of the nations of the continent impel them to stop the consummation of the acts projected [against Paraguay] and . . . the establishment of lamentable precedents." Although a continental balance of power was specifically mentioned in only one of these protests, all of them serve to indicate that the leaders of the west coast nations realized that their own national interests could be affected by threats to the independence of a nation in the Plata power system.

The embryonic sense of a continental balance of power which was evident in the thought of Alberdi and Sarmiento and implicit in the protests of the west coast nations was to become more clearly defined in the decade following the conclusion of the two wars. Contributing to this definition of a continental equilibrium was the resurgence of rivalries among the nations of the Pacific after their victory over Spain. Two major factors were responsible for these renewed rivalries. The first was the expansion of Chilean economic interests into the sparsely populated but valuable desert coastal region of Bolivia. The Chilean government's overt support of this expansion aroused suspicion in both Peru and Bolivia and laid the basis for an entente between them. As Julio Méndez, a Bolivian, wrote in 1872, with Chile obviously in mind, "The absorbent attitude which some South American States have assumed completely disturbs the international equilibrium of those which make up the system of the half-continent."

The second factor which led to the resurgence of international conflicts on the Pacific coast was the superior power position, in terms of navy and defensive installations which Peru had achieved by the end of the war against Spain—a war in which Chile had suffered losses far more severe than had Peru. Peru's recognized superiority had three important consequences: it encouraged Peru to resist Chilean expansionism; it encouraged Bolivia to look to Peru for support; and it encouraged the Chilean Congress to authorize the purchase of two new warships in January, 1872. Finally, in February of 1873 Peru and Bolivia signed a secret Treaty of Alliance which they claimed was designed to contain Chilean expansion but which the Chileans, when they learned of its existence, claimed was for the purpose of destroying Chilean power.

This falling out among the allies on the Pacific coast was one factor which led to the definition of a continental balance of power. A second was Chile's attempt, in the 1870's, to make good its claim to Patagonia. This would not have been so important in developing a continental balance of power, however, had it not been for a third factor—the remarkable upsurge of Argentine wealth, population and political stability which followed the Paraguayan War. Under the impact of this progress Argentina became less preoccupied with the area immediate to the Plata and more intent upon developing its resources in the south—an area part of which was disputed with Chile. Argentine progress put the nation in a better position to contest Chilean claims. The result was increasing tension between the two countries in the years following the end of the Paraguayan War. Chile's dispute with Argentina was another reason why the Chileans felt it necessary to rebuild their naval strength and the existence of the dispute made Argentinians receptive to the idea of cooperation with Chile's Pacific coast competitors.

In mid-1873 the Peruvian government took steps to bring Argentina into the anti-Chilean, Peru-Bolivian alliance. The Peruvian representative in Buenos Aires invited Argentina to adhere to the alliance, pointing out ". . . the tendency which Chile had shown . . . of enlarging its territory to the north and south at the expense of its neighbors and of the South American equilibrium. . . ." Argentine government circles received Peru's invitation most favorably. But at this point a fourth factor contributory to the definition of a continental balance of power became an important consideration. This was the falling out of the allies which had waged war on Paraguay.

Argentina and Brazil, ancient rivals for control of the Plata, had been reluctant allies, each suspicious of the other's designs upon Paraguay. When the war was ended conflict over peace terms had developed and came to a head in 1872 when Brazil violated the terms of the Treaty of Triple Alliance by making separate peace with Paraguay. War between Argentina and Brazil was indeed narrowly averted but tension between them continued. The fact that Argentina was a potential enemy both of Brazil and Chile provided a basis for a possible understanding between these two nations at the very time when Argentina was considering the anti-Chilean alliance with Peru and Bolivia. Although Chile and Brazil concluded no formal entente, Argentina's fears on this score were sufficient to make it hesitate to adhere to the Peru-Bolivian alliance. Peru also began to fear that Argentina's inclusion in the alliance might precipitate a Chilean-Brazilian pact which could compromise Peru's relations with Brazil and endanger its growing Amazon interests. Peru therefore tried to allay any possible Brazilian suspicions by specifically limiting to Chile the application of the proposed Treaty of Alliance. Negotiations lagged while Peru attempted to overcome Argentina's objections to such a restriction and were further bogged down by the injection of an Argentine-Bolivian boundary dispute into the discussions. These delays, plus the delivery of one of Chile's brand new warships, were important factors in preventing Argentine adherence to the Peru-Bolivian Alliance. Nevertheless, these attempts at forming alliances and ententes on a diagonal and intersecting basis as contrasted to a vertical and parallel basis had the effect of bringing about a closer integration of the power systems of the Plata and the Pacific. A majority of the nations of South America had become involved in the balancing of power.

Balancing of power on a continental scale did not prevent the outbreak of the War of the Pacific in 1879, but it was this war which served to involve a larger number of the South American nations more deeply in a balance-of-power system. When it became clear that Chile would defeat its enemies in the War of the Pacific and would demand territorial concessions as the price of peace, the other nations of South America began to sense that the balance of power was being seriously threatened. Colombia's minister in Chile warned his government to prepare to defend itself by increasing its armaments, by strengthening its relations with its neighbors and by securing an alliance with Argentina, a country equally threatened by the growth of Chilean power. A pamphlet by Adriano Páez, published in Bogotá in 1881, was symptomatic of the reaction of many Spanish Americans to Chilean victories over Bolivia and Peru and indicated that Colombians now felt they had a role to play in the continental balancing of power. Chile, Páez wrote, ". . . has destroyed the land and sea power of Peru . . . and has won the predominance of the Pacific. . . . Chile will be master from the Straits to Ecuador, for the present, and, . . . as neither Ecuador nor Colombia has a navy, Chile will rule from the Straits to the Isthmus of Panama. . . . It will be master of the commerce of the Pacific and [will have] more warships than any American nation except the United States. . . ." To meet the Chilean threat the Colombian pamphleteer advocated that Colombia cooperate with other nations of Latin America. "The danger is common," he wrote. "Let diplomacy put itself into the field and raise a unanimous and formidable protest against Chile's pretentions and if that country does not heed the explicit will of America then let there be formed a league of *all* the other Republics so that insane ambition may be returned to its natural bounds."

Venezuelans, whether for reasons of principle or of national interest, were also indignant. The Congress of Venezuela officially protested Chile's conduct. It stated, in a resolution, that ". . . we must profoundly lament the terrible catastrophe of the Pacific. . . . In the name of the great Bolivar, liberator also of . . . [Peru and Bolivia] we solemnly protest against these iniquitous and scandalous usurpations of which they are the victims."

Argentinians also feared the increase of power which victory and the acquisition of valuable territories would give to Chile. The press of Argentina began to advocate the reconstruction of the old Viceroyalty of the Río de la Plata, apparently as a counterpoise to growing Chilean power. The government of Argentina was more practical. It undertook a diplomatic offensive aimed at depriving Chile of its conquests. Among other moves, Argentina worked to obtain the cooperation of Brazil in a joint mediation the specific terms of which would have prohibited territorial conquest. Argentina also attempted to convert an Arbitration Congress sponsored by Colombia into a meeting at which the American nations would condemn Chilean conquests. Moreover, Argentina sent a diplomatic agent to Caracas and Bogotá for the first time in its history, for the apparent purpose of securing cooperation in the diplomatic offensive against Chile.

A Bolivian, Santiago V. Guzmán, published a book in 1881 which aimed at winning Spanish American support for maintaining the territorial integrity of his defeated nation. One of his appeals was the necessity of preserving the South American balance of power. "One can say without fear of [error] ...," he wrote,

that the Bolivian nation is called upon to fulfill in the international politics of these countries the role of regulator which falls to France in the European system; in resemblance to that nation, [which is] the center of equilibrium in the opposition of the Slavic and German races with the Latin and Saxon, Bolivia not only is a necessary element between the Lusitanian race and the Spanish, but it also is among countries of common origin whose territorial sovereignty and whose rights it is destined to preserve. . . .

If in the vast system of South American nations the principle of equilibrium must be one of the fundamentals of its public law, if the axis of the political balance must be the Republic of Bolivia because of its interior and coastal position, it is in the interests of the tranquility of America to assure that nation the full enjoyment of its independence and sovereignty, reëstablishing its territorial limits. . . .

To counteract Spanish American hostility, the Chilean government astutely played upon the antagonisms of the nations most likely to cooperate against it. Particularly important were Chilean efforts to neutralize Argentine activity by working to assure the benevolent neutrality of Brazil, or even to win its active cooperation. One Chilean minister in Brazil was instructed to remind the Emperor's government ". . . that between Brazil and our country there could be formed a powerful league which might affirm our common preponderance on the South American continent."

In spite of much hostility to its policies, Chile emerged from the War of the Pacific stronger than ever and with undoubted hegemony in South America, except for Brazil. It was inevitable, however, that other American nations should attempt to redress the balance of power. In maintaining its predominance Chile was faced with problems on several fronts. Peruvians, as they gradually recovered from the impact of their defeat in the War of the Pacific and as their power position improved, pressed for the return of the provinces of Tacna and Arica, still occupied by Chilean forces. Bolivians insisted on an outlet to the sea before amicable relations with Chile could be reestablished. But the major problem faced by Chilean statesmen was expanding and prosperous Argentina. The two countries were technically still at odds over the question of the demarcation of their boundary—a question which led to several crises and war scares between 1892 and 1902. But in reality, as one Argentinian saw it in 1902, "The Argentine-Chilean boundary question has never existed as a serious motive for conflict. . . . The only question which has agitated the two countries is that of the influence of each in the South American equilibrium."

To improve its position in the power contest with Chile, the Argentine government expanded its naval and armament programs. On one occasion, when war with Chile seemed near, Argentina sought an alliance with Uruguay and Brazil. Moreover, the Argentinians adopted a foreign policy which in the opinion of the Chilean government showed a ". . . tendency to interfere . . ." in the solution of Chile's problems on the Pacific coast by giving Peruvians and Bolivians hope that they would receive support from Argentina.

Chile, once more faced with the possibility of an unfriendly coalition of its neighbors, attempted to preserve its position by exploiting rivalries among the other South American nations. In effect, Chile was attempting to maintain a balance of power among these nations which would enable Chile to retain its hegemony. The Chilean government found potential allies to the north in Ecuador and Colombia. Both nations had long been wrangling with Peru over disputed territory in the Amazon area and their conflicts were intensified at the end of the nineteenth century by the rubber boom. Chile endeavored to capitalize upon these sore spots to win the support of Ecuador and Colombia and thus to create counterweights to growing Peruvian power. To Ecuador, no longer needed Chilean arms and munitions were sold, and arrangements were made for Ecuadorean cadets to study at Chile's Military College and for Chilean army officers to serve as instructors at the military academy in Quito. In Colombia a Chilean legation was established in Bogotá in 1901 which ". . . initiated various efforts with the Government of Colombia directed not only toward creating a current of sympathies between the two countries but also toward strengthening their political and commercial relations." Among other things discussed by the Chilean minister in Bogotá was the sale to Colombia of a Chilean cruiser which, if consummated, would give Colombia ". . . greater military influence in the Pacific. . . ."

The Chilean government also tried to use its influence in northern South America to settle a boundary dispute between Colombia and Ecuador ". . . not only to strengthen the close solidarity which today exists among the three nations but also [because] Chile will thus take one step more to recuperate the influence which legitimately corresponds to it in America because of its organization and progress." In the opinion of the Peruvians, however, "What Chile desired in this matter was, first, that Colombia and Ecuador should reach a peaceful agreement and unite their interests with those of Chile and, second, that Colombia and Ecuador should not reach any agreement with Peru."

Chilean activities were not confined to northwestern South America. Efforts were made to bring both Paraguay and Bolivia into its orbit. Paraguayan youths were encouraged to enter Chile's military and naval academies and at the suggestion of the Asunción government the Chilean minister to Paraguay worked to induce Chilean teachers to come to Paraguay "in order to counterbalance the influence of Argentine teachers, who resist greatly any reform in education which may tend to diminish their preponderance. . . ." To Bolivia there was held out the hope that it might receive part of the former Peruvian provinces of Tacna and Arica as compensation for the loss of its own seacoast to Chile. And finally, the Chilean government continued to work to retain the friendship of the new Republic of Brazil.

But by the beginning of the twentieth century it was becoming increasingly difficult for Chile to maintain its hegemony in Spanish America. One major reason for this was that the armaments race with Argentina, and especially the expensive naval construction program, was becoming a serious financial burden for the relatively small Chilean nation. Argentina also felt the economic strain of the armaments contest and the result was the coming to terms of the two governments. This was accomplished in the famous *Pactos de Mayo* of 1902 and a supplementary Act of July 10 of the same year. These agreements sought, in effect, to establish a balance of the forces of Argentina and Chile by providing for the limitation of naval armaments. Equally important, it was agreed by implication that Argentina would not interfere in the affairs of the Pacific and that Chile would keep out of Atlantic and Platine affairs. Even though these agreements seemed to give Chile and Argentina a free hand on the west and east coasts respectively, they in fact aimed at the maintenance of the continental balance of power because in them each nation explicitly promised not to expand territorially. Although the Argentine-Chilean agreements were not to stabilize for long the balance of power in South America, they were a further indication that the idea of a balance of power had become an accepted part of the international life of South America by the beginning of the twentieth century.

The preceding admittedly sketchy outline has brought together evidence that the concept of a balance of power played a role in the international relations of the South American nations during the nineteenth century. Although space limitations have at times made it necessary to oversimplify, the evidence presented would seem sufficient to permit the formulation of the hypothesis which follows and which is presented as a guide for more intensive investigation.

The concept of balance of power first assumed importance in South America on a regional basis. In the 1820's a regional balance-of-power system developed in the Plata region when rivalry between Argentina and Brazil over the Banda Oriental was resolved by the creation of the independent Republic of Uruguay. This Platine power system was expanded in the 1840's when Paraguay emerged from its isolation and developed contacts with the other nations of the Plata. A second regional balance of power began to take form on the west coast of South America in the 1830's as a reaction to the powerful Peru-Bolivian Confederation. The basic element in this west coast power system was rivalry between Chile and Peru. The independence of Bolivia and Ecuador was essential to the equilibrium between these two powers. Colombia became involved in this west coast system because of its interest in preserving the independence of Ecuador.

While these two regional power systems were independently developing, the extension of Chilean influence toward the Atlantic, the increasing importance of the Amazon area, the Paraguayan War and the war of the west coast countries against Spain all resulted in increasing contacts among the individual nations of the two systems and in the creation of a network of interlocking interests which laid the foundation for the fusion of the two regional power systems. This fusion actually began in 1873 when Peru, a major west coast power, sought aid in its contest for power with Chile from Argentina, thus encouraging an entente between Chile and Brazil and an interplay of the power politics of the Platine and west coast systems. Thus was the framework constructed for a continental balance-of-power system involving a majority of the South American nations. Further impulse was given to this development by the War of the Pacific. Chilean victories aroused fears in most of the South American countries, excepting Brazil. Colombia was in particular made more aware of the growing power of Chile following the collapse of that Peruvian strength which had provided a bulwark between Colombia and Chile. The disturbance of the South American equilibrium caused by the growth of Chilean power resulted in an effort by the other South American nations to restore the balance of power. Argentina took the lead and was aided by a gradual revival of Peruvian power in the 1890's and, probably, by the improvement in Argentine-Brazilian relations which followed the overthrow of the Empire. Then, although Chile tried to counteract mounting Argentine and Peruvian power by developing closer relations with Paraguay, Bolivia, Brazil, Colombia and Ecuador, it finally came to terms with Argentina in 1902. The *Pactos de Mayo* of that year contributed to the stabilization, however short-lived, of the balance of power among the nations of South America.

Further elaboration and testing of this hypothesis, and its extension into the twentieth century, would require much investigation. Such research should throw light upon the "national interests" of the countries of South America and would contribute to the evolution of a more integrated pattern for the study of the history of the international relations of the continent.

Other Articles of Interest

Frazer, Robert W. "The Role of the Lima Congress, 1864–1865, in the Development of Pan-Americanism." XXIX (1949), 319–348.

The Lima Congress of 1864–1865 was the final attempt to achieve inter-American cooperation on the basis of confederation. The desire for cooperation was manifested most strongly when Latin America was menaced by foreign aggression, and in the early 1860's the majority of the New World nations were involved in some way with European states. The invitations to the Latin American nations to join the Congress and their responses to these invitations reveal the several situations in which these nations found themselves. Four treaties were concluded by the Congress but the proposed confederation of American states was not achieved. The Congress failed to accomplish more than it did because of the overprominent position accorded to the Hispano-Peruvian question, because of the attitudes taken by the United States and Argentina, and for other reasons. Despite this failure the Congress demonstrates the continuing belief that inter-American cooperation could be achieved.

Nuermberger, Gustave A. "The Continental Treaties of 1856: An American Union 'Exclusive of the United States.'" XX (1940), 32–55.
During the years 1854, 1855, and 1856 a series of events incensed South America against the United States. Ecuador's concessions in the guano trade were widely resented, as were the harshness of California vigilantes against immigrants from the south, and above all William Walker's invasion of Nicaragua. The development of such a hostile attitude by South Americans was not unusual, but their longings for a continental union in this instance were most extraordinary. Chileans took the lead in the movement, but independent trends in the same direction appeared in New Granada and Venezuela. Yet in every country internal dissensions and external rivalries prevented effective action. The treaty finally signed by the envoys of Chile, Peru, and Ecuador on September 15, 1856, provided for no more than a congress of plenipotentiaries; even this, after futile negotiations, came to naught.

Wilgus, A. Curtis. "James G. Blaine and the Pan American Movement." V (1922), 662–708.
Pan-Americanism began in 1822 with Bolívar's proposal and found its first application in the Congress of Panama two years later. Unsuccessful attempts to repeat this were made in 1831, 1838, 1839, and 1840. In 1847, however, five nations met at Lima and by various agreements paved the way for the "Continental Treaty" of 1856. A meeting followed in 1864, and another was called for 1880. Blaine familiarized himself with the matter over a period of years and succeeded in stimulating discussions in the United States Congress. In 1889 he became Secretary of State. The First Pan-American Conference was held in October 1889 under the guidance of Blaine, its first president, who had made an unsuccessful attempt to call one in 1882. The author gives the details of the conference and the opinions concerning it as published in the chief papers of the United States. Though the conference accomplished less than Blaine expected, twenty treaties of reciprocity were signed soon after its adjournment.

5. Science and Politics: Origins and Objectives of Mid-Nineteenth Century Government Expeditions to Latin America

JOHN P. HARRISON

Since the sixteenth century expeditions dispatched to Latin America have collected information on a variety of subjects. Philip II ordered Francisco Hernández to Mexico for the first extensive operation, which produced large amounts of scientific data. Beginning with the revolutionary years in the early nineteenth century, several European governments and the United States began to send expeditions for political as well as scientific purposes. In the following article Professor Harrison, director of the Institute of Latin American Studies at the University of Texas, concentrates on the expeditions to South America organized in Washington in the years between the war with Mexico and the Civil War, when the spirit of Manifest Destiny was a powerful force in the United States. The recent heated discussions on the abortive Project Camelot of the United States Army in Chile indicate that the conflict between science and politics is still present in government research on Latin America.

Expeditions sent by the United States Government to explore foreign lands during the nineteenth century were peculiarly crowded into the years between the end of the Mexican War and the outbreak of the Civil War. These expeditions, all carried out by the Navy and all having scientific objectives as a part of their official instructions, were sent to the Arctic, the Near East, the Orient, and South America during this fifteen-year period. The crest of this spate of government-supported scientific explorations came in 1852 when, in South America alone, naval personnel were to be found in, about to leave for, or just returning from inland expeditions to the Argentine Confederation, Bolivia, Brazil, Chile, New Granada, Paraguay, and Peru.

It has generally been assumed by those who have written about these expeditions that the object of the United States in sending them out was advancement of science and that they had no connection with the spirit of Manifest Destiny which played so conspicuous a part in the politics of the era. The study of the promotion of the expeditions and the interests

From Volume XXXV (1955), pages 175–202.

of those who helped to plan or to execute them, however, suggests that there was an intermingling of scientific, commercial, and even of colonizing interests involved in varying degrees. The expeditions discussed here are: the United States Exploring Expedition, 1838–42; the United States Naval Astronomical Expedition to the Southern Hemisphere, 1849–52; the Amazon explorations of Lt. William Lewis Herndon and Passed Midshipman Lardner Gibbon, 1851–52; and the Expedition to Explore and Survey the Río de la Plata and its Tributaries, 1853–56.

The efforts of interested individuals and organized groups to obtain government funds for scientific expeditions to foreign lands began with the 1st session of Congress, but no money was appropriated for such a purpose until 1836. Select committees of the First and Second Congresses, in reporting on a petition that asked the government to support an expedition to Baffin Bay to prove certain observations and discoveries relative to the northern magnetic pole, said that they believed Congress could support such a project "with great propriety" but submitted it to the House whether the "present deranged state of our finances" made the time appropriate for such a grant. The House thought not. By the time the treasury was able to support such ventures, exponents of states' rights were vigorously resisting anything that tended to increase federal authority so that many Congressmen opposed such an expenditure of federal funds on principle.

Those who opposed federal support for internal improvements also opposed sending exploring expeditions to foreign lands. It seemed to them that if it was constitutional to pay for the survey of a South American river with federal funds it would be difficult to hold that the survey of a river in Ohio was not a legitimate function of the national government. Other Congressmen believed that such expeditions smacked of the foreign entanglements against which Washington had warned. In addition to clearing these obstacles, the proponents of exploring expeditions had to escape somehow the onus of being associated intimately with the program of John Quincy Adams, who, among public men, was the great advocate of government-supported scientific activities. The violent political opposition and personal animosity towards Adams of a large body of Congressmen were matched only by their inability to understand the intellectual New Englander.

In his inaugural address of 1825 Adams, who believed that the planned diffusion of knowledge was one of the first obligations of a republic, asked for federal support of an exploring expedition. A bill embodying the President's ideas on the exploration of the Pacific Northwest was defeated in Congress in 1826. Adams then began organizing an exploring expedition to the Pacific Ocean and the South Seas. After a bill to this effect was passed in 1829 by the House of Representatives, it was referred to the Senate Committee on Naval Affairs. This Committee not only refused to approve funds but seized this opportunity to rebuke the Executive for misuse of regularly appropriated naval funds by preparing ships for such an expedition and hiring an agent to collect information "for the guidance of the expedition." The Committee held that the true cost of any expedition *"must be the whole expense of preparing the vessels for sea, and supporting them while there."* As the Executive had no right to use public funds for purposes other than those designated by the Congress and as the regular naval appropriation provided only for vessels required on cruising stations to protect commerce, this dictum of the Senate Committee on Naval Affairs said, in effect, that the Secretary of the Navy did not have the authority to organize an expedition for scientific purposes without specific Congressional approval. Chairman R. Y. Hayne of South Carolina concluded with the warning that the Committee was well satisfied that its statement would be "sufficient to prevent the recurrence of any similar transaction." A standard for the determination of Presidential accountability to Congress acceptable to both the legislative and executive branches of government has never been devised, but the opinion of the Hayne Committee, though it may not have been binding, did have the effect—at least until the Civil War—of putting the executive branch of government on the defensive whenever outside interests urged executive support for scientific explorations abroad.

The United States Exploring Expedition, 1838–1842

The first of the four expeditions dealt with in this paper had but a slight connection with Latin America, but because it was the first government-supported overseas expedition it was important as a precedent which in various ways prepared the way for those which were to follow.

Jeremiah N. Reynolds, the special agent employed by the Navy to collect information for the expedition proposed by Adams, did not accept the judgment of the Hayne Committee as the last word on federal support of an expedition to the South Seas. For ten years after 1826 he functioned as a publicity agent extraordinary who would not allow either Congress or the press to forget that such an expedition would redound to the intellectual, economic, and political glory of the United States. Reynolds' earliest interest in this expedition was scientific, if the testing of Capt. John Cleves Symmes, Jr.'s theory that the earth consisted of five concentric spheres with a hollow core and polar openings can be called scientific. By 1828 Reynolds' belief in Symmes was sufficiently wilted so that he based his support of the expedition on the necessity of charting obstacles to navigation in the Pacific Ocean and the South Seas for the benefit of the whale and seal fisheries specifically and of an expanding commerce in general.

Reynolds' main promotional effort was to get local interests to petition Congress in favor of the expedition. The culmination of his effort to influence Congress came when he delivered an address on the "Surveying and Exploring Expedition to the Pacific Ocean and South Seas" in the House of Representatives on April 3, 1836. In this speech he emphasized chiefly the benefits the expedition would shower upon commerce and the new markets for manufactures it would open, but he stressed also "the importance of a flourishing state of arts and sciences . . . to national prosperity and reputation," quoting Washington to stress the point. Reynolds used the Lewis and Clark expedition as a precedent to show the legality of the federal government's spending its money on expeditions to foreign lands. He stressed the glory that would accrue to the United States and cited many examples of European nations engaging in similar activities. The inference was clear that the number and size of the overseas exploring expeditions sponsored by a government were a true indication of its status as a world power. Like battleships at a later date, such an expedition was a visible manifestaton of power clear for all the world to see; and, from this date on, both science and commerce were, in the mind of Reynolds, and a large part of the general public, secondary to the overpowering vision of national glory.

Five weeks after Reynolds' oration an amendment to the Naval Appropriation Bill—passed in the House with the help of John Quincy Adams—authorized President Jackson to "send out a surveying and exploring expedition to the Pacific Ocean and the South Seas" and approved a maximum expenditure of $300,000 on the project. The details of the expedition were left to the executive branch, but from all of the agitation that preceded the bill it was clear that the object was to chart and survey those parts of the world most frequented by whalers.

The President appears to have been enthusiastic about the expedition but his Secretary of the Navy, Mahlon Dickerson, although for many years a prominent member of the American Philosophical Society, did his best to kill the project by a policy of procrastination. Dickerson's two main political tenets were a protective tariff and a conviction that the expenditure of money by the federal government under the "general welfare" clause would result in undue centralization of governmental power. His political convictions were stronger than his interest in science and although as early as October of 1836 he received a committee of the APS that advised him on the personnel necessary to the scientific success of the expedition (first on the list was an astronomer and last a historiographer), the exploring squadron did not leave the United States until 1838. By this time J. K. Paulding had replaced Dickerson as Secretary of the Navy. Under Dickerson's direction the period of preparation had become a maladroit juggling act, with naval officers and civilian scientists continually being thrown into the spotlight only to bounce off the stage into the darkened wings of the political theatre. Under this treatment the original enthusiasm for the expedition of scientists such as John Torrey, who had written a friend in September of 1836 that scientific men would be well paid and perfectly equipped, for "they are determined to have a *big team*," soon waned. His protegé Asa Gray, the greatest American botanist of his age, who earlier had expressed pleasure at his princely salary ($2,500) resigned his appointment in disgust. Other prominent scientists either followed Gray's example or were pushed out until those who finally sailed with the expedition, except for the mineralogist James D. Dana, were not of the first rank.

Secretary of the Navy Paulding instructed Lt. Charles Wilkes, commanding, that the purpose of the expedition was discovery, not conquest. "Its objects," he emphasized, "are all peaceful; they are to extend the empire of commerce and science." While Paulding might have found it difficult to recall any commercial empires the boundaries of which had been extended without conquest, it is nonetheless true that there was no indication, either in the public statements or the correspondence of those who sent the expedition out and of those who participated in it, that the United States was interested in acquiring new territory or in exerting pressure on any established society.

The United States Exploring Expedition spent the year 1838–39 in South America, where it stopped at Rio de Janeiro, El Carmen on the Río Negro, the coast of Patagonia, Tierra del Fuego, Valparaíso, and Callao. In Chile and Peru the botanists were the most active of the scientists but they found very few new or rare plants. The hydrographic information collected around Tierra del Fuego and south of Cape Horn, although not what had been hoped for, was of some value. The comments on local society and politics made by Wilkes were both obvious and lacking in perception. He had nothing to say about Chile and Peru that the United States Government had not heard many times before from its diplomatic, consular, and naval officers stationed in those countries. Nothing was done to stimulate United States commerce and there is no evidence that the whaling industry benefited from the voyage. Thus, though the advancement of commerce and navigation was one of the objectives held forth by the sponsors of this expedition to secure public support, it seems, on the whole, to have been carried out primarily in the spirit of an earlier era with a view to making a contribution to useful knowledge. Though its results were meagre (except as the charting of a considerable portion of coast of the Antarctic continent proved important at a later time) it marked the acceptance, at last, of the John Quincy Adams view that the government of the United States might properly engage in this kind of activity, even though it proved necessary to subordinate science to considerations of national prestige and commercial advantage in order to put it into effect.

The United States Naval Astronomical Expedition to the Southern Hemisphere, 1849–1852

No other government expedition in the history of the United States was more completely the work of one man. The idea for the expedition was Lt. James Melville Gilliss' and he was the central figure in the promotion, the planning, the execution, and the preparation of the findings of the expedition for publication.

The purpose of the expedition, as originally conceived by Gilliss, was quite simple. It was to measure more accurately the distance of the sun from the earth, the "most important of all astronomical problems." Following a suggestion made in April 1847 by the German astronomer C. L. Gerling, Gilliss proposed that this distance be determined by "observations of Venus during the period of its retrograde motion . . . especially when the planet [was] stationary," to be made simultaneously from the Naval Observatory in Washington, D. C., and an observatory to be set up in nearly the same latitude in South America.

Gilliss, sorely disappointed at not having been appointed the first Superintendent of the Naval Observatory which he had largely designed and equipped, wanted to make his life "not . . . altogether useless to science" by directing the observations in the Southern Hemisphere. Two aspects of this proposal, besides the personal satisfaction involved, had a strong appeal to Gilliss, and he hoped the attraction would be as great for the administration and Congress: 1) it was an opportunity for the United States to make a major contribution to world knowledge instead of persisting in its customary parasitic role of drawing from the pool of knowledge without adding anything to it; and 2) the contribution would be drawn from "data *wholly American*." The tremendous energy and persistence with which Gilliss carried on his campaign to secure government support for this expedition was generated from the buoyant enthusiasm of fighting for what he considered to be a righteous, patriotic cause.

Gilliss' first step was to write Gerling in July 1847 asking him to have the distinguished astronomers of Germany send letters urging the importance or utility of the project. Gilliss expressed the belief that because "foreigners of intellect carry much weight with us in America," such letters would help him get an appropriation from Congress should the Secretary of the Navy "decline . . . the responsibility of sending me." Gerling replied that all of the astronomers in Germany would support the plan, but if Gilliss ever received such letters he neither presented them to Congress nor mentioned them in his extensive correspondence with scientists in the United States.

On October 22, 1847, Gilliss sent a prospectus to the American Philosophical Society, the American Academy of Arts and Sciences, and Alexander Dallas Bache, Director of the Coast Survey, and asked their support in securing authorization of the expedition by the Secretary of the Navy or, if necessary, by the Congress. The formal statements to the Society and the Academy were accompanied by personal notes to R. W. Patterson and Benjamin Peirce asking their support in securing the endorsement of their respective organizations. In December Gilliss again wrote Bache, this time in Bache's capacity as a Regent of the Smithsonian Institution, enclosing a statement on the object of the expedition together with copies of his correspondence with Gerling and requesting that they be presented to the Regents for their consideration. Gilliss wanted the Regents' opinion of the project in a form that he could present with his application to the Secretary of the Navy. This letter resulted in Gilliss' enlisting the support of Joseph Henry, Secretary of the Smithsonian Institution, a man who had at his disposal both political influence and funds. This correspondence with individuals and groups interested in science brought Gilliss not only support but the benefit of their accumulated knowledge in helping him plan his expedition. Patterson's chief contribution was in urging Gilliss to set up his observatory near Santiago rather than on the Isla de Chiloé. Bache and Peirce, convinced of Gilliss' professional ability, made sure that the expedition was properly outfitted. Bache also believed that "meteorological and magnetical observations should be combined with the astronomical" so that even if the central purpose of the expedition was not successful the ancillary results would be of scientific value.

Armed with formal endorsements of his project from the two most influential scientists in the United States and with strong written support from the leading scientists in Washington, Gilliss wrote Secretary of the Navy John Y. Mason on February 10, 1848. He asked Mason, a Virginia Democrat, to send him and one assistant to Chile to make the observations, to permit them to use specified instruments owned by the Navy, and to allow $5,000 for "the expense of every nature whatsoever," exclusive of instruments. Although in his letter to Mason Gilliss emphasized the project's value to science, he apparently felt it necessary also to justify such an expenditure of federal funds in more material terms. For the first time in any of his correspondence he pointed out that his findings would benefit navigation and thus would aid the merchant marine of the country; he even went so far as to suggest they would advance the United States in its commercial rivalry with Great Britain.

Secretary Mason, however, needed more than these blandishments to overcome his reluctance to accept the responsibility of what he felt was a questionable assertion of executive authority. Instead of acting directly Mason wrote to the Chairman of the Committee on Naval Affairs of the House of Representatives on March 31, 1848, enclosing the supporting documents submitted to him by Gilliss and recommending that Congress appropriate the sum asked for. Without a dissenting vote the Committee reported favorably, and on August 3, 1848 Congress appropriated $5,000 to be expended for "observations . . . recently recommended . . . by the American Philosophical Society and the Academy of Arts and Sciences." Both the report of the Naval Committee and the discussion on the floor of the House made it clear that Congress wanted more from the expedition than observations of Venus alone. A full report on the agricultural, mineral, and commercial situation in Chile was also expected.

Gilliss had sought a specific amount of money to enable him to carry out a limited and well-defined astronomical objective. In securing the support of prominent scientists the scope of the expedition had been extended to include meteorological observations and a study of terrestrial magnetism in a land of earthquakes; and now Congress, without adding anything to the sum originally asked for, required him to make a full report on the agricultural, mineral, and commercial situation in Chile. What should have been the happy culmination of a year's intensive promotional work in the interest of science was instead for Gilliss the beginning of four frustrating years of trying to carry out a scientific task paid for by Congress and administered by three Secretaries of the Navy serving under Democratic and Whig administrations. Perseverance was the only virtue Gilliss claimed for himself while seeking support for his project. It was indeed fortunate for the success of the expedition that he knew himself well.

Congress appropriated the funds for the expedition but the choice of personnel was the province of the Secretary of the Navy. Gilliss, who feared that the influence of Matthew Fontaine Maury—the Superintendent of the Naval Observatory—was being used against him, felt impelled to remind Mason the day after Congress made the appropriation that it was his letter of February 10 that formed the basis of the Secretary's communication to Congress. During August Gilliss made his position less vulnerable by requesting of Mason, both in letters and in a personal interview, permission to go to Philadelphia and Boston to confer with the learned societies that had supported the project, in order to discuss "the collateral subjects to be investigated, as well as the best method of attaining accurate results in all." Mason would not permit Gilliss to make this trip until he received written assurance from Bache that "the two oldest scientific institutions of our Country . . . have at various times been consulted by the Government in reference to scientific movements." It was November 16, 1848, before Mason finally assigned Gilliss to make the astronomical observations authorized by Congress.

Some of the Navy's instruments that Gilliss had counted on using proved to be faulty, and before his expedition was organized others had been rushed to California for use in charting the coast and surveying the golden interior. The funds of the expedition would not stretch to the purchase of instruments in addition to the other expenses; so Gilliss would have had to approach Congress for a supplementary appropriation had not the Smithsonian Institution provided up to $5,000 for the purchase of a telescope and an astronomical clock.

Gilliss had estimated the cost of his astronomical work in Chile in the belief that the salaries and travel expenses to and from Chile of the naval officers attached to the expedition would be covered by the regular naval appropriation. The $5,000 he asked for was to cover the cost of building the observatory and piers, the rent of an office building, the hire of a porter, and all incidental expenses. Although travel expenses of naval officers on duty had always been charged to the annual appropriation, it took the persuasiveness and prestige of Joseph Henry to induce Secretary Mason to relieve the expedition of the cost of getting the officers to and from Chile.

Gilliss' troubles with the executive branch of government were not even then ended. The expedition was scarcely established in Santiago before the new Secretary of the Navy, William B. Preston, reversed the stand of his predecessor and charged travel expenses against the expedition's funds. This decision meant that the expedition would not have enough money to finish its work. Gilliss wrote to his influential acquaintances in government, including the sympathetic chairman of the House Naval Committee, F. P. Stanton, but without any effect on the Virginia Whig, who is reported to have told Bache "that if Navy officers wished to engage in scientific pursuits, they ought to be satisfied with the rewards of science." Fortunately for Gilliss, Preston's custodianship of the Navy lasted only until June of 1850 and the several friends of the expedition in Washington were able to convince his successor, William A. Graham, to return to the policy set by Mason.

The expedition finished its work in 1852, and its findings eventually were published in six volumes. Its original object was frustrated because Matthew Fontaine Maury, perhaps from personal spite, failed to have the necessary simultaneous observations made in Washington. The results of other astronomic observations and the work of the expedition in related branches of science and in reporting on all aspects of Chilean society and economic life were, as A. D. Bache had predicted in February of 1848, "most valuable"; but the fundamental contribution to the mainstream of scientific thought that Gilliss had hoped to make was not achieved.

Gilliss was interested in science, not in Chile, and this redounded to Chile's benefit. Gilliss instructed Chilean students at the observatory, corresponded with European scientists in an effort to help Chile secure trained men for surveys and similar operations, gave the observatory building to Chile, sold to the Chilean Government the astronomical clock furnished the expedition by the Smithsonian Institution, sent many packages of technical books to Chile after his return to the United States, and maintained a fairly regular correspondence with Andrés Bello, then Rector of the National University, at least until the outbreak of the Civil War. The commercial and agricultural tasks with which Gilliss was saddled by Congress he performed with diligence. Here again his broad concept of what constituted international exchange of knowledge was manifest, for he wrote with considerable asperity to W. D. Brackenridge, who received the plants and seeds he sent from Chile, reminding him that exchange meant a two-way traffic and that he expected Brackenridge to send him seeds and plants for the improvement of Chilean agriculture without further delay.

While compiling data for his report on the economic, social, and political life in Chile Gilliss traveled about the country and corresponded with foreigners who had investments in mining and transportation. He reported home on the true purpose of a merchant combine that sent false reports on the local grain market to the United States in the hope of reaping monopoly profits in California. After his return to the United States he acted as a lobbyist for William Wheelwright in that entrepreneur's attempt to secure a federal subsidy for a proposed west coast line of steamships. It can fairly be said, however, that although Gilliss was strongly critical of many aspects of Chilean society his commercial reporting did not bring him into conflict with the local economy and the expedition neither interfered with nor disturbed the Chilean political scene. As the head of the United States' first technical assistance mission to Latin America Gilliss was a great success.

He returned to the United States, however, thoroughly disillusioned as to the possibility that the United States Government would ever support scientific endeavors. Later, when he wanted to go to Peru to observe the great eclipse of September 1858, Gilliss successfully sought support from private individuals, corporations, and the Smithsonian Institution. In a letter of June 8, 1858, to Joseph Henry he deplored the government's lack of true scientific interest, saying, "we rarely seem willing to venture unless a full harvest is probable, and never as pioneers." In 1859 Gilliss was planning to observe the transits of Mars from near Mendoza in 1860 and 1862. This time he asked a wealthy individual to supply the $30,000 necessary to cover the costs of a three-year expedition to Argentina, explaining that government support was not practical because the Executive branch feared to sponsor scientific work without the sanction of Congress and the course of that body was dilatory and unpredictable.

The history of the Gilliss expedition seems to indicate that though the idea of government-sponsored scientific work abroad was accepted in theory it failed to get real support from the government officials concerned and that the accomplishment of the primary objective was compromised by the broadening of the function of the expedition to include reports on commerce and resources. Such interests were to play a major part in connection with the next two expeditions to Latin America.

The Expedition to Explore the Amazon Valley, 1851–1852

Matthew Fontaine Maury, the self-trained oceanographer who directed the Naval Observatory from 1844 until his hurried departure from Washington at the outbreak of the Civil War, is best known for his wind and current charts of the oceans. These were compiled from ships' logs and abstracts of ships' logs that special appropriations of Congress had enabled him to collect in quantity. Maury, whose interest in politics and science was equally intense, was concerned early with the future of the Southern states: especially their lack of industry, the ever decreasing ratio of their commerce in relation to that of the North, and the proportion of Negroes to the total population.

In the compilation of his charts Maury noticed that a log floating to sea from the Amazon River would be carried by the currents into the Caribbean ("this sea of ours"), past the mouth of the Mississippi, through the Florida Channel and into the Gulf Stream. The winds south from the United States through the Lesser Antilles to the mouth of the Amazon were generally favorable. Hence, Maury felt that the Amazon could be considered a natural extension of the Mississippi Valley. He knew the Amazon Valley to be thinly populated, and he confidently stated that it could support a population of 2,400,000,000. He also noted that "the energy, the science and the civilization of the world have always been in the Northern hemisphere," a situation he did not attribute to chance. England, he remarked, was so dependent on Southern cotton that she was scouting about for a cotton producing area of her own where she would be willing to condone even slavery. The South clearly could not be expected to give away its greatest capital investment, slaves. The combination of these beliefs made the colonization of the Amazon Valley by Southern whites, with their Negro slaves, appear to Maury not just an opportunity but a moral obligation.

Maury had his ideas well in mind by 1849 but he felt that his statements would have more weight if they were buttressed by an eye-witness report about the Amazon. To this end he prepared a lengthy memoir on the Amazon Valley, in which he emphasized commercial possibilities, hinted at the possibility of replacing the Afro-Brazilian slave trade with a transfer of Negroes from the Southern states, and said nothing about colonization. On March 27, 1850 he presented this document to Secretary of the Navy Preston with the suggestion that one or two officers of the Pacific Squadron might "return through South America to the United States and . . . descend the Amazon on their way." Enclosing a copy of the memoir, Maury wrote his relative, William Lewis Herndon, on April 20 that the Secretary had that day summoned him "and has come into my views fully." Preston spoke to Maury of giving Herndon permission to make the trip with a Passed Midshipman for a companion.

On May 2, Maury wrote Herndon that Preston had told him the project had been considered favorably by the Cabinet and he believed the matter settled. This information was imparted in a fifteen-page letter explaining to "Dear Lewis" in minute detail what Maury expected Herndon to look for while descending the Amazon. Inherent in the whole letter was the importance of the venture for the future of Southern society. Specifically, Maury said, the question was whether the Amazon Valley shall be peopled with an imbecile and an indolent people or by a go ahead race that has the energy and enterprise equal to subdue the forest and to develop and bring forth the vast resources that lie hidden there? the latter by all means.

And the object of your mission there is to prepare the way for that chain of events which is to bring this result about.

Maury suggested to Herndon that he leave his ship at Valparaíso and wait there for the official instructions, which were sure to follow. Herndon arrived in Valparaíso on September 1, 1851. There, as weeks stretched into months, he was forced to borrow money for bare subsistence. His uneasiness was not relieved when, in October, he received a letter from Maury— dated August 10—telling him that "Preston & Clayton got to disputing about which of the TWO *originated* the Amazon scheme and it fell through. I shall broach the subject to Gov. Graham as soon as practicable. *I intend to have the examination of that river made.*"

The delay was doubtless caused in part by the difficulty in getting the Brazilian Government's permission for the officers to descend the Amazon. In the summer of 1850 Secretary of State Clayton orally requested of the Brazilian Minister permission to explore the Amazon Valley and the Minister wrote his Government requesting that it be given. The continuing reluctance of Brazil to allow official representatives of any nation to enter the Amazon drainage was doubtless heightened by Daniel Webster, Clayton's successor, when he ordered a copy of Maury's memoir on the Amazon Valley sent to the Brazilian Minister. The Department of State, when requesting the passports, stated that the object of the expedition was "to gratify a liberal curiosity and extend the limits of geographical knowledge in which Brazil and all other civilized states have a common interest." It was not until March 8, 1851, that the necessary documents were sent to Herndon and Passed Midshipment Lardner Gibbon, the officer assigned to accompany him. Before this time, however, Herndon's anxiety about his official status had been relieved when he received orders from Secretary of the Navy William A. Graham, a moderate anti-secession Whig from North Carolina, to proceed to Lima. There, while waiting for the necessary passports, he was to occupy himself with research on the Amazon in libraries and monasteries.

Accompanying these orders was another inspired letter from Maury, dated November 13, 1850, and concerned almost solely with the possibilities of colonization. He said that if Herndon "could offer inducement from Peru to colonise that elegant Tennessee-of-a-place, that splendid Mesopotamia country between the Huallaga & Ucayali, why then and there you might have laid the cornerstone to that magnificent gorgeous & glorious structure which is *obliged* to rise up out of that Amazon Country." Maury wanted to know what guarantees the Governments of Peru and Bolivia would give "American Citizens with their *Slaves* to go there and colonise" and especially what guarantees they would "afford the Institution." Herndon's imagination was so inflamed that he wrote Gilliss, then in Santiago, that he had a paper, "written by a Bolivian officer who explored the 'Bermejo.' I hear that this river drains a productive part of Bolivia, is free of obstructions, and empties into the Paraguay. If this be so, here is the shortest way to the Atlantic, and I think I would prefer, if I can get any grants of land & make any settlements, to do it on this river." Speaking of the same region he wrote Secretary Graham on February 8, 1851, what a great thing it would be for the United States "if colonies of enterprising & industrious people were planted in these parts."

The official and confidential instructions authorizing Herndon and Gibbon to explore the Amazon did not leave Washington until after February 15, 1851. This document was drafted at least in part by Maury, for it contains twenty-eight lines of questions to be answered, all of which can be found in his two long letters to Herndon. The greatest emphasis in the instructions was not on the colonization project that had so filled Maury's last letter to Herndon but rather on the possibilities the region offered "a nautical and commercial people." Specifically Herndon was to "indicate the future importance, to this country, of the free navigation of that River. To enable the Government to form a proper estimate of the degree of that importance, present and prospective, is the object of your mission." The two officers were to make "such geographical, and scientific, observations, by the way, as may be consistent with the main object of the expedition," but they were always to bear in mind that these were "merely incidental."

Daniel Webster did not need Herndon's report "to form a proper estimate" of the importance of free navigation of the Amazon to United States commerce. Even before Herndon had read his instructions Webster had directed the new U. S. Minister to Brazil to negotiate for the opening of the Amazon to free commerce. At the same time Webster, to the perplexity of the Brazilian minister, construed Brazil's granting of passports to naval officers for the purpose of extending the limits of geographical knowledge as a commitment to enter into an agreement for the opening of the Amazon.

The explorations of Herndon and Gibbon, then, were in no way essential to the administration's program of opening the Amazon to world commerce. That the purpose of the expedition was to enlarge "the sphere of human knowledge" was understood only by the Government of Brazil. The real object was twofold: 1) to gather data for Maury to use in promoting his scheme for moving a large part of the Negro population of the Southern states to the Amazon Valley; and 2) to try to gain grants of land for Southern agriculturalists. The two Secretaries of the Navy who supported Maury's scheme were moderate Southern Whigs who, although loyal to the Confederacy when war came, did all in their power to avert secession. Their support of Maury's proposal—probably the most extreme version of Manifest Destiny ever suggested by a public official—seems to have been based on the slight hope that it would solve the problems vexing an expanding cotton economy. And, in this hope, they provided on executive authority alone, $5,000 (exclusive of salary and the cost of transportation to and from the scene of operations) to pay for explorations of the Amazon Valley.

The Expedition to Survey and Explore the Río de la Plata and Its Tributaries, 1853–1856

There was no single driving force responsible for the expedition to explore and survey the main tributaries of the Río de la Plata. Instead there were at least five considerations, all contributing to the final decision to send out the expedition; if any one of them had been lacking, it might never have been organized.

First: In 1843 the Government of Paraguay made overtures to Amory Edwards, United States Consul in Buenos Aires, and to Commodore Daniel Turner, in command of the Brazil Squadron, intimating that Paraguay would welcome the sight of the United States flag on the Río Paraguay. All information received in Washington during the years 1843–45 indicated that the administration of Carlos Antonio López preferred to establish commercial relations with the United States rather than with England and France, whose representatives already were on the scene. The United States did not react to these cordial advances until the summer of 1845, when the Polk administration sent a Special Agent to Paraguay to gather reliable information as the basis of a policy. At the same time the Commander of the Brazil Squadron was instructed to send one of his small vessels to Asunción, if it could be "prudently and safely done," for the purpose of gathering information. Without a ship adequate to the task Commodore Lawrence Rousseau could not carry out these orders, but he did report in the spring of 1846 that the Government at Buenos Aires would not oppose the ascent of the Paraná by a United States steamer and that a French steamer was already at Corrientes and an English steamer at Asunción. The United States Navy was occupied in Mexican waters for the next few years but the idea remained well planted in official Washington that a great commercial opportunity awaited the United States in Paraguay and that the Government there was well disposed to grant her special considerations.

Second: Edward A. Hopkins, the Special Agent to Paraguay whose irresponsible actions soon brought about his recall, returned to the United States with the confidence of Paraguayan officials and grandiose ideas for setting up a commercial and industrial empire in that agricultural land. During the six years between his recall and the decision to send out the expedition, Hopkins was a fountain of publicity that inundated the general public, the scientific fraternity, the merchant class, and both the administration and Congress, with information and misinformation about the opportunities in Paraguay for commerce of the United States.

Third: External political interference as one of the obstacles to Paraguay's accessibility was erased in February 1852 when the Argentine caudillo Juan Manuel Rosas, who had opposed the free navigation of the Río Paraná, was defeated by Justo J. Urquiza. Soon afterwards Urquiza opened the river to world commerce in the belief that this act would make the provinces of Argentina less dependent on Buenos Aires.

Fourth: The Whig administration of Taylor and Fillmore, believing as it did that the purpose of government was "to promote the great interests of National Industry," was eager to open new markets to United States trade.

Fifth: John P. Kennedy, Secretary of the Navy from July 1852 to March 1853, was unusual among political leaders of his day in that he had an eighteenth-century concept of the legitimate influence that learning and knowledge should have in government. This belief, combined with his thorough Whiggism, led him to devote his short term in office almost exclusively to the planning of expeditions that would benefit both commerce and science.

In the summer of 1852, when Kennedy took over the direction of the Navy, Hopkins' frenetic activity within the government was at its height. Hopkins was convinced that not even Anglo-Saxon enterprise could develop a commercial empire in Paraguay unless the invested capital was managed by an official representative of the United States Government. For this reason, even though he had obtained monopoly rights for steam navigation on the Río Paraguay and the capital necessary to exploit this concession, he would not begin operation until he obtained a diplomatic or consular appointment. Interviews, petitions, and letters from himself and others were not enough to convince Secretary of State Clayton that Hopkins could be entrusted with diplomatic powers. Grudgingly Hopkins decided to settle for a consular appointment. But in the interim between his nomination as consul to Asunción and confirmation by the Senate, Secretary of State Daniel Webster seems to have learned for the first time of a gratuitously insulting letter that Hopkins had addressed to Rosas as chief of state in Argentina, and Webster refused to give Hopkins his commission. Failing for the time being at the Department of State, Hopkins used his influence with several Senators and the Secretary of the Treasury to have an amendment added to the Civil and Diplomatic Bill of 1852, appropriating $5,000 to send "a commercial agent to explore and examine the country on the Paraguay." The Senators who successfully opposed this amendment said that they did not object to a legitimate exploring expedition but they were against outfitting some gentleman friend of the administration as a commercial agent.

Hopkins' promotional efforts touched the Navy just two months before Kennedy took office. The American Geographical and Statistical Society, after publishing an article by Hopkins on the geography and commerce of Paraguay, sent a memorial to the Secretary of the Navy asking him to take the first step in bringing about a commercial intercourse between the United States and the region drained by the Río de la Plata by assigning a small steamer "to make a geographical reconnaissance, and a hydrographical survey" of the navigable rivers. The Society offered to procure the services of two or more scientists "to assist in the objects of the enquiry," and it volunteered to furnish a full set of instructions. The Society believed that such an expedition would not require a special appropriation by Congress. With his own interest in exploring expeditions, a general assurance that Congress would not oppose an expedition largely devoted to geographical studies, and the knowledge that the Department of State was interested in establishing relations with Paraguay, Secretary Kennedy needed only slight stimulus to organize an expedition to survey and explore the main tributaries to the second largest river system in the southern hemisphere. This was supplied, somewhat obliquely, by Lt. Thomas Jefferson Page.

Promotions, particularly above the rank of lieutenant, were extremely slow in the Navy at this time. With little chance of ever commanding a ship on one of the regular cruising stations, many a lieutenant with scientific pretensions found that he might satisfy his ambitions by promoting a surveying or exploring expedition to some little known part of the globe that might become important to United States commerce. Page returned from a cruise in the Orient with the idea that the Navy should send an expedition to chart the China Seas, increasingly frequented by United States merchant vessels. He had the vigorous support of his fellow Virginian M. F. Maury and the prominent Boston merchant R. B. Forbes. At Maury's suggestion the plans were expanded to include the charting of the Behring Straits, where the New England whaling fleet was currently losing many vessels. W. F. Seward, Chairman of the Senate Commerce Committee, used information solicited from Page to answer the objections raised by fellow Senators. After Congress approved the expedition Page applied for the command. Secretary Kennedy, however, gave it to his fellow Baltimorean, Commander Cadwallader Ringgold, on the grounds that the command should justly go to an officer with longer service and higher rank because the expanded plans called for sending out a small squadron. Page refused a post as second in command.

Kennedy felt himself in Page's debt and within a month he wrote in his journal: "I am setting on foot an exploration of the River Plate. . . . I intend the Water Witch now in the Yard here, for this service and shall assign it to Lieut. Page." Kennedy believed that a special appropriation from Congress was needed to properly equip an expedition he was planning to send to Africa. In this instance, however, although the *Water Witch* was built with an eye to the problems of navigating the Paraná and Paraguay and was equipped for surveying work rather than regular cruising duty, the Secretary felt no compunction in charging all expenses ($220,000, exclusive of the cost of the *Water Witch* and machinery for the smaller

steamer *Pilcomayo*, built at Asunción) against the regular naval appropriation.

In his official instructions to Page, Kennedy said that the principal
object of the expedition was to determine what commercial advantages
the United States could obtain in the region explored. Page was to do
this by determining the navigability of the principal tributaries of the
Río de la Plata and by exploring the country bordering these rivers to
acquire "correct information touching the nature and extent of agriculture, and, consequently, the probable extent to which commercial intercourse may be desirable. . . ." He was to do everything, "not incompatible with the great purpose of the undertaking, to extend the bounds
of science, and promote the acquisition of knowledge." The main base
of operation for the expedition was Asunción, and the understanding of
the Paraguayan Government was that its sole purpose was to "explore,
for scientific purposes, the various sources of the Río de la Plata, as
far as permission was granted . . . by the governments of those countries."

In addition to his official instructions Page received a memorandum
from Maury suggesting what subjects he might properly investigate. The
only intimation in this document that Maury's personal interests in the
Amazon extended to the Río de la Plata is a suggestion that Page find out
whether the two river systems interlocked during high water and that he
determine the lowest elevation between the headwaters of the two rivers.
According to Maury, Page was to send home every article produced in
Paraguay which could possibly be of interest to commerce, including seeds,
roots, and living plants; to observe the velocity and direction of the trade
winds and the variable wind pressures against the eastern face of the Andes;
to note on which side of the rivers driftwood became lodged and on which
bank alluvium was most heavily deposited; and to make a general series
of meteorological observations.

Without a knowledge of Maury's memorandum of unofficial instructions a reader of the log of the *Water Witch* might be puzzled as to why
the position of driftwood and alluvial deposits were so religiously noted.
The memorandum also helps explain Page's insistence on proceeding up the
Río Paraguay into Brazil—an action that ended the previous good relations
between Page and the Paraguayan Government. This document is also
echoed in the instructions that Page gave to his junior officers for their
exploratory expeditions into the interior. Page, without systematic training in any field of science and without artistic sense, tried to report on
Paraguay in the manner of Humboldt. Meteorological observations were
made, soil samples analyzed, specimens of vegetation collected, altitudes
computed, local customs noted, the processing and marketing of commodities remarked upon; all details were covered, but no meaningful picture
of landscapes as a whole emerged. The object seems to have been simply
to note everything, for, as Page stressed in his general instructions to his

officers; "That, which may seem unworthy of note, may eventually become of vast importance."

There is, however, no doubt that Page made a tremendous effort to see that the expedition under his command made a contribution to geography and natural history. He expected that the specimens he sent to the United States would form the nucleus of a national zoological collection. In this he was disappointed because Secretary J. C. Dobbin, Kennedy's Democratic successor, took a strict view of his accountability to Congress and Congress had made no appropriation for such a purpose.

Page's expedition occasioned an international incident when the *Water Witch* was fired upon from a Paraguayan fort on February 1, 1855. Without attempting to resolve the question of national responsibility in this case, one may say that nothing in the origins or objectives of the expedition posed any immediate threat to Paraguay. There was, however, an explosive force inherent in the expedition—the personality and ideas of its commanding officer. Page fairly yearned for glory, and here was his great opportunity. A man with long distance vision but narrow focus, he did not know the meaning of compromise and, unfortunately, there were others in Paraguay with similar limitations.

Page considered that his instructions had the sanction of the civilized world and that anyone who questioned his actions was therefore either blind or selfish. His official despatches and personal letters bristle with indignation whenever his wishes were not immediately granted. Page felt that Brazil's refusal to grant him free access to the Río Paraguay above Corumbá was "an act that would scarcely have been recognized in the dark ages." In his letters to friends at the Naval Observatory Page wrote that although "Brazil is grasping, and *worse* than the Chinese in her exclusive policy. . . . Her claims will not exclude *me*—that is a *fixed fact.*" The officers at the Observatory assured him that he was just the man for the emergency and that they expected him to return home clothed in glory. After the attack on the *Water Witch* Page's recriminations extended to Commodore Salter, in command of the Brazilian Squadron, because this officer did not immediately order the destruction of the fort and thus put the United States and Paraguay "on equal footing for negotiations."

There was a potential threat to Paraguayan sovereignty in the thinking of those who supported the expedition. The objective of Page and of Hopkins, the man most responsible for generating interest in Paraguay, was to make Paraguay another China or Japan by "opening" it to the commerce of the United States. The political thought of Secretary Kennedy as he tried to equate the inherent rights of civilized man with Manifest Destiny held ominous implications for any non-industrial country. A considerable body of public opinion in the United States of course did not subscribe to such views, and the interests of those who did were much too occupied with other parts of the world to support any extensive activity along the Río de la Plata. That Page and Hopkins were well aware of this apathy is shown by their continuous effort to convince officials and the public that Paraguay had more to offer United States commerce than China or Japan. Paraguay, without representation in the United States, could evaluate United States policy only by the actions of such official representatives as Page and Hopkins.

The accounts of this expedition were closed in 1856. Congress, perhaps for reasons of economy, published only Page's formal report to the Secretary of the Navy. In the full descriptive account of the expedition, published commercially in 1859, Page, apparently to make his work seem more important, greatly exaggerated the commercial advantages of Paraguay. In his correspondence scientific observations were pushed aside to make room for comments on local and international politics; trade opportunities for the United States in Paraguay; and recriminations against Hopkins, superior officers of the Brazil Squadron, and the President of Paraguay. Despite the promotional nature of his writings, the local reporting resulting from this expedition, both published and in manuscript, is superior to that of any other nineteenth-century government expedition to Latin America.

The United States had no set policy on the sending out of exploring expeditions during the period covered in this study. Individual Congressmen and executive officials occasionally favored federal support of scientific endeavors; but the planned diffusion of knowledge as a proper function of government, to be supported by federal funds, unless incidental to other more immediate purposes, was never fully accepted. The expeditions resulted largely from the desires of individuals to see particular projects put into effect. The dominant motives for the expeditions discussed in this article were, respectively and in the order of presentation: discovery, astronomical investigations, colonization, and trade. In each case the promotion or protection of commerce was either a secondary or only the ostensible consideration. The advancement of science by itself was not considered a sufficient reason for authorizing any of these expeditions. In the nineteenth century science depended on its contributions to trade for peacetime public support.

John Quincy Adams was the last president to embrace scientific exploring expeditions as part of his political credo. In a society that tended to regard pure science as mere science no Congressman could afford to sponsor federal support of "philosophic" activities while issues such as the tariff, the U. S. Bank, internal improvements, and slavery absorbed the interests of an ever broadening electorate. Under these conditions it became all but impossible to justify the expenditure of federal funds for overseas expeditions on purely scientific grounds. The application of Lt. J. M. Gilliss in 1848 was the last nineteenth-century instance that I have found where the federal government was asked to underwrite the whole cost of a primarily scientific expedition.

Gilliss and Wilkes were the only commanding officers primarily interested in scientific investigations, and Gilliss was the only naval officer on any of the expeditions with sufficient training and experience to make a basic contribution in any branch of science. The others all had had varying amounts of practice in land and hydrographical surveys so that their contributions were largely the more accurate location of places, the charting of coastlines, and the plotting of river channels. Civilian specialists accompanied only those expeditions for which a special appropriation from Congress provided for their support.

Exploring expeditions were sent out during both Democratic and Whig administrations. Democratic Secretaries of the Navy, however, had a much stricter concept of their responsibility to Congress in the expenditure of funds than did their Whig counterparts. For this reason Whig administrative officials were more inclined than the Democrats to send out expeditions on executive authority and pay for them from regular naval appropriations.

Latin American countries always welcomed scientific investigations within their boundaries but were generally suspicious of the expeditions' commercial aspects. Nothing in the official instructions to the expeditions posed any immediate threat to the countries visited but occasionally the commanding officers were guided by more than their official instructions. The published writings of all the commanders show that they had in some degree the idea that Anglo-Saxon institutions were superior to Hispanic ones; and, more important, they believed that the "enterprise" (a favorite word) needed for commercial development was peculiarly the possession of Anglo-Saxons. The aggressive way in which most of the officers of expeditions expressed their satisfaction with the social and economic benefits derived from their political institutions, combined with their conviction that the Anglo-Saxon "race" was the elite in a world of industrial and commercial progress, not only disturbed many thoughtful Latin Americans but caused them to view any activity of the United States with distrust.

Finally, it is clearly evident that the Herndon and Gibbon and the Page expeditions, if not those which preceded them, owed much of their inspiration to the expansionist attitudes prevalent at the mid-century. If this was never an officially acknowledged objective it shows up clearly in the correspondence of Maury and others. This paper, thus, provides some specific evidence of the interrelation of previously disassociated subjects and shows how Manifest Destiny tended to pervade even a sphere of activity apparently distant from the main political arena in which the doctrine played its part in American history.

Other Articles of Interest

Bell, Whitfield J., Jr. "The Relation of Herndon and Gibbon's Exploration of the Amazon to North American Slavery, 1850–1855." XIX (1939), 494–503. Two ideas lay behind the exploration of the Amazon River: that the Amazon region offered a rich field for the development of American enterprise and that some of the slave population of the United States might be used in the undertaking. Brazil, according to Maury, the father of the project, was to be "the safety-valve of the American Union and insurance against race conflict." Popular opinion in England was apprehensive about this plan. In 1855, upon the circulation of Herndon's report, Amazonia lost some of its attraction; the South turned to westward expansion. But, no doubt, the self-exile of Confederates to Brazil at the end of the Civil War can be traced to Maury's influence.

Dozer, Donald Marquand. "Matthew Fontaine Maury's Letter of Instruction to William Lewis Herndon." XXVIII (1948), 212–228.
Matthew Fontaine Maury's letter to William Lewis Herndon, dated April 20, 1850, reveals scientific, commercial, and political interests in the Amazon area. Maury conceived of the region as one of settlement by United States slaves and their masters. He justified the institution of slavery and extended the Manifest Destiny ideology to include the Amazon Valley. The original letter is unknown. The text printed here is from the copyist's record in the Naval Observatory's Letter Book in the National Archives.

Martin, Percy Alvin. "The Influence of the United States on the Opening of the Amazon to the World's Commerce." I (1918), 146–162.
Despite such early journeys of exploration on the Amazon as those of Orellana in 1541 and La Condamine in 1744, the world's knowledge of the great river was very scant. Brazil's policy was long one of exclusion. In 1850 the United States took first official interest as a result of Maury's Amazon project and sent Herndon and Gibbon, with the consent of Peru, to start exploration from the Amazon headwaters. Bolivia was cooperative, though Brazil held back until Agassiz's expedition took place under the patronage of Dom Pedro. In 1867 Brazil agreed to open the river to merchant ships of all nations. The publicity and the scientific exploration initiated by the United States may be largely credited with the opening.

Rasmussen, Wayne D. "The United States Astronomical Expedition to Chile, 1849–1852." XXXIV (1954), 103–113.
Lieutenant James Melville Gilliss, leader of the United States Astronomical Expedition to the Southern Hemisphere in 1849–1852, supervised the astronomical observations in Chile and arranged the exchange of plants, seeds, and scientific publications between the United States and Chile.

6. Foreign Interests in the War of the Pacific

V. G. KIERNAN

Few conflicts in the history of Latin America have had greater repercussions than the War of the Pacific (1879–1883) in which Chile defeated
Bolivia and Peru. Dr. Kiernan of the University of Edinburgh bases his
account primarily on the British Foreign Office records, and proves the
value—indeed, the necessity—of archival research outside Latin America
if the competing economic and political interests of foreign powers in
the war are to be fully understood.

The Pacific War of 1879–1883 has been studied by a number of writers
on the basis of State Department papers and of South American materials.
In this article some of its aspects are discussed in the light of the British
Office records.

Exceedingly tortuous in detail, the causes of the war were exceedingly
simple in essence. Bolivia had nitrate deposits in her coastal province in
the Atacama desert; Peru, her ally since 1873, had guano and nitrates
in the Tarapacá province bordering it on the north. Chile, to the south,
with few deposits of her own, had invested in the development work in
Bolivia and to some extent in Tarapacá. All three countries were hard up,
and run by oligarchies which disliked paying taxes and looked to revenue
from these fertilizers as a substitute. Peru set up a state monopoly, taking
over private enterprises in exchange for certificates. Bolivia put an export
tax on the Chilean company at Antofogasta. Chile denounced this as a
breach of agreement, and in February, 1879, seized the port. Bolivia declared war on Chile, and Peru supported her ally.

Equally simple in outline is the story of the hostilities. In the desert
battles of November, 1879, Peru lost Tarapacá, and the Bolivian army was
eliminated. In December President Prado fled from Lima, and Nicolás
Piérola was carried tumultuously into power as dictator. By the middle
of 1880 his troops in the south, in Tacna-Arica, were defeated in their turn,
and Callao was blockaded. In January, 1881, Lima fell, and he disappeared.
Part of the country was occupied by the Chileans, while Peruvian factions
struggled for power. In October, 1883, the Treaty of Ancón ended the

From Volume XXXV (1955), pages 14–36.

war, and the nitrate territories of both Peru and Bolivia passed to Chile.

For foreigners, as for belligerents, these fertilizers were the grand object of interest. A complicating factor was the huge debt that Peru, on the security of her guano resources, had contracted in Europe. Payment of interest had been suspended in 1876, and in several European capitals since then bondholders had been clamoring for help from their governments. They had organized themselves, but in contending camps; continental, mainly under French inspiration, and British. Towering above the common ruck was the great Paris firm of Dreyfus, with intricate and dubious claims and hydra-headed schemes for enforcing them, and above all the reputation for influence in Paris in the very highest quarters. Its ambitions were repugnant to all ordinary bondholders, French or foreign; and other claimants in Paris had formed the Société Générale de Crédit Industriel, with complicated rival plans.

If competing pressure-groups helped to prevent the French government from forming any very distinct views, in England a much bigger medley of interests was involved. Bondholders there may have welcomed the outbreak of war as at any rate a shake-up for a stagnant situation, in the same spirit as did the Italian bondholders who told their government: "The Creditors of Peru having for a long time past received neither the Capital nor the Interest of their debt, witnessed with marked satisfaction the phenomenon of a war." Chile also was a defaulting debtor, though on a smaller scale; and of some of her creditors it can be said with confidence that they were inclined not only to welcome the war, but to hope for Chilean success. "I believe," wrote Francis J. Pakenham, British minister at Santiago, when Chile seized Antofogasta, "that the prospects of all claimants and creditors of the nation have undergone a great change for the better." Of the "Peruvian Bondholders" it has been alleged that they tried to prevent munitions going to Peru. Sir Charles Russell, chairman of their chief committee, did make one move of this sort at the Foreign Office; but his motive was to stop Peru from contracting a fresh loan to buy munitions, and the Foreign Office itself similarly protested against a scheme for a new Dreyfus loan to Peru as harmful to other creditors. For these, Peru's nitrate-monopoly plan had held out some potential benefit, and Chile's victory would not necessarily do them any good. They were divided among themselves as well as being on bad terms with fellow-sufferers abroad, and Russell and his committee were under bitter attack from dissidents led by James Croyle. The *Economist*, which wrote at the end of 1879 that "the rise in Peruvian bonds is due to Peruvian defeats," also wrote: "The confusion at present existing amongst the rabble of Peruvian bondholders is almost beyond description."

Britain differed from both France and the United States in having a good deal of capital invested in the actual production of nitrate, the newer fertilizer which was soon to take the lead over the older source, guano, now nearing exhaustion. An Englishman, Hicks, was manager of the Chilean company at Antofogasta in 1879, and its funds, Pakenham had written, were "chiefly those of Gibbs, and Edwards and Co., wealthy capitalists of English extraction, and the former connected with the well-known house of A. Gibbs, of London." In the Tarapacá nitrate fields also there had been British capital, estimated at a million pounds. It has been asserted, though on no specific evidence, that the expropriated owners there "formed a powerful group determined to have Tarapacá taken out of the Peruvian monopoly," and that they lobbied at Santiago for a war. At the same time it should be kept in view that anyone who may possibly have encouraged Chile at the outset may have intended no more than a war with Bolivia alone, especially as there was a prevalent notion that the Chilean army was weaker than the Peruvian. In any case, the influence of those sections of British capital that *may* have had something to do with the outbreak of the war lay at Santiago rather than at London. With events developing so rapidly after war began they scarcely needed to seek the ear of the Foreign Office, while the bondholders, who sought it vociferously, had nothing coherent to say.

Distinct again were various commercial interests, more numerous in Britain than in any other country concerned. Merchants were unlikely to welcome a war of which their trade would be the obvious victim, or to favor the most aggressive belligerent, Chile. "The commercial community," wrote Pakenham, "is absolutely bewildered by the sudden war and must encounter heavy loses." It looked as if Englishmen would be "the principal sufferers by this unhappy war." In the summer of 1879 the Foreign Office pointed out to Chile "the irritation which the commercial world necessarily felt at the continuance of a war by which neutrals were suffering so heavily." Shipowners were hard hit, especially those in the guano trade which it was Chilean policy to disrupt; complaints against Chile came in from many British seaports. There was, on the other hand, a mercantile section which held that a Chilean victory would be good for trade in the long run, because Chile was the most efficient and energetic of the Pacific coast republics. This opinion gained ground when Chile's successes proved unbroken and increased trade with her came to make up for trade losses in Peru. By the end of 1881 this view was shared by the British minister at Lima. One more group of interests was represented by British properties destroyed or damaged by military operations, chiefly in Peru, and particularly in the fighting around Lima just before its fall. Numerous claims piled up against Chile; but there were vexatious complications because much British capital was employed in companies of Peruvian register, and its owners could expect little consideration.

Thus, pressure brought to bear on the Foreign Office was multifarious and contradictory; and while the first book on the war published in England, Clements R. Markham's *The War Between Chile and Peru* (1882), was vigorously anti-Chilean, there was not, in a broad sense, any real British "public opinion" to be taken account of. As a rule, the Foreign

Office was free to choose its own line; and it was always calm and correct, usually alert, and sometimes notably good at masterly inactivity. It should be emphasized that the Foreign Office never at any time contemplated any kind of active intervention. At the outset of hostilities one of the staff wrote with engaging frankness: "We may at present claim to be as impartial as ignorance can make us." And, formally at any rate, the Foreign Office continued impartial. It was especially scrupulous in seeing to it that no warships were smuggled out for sale to either side, for it was in mortal dread of another Alabama Award. Arms were sold freely, as by other countries, to whichever side could pay for them; and British nationals were allowed to go on serving in any of the belligerent forces. In 1880 Pakenham, dissatisfied with Chile, reminded her that Britain could put an end to such service by her nationals whenever she chose. "This," he wrote to London, "would prove embarrassing indeed, as I believe almost the entire transport of the Chilean army, their munitions, and supplies of all kinds, besides the coal for their squadron, are directly or indirectly in English hands." Peru made no complaint. A considerable number of the crew of her famous warship, the *Huascar*, at the time of its capture were Englishmen.

Apologias and manifestos put out by the belligerents received very little attention in London. The war was treated as a fact; the Foreign Office did not share the State Department's moralizing interest in the question of who was responsible for it, though a suggestion appears in a memorandum of April, 1879, that Peru had joined Bolivia in order to get control of the Chilean nitrate workings which competed with her own. Reports from Spenser St. John, the British minister at Lima, may have fostered this impression. At first inclined to think the Bolivian tax not unjustifiable, he soon felt that the quarrel had been forced on Chile, and, before long, that Peru had had a hand in it. By August, 1879, he was writing: "It is the want of any fixed principle on the part of the Bolivian authorities which has been the cause of the present war." These were, no doubt, one-sided views. Pakenham's reports from Santiago before the war had been nearly as critical of Chile as his colleague's were of Peru, and he and other British representatives in Chile remained censorious throughout. However, Chile was at least fairly stable, and knew how to fight. As to Bolivia, Britain, unlike the United States, had no legation there, and showed very little interest in the country or its fate. General Daza was a bad president, and unfriendly to Britain; there was tacit agreement with a Dutch dictum that Bolivia was "but little removed from a state of semi-barbarism."

Peru, in 1879, had just emerged from the "guano epoch" of her history, with an expensive set of railways, a moribund revenue, a demoralized public life, and a heavy foreign debt. St. John warned her, before she began to fight, that war would mean financial ruin. Her people did not even seem to be eager to win the war, whereas the Chilean public was undeniably enthusiastic. One early report, for instance, from the vice-consul at Caldera described the spirit of soldiers in training as very high. ("They are only waiting," it added, "for their trousers to arrive in order to leave for the seat of war.") In the case of Peru, St. John felt from the start that enthusiasm was merely artificial, and that, as he wrote in a later despatch, the patriots were "satisfied with shouting 'war to the death' but doing nothing whatever." One of his first reports was that "The mass of the people view the prospects of the war with deep discouragement," and in June, 1879, he thought that "the desire to terminate the war is spreading. . . . As recruits are not forthcoming, the police are employed to capture men of the working classes." In the ruling circles he saw only "ignorance or frivolity. . . . On all sides incapacity appears to be in possession of every important post . . . Peru appears struck as with paralysis; the people themselves seem as indifferent to the future as the governing classes." By the end of October he had made up his mind that "the cause of Peru is hopeless," an opinion in which he never wavered. When the president's "disgraceful flight" took place, St. John commented that he had "ever thought General [Mariano Ignacio] Prado to be totally unworthy of his position."

Foreign interests were heavily involved in the War of the Pacific, and the war was not long in producing ideas of consultation among the main European powers, with a view of limiting the hostilities or their destructiveness. What was felt, if only in a very indistinct way, to be needed was an extension to this new region of the well-tried mechanism of the "Concert of Europe," which had just been brought to bear on a first-rate crisis, the Russo-Turkish War. A "Concert of Latin America" would no doubt have been even more appropriate, but although neighboring South American governments from time to time made, or contemplated, moves toward mediation, and although Peru in defeat felt that there ought to be a common consensus in Latin America against the vicious "European" principle of territorial seizures, no practical results followed. Argentina was on bad terms with Chile; Brazil's attitude was ambiguous; no other country could carry any weight. There is no sign of England's attaching any value to coöperation with them. In London, and in Europe generally, it was taken for granted that Britain must be a chief element in any effort to moderate the war; but also that the "Concert of Europe" ought, if possible, to be extended in this case to include the United States. London was not, however, desirous of seeing Washington act alone, and settle things unilaterally.

This, on the other hand, was just what Washington soon showed itself to be bent on doing. Dexter Perkins has come to the conclusion that there is no evidence, in this whole period, of Latin America being "in any peculiar peril from European ambition." But the United States government cannot be called irrational because it was perturbed by possibilities of European meddling in the Pacific War, in a manner subversive of the Monroe Doctrine. Europe was approaching the heyday of its age of imperialism. When the war broke out England was at war with Zululand

and Afghanistan; in 1882 she occupied Egypt, and France at about the same time was attacking China.

At Washington two hypotheses were afloat, really inconsistent though often apparently combined; one of a collective European intervention, and the other of an engineering of events by secret processes from London. Of these the first can be disposed of more easily. Not even a collective influence, to say nothing of intervention, emerged in fact. There was no common outlook among the powers, unless at odd moments, when it was chiefly inspired by common dislike of the seeming wish of the United States to monopolize South America. Near the end of 1881, for instance, when Washington pressure in favor of Peru was strong, St. John found his colleagues at Lima more or less in agreement that Chile was more deserving than Peru, being the only state in that region capable of anything better than anarchy; and Viviani, the Italian, had advised his government in favor of strengthening Chile as a counterpoise to the United States in the Pacific. St. John himself considered that American talk about sinister European influence was overreaching itself; South America was coming to feel, rather, that it would have to lean on European support against the United States, and most foreigners there would stand together against this common opponent. His successor, James Reginald Graham, said the same things a little later in the course of a discussion with his colleagues. Peru, he argued, had gained nothing by ignoring them and throwing herself into the arms of Washington; talk of "America for the Americans" really meant "America for the U.S.A.," and Britain had far greater interests south of the Isthmus, which she meant to defend. Graham's sentiments were cordially endorsed by the other Europeans and, if a shade less heartily, by those of Argentina and Brazil.

Otherwise, no common motive united Europe, and it is a noteworthy fact that those states whose coöperation England desired, especially Germany, hung back, while those which thrust themselves forward usually found England hanging back. Germany was reserved and non-committal from the moment when Washington's displeasure became clear. As Perkins has observed, Berlin was always in this epoch on its guard against giving offence to the United States. Italy had bondholders, nitrate investors, emigrants, and a desire to cut a figure in the world. A Garibaldi Legion of Italians fought in defence of Lima in January, 1881. Rome was active in promoting protests to the belligerents over this and that; London was standoffish, and suggestions made from time to time by Holland were also received there politely rather than cordially. Neither the Dutch Consul-General, Boonen, at Santiago, nor his Lima colleague, a Peruvian of the Canevaro family, were considered by the British to be free from private interest in guano. When Spain expressed a wish to take part in mediation, in October, 1881, Pakenham pointed out that Spain and Chile had had no diplomatic relations since their contest in 1866.

Britain and France were the two countries with most at stake. They were also the two chief world rivals, with a series of quarrels on hand running across Africa and Asia. "The risk of a war with France about Tunis is appalling," Lord Granville was writing to Lord Hartington in April, 1881. Washington might have been less apprehensive if it had taken due note of this. Another factor weighed heavily on the same side. For both the two great French interests, Dreyfus and the Crédit Industriel, it was essential that Peru should retain her guano and nitrate resources, which they hoped to control. Now it was the United States, not Great Britain, that emerged as Peru's protector; hence it was with the United States that these French interests thought of collaboration. In January, 1881, if not earlier, the Crédit Industriel was pressing the State Department to help in keeping Tarapacá for Peru. No such approach was ever made to the Foreign Office. As an inducement the lucrative guano export agency would be given to a United States firm. A little later, on the basis of an arrangemen with Piérola's successor, Francisco García Calderón, the agency was in fact promised to the firm of Levi P. Morton, a pillar of the Republican Party, who went to Paris that year as United States minister. Very soon, however, Paris was trying to manipulate Washington on behalf of the rival Dreyfus firm. In August and September approaches were made to Morton by no less a person than President Grévy, whose legal services had formerly been retained by Dreyfus. Secretary of State Blaine now took a high tone, talked of the pre-eminent position of the United States in South America, and declined any agreement. Nothing was known of these exchanges at the time in London; but they should have dispelled any fears at Washington of a European front. It is fairly clear, indeed, that the United States held all the cards she needed to isolate England over the Pacific War; she could not play them because she was bent on isolating herself instead.

The second of Washington's two besetting suspicions was expressed most dogmatically by James G. Blaine when defending his recent conduct as secretary of state in a Congressional enquiry in 1882: "It is a perfect mistake to speak of this as a Chilean war on Peru. It is an English war on Peru, with Chile as the instrument." It followed from this view that the United States ought to protect Peru. Especially during Piérola's régime, Peru was quick to realize that the worse terms she was on with London, the better terms she could hope to be on with Washington. So far as the British government was concerned, in this particular case, Blaine's suspicion was unfounded. But it could easily lead to unpleasantness between London and Washington, such as had developed in 1865-1866 during Spain's raid on the Pacific coast. Since then the vexed question of an interoceanic canal had been coming to the front; work started on the French Panama project in 1881, and Washington was trying to rid itself of the irksome Clayton-Bulwer Treaty. Britain could return American distrust by suspecting deep-laid schemes for ousting her legitimate interests on the Pacific coast. Commercial ambitions were now coloring the Monroe Doctrine, and challenging Britain's trade supremacy in South America. "Everything that can possibly be thought of," said a British trade report from Washington in 1879, "is being carried out to obtain foreign markets for United States products and manufactures." Obvious opportunities were offered by the Pacific War; and at one of its critical points, late in 1880, the British chargé at Washington felt convinced that the grand object there was "to obtain the trade of South America, now in the hands of European countries, for the United States, which considers that the whole of the South American trade should belong to her . . . and undoubtedly by her ingratiating herself with both Chile and Peru in the present juncture of affairs there, trusts to gain commercial advantages over the nations trading with them." When Blaine in 1881 worked for a Pan-American conference, one of his motives was to promote United States exports. In 1883 a circular was sent to British legations on "the steps the government of the United States are about to take to promote the commercial relations of the United States with Central and South America"; and a report came in from Chile of stiff competition in the sale of railway materials.

As things then stood, United States commercial interests on the Pacific coast might reasonably be suspected of resorting to political weapons, because American trade lagged so far behind European, especially British trade. This lack of a firm basis of local interests and connections was one of the handicaps of United States diplomacy, which was working, so to speak, in a vacuum. Moreover, speculation, flourishing like a beanstalk in the rank soil of guano, outstripped legitimate business. It became mixed up with the party politics of the United States, most of all in the time of Blaine, who gave his backing to a diversity of unsavory claims on Peru, and by what has been called his "excessive lust for riches" imperiled both his own and his government's reputation.

If Blaine had not developed such a definite concern with Pan American affairs, the Foreign Office's interest in the war might have been much smaller. Its opening moves were very tentative, and inspired by a normal fear of interruptions to trade. When Peru, just before entering the war, toyed with the idea of arbitration, St. John unofficially suggested the president of the United States as a suitable umpire. Only after Peru had become involved in war, and in response to a private hint from Carlos Piridal, Peruvian minister in London, did the Foreign Office inform the belligerents that it was "most anxious to avert an outbreak of hostilities between Chile and Peru," and to tender "friendly offices." When both sides declined, Sir Julian Pauncefote (then assistant under-secretary) noted: "It seems to me that it is almost worth making another attempt at pacification in the interests of British commerce which must suffer very much by a continuance of hostilities between such fiery and unscrupulous belligerents." Lord Salisbury, the foreign secretary, assented. But when, in June, the German ambassador in London proposed a joint approach to the United States for combined mediation, and the Foreign Office sounded Washington, it was surprised by its cold reception. Sir Edward Thornton, the British minister, was told that while Washington was ready to tender good offices, it did not favor any joint *démarche*, as that might savor of coercion. It was left to the United States to make the next moves, which were initiated not so much by Secretary of State Evarts as by her ministers to the belligerent countries. Their ill-coördinated efforts came to nothing. When asked in September whether or not he was trying to mediate, William M. Evarts returned an answer in what seemed to Thornton "intentionally obscure language."

From the beginning the British government had expressed itself in favor of peace, but showed no inclination to put pressure on the winning side to forego its gains; and since Chile was, from the first, in possession of Bolivian territory, any *status quo* peace might be held, at Lima and La Paz, to favor her. Bondholders might be expected, in view of Peru's military failure, to pin their hopes on her rival, and Chile was intelligent enough to play on their hopes and fears. When Pakenham was told, in December, 1879, to seek recognition by Chile of the creditors' claims on Peru's resources, Chile made proposals which Pauncefote approved, noting that they were "received with acclamation" at a City meeting on February 2, 1880; they were embodied in a decree of the same month, assigning to the bondholders the proceeds of the Tarapacá workings. "The Chilean Govt. have behaved very well in this matter," Pauncefote commented, and the *Economist* had come to feel that a Chilean annexation of the guano islands could not be bad for the bondholders. This was also, by now, more or less the opinion of Sir Charles Russell. Peru had protested in advance against any arrangement between her creditors and Chile, and naturally resented it when it was made, even if Britain did not consider it as implying any recognition of Chile's territorial demands. In these ways, though the Foreign Office would still have disclaimed any partiality, Britain might seem to have slipped into a position of something less than absolute neutrality.

It was while Piérola was in power that estrangement between England and Peru went furthest. This came about partly through the United States taking sides with Peru, and partly through other causes. An incident in Piérola's stormy career was remembered against him in London; and before long the press of Lima, taking its tone from his secretary in *La Patria*, was loudly Anglophobe. "The hatred of the Piérola party to the English," St. John wrote, ". . . is notorious . . . there is not a club or society in Peru in which abuse of the English is not of constant occurrence." Moreover, Piérola was regarded in London as a politician very closely linked with the firm of Dreyfus, and on that account inimical to the interests of Peru's other creditors. St. John credited him with personal motives for this. Britain was averse to Peru's raising any fresh money abroad, and Piérola could raise little at home. This involved St. John in an unpleasant scene with the Foreign Minister, who complained too loudly of British hostility. Disliking the man's "ill-bred excitement," St. John forbore to visit him again for some time. Of Piérola himself, who both before and after the war left his mark on Peruvian history, few have ever made a lower estimate than the British minister did. "The Supreme Chief," he reported, "passes the principal portion of his time in preparing decrees at which the public smile," and manifestos "bombastic and absurd." As to his new troops, many were "Indians caught in the interior and sent tied together to the capital; at the first opportunity they will desert and return home." Similar comments came from British officers attached to the staffs of the rival armies.

However just some of his strictures may have been, a touch of prejudice peeps out in St. John's statement that "the Government of Mr. Piérola rests entirely for support on the lower orders." Piérola was always for him a vulgar demagogue. The "democratic party," the British envoy at Lima remarked in 1884, "might perhaps be styled more briefly as the mob." St. John, it is worth recalling, had passed most of his active life in Borneo, partly as Rajah Brooke's lieutenant, and in Haiti, where he "frequently took violent measures against native disturbers of the public peace." More important still, at the moment, it was only a decade since 1871, and he was in fear of the emergence of "a kind of organized commune." Pauncefote likewise felt that the legation was in a "serious position," the Pierolistas being such "desperate fellows." This anxiety continued to haunt St. John and his successors in the years of disorder after Piérola's fall. Hence, though they found the Chilean occupation forces lawless and arrogant, they felt that men of property preferred the occupation as the lesser evil. "There exists a vast amount of distress and poverty," we hear in 1882. Many Indians had been "driven to desperation by the outrages . . . committed upon them by the invaders . . . it would be a serious matter if the lower orders were to rise." A year later it was the same story. "The poor Indians have been the greatest sufferers throughout the war." In several provinces they revolted. African and Chinese laborers were another peril. All this had the effect of making Englishmen blame what one of them called "the wilful stubbornness" of Peru, rather than Chilean greed, for the long-continued deadlock after 1880, and dislike any moves that might encourage the "easily deluded Peruvians" in their obstinacy. Such a trend of thought might lead far. Admiral Lyons wrote from Peru in 1882: "The annexation of the country by Chile is not improbable, and I imagine that this measure would be popular with the large foreign population."

These, however, were the feelings of men on the spot. In the Foreign Office it seems to have been felt at more than one juncture that the Chileans were being at least as obstinate as their opponents. While Piérola was in power he received various offers of good offices from Britain and other European powers. Even supposing Britain to be in favor of the nitrate areas going to Chile, she could have no such desire to see Chile prolonging the war in order to secure Tacna and Arica, which had no nitrates and could serve no purpose unless to strengthen the Chilean frontier. Piérola wanted active support, not mere good offices, and could only look to Washington for it. Washington was ready at least to obstruct any moves from other quarters. St. John was surprised in May, 1880, at the hostile attitude adopted by Isaac P. Christiancy, the United States envoy (for whom he made allowances as "a lawyer from the Western States but little acquainted with the usages of his new position"), and at being told by Christiancy that his orders were to prevent any foreign interference. "As far as we are aware in Lima," he wrote, "no foreign power has ever thought of intervention in the affairs of the Republics." Acting Secretary John Hay at Washington made it clear to the Italian representative, and Evarts repeated the warning a little later, that they were going their own way and would not coöperate with anyone else.

When, in the autumn of 1880, arrangements were made for a conference to discuss peace on board a United States warship at Arica, St. John felt that England's efforts had been brushed aside with little courtesy; he considered Chile's conduct as "very underhand," and Osborn (the United States minister at Santiago) guilty of "a great want of straightforwardness." In spite of this irritation, the British and other European diplomats at Santiago agreed that, since they all desired peace, they should do nothing to hamper the negotiations. They even tried to be helpful by urging Chile to take part in the conference.

Its failure, and the recriminations that followed, ushered in the 1881 period during which suspicions between London and Washington were at their worst. St. John concluded that at Arica Washington tried to throw dust into the eyes of both parties in order to smuggle through a peace on its own terms; and that Thomas A. Osborn had "completely thwarted his European colleagues" by making Chile think they were trying to interfere against her on behalf of their holders of Peruvian bonds. Lord Granville told Italy he "did not think we could admit a doctrine that European countries were to be debarred from endeavors to put an end to conflicts which seriously affected their commerce and the interest of their subjects." At the same time rumors of financial maneuvers by the United States came to reinforce dislike of its political activity. A series of "secret" telegrams to the Foreign Office announced that Consul-General Archibald at New York had discovered "very astonishing and important proofs" of a most "nefarious transaction." A scheme was afoot, it appeared, to transfer control of Peru's guano to a ring of United States speculators with President Hayes' secretary as "a principal mover." Peru would be given a loan secured on guano to enable her to pay Chile an indemnity instead of ceding territory. What Archibald had stumbled on must have been connected with the plans of the Crédit Industriel. St. John found the story quite plausible. He had himself got wind in October of some such stratagem, by which the wealth of Tarapacá would in effect belong to the United States, and he took comfort in a conviction that Chile was not likely to let herself be bullied into giving up the province. Christiancy, he said, was aware that the other envoys distrusted him; his private secretary had been connected with railway concerns in the United States and his own reputation was not above suspicion.

Blaine took office as secretary of state in March, 1881, when his friend James G. Garfield became president, and by the summer was getting into his stride. Both his anti-British bias and his financial connections helped to make him the most adventurous of the three heads of the State Department during the war years. Speculators' intrigues were soon blossoming into what Perry Belmont was to describe in Congress as the idea of "a protectorate and guarantee of Peru by the United States." This was now a possibility to be reckoned with, one whose fulfillment would have altered history. The Dutch representative at Washington was among those who thought that Blaine, by erratic and irresponsible tactics, was carrying his country to the edge of war for the sake of making Peru a United States dependency. By November Santiago was full of rumors about Washington-inspired schemes, including especially that of Stephen A. Hurlbut, Blaine's minister at Lima, to lease the Peruvian port of Chimbote as a United States naval base. At the end of the year Blaine's activity culminated in the despatch to Chile of a special commissioner, William H. Trescot, and a squadron of warships.

Before this, in August, St. John brought about a meeting in his house between Chilean and Peruvian spokesmen; he was perhaps hoping to get things patched up before the United States could go too far. No agreement resulted, and he privately told J. Godoy, the Chilean, whom he knew well, that his demands were extravagant. Nothing like an Anglo-Chilean alliance developed in the critical months following; but Chile naturally did her best to play off Britain against America. At and after the Arica conference she had expressed a tactful sympathy with the British bondholders; and now, with Trescot in the offing, José Manuel Balmaceda, the Chilean foreign minister, made them another well-timed offer out of the proceeds of guano sales from the occupied territory. He also played upon British misgivings about Chimbote, asserting that the United States had promised to pay or guarantee a war-indemnity and oblige Chile to evacuate Peru. In London the Law Officers considered that a lease of Chimbote by the United States would not be an infringement of the Clayton-Bulwer Treaty; but both Foreign Office and Admiralty were disturbed. Pakenham, however, quietly evaded the question when Balmaceda asked him one day "what was the opinion of Her Majesty's Government with reference to the intervention of the United States government in the affairs of the South American Republics"; and the fall of Blaine and his replacement by Frederick T. Frelinghuysen brought the crisis to an end in January, 1882.

One reason for England's self-restraint must have been the fact that Chile's position was less dangerous than it seemed, because the naval strength that the United States could bring to bear on her was in reality surprisingly small. In Britain, where the most up-to-date warships were built and sold to all comers, this was understood more clearly perhaps than at Washington. The United States warships sent down the Pacific coast were reported by the Admiralty to be "old wooden steamers, armed with smooth bores, and very slow"; St. John remarked that the "naval demonstration" at Valparaíso had gone almost unnoticed. Chile's naval power, as displayed in the war, had been "a complete revelation to South America," and naval warfare was evolving so rapidly that a small state with a handful of new ships was for the moment a match for almost anyone. As the British Admiralty observed in 1881, "The Chilian Government . . . having three ironclads, and the United States Government being deficient in that particular, it would be out of the power of the latter effectively to coerce the former Power."

After Trescot got home he told Sir Lionel Sackville-West, the new British minister to the United States, that Washington's claim to an exclusive right of mediation had been a great blunder: "European Powers had acquired an influence in the South American Republics which it was folly to ignore." Sackville-West suspected sour grapes, and refrained from asking why with such opinions he had undertaken his mission at all. Meanwhile, Frelinghuysen's three new envoys to the belligerent countries—James R. Partridge, Cornelius A. Logan, George E. Maney—quickly fell into the same eternal triangle of quarreling and bungling which had characterized their predecessors. Britain continued to look on. Occasionally there was discussion as to whether Washington was likely to resent any fresh British initiative towards peace, and if so whether her feelings ought to be ignored. Alfred St. John (Sir Spenser's nephew, who was in charge at Lima after Graham fell ill) wrote early in 1883, when Partridge had been recalled in disgrace for discussing a joint *démarche* with the other diplomats, that Washington seemed to be "still animated with an intense jealousy of European interference to bring about peace. The Government of the United States are conscious that the prestige of their country has greatly suffered after the several signal failures their diplomacy has suffered on this coast. . . ." Sir Spenser St. John, who had returned to Europe, had been asking why Britain should admit any United States primacy, or bother about Germany, and he believed that Chile ought to be made to conclude a peace. Sackville-West likewise saw no reason why Britain should not act alone. "The United States Government," he said, "are at their wits' end to get through with the question. . . . They have thought more than once lately of devising means to obtain assistance in settling it without sacrificing their own 'amour propre' in the matter." Later, in 1883, when General M. Yglesias emerged the winner among the Peruvian factions, and was ready to sign peace terms, the Foreign Office wondered whether to strengthen his hand by recognizing him. Alfred St. John thought him well-meaning and unambitious, though surrounded by low intriguers. Harry

S. C. C. Jervoise at the Foreign Office (the senior clerk concerned) pointed out that Washington was "thoroughly discredited" in South America, and chagrined at the upset of the balance of power there; and Philip H. Currie (assistant undersecretary) thought it would be good for England's prestige to act without consulting other governments. In fact, however, recognition of Yglesias was delayed. Even at this late stage there was apparently a reluctance to offend Washington unnecessarily.

United States diplomacy had been far too poorly equipped to succeed in emulating the new German system, of fostering commercial influence by political strategy. The British service had the easier function of watching over commercial interests already solidly established, and its men were adequate to their task. If Pakenham was addicted to long and frequent leaves of absence, his Valparaíso consul, James De Vismes Drummond-Hay, could fill his place. At Lima Alfred St. John, though a very junior officer, kept things going satisfactorily for nearly two years. United States diplomats were ill-paid, ill-trained, and ill-tempered. After the Arica conference, for instance, both Christiancy of Lima and Adams of La Paz grumbled indiscreetly to outsiders about Osborn at Santiago; Adams told Sir Spenser St. John later at Lima that he had never met "a more thorough Chilian" than Osborn. St. John reflected that American envoys were apt to see things in the same light as the governments they were accredited to. "The explanation usually given is not complimentary to their disinterestedness." When some of the State Department's correspondence was published, he wrote a long and bitter critique of it, among other things accusing Christiancy of having filled Washington with groundless suspicions of Europe. "The result of the interference of these untrained men in international affairs, which they did not fully understand, was a remarkable display of pretentious incapacity."

Like Osborn in 1880 and Hugh J. Kilpatrick in 1881, Logan in 1882 showed a disposition to fall in with the Chilean point of view that quickly aroused comment. Frelinghuysen himself was despondent enough at one moment to confess to the British minister how much he was hampered by finding all his agents turn into partisans of the countries they went to, and even asked Sackville-West whether he personally had any notion of how peace could be brought about. It was indeed only too apparent that the eyes of the State Department at Lima and Santiago were usually squinting in different directions. "The explanation is very simple," wrote Sir Spenser. "Most of the American agents I have known have been either directly or indirectly bought by the Governments to which they were accredited. I could give details of names and circumstances, should it be considered useful." Only one American agent enjoyed the respect of his British colleague: Partridge, at Lima in 1882, who was described as "a very superior person to the sort of ordinary office-hunters who are too often named by the Government of the United States to fill Diplomatic and Consular positions in South America." Partridge committed suicide a year after his recall. The United States minister in London from 1880 to 1885 was James Russell Lowell; but so far as Pacific War business with the Foreign Office was concerned, no use was ever made of him by the State Department.

The United States practised an "open diplomacy," and publicity made its failures more resounding. It was prone to invoke moral principles, and Blaine spoke of the Monroe Doctrine he was engaged in expanding as "humane and disinterested." But a Monroe Doctrine extended by such men to cover such designs could not seem to others so "absolutely disinterested and unselfish" as it must, James Bryce pointed out in 1912, if it was not to arouse resentment in Latin America. Historians in the United States have not failed to recognize this, and Millington sums up the Pacific War as "one of the most unfortunate chapters in American diplomatic history."

At the end of the story, when the Treaty of Ancón was signed in October, 1883, the country which made the most flurry was neither Britain nor the United States, but France. By the treaty the Peruvian bondholders were to get half the net profits from existing, but not from future, nitrate workings in the territory annexed by Chile. Jules Ferry, the French premier, called this "absolutely inacceptable." France had, of course, no more sympathy than Britain with the reluctance of many Peruvians to cede territory—"the usual rhodomontade about the Honour of Peru," as someone at the Foreign Office had dismissed it. Alfred St. John thought the terms not bad; he argued that Peru, if she had kept Tarapacá, would have treated her creditors no better than before. But on the whole the creditors were disappointed. Now, as when the war started, the Foreign Office was beset with much contradictory advice. A pro-Chilean trader wrote to warn it that he thought the United States would rejoice to see England committed to any risky course, and would make capital out of it. Seventeen merchant houses of London and Liverpool wrote that rumors of intervention on behalf of the bondholders were injuring trade, and that Yglesias ought to be recognized. Several governments did in fact protest, including the British and French but not Germany or the United States. In March, 1884, none the less, the treaty was ratified as it stood, and in April Yglesias, on the ground that he had not been recognized, abruptly broke off relations with the diplomatic corps. Paris reacted violently. Already some months earlier the Marquis de Tallenay, French envoy at Lima, and a man of truculent disposition, had begun threatening that France was about to break off relations with Chile, and that this would presage armed intervention. Now France pressed Britain to join in the kind of "European intervention" so long feared at Washington, by taking up a firm attitude to both Chile and Peru, sending ships to Callao, and embargoing all exports of guano and minerals. As little disposed as ever to pull French chestnuts out of the fire, the Foreign Office adhered to its sober policies. Pauncefote directed this "wild programme" to be answered with "some cooling and sedative language." On April 23, 1884, St. John was told to recognize Yglesias; the United States did so at the same time, and other powers followed.

British interests, because they were the biggest and most varied, suffered more losses in the course of the war than those of any other country; for the same reason, on the other hand, they came off best in the long run. Proceedings against Chile for compensation for war damages proved tedious, vexatious, and in the end disappointing. Certainly Chile did not emerge from the war in any mood of gratitude or docility towards England, nor England in any mood of admiration or respect for Chile. The bondholders were left with an arbitration case against Chile, which they lost by the Rapperschwyl Award of 1901, and a case against Peru which brought them in 1890 appreciable concessions. The nitrate-miners were the luckiest. And the shift away from the purely financial type of investment represented by guano loans to the industrial type represented by nitrate mines implied, at the same time, a change favourable to Britain as against France. French and other bondholders, besides British, profited by the 1890 agreement with Peru; but the sweeping projects nourished by French, and more intermittently by American, speculators had collapsed. Over France commercially, and over the United States politically, Britain had increased her already long lead. Germany, still far behind, utilized the war and post-war years to look out shrewdly for trade openings.

Few of the wider consequences of the war could have been foreseen when it began—a fact which tells against Blaine's idea that this was an "English war." So far as his suspicions were concerned with the British capital established in Chile in the nitrate-fields, there must remain—as with many analogous problems—an element of doubt. This capital had close connections with Chilean financial and political interests, and through them could exert behind the scenes an influence of the sort that tends to leave little positive record of its activity. The Scottish legal verdict of "not proven" may be the most suitable one here. Blaine's suspicions, however, extended much further, to the aggregate of British interests, and the British Government as their representative; and here the verdict can only be "not guilty."

Other Articles of Interest

Bastert, Russell H. "A New Approach to the Origins of Blaine's Pan American Policy." XXXIX (1959), 375–412.

Brown, Joseph R. "The Chilean Nitrate Railways Controversy." XXXVIII (1958), 465–481.

————. "Nitrate Crises, Combinations, and the Chilean Government in the Nitrate Age." XLIII (1963), 230–246.

Hardy, Osgood, "The Itata Incident." V (1922), 195–226.

The *Itata* attempted to secure arms in the United States for the use of the Congressional party against President Balmaceda in the Chilean Civil War in 1891. The adventures of the *Itata* after its seizure in San Diego are followed: its escape, transhipment to it of supplies from other ships, its return from Chile to California, and the resulting trial and vindication in the courts of California with the participation of some of the finest California legal talent.

————. "Was Patrick Egan a 'Blundering Minister'?" VIII (1928), 65–81.

Egan's great sin was that of representing a government which, "unable to act in such a way as to secure the friendship of both parties to a civil war, had made the mistake of picking the loser." Egan's worthiness was largely a matter of public opinion in the United States. The attack against him was led by the *New York Evening Post*, the *New York Times, Harper's Weekly,* and the *Nation.* Three episodes, the "Itata Incident," the "Cable Affair," and the "Quinteros Bay Episode," were beyond his control. Facts to be considered are these: (1) he was *persona non grata* to British representatives; (2) he committed no unneutral act; (3) the charge that he did not make complete reports to his government can be proved wrong; (4) the accusation of corruption must be borne by his son, since the father tried only to find a place for American capital.

Stewart, Watt. "Federico Blume's Peruvian Submarine." XXVIII (1948), 468–478.

After engineering experience and travel in Germany, Venezuela, Cuba, and the United States, Federico Blume made his home in Peru in 1855. He developed his submarine plans in connection with the war with Spain, 1864–1866, but the opportunity for effective demonstration came only with the War of the Pacific. The submarine was launched and operated in 1879 but was never used against the enemy. The principles of submarine construction were arrived at by Blume independently of any connection with Holland's later perfection of the submarine.

7. The Latin-American Republics and the Suppression of the Slave Trade

JAMES FERGUSON KING

Professor King of the University of California, Berkeley, and former managing editor of the *HAHR*, presents in this article a solid study of the patient diplomatic efforts Great Britain made to suppress the traffic in Negro slaves. Britain ended the traffic to her dominions in 1807, and thereafter tried to influence other governments to follow her example. She was particularly eager to ensure that slave ships should not be allowed to sail under the flags of the Latin American republics, and this article shows how her objective was accomplished.

Great Britain's abolition of the slave trade to her dominions in 1807 marked the end of one period in the crusade against the "abominable traffic" and the beginning of another. For the British anti-slavery leaders scarcely paused to celebrate this domestic victory of their cause, so anxious were they to carry the struggle into the world at large. And now, ironically enough, the humanitarian initiators of the movement were potently reinforced by their erstwhile enemies, the British plantation owners, who experienced a sudden conversion when faced with the prospect of a continuing slave trade to competitive foreign areas as the replenishment of their own labor supply was cut off. Thus the stage was set, as Viscount Palmerston later put it, to enlist in a "league against slave trade every state in Christendom which has a flag that sails on the ocean. . . ."

The major outlines of Britain's long and arduous struggle to exterminate the foreign slave trade are well known. The campaign was directed primarily against the traffic to Brazil and Cuba, the two areas of the western world that continued to import slaves on a large scale following the decline of the illegal trade to the United States after 1825. The story has been told heretofore in terms of the pursuit of international slavers from one flag to another as Britain succeeded in making reciprocal search treaties with the nations whose sovereignty successively protected the trade. As such, the account is primarily one of remedial action to suppress existing abuses. There is, however, one neglected aspect of the matter that remains to be

From Volume XXIV (1944), pages 387–411.

studied: Britain's *preventive* campaign to bind the new Latin-American republics by treaties made for the most part in anticipation of attempts to prostitute their flags to the purposes of the trade, as slavers were forced to relinquish the protection of other nations.

The Slave Trade and British Recognition

During the decade from the beginnings of the struggle for Spanish-American independence until the outbreak of the Spanish revolution of 1820, Great Britain sought to mediate between Spain and her revolted colonies. This policy was dictated at first by the Anglo-Spanish alliance against Napoleon, subsequently by dislike of New World republicanism and by the expectation that existing quasi-legal British trade could be maintained even within a restored Spanish Empire. During this period only one substantial consideration argued in favor of Spanish-American independence: the willingness of the revolutionary governments to abolish the Negro traffic. But until Britain learned the full recalcitrance of Spain in slave-trade matters, she hoped to secure the abolition of the Spanish traffic by dealing with the mother country herself. In 1817 she went so far as to make abolition of the trade one of the conditions of her mediation between Spain and her colonies.

Nevertheless, there was no blinking the fact that liberal revolutionary philosophy placed the new American regimes considerably in advance of Britain, whose slaves were not freed until 1833; for their measures struck not only at the Negro traffic, but frequently at slavery itself. British statesmen could not fail to note that a Mexican deputy, for example, had been a leader in the abortive attempt to secure the abolition of the traffic and gradual emancipation of slaves in the Spanish Empire at the Cortes of Cádiz in 1811. Venezuela led the Latin-American nations in proscribing the Negro traffic in a decree issued by the Supreme Junta of Caracas on August 14, 1810; and the prohibition of "the vile traffic in slaves" was incorporated into the first Venezuelan constitution, promulgated December 21, 1811. The Curate Hidalgo proclaimed the abolition of slavery in Mexico on December 6, 1810; and when José María Morelos assumed the leadership of the revolution there, he repeated Hidalgo's decree in a *bando* of January 29, 1813. Chile had already followed suit in legislation of October 15, 1811, which ended the Negro trade and provided that the children of slaves should subsequently be born free. The government of Buenos Aires issued an executive decree on May 15, 1812, confirmed by legislation of February 4, 1813, ending the Negro traffic to the provinces under its control. The constitution of the State of Cartagena of June, 1812, likewise proscribed the trade. Simón Bolívar, whose strong opposition to slavery was well known both in Europe and America, declared the freedom of slaves in northern South America beginning in 1816 and sought, without immediate success, confirmation of his acts at the Congress of Angostura in 1819. José de San Martín signed laws on August 12 and November 24, 1821, proclaiming respectively the freedom of children subsequently born of slave mothers and the cessation of the slave trade.

Such evidence of creole attitudes toward slavery and the slave trade was not lost upon British statesmen, particularly at a time when the campaign against the Negro traffic was meeting extensive foreign opposition. The contrast between the policy of the revolutionary governments and that of the mother country was particularly striking. True, Spain had joined other European powers in giving lip-service to a denunciation of the traffic at the Congress of Vienna; and in 1817, in response to British pressure and a subsidy of £400,000, she even signed a treaty providing for the suppression of the Spanish slave trade by 1820, reciprocal search of merchant vessels, and mixed courts to try offenders. But Spain proceeded to demonstrate the evasion and obstruction that were to minimize the effect of this and later agreements with Great Britain.

It is not strange, then, that British statesmen recognized the disposition of the Latin-American republics spontaneously to abolish the slave trade as an important point in their favor, even though other considerations as yet made recognition inexpedient. Writing from his observation post at Rio de Janeiro in 1814, for example, the British minister to the Portuguese court advised Viscount Castlereagh:

> ... I should fail in my duty did I not state to your Lordship that upon one point at least the Government of Buenos Ayres seems to have a just and strong claim to our good offices, and that the noble example which they have shown to these countries by the abolition of Negro slavery [i.e., the slave trade] throughout the Provinces under their authority does appear to entitle them to the favour and sympathy of the nation whose principles on that subject they have proclaimed and whose practice they have adopted.

By 1815, when events in Europe had improved Spain's prospects of suppressing colonial revolt, the same observer warned: "In the event of Spain's recovering her footing in South America, the Slave Trade, which the new Government has put down, chiefly in compliance with the sentiments and example of Great Britain, will undoubtedly be revived, and the beneficial effects which might have been expected from the introduction into this hemisphere of a liberal and virtuous policy on that question will be suddenly and completely checked."

It is true that political and general commercial considerations were the basic determinants of Britain's preparation to recognize the new republics after 1820, but there is good evidence that the slave trade also figured significantly in this shift of policy. "Of one thing the Allied Powers may be perfectly assured," wrote Foreign Secretary Canning to Britain's representative at the Congress of Verona, ". . . no State in the New World will be recognized by Great Britain which has not frankly and completely abolished the trade in slaves." When instructions were prepared for the

British commissioners sent to Mexico and Colombia in 1823, they were directed to report whether four prerequisities of recognition had been met. The first three concerned formal declaration of independence from Spain, ability of the regimes in power to control and defend the countries, and their acceptance by the people. The fourth read: "Has it [i.e., the government] abjured and abolished the Slave Trade?" Copies of these instructions were likewise provided for the guidance of the consuls who were sent about the same time to Chile, Buenos Aires, and Peru.

In the cases of Mexico, Colombia, and Buenos Aires, the replies were satisfactory; and negotiation of treaties of amity, commerce and navigation was shortly begun. So far as Buenos Aires was concerned, the slave trade had long been forbidden. Much local legislation against the slave trade had already been adopted in the component states of "Great" Colombia, and the British commissioner in Bogotá was able to report that this had been incorporated into the comprehensive law passed by the Congress of Cúcuta on July 19, 1821, which not only reiterated prohibition of the traffic, but provided for free birth of slave children and for gradual compensated emancipation of those previously born. Although the prospect of earning Britain's favor may to some extent have influenced the Colombian legislators, the strong creole anti-slavery movement in the country, which dated at least from the *Comunero* uprising of 1781, is itself sufficient to explain the step. From Mexico, Commissioner Hervey reported that "The Slave Trade was solemnly abjured and abolished throughout the Mexican dominions by a public declaration of the National Congress, voted almost unanimously on the 15th instant." Such legislation, passed almost immediately after the arrival of the commission when Mexicans felt "the necessity of the support of some great maritime Power to protect their rising Independence," strongly suggests British pressure. But on the other hand, no appreciable slave trade to Mexico had existed since 1739; and compliance with British wishes not only represented no sacrifice of local interests, but probably reflected Mexican desires.

Domestic anti-slave trade laws in the new republics were all to the good, but the British Foreign Office had no intention of relying upon them alone. Such legislation might be revoked or left uninforced; and in any event, the new states were without adequate naval forces to maintain the maritime patrol which British experience was demonstrating to be the best method of coping with slavers. The negotiation of treaties of amity, commerce and navigation provided the opportunity for placing the suppression of the slave traffic on a bilateral basis and for giving Great Britain wide, though as yet unspecified powers, which might be invoked in the future should circumstances warrant such a course. Hence standard slave trade articles were incorporated into the treaties—part of the price of recognition. Article XIV of the treaty of February 2, 1825, with the government of Buenos Aires was substantially similar to those contained in the pacts signed shortly thereafter with Colombia and Mexico:

His Britannic Majesty being extremely desirous of totally abolishing the Slave Trade, the United Provinces of Rio de la Plata engage to co-operate with His Britannic Majesty for the completion of so beneficent a work, and to prohibit all persons inhabiting within the said United Provinces, or subject to their jurisdiction, in the most effectual manner, and by the most solemn laws, from taking any share in such trade.

Though treaty relationships with the remaining Latin-American republics were perforce delayed by unsettled conditions and other factors, these three agreements set the pattern and provided a foundation for special anti-slave trade treaties subsequently negotiated.

The Palmerstonian Crusade

For nearly a decade after the conclusion of the treaties with Buenos Aires, Colombia, and Mexico, Great Britain gave scant attention to slave trade matters so far as the Latin-American republics were concerned. After its cessation during the struggle for independence, the Negro traffic to these countries at first showed few signs of being resumed. The use of the republican flags to protect the trade to Cuba and Brazil was unnecessary and inconvenient, so long as slavers could obtain the protection of more powerful nations. Accordingly, for the time being Britain concentrated her efforts on securing effective treaties with the erring powers.

With the coming of Viscount Palmerston to the Foreign Office in 1830, the British campaign got into its stride. The new Foreign Secretary was forceful, able, and passionately intent upon suppressing "this diabolical slave trade." He knew from the experience of his predecessors that pious denunciations of the traffic by foreign powers were insufficient, and that even the principles of reciprocal search and mixed tribunals, which gave British cruisers the power to intercept slavers on the high seas and to bring them in for adjudication, were not enough unless accompanied by an "equipment clause" permitting seizure of slavers with no Negroes aboard, and a stipulation for the breaking up of condemned slave vessels. Hence Palmerston immediately began the negotiation of a new series of treaties with the principal slave-trading powers to supersede imperfect prior agreements.

France, hitherto recalcitrant, led the way by agreeing to satisfactory conventions in 1831 and 1833, after the liberal regime of Louis Philippe was set up. When the slavers sought refuge under the Spanish flag, Palmerston countered by obtaining a new and more stringent treaty with Spain in 1835. Next the slavers resorted to Portuguese colors; and the Foreign Minister, finding that government unwilling either to live up to former treaties or to negotiate a new one, high-handedly but effectively employed an act of Parliament of 1839 to remove the flag of Britain's ancient ally from slave vessels. Satisfactory agreements were made with other European powers, whose flags were already ceasing to be used for slaving purposes.

And finally, the Republic of Texas was forced to accept a treaty negotiated in 1840 as part of the price of British recognition. Despite the inability of Great Britain to secure an equipment convention to supplement the Anglo-Brazilian treaty of 1826, and the refusal of the United States to concede the right of search until 1862, the British program after 1830 was clearly making the Negro traffic a highly desperate enterprise. The obvious strategy of the slave traders was to seek the protection of other flags still untrammeled by precise treaty obligations. The national colors that could best meet this demand were those of the Latin-American republics. Given the background of her relations with these new states, it was natural that Britain should next turn her attention to the prevention of this development.

The Traffic Renascent in
the Río de la Plata

The two Platine states of Uruguay and the Argentine Confederation represented the most immediate danger to the program for the suppression of the slave trade, and upon them Great Britain concentrated her first efforts. Adjacent to the great slave market of Brazil and facing Africa across the South Atlantic, their location was itself a powerful inducement to lend their flags to the lucrative traffic. Moreover, domestic slavery still subsisted in both countries. Uruguay, alone among the Spanish mainland countries, seems actually to have experienced an increase in the slave population during the revolutionary period, doubtless because of the influx of bondsmen during the periods of Portuguese and Brazilian domination. Though there were only three hundred slaves in the Argentine provinces when an official British estimate was made in 1843, the total colored element was reported to comprise one fourteenth of the population. Domestic conditions in both countries were thus favorable to slaving enterprises.

Uruguay was the worst offender in British eyes. True, a law passed in 1825 at the outset of the war to drive the Brazilians from the country had proclaimed the end of the slave trade and the freedom of children of slaves; and this legislation had been incorporated into Article 131 of the Uruguayan constitution, promulgated in 1829. Yet as early as 1833, the British consul-general in Montevideo reported acts of Uruguayan officials, "which strongly indicate an underhand desire . . . to evade the law by allowing slavery to be carried on under simulated character." The same despatch brought news that the recent arrival of a Portuguese schooner at Montevideo, allegedly to repair damages but actually to refit for the traffic, "had awakened the dormant spirit of Slave Trading in certain Subjects of this Republic . . ."; that accordingly a Montevidean vessel was already fitting out for the Congo, and that other fast sailers were in demand for like purpose.

The consul-general's accusations were confirmed by a British cruiser's seizure, in November, 1834, of the brig *Río de la Plata* under Uruguayan colors, with a cargo of 521 slaves aboard, bound ostensibly from Loanda to Montevideo. Found among the slaver's papers was a contract between the government of Fructuoso Rivera and two individuals, one with a suspicious Portuguese name, granting them permission to import 650 African "colonists" within two years in return for 30,000 *pesos*. The vessel was brought before the mixed Anglo-Brazilian tribunal at Rio de Janeiro and condemned on the ground that she was a Brazilian slaver masquerading under the flag of Montevideo. *A propos* of this episode, the British minister at the same capital observed:

There has all along been a strong probability . . . that the unfortunate Negroes, nominally embarked in Africa as free Colonists for Monte Video, and under license from the Monte-Videan Government, are in fact destined as Slaves for the Brazilian market. Many of these cargoes are clandestinely landed on the Coast of Brazil, without being carried to the Oriental Republic at all; others, that in conformity with the License are marched into the interior of the Oriental Territory, have from thence been easily passed over into Brazil as slaves; and there is good reason to believe that the Brazilian dealers on the Coast of Africa keep open a regular debtor and creditor account with their correspondents in the town of Rio de Janeiro for the value . . . of the identical Blacks shipped apparently as free Colonists for the Uruguay.

The rising up thus of the African Slave Trade under the Flag of Monte Video is peculiarly galling to Great Britain. When the Slave Trade Conventions were entered into with Brazil, the Territory of Monte Video was a Brazilian Province, and its inhabitants bound by the Laws and Obligations of this Empire. It was at the suggestion of Great Britain, and under her mediation, that the subsequent war between Brazil and Buenos Ayres was terminated by raising the Banda Oriental into a separate State; and by virtue of this Act of Mediation, the Monte Videans are now enabled, as an independent community, to escape from the engagements contracted for them when subjects of Brazil. . . .

Meanwhile, the British chargé d'affaires in Buenos Aires had felt obliged to protest to the government of Juan Manuel de Rosas against infractions of Article XIV of the treaty of 1825 arising from the Argentine slave trade, "which," he observed, "I have strong reason to believe, has latterly been carried on pretty largely at Buenos Aires, in contradiction to that treaty, and in defiance of the laws of the country." Negroes imported from Brazil, Uruguay and directly from Africa were being "sold with little concealment" in Buenos Aires, the chargé further reported, but he had no evidence that the Argentine flag was being used as yet in the trade to other countries. During the next two years, the Rosas government at the request of local British diplomats stopped the fitting out of several slavers at Buenos Aires; and by 1836 the new British minister believed the laws against the slave trade were being "honestly executed."

Whether the Negro traffic flourished because of apparent negligence on the part of the Buenos Aires authorities, or because of obvious collusion between the Uruguayan government and slavers, it was clear that the Río de la Plata trade was so extensive and dangerous that it could only be suppressed permanently by British action under treaties with the two republics concerned. Accordingly, Hamilton Hamilton, the British minister at Buenos Aires accredited to both Uruguay and the Argentine Confederation, was instructed to submit to them Foreign Office drafts of a comprehensive anti-slave-trade treaty providing for mutual search and mixed courts, and including the all-important equipment and break-up articles. "You will represent to the Monte Videan Authorities," wrote Palmerston, "the deep disgrace to which they are exposing their country, by affording fresh facilities to a Traffic which has been denounced by every civilized Power in Europe and America."

Neither Montevideo nor Buenos Aires at first favored the proposed treaties, and negotiations dragged out interminably. Hamilton, who in September, 1835, broached the matter to the Argentine foreign minister, received a dual answer: namely, that the proposed treaty unjustifiably implied Buenos Aires' failure to live up to the slave trade article of the Anglo-Argentine pact of 1825; and second, that if his government should overlook this slur in concluding the proposed treaty, it could only be on condition that the commercial agreement of 1825 should be simultaneously revised along lines more favorable to his country. J. H. Mandeville, who superseded Hamilton as minister at Buenos Aires the next year, countered the Argentine stand by pointing out that even if the Buenos Aires government *was* enforcing its laws against the slave trade domestically, it was likewise obliged by treaty obligations to coöperate in the suppression of the traffic on the seas, and that this could only be accomplished by concluding the proposed supplementary treaty. As to the second point, the British minister observed that there was no logical reason why Great Britain should mix two such separate matters as the slave trade and commercial treaty revision. Thus matters reached an impasse, against which the patient diplomacy of the Briton was powerless for over two years.

The capitulation of the Rosas government coincided significantly with the coercive blockade thrown about the mouth of the Río de la Plata in 1838 by France to secure better treatment of her subjects. In January, 1839, the Argentine dictator, who needed British support in the crisis, proclaimed his intention to conclude the slave trade agreement. The treaty was signed in Buenos Aires on May 24, 1839, and ratifications were exchanged on May 16 of the following year.

Negotiations with the Montevideo government were even more protracted and difficult. Consul-General Hood reported additional evidence of the Rivera administration's implication in the slave trade, though he likewise noted increasing popular indignation at such activities. "Every fresh arrival from South America brings additional proof of the urgent necessity of putting a stop to these acts by which, under the cover of the Monte Videan Flag, a new Slave Trade is growing up . . . ," Palmerston wrote the British minister. At the same time he transmitted a threat: "you will plainly declare . . . that you do not believe that your Government will be disposed to tolerate such attempts to render null the Stipulations of Treaties between Great Britain and Brazil." Meanwhile the efforts of local British agents had been unable to end official collusion with the slavers, much less to secure a treaty.

When Manuel Oribe assumed the presidency early in 1835, however, he put an immediate end to government participation in the slave trade. This "laudable conduct," as the British minister in Rio de Janeiro suggested, perhaps arose from "the fortunate circumstance of the capture and condemnation of the Monte Videan brig *Río de la Plata*, by which it was made manifest that the [slave trading] Licences, now so promptly disowned, did not . . . secure the nefarious holders of them the impunity which had been anticipated." But Oribe proved as obdurate as Rivera in the matter of the treaty. Although Mandeville soon re-opened negotiations, the Oribe government repeatedly put the matter off, alleging inability to meet the naval and judicial expenses thought to attend the proposed compact, and requesting prior settlement of Uruguay's pecuniary claims in the case of the *Río de la Plata*, whose condemnation as a Brazilian slaver was repeatedly protested.

In the meantime, negotiations had been periodically interrupted by the bitter strife of the incumbent *Blanco* party with Rivera and his *Colorado* followers, who had revolted against the Oribe government in 1836. But the conflict eventually cleared the way for the treaty; for when mutual enmity to Rosas led the French blockading forces to help Rivera back to power late in 1838, the latter sacrificed his penchant for licensing the importation of African "colonists" and even agreed to conclude the treaty in order to gain British favor. The pact was accordingly signed at Montevideo on July 13, 1839; and after further vain attempts on the part of Uruguay to obtain monetary compensation for the *Río de la Plata*, ratifications were at length exchanged on January 21, 1842.

The Diplomacy of Prevention

Prompt British pressure, supplemented by direct action upon occasion, had checked the renascent slave trade of the Río de la Plata until the treaties of 1839 with Uruguay and the Argentine Confederation gave Great Britain the permanent right to patrol the seas against slavers flying the colors of these nations. Although elsewhere among the new Spanish-American republics no attempt had yet been made to renew the Negro traffic, the danger of such a development was clearly imminent. As the British minister in the Brazilian capital warned:

I believe that the African Slave Trade is not at present carried on by any of the Spanish-American Nations on the Coast of the Pacific; but this guilty traffic in human beings continues to be so enormously profitable to those who engage therein, and the ingenuity of the traders is consequently so keen and extensive, that if ever by good fortune the trade were effectually put down under the Flags of the Nations on this side of America, I entertain little doubt that the same infamous occupation of supplying Brazil with contraband Slaves would soon begin to be followed under the Flags of Chile and Peru . . . unless sufficient preventive measures shall have been adopted in time by the Governments of those countries.

Much the same could have been said regarding the danger of participation by the Latin-American republics in the Cuban slave trade. Consequently the watchdogs of the Foreign Office moved to forestall such developments even before the conclusion of the treaties with the Platine states.

At this juncture, British diplomacy received unexpected and welcome aid from Brazil. When in 1830 the slave trade to that Empire became illegal under the terms of the Anglo-Brazilian treaty of 1826, the bedevilled Imperial Regency was subjected to strong British pressure for the addition of an equipment clause to facilitate the suppression of the traffic. Itself inclined to comply with Britain's demands, the Regency was nevertheless powerless to do so because of the well-nigh universal opposition of the politically powerful classes of the Empire. As an earnest of its good intentions, and possibly also to divert the attention of the importunate crusaders in London, the Regency proposed in 1835 that Brazil and Great Britain unite to persuade the governments of Spanish America to enter into anti-slave trade treaties. Palmerston embraced the proposal with alacrity, and late the same year addressed a circular instruction to the British agents in Mexico, Venezuela, Colombia, Peru, and Chile, which read in part as follows:

> His Majesty's Government, and the Government of Brazil, being mutually desirous to put an end to the Slave Trade, have agreed that their Agents in Spanish America shall unite in a joint effort to persuade all the Spanish American Governments to enter into treaties for abolishing that trade, and for declaring it to be Piracy. I send you a Draft of a Treaty which has been proposed for this purpose to the Governments of Buenos Ayres and Monte Video. You will immediately enter into Negotiations with the Government of ————— for concluding a Treaty between Great Britain and that Country on this basis.

Subsequent failure of Brazilian diplomatic representatives in Spanish-American capitals to give more than nominal support to the ensuing negotiations, and the unwillingness of Brazil to become a party to the proposed treaties or to sign a general convention, are strong evidence that the Imperial government was not profoundly interested in the plan. But Brazil's initial support may have been of some aid in opening negotiations with certain of the Spanish-American countries. Of similar assistance in dealing with these governments was the papal brief issued by Gregory XVI on December 3, 1839, to denounce the slave trade, which British agents caused to be widely published in Latin America.

When Sir Richard Pakenham, British minister to Mexico, opened negotiations with the government of Justo José Corro in March, 1836, circumstances seemed to favor the rapid conclusion of a treaty against the slave trade. Mexico had abolished slavery in 1829, and since the law had not

been observed by the Anglo-American colonists in Texas, she now proceeded to issue a new abolition decree on April 5, 1837. More important
was the Mexican government's reliance upon Great Britain for support in
thwarting the annexation of rebellious Texas by the United States. Hence
it is not strange that Pakenham was able to conclude on April 16, 1837, a
treaty based on the standard draft sent him by the Foreign Office. But
Anastasio Bustamante, who became president three days after the treaty
was signed, failed to press its ratification in the Mexican Congress. The
Committee on Foreign Affairs of the Chamber of Deputies, though protesting Mexico's devotion to "so grand an object as the abolition of the
Slave Trade," nevertheless recommended rejection, primarily because of
its fear of the reciprocal search feature. "This right," it reported, ". . . is,
in the opinion of the Committee, odious."

It would oppose obstacles to the advancement of our infantile mercantile navy,
seeing that it would thereby be exposed to dangers into which it might in-
advertently or innocently fall, by not fulfilling the conditions which are stipulated; and the detention of a Mexican vessel could never, in any case, be just,
inasmuch as by the Laws of the Republic, and state of its navy, it is not possible
that any one of its citizens should engage in the Slave Trade.

There followed nearly four years of laborious negotiations, interrupted by the "Pastry War" against the French in 1838 and by chronic
domestic disturbances. A second treaty, signed in May, 1840, was rejected
by the British government because it was limited to eight years' duration.
When, finally, a compromise agreement was signed on February 24, 1841,
the time limit was omitted, but Mexican vessels were granted freedom from
search within prescribed zones, notably along the Gulf coast of the republic and in Mediterranean and European Atlantic waters. Even then, Mexican resentment at British recognition of Texas delayed acceptance; and not
until Antonio López de Santa Anna seized power and dissolved Congress
was the way opened for exchange of ratifications in London, on July 29,
1842.

The experiences of Sir Robert Ker Porter, British chargé d'affaires in
Venezuela, were similar to those of his colleague in Mexico when he opened
negotiations with the government of José Antonio Páez in March, 1837.
Venezuela, like Mexico, was in no way adverse to binding herself not to
engage in the Negro traffic. Although the census of 1837 indicated that
there were still 37,689 slaves in the republic, her government had reënacted
the essential features of the Colombian anti-slave trade and manumission
law of July 19, 1821, immediately after her secession from the parent state.
There was no illegal traffic. After less than three weeks of negotiation, a
treaty was signed on May 19, 1837. But as in Mexico, the Congress refused
ratification, despite a "full sense of admiration of the philanthropy of
Great Britain," on the grounds that Venezuela was already living up to the
anti-slave trade article of the Colombian treaty of 1825, that she could not

afford the expenses of the proposed agreement, and that reciprocal search was unnecessary and dangerous to her commerce. Accordingly the next two years were spent in negotiating a compromise treaty, signed on March 15, 1839, by which Venezuela consented to the right of search only on the West African coast and within twenty-league zones off the coasts of Cuba, Puerto Rico, Brazil and Madagascar. "This Treaty indeed is not all that could be wished," wrote Palmerston, "but it is a very important step gained."

Negotiations with New Granada, delayed until 1838, apparently by shift of British legation personnel in Bogotá, proved to be even more protracted and difficult than in Mexico and Venezuela. British diplomats were unanimous in reporting that Granadian opposition to the proposed treaty in no way reflected implication in the slave trade. Following the gradual emancipation law of 1821, which had prohibited the traffic, the parent state of Colombia had made the African slave trade piracy by legislation of 1825; and in 1829 it had agreed to an article in a treaty with Peru providing for the mutual punishment of African slavers as pirates. True, New Granada authorized the exportation of her own slaves in 1843, to rid herself of Negro rioters in the Cauca Valley, but the law was revoked in 1847. Slavery itself was in process of extinction as a result of non-importation, manumission and free birth; and the census of 1835 showed that the once numerous slave population had declined to 38,940. Much more important to Great Britain was the lack of any substantial evidence that the Granadian flag was being used to protect the trade to other countries.

Clearly, New Granada's objections to the proposed treaty were based upon fear of permanent commitments to a strong naval power, who might harm her commerce and outrage her sovereignty. To overcome these fears, the British chargé in Bogotá accepted, in a treaty signed in February, 1842, drastic geographic limitations on the right of search, the substitution of national for mixed tribunals, and a duration of only fifteen years. The pact was rejected by his government. After additional lengthy negotiations in Bogotá, Palmerston sought vainly to secure a satisfactory treaty by dealing directly with the Granadian minister in London. Little attempt was made to break the resulting deadlock until 1851, when Daniel F. O'Leary, a later British chargé in Bogotá, seized upon the enthusiasm of the new Liberal administration of José Hilario López for the complete abolition of domestic slavery as a favorable basis for renewed negotiations. A treaty substantially similar to that with Venezuela was concluded at Bogotá on April 2, 1851, and ratifications were exchanged on December 16 of the same year. "Thus has terminated a long-protracted negotiation," reported O'Leary, "owing to the more enlightened feeling that now prevails in this country and to the philanthropic sentiments of the President, General López. . . ."

Ecuador made few of the usual objections when the British consul, Walter Cope, presented the draft treaty sent out to him by Palmerston; and six months later, on May 24, 1840, the agreement was signed. But Cope accepted an additional article required by Ecuador to protect a curious local slave trade sporadically carried on ever since the republic's secession from Columbia in 1830. At that time, there were still slaves belonging to Ecuadorians in the Granadian part of Gran Colombia; and consequently a law was passed on September 26, 1830, to permit their introduction under government regulation. But the additional article excepted from the effects of the treaty the slave trade to Ecuador from Pacific South American ports in general, and Palmerston rejected it on the ground that it could be used to facilitate a renewed African Negro traffic. Ecuador, whose slave population had declined to a mere 4,960 by 1843, remained adamant, particularly after the Granadian legislation of that year promised a considerable influx of Negro workers from the neighboring republic. Her government withstood British pressure until 1846, then signed the treaty without the objectionable article. The agreement entered into effect upon the exchange of ratifications on July 5 of the following year.

Negotiation of anti-slave-trade treaties with Peru and Bolivia was rendered difficult by the fact that Belford Hinton Wilson, the British minister to these countries, received Palmerston's circular instruction in 1836, just as the Bolivian dictator Andrés Santa Cruz had defeated the rival Peruvian *caudillos* and was erecting his Peru-Bolivian Confederation. True, Santa Cruz, Wilson's companion in arms during the war of independence, was favorably disposed toward Great Britain and the crusade against the slave trade. Article XIV of the treaty of amity and commerce signed on June 5, 1837, pledged the Confederation to coöperate in the suppression of the traffic. But when Wilson sought to negotiate a supplementary treaty for this purpose, he was informed that the Chilean army then invading Peru and its local supporters "would represent this measure as one destructive to the interest of agriculture; and consequently . . . [would convert] a principle of eternal justice into a pretext for exciting a feeling against the Protectoral Government." Thus matters stood until the Chilean victory over Santa Cruz at Yungay in 1839 broke up the Confederation and made it necessary to negotiate separately with the reëstablished states of Peru and Bolivia.

Unfortunately for the prospects of the treaty with Peru, Agustín Gamarra, who came to power after the defeat of Santa Cruz, was influenced by a landed gentry dependent upon the fast dwindling number of Negro slaves to work their coastal plantations. The Congress of Huancayo, dominated by Gamarra, accordingly passed a law on November 27, 1840, which reversed San Martín's anti-slave trade decree of 1821 in order to permit the importation of slaves from other American countries. The pro-slavery reaction in Peru under Gamarra and his successors was considerably strengthened by the importation of slaves from New Granada after 1843. In 1841 the Peruvian government even considered seriously a petition presented by an Havana merchant on behalf of twenty-four "persons of consideration" in Lima to request the resumption of the African slave trade; and the proposal was rejected only after strenuous British protests. It is not strange that successive British negotiators found it quite impossible to obtain Peru's consent to the desired treaty. The most that could be secured was a general article condemning the Negro traffic in the commercial treaty concluded with the government of Ramón Castilla on April 10, 1850. The reconstituted republic of Bolivia, on the other hand, agreed immediately to the draft proposed by the British minister in Lima; and the treaty was accordingly signed at Sucre on September 25, 1840. Ratifications were exchanged during the course of 1842.

When Consul-General John Walpole began negotiations with Chile in 1837, he encountered no opposition from partisans of the slave trade, "every vestige of that commerce having been extirpated throughout the Territories of this Republic at the period of its first Independence of the Mother Country, and its total abolition recognized and confirmed by every successive Constitution." He might have added that the less than 4,000 slaves still remaining in Chile in 1823 had been freed by legislation of July 24 of that year, a fact of which Chileans were proud. After some delay resulting from Chilean preparations to send an expeditionary force against the Peru-Bolivian Confederation, the foreign minister agreed to the British draft treaty with minor changes on January 19, 1839. But Walpole was subsequently forced to report that the Chilean Senate had attached a ten-year limit to the treaty as the price of ratification, "an act marking the insurmountable aversion, entertained by the influential portion of this State, to the conclusion of a Treaty with a European . . . Power, or to the imposition on themselves of any obligation, binding them for more than a period exceedingly circumscribed." Though the Consul-General agreed to this stipulation in a supplementary convention of November 25, 1840, his act was rejected in London. "After much patient endurance and vexatious discussion," Walpole finally concluded a compromise "additional and explanatory convention" on August 7, 1841, in which Chile accepted unlimited duration in return for the restriction of the right of search to the African coasts and to twenty-league zones off the shores of Brazil and the Spanish Caribbean colonies. Ratifications of the treaty and convention were exchanged at Santiago on August 6, 1842.

For reasons not entirely clear, Great Britain did not make special treaties with the remaining smaller republics of Latin America. In Central America slavery and the slave trade had been totally abolished by the constituent congress of the five United Provinces in 1824, shortly after independence was proclaimed; and following the dissolution of the Confederation, the component states adopted the same policy. Article XIV of the similar commercial treaties which Britain signed with Guatemala and Costa Rica in 1849 contained a pledge of these republics' coöperation in suppressing the traffic. But no agreement whatever was made with the remaining Central American countries of Honduras, Nicaragua, and El Salvador. Paraguay, the only South American republic without direct access to the sea during this period, nevertheless agreed to a general article against the slave trade in the commercial treaty signed with Francisco Solano López on March 4, 1853. Presumably more specific commitments could have been obtained from these smaller countries had it been judged necessary.

The proximity of the two island countries of Haiti and the Dominican Republic to Cuba made more detailed agreements with their governments desirable. Haiti, in view of her Afro-French background and natural animus against slavery, enthusiastically adhered to the Anglo-French conventions of 1831 and 1833. Following her independence from Haiti, the Dominican Republic conceded the unilateral right of search to Great Britain in Article IX of the commercial treaty signed on March 6, 1850.

The Anti-Slave-Trade Treaties in Operation

The treaties signed by Great Britain between 1839 and 1851 with the Argentine Confederation, Uruguay, Mexico, Venezuela, New Granada, Ecuador, Chile, Haiti, and the Dominican Republic were admirably calculated to forestall the use of the flags of these nations for the slave trade. With the exception of the Haitian and Dominican agreements, they were based upon a standard British draft and differed significantly only in cases in which limitations of jurisdiction or the areas of search were stipulated. The treaties typically obligated the contracting republics to declare the slave trade piracy; established reciprocal search of merchant vessels by each party's naval vessels; set up mixed courts to try slavers, one in British West Africa and the other in the contracting republic; specified slaving equipment that made ships liable to capture even without slaves on board; outlined procedure for claims by the injured nation in case of unjust detention; and decreed the breaking up of condemned slavers. Three annexes were ordinarily subjoined to the treaties: Annex A contained precise instructions for naval vessels on patrol; Annex B prescribed the personnel and procedure of the mixed courts; and Annex C established rules for dealing with captured slaves. Additional articles declared the sentences of the British judge and arbitrator of a mixed court valid in the absence of their colleagues of the republic concerned and provided that the latter could avoid all judicial expenses by exercising its right not to appoint such officials.

Despite the formal reciprocity of the treaties, their practical effect was to give Great Britain a free hand to seize and bring to trial suspicious ships of the contracting republics. Britain in all cases named Sierra Leone as the seat of her West African court, and the same British officials officiated there under all the slave-trade treaties. By mutual agreement with Britain, most of the republics waived their right to establish mixed courts in their own territory, and none appointed officials for service at Sierra Leone. Nor were any of these nations in a position to fit out cruisers to exercise the right of reciprocal search outside of their own waters.

The best proof of the efficacy of the treaties lies in the fact that in the crucial period from 1840 to 1847, during which most of the treaties entered into effect, no vessel flying a Spanish-American flag was brought before the court at Sierra Leone. Nor is evidence available that any of the republics bound only by general articles in commercial treaties broke their pledges. By the treaties here described Great Britain not only secured her immediate purpose of preventing the recourse of slavers to the flags of the Latin-American republics, but through her patient diplomacy enhanced her prestige among them as a powerful defender of international morality and encouraged domestic abolition movements where slavery still existed.

Other Articles of Interest

Bierck, Harold A., Jr. "The Struggle for Abolition in Gran Colombia." XXXIII (1953), 365–386.
Bolívar decreed the abolition of slavery in a proclamation of 1816 and in later orders to 1828, but both the abolition and the anti-slave-trade laws were repeatedly violated. Bolívar saw in liberation both an inherent good and a political lever against the enemy, but he also saw in armed service an opportunity to lessen the number of Negroes. Pro-slavery interests were abetted by lax enforcement officers, and gradual emancipation was established in law and partially in practice.

Hill, Lawrence F. "The Abolition of the African Slave Trade to Brazil." XI (1931), 169–197.
Anglo-Portuguese agreements of 1810, 1815, and 1817 provided for the end of the slave trade to Brazil. However, in view of her shortage of labor, Brazil's importation of slaves doubled between 1820 and 1827 and trebled in 1829, probably the result of the anti-slave-trade convention of 1826 between Great Britain and Brazil, which was to be active in three years. The Aberdeen Act of 1845 followed. But the obstacles to abolition in Brazil were very real: the traffic had been continuous since the early sixteenth cenutry; conditions for illicit trade were favorable; the traffic was profitable. Between 1835 and 1853 thousands of Negroes were imported with the aid of Yankee traders. As for the British, they refused to destroy factories on the African coast and themselves used slaves in the West Indies and Guiana.

Jones, Wilbur Devereux. "The Origins and Passage of Lord Aberdeen's Act." XLII (1962), 502–520.

Martin, Percy Alvin. "Slavery and Abolition in Brazil." XIII (1933), 151–196.
A brief survey of the origin of Negro slavery in Brazil, its gradual extension, the place which it occupied in the social, economic, and political fabric of the state, and the successful efforts of the Brazilian people to free themselves from this incubus without bloodshed or serious economic dislocation. The tension over the slave trade between Great Britain and Brazil overshadowed the whole period from 1807 to 1888.

CHAPTER THREE

MEXICO AND CENTRAL AMERICA

8. José María Luis Mora and the Structure of Mexican Liberalism

CHARLES A. HALE

The intellectual history of Latin America has sometimes been portrayed as a simple transplantation of ideas from abroad, principally Europe. Other studies interpret developments in the various countries of Latin America as almost completely resulting from their own history and their own thinkers. The special contribution this article makes is to examine and weigh both foreign and national influences, and to treat comprehensively one of the dominant themes in Mexican history, liberalism. The occasional comparisons of nineteenth-century events with those of contemporary Mexico are also valuable.

Modern Mexican history can be and has been viewed as a continuing liberal struggle of epic proportions against the forces of political reaction, social privilege, and economic exploitation. In no Latin American country has ideological conflict, revolutionary fervor, and open civil strife been so intense as in Mexico since 1810. The Mexican experience forms the exception to the common generalization that the independence movements in Latin America were Creole efforts, devoid of social content, and aimed at mere political independence from Spain. The *Reforma* of mid-century has affected our entire view of liberalism in the rest of Latin America. Similarly, the Mexican experience has provided the basic point of departure for considering the revolutionary changes of the twentieth century.

Yet the very dramatic and heroic quality of this continuing struggle, culminating in the great Revolution, has made a critical analysis and assessment of nineteenth-century liberalism difficult. Besides this entanglement of liberalism with the Mexican revolutionary tradition, there is a tendency to associate the liberal movement with the unfolding of national ideals. The equation *liberalismo-patria* has distracted us from a dispassionate consideration of the nineteenth century.

If we are to avoid these pitfalls and view liberalism other than as a chronicle of progress toward fulfillment of national and revolutionary

From Volume XLV (1965), pages 196–227.

ideals, it is necessary to identify Mexican liberal thought and policy within the context of what R. R. Palmer calls Atlantic Civilization. My chief concern is not to trace foreign influences in Mexico, but rather to seek out some affinities of structure between European society, politics, and thought, and those of Mexico.

I. The Structure of Liberalism

If we may abstract the composite liberal program at mid-century, we find that it included two conflicting objectives. On the one hand there was the basic drive to free the individual from the shackles which bound him under the Spanish system. The liberties of the individual must be guaranteed against irresponsible power: thus, freedom of the press, speech, and even worship were of great significance. Federalism, an irradicable part of the ideology of liberalism, falls in this category, as does municipal liberty, often advocated by liberals. Property rights of the individual (including property qualifications for voting), as well as the freeing of the individual economically through the regime of laissez-faire, both were aimed at the overriding objective of individual freedom.

On the other hand the liberals were concerned with freeing the new nation from the regime of corporate privilege. A modern, secular, progressive nation must be juridically uniform; its citizens' allegiance to the civil state must not be shared with the Church or army or with any other corporation, for instance the university or the Indian community. This objective included educational reform, the attack upon the *fueros*, secularization, colonization, and even land reform.

Did these two aims of liberalism really conflict, it might be asked? Let us attack the question obliquely by turning to some of the comparisons which emerge between Europe and Mexico.

In France, as Alexis de Tocqueville showed so clearly, it is impossible to understand the development of a liberal and revolutionary ideology without considering the nature of the Old Regime. The same would be true for Mexico. The fact which emerges from any comparative study of social and political institutions in the Atlantic world is the marked similarity between New Spain and pre-revolutionary France and Spain. In the three areas a pattern of centralized administration under absolute monarchy held sway. The French monarchy in the seventeenth century drew heavily upon Hapsburg practices of the sixteenth, and in turn stimulated Spanish Bourbon administration in the eighteenth century.

New Spain represents from its foundation what developed in France in the seventeenth century, namely a privileged feudal society without the corresponding feudal political institutions. In England after 1688 the landed aristocrats having large private incomes controlled the Parliament and constituted a true governing class within a constitutional monarchy. The French aristocracy, on the other hand, was politically ruined under the Cardinals and Louis XIV, as the Spanish nobility had been under Philip II and earlier. This remained true in the eighteenth century despite the "aristocratic resurgence" which culminated in the events of 1789. Feudal political institutions in France and Spain—Cortes, Estates General, provincial assemblies, municipal governments—had been allowed to wither between 1500 and 1789; in New Spain they were never created. The exception of course was the cabildo, which, it must be added, enjoyed little political potency between 1550 and 1790. Though the Crown prevented political feudalism in the New World, it encouraged the establishment of a highly stratified society, dominated by a landed and mining aristocracy. In short, in New Spain as in France and Spain, the aristocracy retained its social and economic privileges while it lost its political initiative. Royal undermining of the political and military potentialities of the encomienda exemplifies this process. Functional corporations became the institutional focus for much of this privilege and thus epitomized the Old Regime to liberals by 1833. Furthermore, like Spain though unlike France, the revolutionary movement did little to alter the position of the strongest corporations. Church and army were stronger in Mexico after 1821 than they were before 1810, at the same time that viceregal government collapsed.

Turning briefly to the development of liberal political ideas, it can be demonstrated that the two aforementioned objectives of Mexican liberalism reflect a more general conflict within liberalism in Europe. Political liberalism in part sprang from the tension between medieval, feudal, contractural traditions on the one hand and absolute monarchy on the other. In France, the former involved the "Ancient French Constitution," made up of Estates General, provincial *assemblies*, and *parlements*, all of which the monarch must respect. This "constitution" was defended during the Fronde of the seventeenth century, by Montesquieu, and after him by the lawyers of the parlements during the eighteenth century. Absolute monarchy, on the other hand, was new, irresponsible, and defiant of medieval Natural Law. It strove to attack corporate privilege, to unify, theoretically to reduce society to sovereign and subjects. We know, of course, that in practice seventeenth- and eighteenth-century monarchs made all manner of practical compromises with special privilege.

As it emerged in those critical last years under Louis XIV, liberalism, with its concern for individual rights and legal equality, oscillated between these two conceptions of government, between the unified sovereignty of the monarchy and the limited sovereignty of the "representative" bodies. Liberalism was, as Guido de Ruggiero says, not connected with either party to the conflict between monarchy and the "regime of privilege," but "with the conflict itself."

Without the effective resistance of particular privileged classes, the monarchy would have created nothing but a people of slaves; without the levelling effected by royal absolutism, the regime of privilege, however widely extended, would never have bridged the gulf which divides privilege from liberty in the proper sense of the word—that liberty which universalizes privilege to the point of annulling it as such.

This kinship between *privilege* and *liberty* is particularly apparent in England which comes to symbolize one current within liberalism, that view which conceives of liberty as based upon historically acquired rights. These constitute specific limitations on the sovereign in favor of the individual (or at least certain individuals). This is the regime of parliamentary rights and privileges for which John Locke was the spokesman in 1688. They were defended by the aristocratic governing class of eighteenth-century England and even more militantly by Edmund Burke in 1790.

It was France which symbolized the other current within political liberalism. Liberty was conceived of as universal, discoverable through reason, and applicable to all men. Whereas John Locke's idea of the inalienable rights of the individual had the effect in England of sanctifying traditional liberties, in France his idea was interpreted more theoretically, largely because of the weakness of traditional institutions below the monarchy. Thus in France, the abstract conception of liberty, particularly as expressed by Rousseau, led to political equality and to the sovereignty of the people. Yet as Ruggiero points out (in a passage reminiscent of Tocqueville), the new French liberalism was like the monarchy egalitarian, "but its egalitarianism was inspired and ennobled by a broader rationalistic consciousness attributing to all men one identical spiritual and human value." This was the conception which Burke so deplored in 1790 when he saw it being used by the revolutionaries to assault their past.

Thus these two conflicting tendencies within liberalism, the French and the English, reached a climax in the era of the French Revolution. The French pattern not only came to epitomize liberty as an abstract conception, but also the centralized state—with sovereignty lodged in a monarch, in the people, or in a Napoleon—as the vehicle of change. The course of Spanish liberalism, first under Charles III and later under the centralized popular government of the Cortes of Cádiz, was generally parallel to that of France.

There was much interpenetration of these two tendencies. Montesquieu had brought "English" liberalism to bear upon France, just as later Jeremy Bentham applied continental modes of thought to England. A further pertinent example were the French constitutional liberals of the restoration period. Reacting against the way the abstract conception of liberty had been used to serve the interests of a new centralized despotism under the Convention and Napoleon, Benjamin Constant and his followers found English liberalism particularly attractive. Inspired partly by Montesquieu and even more by a fresh study of English representative government, the constitutional liberals advocated a system which would guarantee the individual against tyranny.

Returning to Mexico, we can find in the liberal movement of the 1820's and 1830's a key to further understanding of the nineteenth century.

Though I am fully cognizant of the variety within Mexican liberal thought and of the efforts of Mexican historians to plumb the documents for early indications of social radicalism, it seems to me that José María Luis Mora remains the most significant liberal spokesman. This is true because of the depth of his thought, his influence, and the way he epitomizes the nineteenth-century liberal tradition. Mora's writing, almost entirely done between 1821 and 1837, demonstrates clearly the tension within Mexican liberalism and its central orientation.

Mora's thought must be viewed in stages. The first began in 1821 and ended roughly in 1830. The second encompasses the essay on church property of 1831 and the writing emerging from his association with the reform regime of 1833–1834.

There is a striking parallel between Mora's political ideas of the 1820's and those of the contemporary French constitutional liberals. Besides the indications of overt intellectual influence, I think it can be suggested that Mora associated the problems of his country with those of post-Napoleonic France. Analogies were present to be seized upon: the revolutionary experience which in both countries had entailed social violence; the apparent break with monarchy and corporate power in the hopes of instituting representative government based on a regime of uniform legislation; the emergence of military dictators as self-styled "emperors." Mora showed considerable knowledge and understanding of French and Spanish history of the Revolutionary Era, and it is probable that he developed his ideas within the comparative context.

Mora's writing of the 1820's, like that of the constitutional liberals in France, centers on the defense of individual liberties against despotic power. He emphasized that despotism could come in many forms, and attacked variously the theories of Rousseau, the politics of Iturbide, and the arbitrary actions of the Mexican congresses of the 1820's. Mora quite frequently criticized the democratic doctrine of popular sovereignty which he said was introduced into Mexico with the Spanish Constitution of 1812. Mora felt that only property-owners should be citizens. Yet he, like the French constitutional liberals, accepted change ("the revolution of the century" as he called it), and hoped to consolidate the gains of the Revolution for Independence, the gains for individual liberty at the expense of privilege and absolute power.

Specifically, he emphasized freedom of the press, the necessity of an independent judiciary and citizen juries, and federalism. Mora was always a strong advocate of federalism, and despite certain reservations, supported the Constitution of 1824. He became deeply involved in the politics of the State of Mexico and looked upon provincial and even municipal liberties as essential. Yet it is significant that he, unlike most of the federalists, made little if any reference to the experience of the United States. Moreover, at one point, Mora cited as a precedent for federalism the French reformer Turgot's effort in 1774 to establish provincial assemblies based on property-ownership. Dr. Mora's enthusiasm for federalism was advanced in the spirit of the French liberals, seeking a check on the predominant tradition of central power. The example of the United States seems to figure little in Mora's thought, in fact, it may be a far more superficial element in Mexican liberalism than is generally supposed.

Although most of Mora's writing of this era is markedly abstract in tone and seldom brought down to the level of Mexican realities, he did bring his "constitutional liberalism" to bear upon one vital Mexican issue: the expulsion of the Spaniards in 1827 and 1829. Though Mora was unable to stem the tide of anti-Spanish fanaticism which emanated from Congress and the states, he did defend the civil rights of Spaniards vigorously in a series of articles in the *Observador*. This was a courageous stand in the 1820's, since the popular liberal position was to reject the Spanish heritage and all that it represented.

After 1830 there was a decided shift of orientation in Mora's thought, coinciding with the political turmoil which brought Vicente Guerrero and then his vice-president, Anastasio Bustamante, to power. Mora soon rejected the regime in which Lucas Alamán was a prime mover, and during the next four years his discussion of guarantees for the individual gave way to a defense of extraordinary power. This shift reached a climax in 1834 when Mora criticized his friend and collaborator, Vice-President Gómez Farías, for not using the full power of government against Santa Anna and other rebels. Gómez Farías, lamented Mora, would not take an unconstitutional step. Mora in four years had abandoned his constitutional liberalism. How do we explain this reversal of position?

Mora probably realized about 1830 that Mexico's basic problem was not to guarantee individual liberties against irresponsible power, but rather to liquidate the Old Regime so that individualism could have some meaning. Constitutional liberalism was more significant in France than in Mexico during the 1820's because the regime of corporate privilege had been largely destroyed by the Revolution. In Mexico it was still intact. After 1830 Mora began to complain about the deficiencies of the Constitution of 1824, namely that it said nothing about the fueros of Church and army. Particularly eloquent were his famous passages condemning the *espíritu de cuerpo* which led significant numbers of men to identify themselves with some corporation or other and only vaguely with the nation. Under Mora's intellectual leadership the 1833 reformers sought to root out the *espíritu de cuerpo*.

It is significant that Mora's reform writings of these years contained numerous references to the Spanish Bourbons and their policies. While no apologist for the colonial regime, Mora showed obvious admiration for the Bourbon reforms, especially the assertion of royal control over the Church. This admiration is evident in his 1831 *Disertación* on church property, which was probably the point of departure for nineteenth-century anticlericalism. In this essay Mora gave an historical account of regalian rights over church property and attacked sharply the claims of the Church that its property was inalienable because it had become "spiritualized." Mora referred to the decree of 1804 which disentailed some church property in Mexico to back a royal bond issue in Spain. He even claimed that this decree served as a precedent for the reform laws of 1833.

Was not Mora turning to Bourbon traditions when confronted with the resurgent corporations? Here in Mexico's own past were the foundations of a policy which could secularize society without encouraging dangerous popular democracy. In his historical writings, Mora singled out the enlightened reforms within Mexico itself, the bishop Abad y Queipo and the intendants Riaño and Flon, all Spaniards who in the years just prior to independence had called for political and economic change. Mora even looked more charitably than he had previously upon the radical Spanish Cortes of 1810 and 1820; for though he never accepted their democratic doctrines, he admitted that their work had introduced the seeds of liberty into the colonies. Thus José María Luis Mora in this second stage epitomized what was to become the major orientation of Mexican political liberalism: its adherence to continental—i.e., French and Spanish—modes of thought, particularly the reliance upon state power to achieve liberty.

One element remains to be considered—utilitarianism. So great was the impact of the utilitarian idea that at least one student of European liberal thought accords it central importance in his interpretation. Let us examine how utilitarianism was grafted on to Hispanic conceptions of reform to give the Mexican liberal tradition its peculiar character.

Although the main influence of utilitarianism in the Hispanic world came through its principal exponent, Jeremy Bentham, it is necessary to say a few words about its earlier history. In very general terms the utilitarian ideal was built upon the secularism of the Renaissance, the scientific spirit of the seventeenth century, and the intense questioning of moral principles derived from revealed religion, that took place in the last years of the reign of Louis XIV. For our purposes, however, utilitarianism can most conveniently begin with John Locke, who developed the idea that human understanding with based upon sense perception rather than upon innate ideas, such as the existence of God.

This new psychology of sense experience developed in the eighteenth century, both in England and on the continent, but perhaps most significantly in France. As formulated particularly by Helvetius in his work *Essays on the Mind* (1758), human behavior was subject to two motive forces, desire for pleasure and dislike of pain. Man was searching happiness and he was not "bad" as traditional moralists had said. Badness among men was merely being subject to their own interests and pleasures. Knowledge was the key to happiness which was now the supreme good. "Ignorance was man's only limitation and science offered unlimited possibilities." The basic problem in society was to put individual interests into harmony with the general interest, which Helvetius and Bentham after him believed was the proper sphere for legislation. The greatest good for the greatest number (or utility) was the standard by which one could judge the worth of social institutions. The special good of a particular class or of a corporate body impeded the association of individual interests with the general interest.

Actually, the principle of utility was quite distinct from that of self-evident inalienable rights, which also came from Locke and which formed the basis of the abstract or generalized conception of political liberty in France. Rights would logically have to be judged by their utility, and therefore could not be inalienable or self-evident. The problem, however, was avoided because the political reformers in France could atttack corporate privilege, class distinction, and archaic legislation in the name of both utility and the natural rights of man. Jeremy Bentham, for instance, who rejected the French Declaration of Rights of 1789 as 'mere bawling on paper,' ended up justifying on the basis of utility "the very rights which the French were claiming on grounds of nature."

Jeremy Bentham went to France in 1770 and absorbed French utilitarianism, especially as formulated by Helvetius. Though in a sense utilitarianism had English roots, Bentham's approach to political problems at least was decidedly continental in spirit. The weight of his criticism always fell upon established institutions. For Bentham as for Adam Smith in the economic sphere, it was the spirit of corporation which was the greatest obstacle to utility, or the harmony of interests in society. According to Halevy, Bentham's great passion for legal codification was "a continental and not a British idea."

His approach to English institutions was the antithesis of that of Edmund Burke. Bentham was a simplifier, Burke sanctified the complications of the British system. It is significant that early in his life, Bentham was a Tory and an admirer of Enlightened Despotism. In fact, Halevy maintains that in his impatience for legal and judicial reforms Bentham was never a liberal in the English sense: "he merely passed from a monarchic authoritarianism to a democratic authoritarianism [after 1815] without pausing at the intermediate position, which is the position of Anglo-Saxon liberalism." It was doubtless because of Bentham's affinity for the French reformers that he was so influential in the Iberian world. Halevy says he "became a kind of demi-god in Spain," and his ideas strongly influenced the discussions of a single-chamber system and a new civil code in 1821. He exercised a similar influence in Mexico.

The political and juridical applications of utilitarian doctrine were only part of its significance; it also dominated the economic and social aspects of liberal thought. From the motive force of individual interest, enlightened through knowledge and freed from institutional bonds, would come wealth, prosperity, and the good society. The system of the Physiocrats in France, which promoted the freedom of the individual landowner and attacked manorial customs and internal restrictions on trade, was one variation of utilitarian economic thought. Adam Smith's expanded view of individual economic liberty and its benefits (which incidentally criticized the Physiocrats for their scorn of manufactures) was undoubtedly the most important and influential.

In Spain, utilitarian doctrine is contained in every paragraph of Gaspar Melchor de Jovellanos' *Informe de ley agraria* (1795), the ideas of which permeate agrarian thinking in nineteenth-century Mexico. Jovellanos, having absorbed physiocratic thought, set about to probe the agrarian regime in Spain, concluding that "the laws for aiding agriculture ought to be reduced to protecting the individual interest of its agents." The "only means of protecting this interest," he continued, "is by removing the obstacles which hinder the natural tendency and movement of its action." The essay then isolated the various obstacles, physical, moral, and political, which, if removed, would allow the free play of individual interests, the basis of general prosperity.

In Mexico, utilitarianism pervaded the thought of Dr. Mora. We find him speaking in 1827 of "the wise Bentham" and agreeing that "not only is utility the origin of all law, but also the principle of all human actions." Throughout Mora's anticlerical writing runs the thread of utilitarian ethics. It appears that Mora's general attack on corporate privilege is carried through in the name of utility rather than from the natural rights position. Mora seems close to the spirit of Bentham on many occasions, especially when he championed the need for a thoroughgoing secular mentality in Mexico. He deplored the confusion by the masses of religious sins with civil crimes; the official intolerance of non-Catholics led people to regard the Protestant foreigner as a political criminal. When Mora spoke of progress he did so in utilitarian terms, basing it in the free individual identifying his interests with the general interest of society.

To reconstruct Mexico on a secular basis, it was necessary to do more than tear down the corporate structure of society; positive measures must also be taken. Thus Mora turned to education and as minister in 1833–1834 laid the groundwork for a system which would train an *hombre positivo* —that is, a progress-minded citizen of the nation. The outcome was the abolition of the university and the brief inauguration of a nationalized system of secular higher education. It is interesting that in the *Indicador*, a weekly journal Mora was editing at this time, notices of the new educational reforms were interspersed with reprints from the educational proposals of Jovellanos, written in Spain between 1780 and 1800. Thus an analysis of the 1833 program reveals that utilitarian philosophy was intertwined with a conception of reform which followed Bourbon regalist traditions.

It was through the general acceptance of the doctrine of economic liberalism that utilitarianism had its greatest impact. Aside from the industrialist Esteban de Antuñano, the editors for a time of *El Siglo XIX*, and the defenders of artisan industries like Francisco García of Zacatecas, the economic thinking of Mexican political liberals was dominated by laissez-faire. Mining, free commerce, and agriculture were to be the bases of Mexican development. "Forced industry," and the accompanying tariffs and government investment were attacked violently.

Continental liberalism, as expressed by the Physiocrats, by a Jovellanos, by the middle-class victors of the French Revolution, projected the new society as being rooted in the property-owning citizen. Tocqueville maintained that the French Revolution abolished all privileges save that of property which to a degree became associated with equality in an agricultural society like France. In Mexico Mora, Lorenzo de Zavala, and their colleagues of 1833 sought to create a rural bourgeois society by insisting upon property qualifications for voting and citizenship, and by advocating schemes of rural colonization by European peasants. Even Mora's constitutional liberalism of the 1820's follows what Ruggiero calls a "continental" orientation, having "its origin in the economic and legal institution of modern or bourgeois property . . . universalized and codified by the French Revolution." Yet the example of France was misleading, for Mexico was essentially a society of latifundia and depressed Indian peasantry, a structure which was basically undisturbed by the Revolution for Independence. Reluctant to attack private property, the reformers had to base the new society of small proprietors upon the disentailment of Church property, legislated in 1833 and again in 1856.

By 1834 we see an apparent contradiction between the liberal political emphasis upon a strong state to attack corporate privilege and the economic tendency toward unfettered individualism. Here a further consideration of utilitarianism in Europe may point the way. Elie Halevy, the foremost student of the subject, has emphasized a perpetual problem which existed between the "artificial" and the "spontaneous" identification of individual interests. Was the fusion of interests for the general good natural and spontaneous or was it necessary to impose an artificial identification? Jeremy Bentham, concerned primarily with political and juridical questions, came to advocate the artificial identification of interests and the significance of state action. The conclusion of the economic theories stemming from utilitarianism, however, was that the identification of interests came about spontaneously, by action of the laws of nature. Adam Smith and the Physiocrats argued this way, as did Bentham in economic matters; yet all advocated a strong state to attack political privilege. Jovellanos in Spain likewise supported the regalism of Charles III.

The "double way in which they [the utilitarians] understood the identification of interests" is particularly applicable to Mexico. Economic privilege, still deep-rooted after Independence, found little threat from utilitarian economic theories. Political privilege, on the other hand, was consistently and even effectively attacked. Did not the contradiction within early liberalism (and within the Porfirian system later) between a strong political state and rampant laissez-faire stem partly from the dichotomy within utilitarian doctrine? Does not a similar contradiction exist within industrial Mexico today?

II. Liberalism and Conservatism

At this point it would be revealing to shift our focus to try to discern the distinctions between conservatism and liberalism by mid-century. If it is true that we tend to generalize about liberalism in Latin America from the experience of Mexico, the reason may be because Mexico was the classic battleground between liberalism and conservatism. What exactly was the conflict?

The traditional view, restated recently by Jesús Reyes Heroles, describes liberalism and conservatism "as the two faces of the political evolution of Mexico. The one is inconceivable without the other." This interpretation, which essentially perpetuates the progress vs. reaction theme of the liberals themselves, must be questioned critically.

Any discussion of nineteenth-century conservatism must focus first upon Lucas Alamán, undoubtedly the great figure of independent Mexico until his death in 1853. Alamán in many ways epitomizes Mexican conservatism. Consider for example: his wealthy Creole background, intimately tied to Guanajuato mining; his ready predilection for centralism and authoritarian government; his consistent defense of the Spanish heritage, climaxed by his effort to defend the vast property holdings of the Sicilian duke who was the nineteenth-century heir to the patrimony of Cortés; his support of the Church, temporal and spiritual, against liberal attacks; finally, his outright advocacy of monarchy in 1846 and his more cautious argument in the years 1848–1853. Still, Alamán remains ambiguous and it is misleading to categorize him, as Reyes Heroles does, an "integral conservative."

What confuses the distinctions between liberal and conservative which rely upon Alamán as epitomizing the latter, is the entrepreneurial side of his career. Alamán was the foremost nineteenth-century pioneer of national industry. His entrepreneurial activities, first as mining promoter, then as originator of the government Banco de Avío in 1830 to aid incipient industry, and finally as an active industrialist himself, have been well studied and need no further elaboration. In short, Alamán's vision of economic development for Mexico, while departing from laissez-faire, was dynamic and progressive. The contemporary industrial revolution in Mexico, whether it be called "liberal" or "conservative," owes a good bit to Lucas Alamán, the nineteenth-century archetype of political conservatism.

Unlike laissez-faire, which attracted the majority of liberals, national industry was not built upon a philosophical argument, but rather upon tradition (the artisan enterprises of the colony) and upon an instinctive realization that a country cannot live completely by importing and exporting. Returning to Alamán, his position is obviously paradoxical and inconsistent, for the Alamán who left church lands untouched, who tolerated the special privileges of the military, who favored authoritarian government, also promoted an industrial development which would undermine the Old Regime. In searching for the analogy which might help understand Alamán, I come back, not as Reyes Heroles does to Edmund Burke (who obviously was an inspiration for Alamán's political and social views), but to Bourbon Spain.

Alamán's early days in Guanajuato under the enlightened intendant Riaño experienced the revival of the mining industry through government loans and encouragement. The Banco de Avío of 1830 was undoubtedly derived from the Banco de Avíos of the 1780's. This affinity for Bourbon policies raises an interesting question: have we not found that the liberals of 1833, led by Dr. Mora, also turned to Bourbon traditions in their reform policies? The fact is that Bourbon policies inspired both political camps in nineteenth-century Mexico.

Would not a further study of political and economic currents in Spain from 1760 to 1800 help to understand the nature of the liberal-conservative conflict in Mexico? For instance, Richard Herr has shown that Charles III's economic policies were really mercantilist in orientation; physiocratic and laissez-faire ideas had not found their way into policy. The influence of Jean Baptiste Colbert was strong, and government-supported commerce and industry flourished, particularly cotton textile manufacturing. By 1792 this latter industry at Barcelona had overtaken the French and rivaled that of England. Following mercantilist ideals, agriculture was distinctly secondary; thus the utilitarian and physiocratic *Informe* of Jovellanos was a radical departure.

In Mexico, one point which distinguishes Alamán (and perhaps Esteban de Antuñano also) from the liberals is the former's adherence to mercantilist conceptions as opposed to the economic ideas derived from utilitarianism. In fact, Alamán seems to have been untouched by Benthamite or laissez-faire ideas in any aspect of his thought. In this respect, he was unlike Edmund Burke, who was a close follower of Adam Smith in the economic realm. This interpretation would lend some support to Reyes Heroles' assertion that by promoting industry, Alamán was trying to develop an industrial class to round out the regime of privilege in Mexico. Alamán's idea, however, was not drawn from Edmund Burke, as Reyes Heroles maintains, but rather from Bourbon mercantilism. This would suggest that Mexico's industrial tradition, stemming from Alamán, has developed within a mercantilist framework.

From the above it is clear that one has to be wary in distinguishing between liberals and conservatives on the basis of their attitude toward Mexico's Spanish heritage. We have been too ready to take liberal pronouncements against things Spanish and colonial at their face value, and to assume that liberalism was therefore primarily an effort to build a new society based on French, English, and American models. Spanish traditions were important for the liberals, just as they were for the conservatives. The difference, of course, was the degree of adherence to Spanish and colonial policies, and which policies were emphasized. Both Alamán and Mora were defenders of Hernán Cortés and of the importance of the Spanish Conquest, but Alamán carried his defense much further and wrote three volumes on the subject. Much of Mora's historical discussion of New Spain focused on the efforts over three centuries to obtain independence. Alamán was clearly an apologist for Mexico's Spanish heritage; Mora was not. What Mora did do was to perpetuate the Spanish tradition of state power and turn it to the uses of reform under the aegis of the new utilitarian philosophy.

How did liberals and conservatives differ in their social attitudes? This immediately raises the question of private land tenure. The search for "social liberalism"—in particular nineteenth-century precedents for the radical agrarianism of the Revolution—has intrigued Mexican historians, most recently Jesús Reyes Heroles who has brought forth a wealth of documents, many heretofore obscure. Scattered through the nineteenth century were spokesmen for agrarian reform who attacked directly large private holdings—Hidalgo and Morelos, a few radicals in the Constituent Congress of 1823–1824, Francisco García, Mariano Otero, and Ponciano Arriaga, to cite the most prominent. Yet the contemporary significance of these radicals can easily be overemphasized, and I find it difficult to agree with Reyes Heroles that "seeing land as a problem is almost equivalent to [*consustancial a*] our struggle for liberty."

Of these spokesmen Ponciano Arriaga delivered the most forthright attack on the large landed estate. The occasion was a dissenting opinion given on June 23, 1856, as a member of the constitutional committee drawing up Article 17 which made property rights conditional to the right to work. Arriaga, along with José Castillo Velasco, dissented because the law did not go far enough. Arriaga could not accept the doctrine of private property. What meaning did such a theory have, he asked, in a country like Mexico where land and thus power were concentrated in few hands? He chided his colleagues: "ideas are proclaimed and facts are forgotten. . . . We digress in the discussion of rights and we set aside positive acts." He then proceeded to detail the abuses of *latifundismo*—debt peonage, monopoly of unused lands, encroachment with impunity upon defenseless Indian communities, political and juridical power inside the hacienda rivaling that of the state—all the abuses which Andrés Molina Enríquez attacked again in 1909 and which provided the impetus to reform after 1915.

Arriaga had clearly moved beyond doctrinaire individualism; social obligation was his motivating concern. Individual right, he maintained, does not include the right of economic and social oppression which violates the "sanctity of man's freedom." He and his fellow dissenter Castillo Velasco accepted the legitimacy of private property, only if subject to social function. Arriaga concluded his discourse with ten specific measures for rationally reorganizing the system of land tenure in Mexico, measures which were characteristic of twentieth-century reform programs.

Proposals such as these, and others can be cited as well, constitute what Reyes Heroles rightly calls a "socialist" current in the Reforma. Yet these views represented only a radical fringe, contrasting sharply with the Ley Lerdo of May, 1856, and its subsequent incorporation into the Constitution. The Ley Lerdo and the laws of 1859, concerned primarily with the disentailment of Church property, did not undertake "the restructuring of social classes nor the de-concentration of lay property." The aim was rather political—further removal of the Church from a position of power—and financial, to increase government resources and to secure foreign loans. Neither Mora, nor Zavala, nor later leaders like Lerdo and Ocampo favored the regime of latifundia. Mora stated on several occasions that he advocated a society of small independent holdings. Melchor Ocampo hoped that the nationalization laws of 1859, if properly instituted, could carry out what the Revolution had done in France: produce a landed middle class, tied to the cause of reform.

Yet we must conclude that there was little tangible difference in reality between liberals and conservatives on the question of the private hacienda. The predominance of utilitarianism and its emphasis upon the sanctity of property prevented them from meeting the problem of land concentration. Conservatives, naturally enough, took the latifundia for granted and had little to say on the matter. The role of the hacienda in politics and ideas is a subject which demands further study.

Closely related to the agrarian question is that other great preoccupation of twentieth-century Mexico—the status of the Indian population. Was there a significant difference between liberal and conservative attitudes and policies toward the Indian? The first problem we encounter in such an inquiry is the absence of concern for the Indians as a group. Liberals were apathetic toward the Indian and toward problems of social integration presented by cultural differences. Dr. Mora expressed a generalized liberal sentiment when he said that the Gómez Farías regime "did not recognize in government acts the distinction of *Indians* and *non-Indians*, but it substituted *poor* and *rich*, extending to all the benefits of society."

Francisco López Cámara, in a recent provocative book on the origins of the liberal idea, argues that concern for the native element was inherent in the Creole use of "America" and "Americans" during the Revolution for Independence. Men such as Hidalgo, Cos, and Morelos conceived of a "national community" of Indians and Creoles, united against the Spaniards and the colonial past. He concludes that a "vindicating nativism [*indigenismo reivindicador*] becomes fused with the ideals of liberalism, as one of its social elements." Whether or not López Cámara's thesis holds for the revolutionary years, one thing is clear: after 1821 whatever concern there had been for the Indian subsided. The liberals rejected the notion that the

Indians, who made up the majority of the population, might represent the core of Mexican nationality. Dr. Mora, though denying a belief in racial superiority, betrayed a deeper conviction that the Indian was inferior and that there was little hope of bettering his status. Guillermo Prieto, writing in 1850, stated categorically that "it is not in it [the Indian race] that nationality resides today." This early nineteenth-century attitude is exemplified further by the dearth of historical or archeological interest in Aztec civilization.

There is little evidence of a clash between liberals and conservatives on the Indian question until the shocking outbreak of the Caste Wars in the years 1847 to 1853. During this period the Indian problem was added to the other major issues which made up the great debate preceding the Reforma. In the wake of the Caste Wars there was a considerable effort, expressed through the vigorous newspapers of the day, to explain the rebellions, their origins, and their implication for future social policy.

Liberal spokesmen, especially in *El Siglo XIX* and *El Monitor Republicano*, attributed the upheavals to the accumulation of abuses under the oppressive colonial regime, abuses which the liberal institution of equal rights and opportunity since 1821 had not as yet been able to rectify. On April 1, 1853, *El Monitor* charged Spanish policy with "systematizing by means more or less hypocritical, the divorce of the races." Many liberal spokesmen admitted that, despite legal innovation, the basic status of the Indian remained unchanged; nevertheless they insisted that he was better off under the Republic than in colonial times. *El Monitor*, reacting to the social violence, presented two alternatives in dealing with the Indian race: "either exterminate it or civilize it, mixing it with the others." This conclusion is similar to the one reached by Francisco García Pimentel in 1864.

Extermination or forced removal of Indians following the United States pattern did have some advocates, particularly in the areas directly affected by the rebellions or in the northern regions where incursions of *indios bárbaros* had been a continual menace. The conservative daily, *El Universal*, triumphantly reprinted such an extreme statement, taken from a Vera Cruz newspaper. The article had praised the Anglo-Saxon policy for at least assuring self-survival "which is the primary law." Moreover, the article had maintained that conflict between the races was inevitable and that humane measures would merely postpone the day of reckoning. An even balder statement came in 1851 from the frontier state of Coahuila which was regularly menaced by Indian attacks. The writer was a cleric, an overseer on the gigantic Sánchez Navarro hacienda:

If the legislature resolves to decree that 25 pesos be paid for every scalp, I swear I will grant each member of the legislature a plenary indulgence as soon as I am ordained, and it matters little that the legislators be excommunicated by those profound politicians in Mexico City, who, preoccupied with their European theories, know nothing of the necessities which unfortunately, must be adopted by our northern states.

This frontier attitude, which bore little relation to political affiliation or principles, was undoubtedly quite generalized.

Nevertheless, there was none of this talk among "those profound politicians in Mexico City." The liberal newspapers spoke of fusing the races, of education, even vaguely of land reform; but one is struck by the mildness of the measures suggested. The policy advocated most enthusiastically was colonization, a perennial liberal concern which was reactivated in the post-war years. There were several colonization schemes which were proposed in the legislatures of 1848–1850; but they failed to pass, largely because of the opposition to religious tolerance, a prerequisite to foreign immigration.

The conservative response to the Caste Wars proved more vigorous and less confused than that of the liberals. Numerous articles appeared in the conservative press, particularly in *El Universal*, which used the Caste Wars as an opportunity to discredit the Republic and to contrast its failures with colonial peace and stability. More than mere polemic, *El Universal* presented a forceful and well-reasoned explanation for the Caste Wars, a devastating criticism of the Indian policies of the Republic, and an impassioned defense of colonial paternalism. Spanish policy, argued the conservatives, did not need to rely on physical force to control the Indian population; it rather extended, under missionary guidance, a system of "moral force" which depended on the "development of the religious principle" and a "profound respect for authority."

The system that had proved itself so successful for three centuries broke down, argued *El Universal*, when the caudillos of the Revolutionary era incited the Indian against his former masters, and later when he was made "free and independent, a citizen of a great Republic." The Creole leaders of Independence had "denied their own race and condemned it to extermination," since the Indians, hearing incitements to rebellion, freely associated present-day Creoles with former Spaniards. Thus the Caste Wars were not the delayed reaction to colonial oppression, but rather the direct result of liberal attacks upon the colonial structure and the injection of new doctrines of equality and individualism into Mexican society. The conservatives were advocating a return to Spanish paternalism, the re-establishment of missions, the re-institution of the tribute, and the preservation of the Indian community.

The issue of communal property was one which evoked a particularly spirited debate. In one instance, August, 1853, there was a sharp exchange between *El Orden*, a conservative daily, and *El Siglo XIX*. On August 13 *El Siglo* suggested (the article was probably written by Francisco Zarco, the editor) that the recent Indian rebellions were stimulated by those who presently live, frustrated by the lack of private ownership, under the "cruel yoke of the community." The "communal vice" was largely responsible for the presence of two societies in Mexico and for the lack of an industriousness which could only be stimulated by individual initiative. The communal system, maintained the writer, citing no less an authority than Jovellanos, was outmoded and must be suppressed. These ideas of 1853 suggest the spirit present in the Constituent Congress, which was responsible for the fact that the Indian community emerged unprotected in the 1857 Constitution. It is important in this regard that Ponciano Arriaga and José María Castillo Velasco showed considerable respect for the Laws of the Indies, which had provided for the protection of communal property. Here the agrarian radicals seem closer to the conservative than to the dominant liberal position. Have not twentieth-century agrarianism and *indigenismo* reflected a similar affinity for Spanish colonial paternalism?

The Indian problem clearly revealed differences between conservatives and liberals. The liberal argument was based on individual liberty, legal equality, and, following the utilitarian bent, an antipathy toward protective legislation for any group and even less for a "corporate body" such as the Indian community. Mexico was to be a country in which the Indian would gradually disappear, hopefully through European colonization, a country in which small property holders would triumph under a regime of equal rights, individual opportunity, and administrative uniformity.

The conservatives opposed this passion for uniformity and utilitarianism. Their ideal was bound to a tradition which included "privileged" legal entities. It also included a strong religious establishment infusing society with hierarchical principles, presided over by a paternalistic state which could provide justice against exploitation. Neither position showed real concern for the freedom and progress of the indigenous population.

In conclusion, this debate over the Caste Wars suggests that liberals and conservatives, each for different reasons apathetic toward the progress of the indigenous population, were arguing about Indian policy only within the context of greater concerns—the colonial heritage, the Church, and the form of government itself.

Considering the ideological intensity of Mexico's civil war of the decade 1857 to 1867, it is doubtful that the issues thus far raised could provide grounds for an irreconcilable conflict between liberals and conservatives. The most obvious political question of the Reforma and Intervention period was the form of government, whether Mexico should be monarchy or republic. This issue may be less crucial to the conflict than it appears on the surface, and I will return to it later. There remains one major question to pursue—the Church—which I think provides the key.

Seeing anticlericalism as the chief issue in the Mexican liberal-conservative conflict is anything but novel. In fact the traditional place of the Church in Mexican historiography has produced a recent effort to search out other ingredients of nineteenth-century liberalism which may have been slighted. The results, as Daniel Cosío Villegas wrote in 1957, are reinterpretations of Juárez and the Reforma which seek the "enduring" features of the liberal movement as opposed to the "superficial" tendencies such as anticlericalism (superficial because they seem to have receded today).

Cosío dubs such reinterpretation a kind of historiographical sleight-of-hand. I agree with Jesús Reyes Heroles who argues that we cannot understand the liberal movement "as simply anticlericalism," and that anticlericalism was part of a broader effort to achieve the secularization of society, and to obtain political and civil liberties. Nevertheless, if we are seeking the basic point of division between liberals and conservatives, and incidentally the issue which gave Mexican liberalism its central orientation, we cannot subordinate the traditional question of the Church.

Returning to Dr. Mora, it was the 1831 essay on church property which separated his constitutionalism from his second phase during which he joined battle with the corporate reality of Mexico. It was always the Church question which aroused the strongest passions on both sides. The 1833 government was brought down with the cry, *religión y fueros*. A genuine conservative-liberal split did not become apparent until after 1830, and became blurred again in the years 1835 to 1846, at a time when anticlericalism subsided.

The struggle to secularize society by weakening the power of the most powerful of the corporations—the Church—was a distinctive feature of continental liberalism. It was the Civil Constitution of the Clergy of 1790 in France that led to the irreconcilable divisions between revolutionaries and counter-revolutionaries. The French Revolution aroused a similar division in Spain and provided Spanish liberalism with one of its central issues. Later in 1820 and 1823 Spain became a focus of European politics, inspired liberal movements throughout Southern Europe, and incidentally gave us the English word "liberal" as a political term. The role of anticlericalism points up again the affinity between Mexican experience and that of the continent.

The drive to free Mexico from corporate influence was not limited to the Church; the army was also of concern. Dr. Mora and his colleagues attacked military privileges in 1833. The reformers even advocated a system of civil militia, organized by the states, a suggestion that was put forth again in the years following the war with the United States. Military fueros were outlawed in the Ley Juárez of 1855, a provision which was written into Article 13 of the Constitution of 1857. Despite the fact that Mora and later reformers deplored the *espíritu de cuerpo* of the army and the evils of militarism, army reform always carried less conviction than reform of the Church. The need for military support of the liberal cause—repeatedly civilian reformers turned to Santa Anna and other untrustworthy generals for leadership—blunted the edge of the liberal attack.

Returning to the Church, the Ley Lerdo of 1856, Article 27 of the Constitution of 1857, and the Nationalization Decree of 1859 were clearly derived from the proposals of Lorenzo de Zavala and Dr. Mora in 1833. In each measure the same objectives prevailed—secularize society, strip away the political power of the Church, disentail its vast capital for free circulation. The conservatives made little reference to the Church except when they were aroused by liberal attacks. Veneration for the Church was inherent in the conservative program. The strength of conservative sentiment, with its focus on the defense of the Church, was greater in the 1850's than is apparent from the overemphasis on liberal doctrines and on liberalism's progressive triumph. There had been a conservative resurgence following the war with the United States, which included the appearance of *El Universal*, the organization of the Conservative Party (which captured the Ayuntamiento of Mexico City in 1849), and the appearance of Alamán's influential *Historia de Méjico* between 1849 and 1853.

Edmundo O'Gorman, in one of his independent-minded essays, writes that conservatism, contrary to the "official jacobin view," was not the work of a few perverse and intelligent leaders who managed to trick the public. Rather, he maintains that popular support for conservatism (in 1854) was stronger than for liberal ideas. This sentiment was manifest in the reaction to the debates on projected Article 15 of the Constitution, providing freedom of worship. These debates were the most passionate in the whole convention and the most avidly followed from the galleries. Finally, the central place of the Church in the ideological conflict can be demonstrated by comparing the extremist provisions of the conservative Plan of Tacubaya of 1857 with the liberal Reform Laws of 1859.

III. The Transformation of Liberalism

If we follow the liberal and nationalist interpretation of Mexican history referred to earlier, the Reforma becomes a kind of climax, culminating in 1867 with the defeat of the forces of clericalism, monarchy, and foreign intervention. From this point of view, the period 1867–1910 emerges as an inglorious hiatus between the Reforma and the Revolution. The Cosío Villegas volumes have demonstrated the inadequacy of this interpretation, one which construes liberalism only as ideology.

In exploring the engaging question of continuity between the Reforma and the Porfiriato, we must ask what elements passed from the scene in 1867. First of all, there was no serious advocacy of monarchy after the death of Maximilian. Following José María Gutiérrez de Estrada's sensational "letter" to President Bustamante in 1840, which advocated a constitutional monarchy for Mexico, conservatism became increasingly associated with the monarchist idea. The newspaper *El Tiempo* openly called for monarchy in 1846 and *El Universal* less openly after 1848. Lucas Alamán, likely the editorial spokesman in both newspapers, was clearly an avowed monarchist by the time of his death in 1853. Culminating in the rule of Maximilian in the 1860's, conservatism and monarchism became inseparable, and both were equally discredited with the fall of the Empire in 1867. The sudden demise of the monarchist idea suggests that despite the actual brief presence of a monarch on a Mexican throne, the issue itself was more ephemeral as a point of division between liberals and conservatives than one might believe from the polemic of the era. The liberals' attachment to strong central authority, an emphasis they shared with monarchists, implies further that the cause of contention was less the structure of government that the outward form and what it symbolized.

With the passing of monarchy went foreign political tutelage, never a serious issue thereafter. Though national integrity had been vindicated in the political sphere by 1867, it would be difficult to argue that economic and cultural tutelage were absent through the remainder of the century. A still more compelling reason for the apparent break in 1867 is that the Church question was temporarily resolved. The Reform Laws were incorporated into the Constitution in 1873; and, despite the considerable material recovery of the Church during the Díaz regime, anticlericalism became an undercurrent until the Revolution.

With the removal of the Church question, foreign political tutelage, and monarchy, the interesting question arises—what happened to conservatism? To what extent did the spirit of Alamán live on in post-1867 Mexico? What became of prominent conservatives of the Maximilian era? Did they turn to economic activities like those of Alamán earlier? What was their relationship to the regimes of Lerdo and Díaz? Could they reconcile the kind of philosophy represented by Alamán with the reigning positivism of the post-1867 era, philosophies conflicting in so many respects? Andrés Molina Enríquez in 1909 referred to Alamán as a precursor of the *política integral* of Díaz. Perhaps many elements of the era of Alamán were incorporated into the transformed liberalism of the Porfiriato. There is a wide area of study open to those who would understand the patterns of continuity in nineteenth-century Mexico.

In examining the political liberalism of the Reforma and Restored Republic, I believe there is evidence of the same inner tension noted in the earlier period. The constitutional convention of 1856–1857 was greatly concerned with guaranteeing the liberties of the individual. Federalism triumphed, and its identification with the ideology of liberalism was so close as to be little questioned. Centralism, which had commanded considerable support among liberals in 1824, found little if any in 1857. In fact, the anti-centralist sentiment was particularly strong after the de-facto centralism of the Santa Anna dictatorship (1853–1855). Centralism, said Ponciano Arriaga in presenting the *proyecto de constitución*, tended clearly to despotism. The direction of dissenting opinion, more extreme yet, is revealed by Isidoro Olvera who proposed that the capital of the country be removed from Mexico City. All the elements of "the *status quo* and reaction," he said, cluster in Mexico City which in this respect is "like Madrid and all the capitals of the Catholic world."

This resurgence of federalism is explained partly by the fact that the strength of the liberal movement had always come from the provinces.

This was the case in 1833; it was true again in 1856. Juárez, Degollado, Ocampo, and their like were regional leaders first, who then captured power on the national level. As Justo Sierra put it, the reformist tide flowed back from the provinces to the center. The Three Years War (1858–1861) and the resistance to the French had to be directed from the provinces, since the enemy held Mexico City for most of a decade. Could this regionalist sentiment, which necessarily gave federalism its vitality, remain strong once the Republic had been restored and triumphant liberals had recaptured the capital? According to Cosío Villegas, one of the major political themes of the years 1867–1876 was the increasing effort to suppress regional revolts and bring peace to the country, an effort which might be said to have culminated under Díaz. Federalism as a reality had vanished by 1876.

The movement to guarantee liberties also included an attempt by the 1857 constitution-makers to introduce a cabinet system of government responsible to a single-chamber assembly. Strong executive power was associated with Spanish monarchy or dictators such as Iturbide and Santa Anna (the constitutional convention in its early phases was obsessed with Santa Anna). Thus, the liberals of 1857 sought in a democratic legislature a guarantee of political liberty. The system worked briefly in a modified fashion in 1861–1862 when various cabinet ministers were more significant than President Juárez. But, according to Frank A. Knapp, parliamentary government was an exotic form that was doomed to failure. The demands of reform, of war, and later of peace, forced the liberals to revert to a strong executive. It is revealing that Sebastián Lerdo de Tejada, an early supporter of cabinet responsibility in theory, dealt it a death blow as President, and "provided a precedent for the still stronger rule of Porfirio Díaz."

Nevertheless, the post-1867 years reveal that political and civil liberties were not completely overwhelmed by the dictates of a strong state. Cosío Villegas argues that these years represented in a political sense as vitally free and democratic a period as Mexico has known. Freedom of the press, guaranteed by the Constitution of 1857, meant the existence of a great variety of opposition newspapers at the same time that an official press was absent. The Supreme Court was more independent between 1867 and 1884 than at any other time.

In effect, then, the political drama of these years was the contention between increasing state power on the one hand and constitutional guarantees on the other, the same political problem reflected in Dr. Mora's thought. Benito Juárez assumed dictatorial powers during the war years. The anticlerical drive gave the state expanded authority. The government now had to administer church property, a civil register, education, and cemeteries. Secularization, as in France during the Revolutionary Era, was an integral part of the expansion of state administrative machinery. The initial triumph of secularization meant also that the work of legal codification was free to proceed. Many of the codes of modern Mexico are the product of the Restored Republic. Yet the advance of the administrative state entailed what Cosío terms "constitutional relaxation." A gradual tightening of state authority, an expansion of extraordinary presidential power, even the restriction of liberties, was the experience of the early 1870's. In fact, in this respect the Restored Republic

. . . dovetails perfectly with the Porfiriato. Between the one and the other there is no break in continuity, nor much less is there an historical "fault."

The resolution of the Church-State relationship by 1873 further demonstrates the orientation of transformed liberalism. The Reform Laws of 1859 instituted separation of Church and State. But it is "separation" only in a peculiar Mexican sense. It is a system somewhere between the extreme French gallicanism of 1790 (where not only did the property of the Church come under civil jurisdiction but priests became state employees) and extreme separation as has prevailed in the United States. What Mexico achieved in 1873, a solution anticipated by Mora in 1833, was comparable to the Italian Cavour's formula of a "free Church in a free state." But the "free state" meant vast state power over Church property, the suppression of monastic orders, and severe limitation of church-supported education.

The transformation of liberalism is enmeshed with the entry of positivism which dominated the intellectual scene by the end of the Restored Republic. Positivism provided a philosophical underpinning for the general climate of thought and opinion after 1867. Particularly noticeable was an increasing desire for peace and political order on the one hand, and economic progress on the other. An erstwhile jacobin liberal of 1857, Francisco Zarco, could write in 1868 that "the time for merely abstract questions has already passed and the hour for practical questions has arrived." Symptomatic of the climate of the times was a surge of foreign capitalist promotion and railroad building.

Mexico's positivist pioneer was Gabino Barreda, Juárez's minister of education, who had attended Auguste Comte's lectures in Paris. In his famous *Oración cívica* of 1867, which included an interpretation of Mexican history in the three familiar positivist stages, Barreda emphasized that social reconstruction was now the order of the day. Mexico was entering the positive stage of her evolution and further constitutional reform by revolutionary means would be "useless and imprudent, not to say criminal." Economic development, a scientifically-based education, and more political order were to replace the anarchical and utopian character of the earlier liberalism. As Justo Sierra put it, Mexico needed a realistic liberalism of order, more "practical liberty," or a "liberal conservatism." The mandate for strong government was obvious: Federico Cosmes even called openly for an "honorable tyranny."

This continuity of nineteenth-century liberalism can be further demonstrated by considering the relationship between positivism and the earlier utilitarianism. Both were empirical, emphasizing the primacy of experience or sensation as the determinant of ideas. Both were equally hostile in the name of science to inherited dogma, tradition, or custom. The test of utility —producing the greatest good for the greatest number—was akin to the emphasis inherent in positivism upon tangible achievement and material progress. The central change in orientation was the shift from the atomistic to the organic view of society. The individual, whose interests if allowed free play would fuse with the general interest, was no longer the central category. It was now society, which evolved as an organism by interaction with the environment. Thus the Mexican positivists emphasized social reconstruction and regeneration rather than the removing of obstacles which blocked individual freedom.

Leopoldo Zea has justly called Dr. Mora the precursor of positivism in Mexico. Mora's utilitarian liberalism, his vision of a secular society, directed by middle-class property owners who would be the beneficiaries of a state-controlled educational system, foreshadowed the ideas of Gabino Barreda and his followers. Moreover, the influence of Mora's analysis of Mexican society upon Justo Sierra is apparent in the early pages of the latter's *Juárez*. Sierra's search for a Mexican bourgeoisie which would oversee the material and moral progress of the nation seemed an extension of Mora's vision and that revealed in the Ley Lerdo.

Our search for continuity within the nineteenth-century liberal tradition must not obscure the vital distinction between the positivists and the earlier liberals. The latter, despite their ultimate reliance upon a strong state to attack corporate power, always kept alive the struggle for liberties, free political institutions, and the basis of political democracy. The positivists, however, despite their ostentatious use of the word *libertad*, inherited the great political defect of Auguste Comte's philosophy, its absolute lack of concern for individual liberty. They supported Díaz much the same way that Comte welcomed Napoleon III in France.

The continuity from utilitarian liberalism to positivism is even more apparent in the economic sphere. Here Comte's philosophy was inadequate, for his exalting of society left little room for individual initiative. In Mexico, as in Europe and the United States, it was rather the positivism of Herbert Spencer, deceptively appearing to be a mere extension of laissez-faire liberalism, that gave economic enterprise its support. The conflict between Comte and Spencer within Mexican positivism has been pointed to by Leopoldo Zea, but it deserves further study. To both Comte and Spencer, society and not the individual was the highest entity. Where they diverged was in their attitude toward the state. As could be expected from the French tradition, the state was of great importance for Comte, and he made it synonymous with society. For Spencer, the state was merely an obstruction to social evolution, an obstacle to Nature itself, the perfection of which resulted from the free adaptation of individuals. The followers of Barreda had already begun to take up Spencer's ideas with the founding of the journal *La Libertad* in 1876. They were to provide the ideological buttress for the economic development, and incidentally, the social exploitation, of the Porfiriato. It is significant to add, however, that Spencer's Darwinism was considerably modified in Mexican social thought. Concern for the Indian, inherited from Las Casas and Spanish paternalism was not completely subverted, either by doctrinaire liberalism or by Spencerian positivism.

Thus we can speak of a transformed liberalism with the emergence of the regime of Porfirio Díaz. In the political sphere the struggle within liberalism had ended in favor of the authoritarian state, reminiscent of the Bourbons. Individual guarantees and free political institutions were submerged. The ideology of federalism had given way to the reality of centralization. In Cosío's words, "only an astute archeologist could discover at the end of the Porfiriato vestiges of a federal organization." The political synthesis may also have included elements of the conservatism of Alamán, thus passed on as a legacy to contemporary Mexico. Yet the autonomy of economic interests remained. The earlier contradiction within utilitarianism cropped up again in the conflict between Comtian and Spencerian positivism. The latifundia remained unchallenged; foreign capital was accorded vast privileges; even the Church revived economically.

In conclusion, we must ask: have not the elements of this structure emerged again in a new guise, despite the social revolution of our century?

---

9. Diplomatic Futility

JOSEPH B. LOCKEY

Diplomatic history is not often recounted with such vivacity, and even humor, as the author of the following article brings to the sorry record of U.S. diplomats in Central America in the second quarter of the nineteenth century. Those diplomats who did not die *en route* to their posts were largely ineffective, at least partly because conditions were at times so chaotic that one "travelled over the length and breadth of the country, unable to find a government to receive him." Professor Lockey, who taught for many years at the University of California, Los Angeles, has produced a substantial and fascinating article based on a wide variety of sources.

From Volume X (1930), pages 265–294.

Futility marked the early relations of the United States with Central America. Nothing went right; everything went wrong. The very agents of the Washington government seemed to move under an evil star. Physical hardships, vexations of spirit, dread diseases, and in some cases death itself attended them. Of the eleven appointees before 1849, three died *en route;* another succumbed before he started on his mission; one escaped with his life by being dismissed before he embarked; another survived by contriving to draw his salary for more than a year without going near the Central American capital; and another traveled over the length and breadth of the country, unable to find a government to receive him. Though the remaining four reached their destination and were received, only one of these prolonged his stay beyond a few months, and he committed suicide soon after his return to the United States.

Nor is this the whole story of adversity. The country to which the ill-starred agents were accredited, was itself the victim of misfortunes of the greatest magnitude. Organized in 1824 under a constitution similar to our own, the Central American federation was confronted from the beginning by obstacles which it could not surmount. No strong sentiment of nationality bound the parts together; communication was slow and difficult; the mass of the population was ignorant and indifferent; many of the upper class were frankly reactionary; and the leaders of the enterprise were themselves torn by conflicting personal interests. Civil war, secession, foreign encroachments, political chaos, and a whole train of accompanying evils left the country hopelessly prostrate.

Misfortune on the one hand; disaster on the other. Is it possible that some fatal connection existed between the two? It is evident that the elements of salvation for the Central American republic did not lie within itself. Could external aid have saved it from destruction? The United States alone was in a position to render this friendly office; yet it failed utterly to perform its neighborly function. Was the failure a mere matter of mischance, the result of unforeseeable and inevitable misfortunes? Could it have been caused, in part at least, by a certain unawareness at Washington of the nature and magnitude of the Central American problem? In part by ignorance of the climatic, topographic, and social conditions which prevailed in the new state? In part by diplomatic awkwardness? In part by the subservience of diplomacy to party politics? Perchance by a combination of a number of such causes? Let the sombre details speak for themselves.

The first agent designated was Thomas N. Mann of North Carolina. Bred to the law and limited in outlook to the horizon of his native state, he was ignorant of the language, customs, and institutions of Spanish America, and even of the very location and extent of the country to which he was to be sent. Be it said to his credit, however, that he was eager to learn. Immediately after his appointment in April, 1824, he went to Washington and had interviews with President Monroe and Secretary of State Adams. He wanted enlightenment not only on the geographical, social, and political conditions of Central America, but on matters of high personal interest to himself: he wanted to know by what means he was to reach his destination, and how long his exile in that far country was to continue. On this last point Adams, whose duty it was to satisfy the agent's curiosity, appears to have had nothing to say. Perhaps he had a premonition that talk of returning from Central America before one arrived was a bit premature. On the other points the secretary of state was more explicit, though in matters of detail he was himself somewhat confused.

I told him [says Adams] of the principal objects of his mission: that the first of them was to obtain and transmit information respecting the country to which he was going—a new central South American, and as it would seem, confederated republic, situated at and including the Isthmus of Panama, a position of the highest geographical importance—important also by the commercial connections, and lodgements on the soil by the British, with the neighboring Bay of Honduras and Mosquito Shore. It was furthermore interesting from the step once taken by St. Salvador, now forming a portion of the republic, to connect itself directly with the United States. It was understood that one of the deputies who came here on that occasion was now, or recently had been at the head of the new Guatemalan Government. By the public newspapers it appears that they had appointed a public Agent or Minister to come to the United States. The republic bordered on those of Mexico, Colombia, and Peru; but our information concerning it was scanty, and we expected to receive much from his Agency.

Adams's information was obviously scanty. It did not greatly matter, however, that the new republic did not extend to South America nor include the Isthmus of Panama; for, reduced to its proper limits, it occupied nevertheless a position of the highest geographical importance. It did not matter that the British at the moment had no lodgement on its soil; for they did have an establishment at Belize which served as a base for commercial connections, and as a point of departure for later territorial encroachments, including a reassertion of old claims on the Mosquito Shore. It did matter that Adams hit upon two of the essential elements—geographical importance and lodgements of the British—of what in years to come was to be known as the Central American question. His mention of the proposed annexation was intended to convey some notion of the friendly reliance of the weak on the neighborly protection of the strong. This amicable relationship was to form the basis of a third element of the question; that is, championship, by the United States, of the Central American cause.

Unfortunately, Adams did not clearly apprehend the significance of a unified and stable republic of Central America as a factor in the contest which he vaguely foreshadowed. Neither in his conversation with Mann nor in his formal instructions, which were but an elaboration of the main points of the interview, did he propose any steps to aid the leaders then engaged in framing what to them was a strange form of government. This was the time to render assistance; but the golden opportunity was allowed to pass. When the real meaning of the federation was finally perceived, the good offices of the government at Washington were powerless to prevent dissolution or to effect restoration. Internal chaos and foreign aggression was the result.

How to reach Guatemala was a perplexing question. The prospective traveler could not avail himself of any regular sailings to the Central American coast, for their were none. He could occasionally obtain passage to the Isthmus of Panama, but his progress from there northward on the Pacific was extremely uncertain. He had even less opportunity in these days to go by the Nicaragua route, for vessels seldom touched at San Juan del Norte. Of the other more or less direct ways, the only one open to him was the trail which led inland from Izabal, farther up the coast, on the Golfo Dulce. But to get to Izabal was a problem. If he had the good fortune to be taken aboard by a ship going in that direction, perhaps after a round-about course, he had to disembark at Omoa on the coast of Honduras or at the British port of Belize, to continue his voyage on a chance vessel of light draft capable of navigating the shallow waters of the gulf. Delays at every point, exposure to the diseases prevalent on tropical shores, and the discomforts of the land journey from Izabal onward, rendered his undertaking arduous and perilous to the highest degree.

Mann knew little of these matters, and in his ignorance he applied to the department of state for assistance. But to Adams the subject was annoying. It irked him to attend to such details. "These private economies of our public Ministers and Agents," he confided to his diary, "are among the most disagreeable appendages of my public duties." Yet the harassed secretary went through with the unpleasant task, and while Mann returned to North Carolina to attend to private business and prepare his "baggage and library" for shipment, Adams succeeded in arranging the desired passage on the United States ship of war *Hornet*, soon to depart on a cruise in southern waters. Two months later Mann embarked at Norfolk, and the *Hornet* turned its prow, not toward Omoa or Belize, but toward La Guaira, Venezuela. Other interests took precedence, and as the vessel cruised Mann fell sick and died on board. His mission ended before it had well begun.

William Miller, also of North Carolina, and a former governor of that state, was designated in March, 1825, as Mann's successor. He was commissioned as chargé d'affaires, recognition having been accorded the Central American federation in August of the preceding year. His instructions were ready in April, exactly a year after the date of Mann's appointment. Two months later Miller was in Washington seeking aid of the department of state in reaching the Central American capital. Whether the memory of Mann's fate on board a public vessel had anything to do with the matter or not, the new agent was left to make his way as best he could by such means as chance might afford. Accordingly he sallied forth and for months was lost to view. How he traveled, what difficulties he encountered, and what hardships he endured the records do not reveal. They only show that he reached Key West, and that there he fell, in September, 1825, a victim of yellow fever.

John Williams of Tennessee, the next in order, was more fortunate. At the time of his appointment, in December, 1825, he was in the prime of a vigorous manhood. His career had been active and varied. At the age of twenty-one he was a captain in the United States infantry; at twenty-five he was admitted to the bar; at thirty-four he raised a regiment of mounted volunteers, and by conducting a successful campaign against the Seminoles won a commission as colonel in the regular army. After serving throughout the War of 1812, he was elected United States senator from Tennessee, and in this capacity remained at Washington until 1823. He was one of General Jackson's bitterest adversaries, which explains at once his descent from the senate and his elevation to a diplomatic post. If he had been less valiant he might have quailed before the mission to Central America. But his courage was a matter of record: he had faced death on the battlefield, and for good measure he had defied Andrew Jackson. It was no wonder that such a man should be the first to reach Guatemala and return alive.

In March, 1826, three months after his appointment, Williams was at Norfolk awaiting passage on the sloop of war *John Adams*. In April he was at Havana, and in May he reached Guatemala. But this was six months after his appointment, and a full two years after the first agent's appointment. Precious time had been lost. We learn from Williams's communications that the federation was already in a process of dissolution; that the federal and state governments were in constant collision; that the house of deputies, recently in session, had adjoined without passing the appropriation bill; that a forced loan was being talked of; that seizure of church property was contemplated; that a territorial dispute with Mexico threatened war; and that the British were extending their trespasses. Williams warned the Central American officials that their country was on the brink of an awful gulf, and he recommended as a possible means of salvation the adoption of the writ of habeas corpus, trial by jury, and Livingston's Louisiana code. He urged also the founding of a national bank with a metallic basis, and on request drew up a charter for such a bank. These were, after all, mere devices, and Williams had little hope of seeing the republic saved from destruction. "They have no master workmen among them," he said, "& the whole machinery is badly contrived." Under conditions so disheartening, he made his stay short. In December, six months after his arrival, he turned the affairs of the legation over to the acting consul, and set out on the return journey to the United States.

William B. Rochester of New York was commissioned in March, 1827, to succeed Williams. He it was who managed to reap the fruits of office without rendering any useful service. He was an adept in this art. For nearly a year he had been the recipient of a salary as secretary of the mission to Panama without budging from his native state, and at the time of his appointment to the Central American post, he was in Mexico to attend a second meeting of the congress, which never materialized. Under his instructions for the new post, which he received in May, 1827, he had two courses open before him: he could go promptly to Guatemala and assume the duties of his office; or, if his private affairs demanded, he could first visit the United States, and then proceed to his destination.

Rochester had, it must be admitted, an intellectual perception of the nobler course. He had been told by agents of the Central American republic in Mexico, so he wrote the secretary of state, that the situation was urgent; that the departure of Colonel Williams had been viewed with great regret; that the government and people were most friendly toward us; and that it was their sincere desire to cultivate and maintain a good understanding with our country. His fervent account leaves us almost convinced that his emotions were touched, and that his sense of duty was aroused. He informed the secretary of state that it was his intention to go to his post at once; and he made his way promptly down to Vera Cruz, to proceed by way of the Bay of Honduras for Guatemala. But the flesh was weak. He embarked instead for New Orleans, and once there he was loath to quit again his native soil.

The movements of Rochester during the next year were amazingly dilatory. From New Orleans, where he arrived early in June, 1827, he wrote that having failed to obtain an early passage to the coast of Central America, he had resolved to send his baggage to New York, from which city he would sail after paying a visit to his family. In July, he was at the ancestral home in Rochester; in September, he spent some days in New York, where he professed to be making preparations for his departure; in October, he was back at Rochester; in November, he missed sailing from New York on the *John Adams;* in December, he promised to "use due diligence in getting to Norfolk by means of steamboats & stages" to meet the sloop of war *Falmouth*, in which he now proposed to sail; in January, he was in Washington where the president could observe his snail-like pace; in February, his perseverance brought him to Norfolk; and in March he at last embarked. After a long and restful cruise on the *Falmouth*, he went ashore, in May, at Omoa. Here he faltered still. Instead of hurrying away to the Central American capital, three hundred miles away, he embraced the first opportunity to take passage for the United States. In June, he was back, and in October, his diplomatic career was closed with commendations from the secretary of state.

This strange affair becomes stranger still on examination. Rochester owed both his appointments to family connections with Secretary of State Clay. In itself this is not remarkable. Public servants have often been selected on such grounds, and thus selected have frequently failed to render any corresponding service. But the acquiescence of the austere and correct president in proceedings so sterile and so oblique is beyond belief. Adams knew that Rochester while nominally secretary of the mission to

Panama was busily engaged in efforts to promote the political interests of Henry Clay in the state of New York; he knew that to permit Rochester, after a brief and fruitless residence in Mexico, to travel over half a continent before assuming duties that lay close at hand, was a waste of public funds and a damage to the public interest; he knew that Rochester's delay in New York during the summer and fall of 1827 was still in the interest of party politics; and finally, he knew that Rochester set out in the spring of 1828 with no intention of establishing a residence in Central America.

The following excerpts from Adams's *Memoirs* bear witness to these facts, though they do not remove our wonder that he could have been a party to conduct so reprehensible.

January 8, 1828. Mr. Barnard, a member of the House of Representatives from New York, came with Mr. Rochester, the Chargé d'Affaires to the Central Republic of Guatemala, who is going with lingering step to Norfolk, to embark for the port of his destination. This gentleman was at the last election of Governor of New York a candidate for that office against DeWitt Clinton, and has an earnest craving to be a candidate again. . . . But upon the vulgar adage, "a bird in the hand is worth two in the bush," he goes to Guatemala, looking back to New York—like Reynolds's picture of Garrick, between Tragedy and Comedy.

March 19, 1828. Mr. Brent came from Mr. Clay, and mentioned that Mr. Rochester, the Chargé d'Affaires to the Central republic of Guatemala, was still at Norfolk, waiting for his passage. By the accounts recently received from that country, a desperate civil war is raging among them; and Mr. Clay proposed giving an instruction to Mr. Rochester, if he should find upon his arrival at Omoa that no useful purpose would probably be attained by his proceeding to his destination, to return immediately to the United States.

I assented to this, but desired Mr. Brent to present to the consideration of Mr. Clay the expediency of suspending for the present the mission to Guatemala and directing Mr. Rochester not to proceed on the voyage. . . . Mr. Clay was here. . . . He spoke of Mr. Rochester, and thought it would be most expedient to instruct him to proceed to Guatemala, the letters from the Consul at Omoa, Phillips, expressing much solicitude for his arrival, in the hope that his presence might afford protection to the persons and property of our citizens there. Mr. Rochester has been so long at home, waiting for a passage, that Mr. Clay thought it would be more satisfactory to him, and also to the public mind, that he should go to the place of his destination, rather than that his mission should now be abruptly terminated. But he agreed that it would be advisable shortly to abolish the mission to the central republic; and rather because he had this day received a letter from Mr. Gonzales, their Chargé d'Affaires in this country, now at New York, announcing that in consequence of the disastrous state of his own country he found himself compelled to embark for home. . . .

June 23, 1828. Mr. Brent sent me several dispatches, received since Mr. Clay's departure yesterday morning—among them letters from William B. Rochester, Chargé d'Affairs to Guatemala, who has returned and landed at Savannah. The republic of Central America is in a state of Civil War, and the Government is virtually dissolved. . . .

July 7, 1828. Mr. Southard brought me a bundle of letters and enclosures from Master-Commandant Charles W. Morgan, commander of the sloop-of-war Falmouth, just arrived at Pensacola, from a cruise in the Gulf of Mexico and the Caribbean Sea. This vessel was sent to take W. B. Rochester . . . and John Mason, Jun., the Secretary of Legation to Mexico, to the countries of their respective destinations. He landed Rochester at Omoa, but, instead of proceeding to his post, he posted off to the British settlement in the Bay of Honduras, and thence back to the United States, where he arrived some time sooner than the Falmouth, which carried him out. Morgan, in a private letter to Mr. Southard, intimates that Mr. Rochester was quizzed into very unnecessary panic by a British Agent at Omoa, and describes his agitation and movements in a manner somewhat ludicrous. Rochester's masterpiece of diplomacy seems to have been in changing his ships, and coming back in a different vessel from that in which he went out.

The office of chargé d'affaires to Central America was now left vacant for a while. The Adams administration ran its course and two years of the reign of Andrew Jackson passed before a successor to Rochester was appointed. In the meanwhile Clay yielded the office of secretary of state to Martin Van Buren and Van Buren to Edward Livingston. It was Livingston who was responsible for the restoration. His long residence at New Orleans where his gaze was constantly directed toward the south (his knowledge of the language, customs, and institutions of Spanish America, his preparation of a universally praised code of laws thought to be peculiarly adapted to the needs of the new republics, his exceptional opportunities for observation, and his habit of intelligent reflection on the phenomena presented to his view, gave him a profound understanding of Central American problems, and a sure grasp of the importance of the region to the world in general and to the United States in particular).

The reasons assigned by the preceding administration for discontinuing all efforts to maintain contact with the crumbling republic did not appeal to Livingtston. He set his hand with zest to the preparation of fresh instructions in which he substituted for the earlier vague generalities clear-cut and specific injunctions. He gave "geographic importance" a concrete meaning. He made it signify a transisthmian ship canal—a stream of interoceanic commerce—and an awakened Central America with free ports, good roads, and a growing trade, from all of which the United States, because of its proximity to the scene and because of the enterprise, the wealth, and the proficiency of its citizens, would derive great advanges. And in closing his instructions he touched with feeling upon the peculiar regard which Central America merited as a neighbor and sister republic.

But neither time nor Livingston's fresh enthusiasm brought better luck. The new agent, William N. Jeffers of New Jersey, appointed in June, 1831, set forth, but got no farther than Pensacola. There he was overtaken by ominous communications. Accusations against him had been lodged at the department of state, and when, after some months of interchange of correspondence, the matter came to a head, Jeffers resigned his commission to disguise virtual dismissal.

A worse fortune befell his successor, James Shannon of Kentucky. He accepted the appointment and set out on the hazardous journey with a hopefulness which passes all understanding. Accompanied by his wife, his son Charles, and his niece, Miss Shelby, he embarked in June, 1832, at Pensacola on the sloop of war *Vincennes*. After a short and uneventful voyage, he landed at Omoa, where he expected to take passage for Izabal. Disappointed in his expectation, he availed himself of an opportunity to pass with his retinue across to Belize, whence the superintendent, Colonel Cockburn, sent the party forward—unwittingly to a tragic dénouement. At Izabal James Shannon and Miss Shelby were stricken with yellow fever, and within a few days both were dead. The survivors laid the bodies to rest in the damp soil, and, burdened with sorrow, returned by way of Belize and New Orleans to their home in Kentucky.

No perfectly normal person would now accept the post. Charles G. DeWitt of New York State, who did accept it, was undoubtedly a bit queer. It required six months of search to find him and agree upon his appointment, and nearly twice as many months of prodding to get him past Shannon's grave and on to Guatemala. The story would be amusing if it were not so pathetic. DeWitt was appointed in January, 1833, and being "extremely anxious to depart", went to New York City for that purpose. In April he wrote that he was still detained for the "want of an opportunity to proceed". It is not unlikely that something else besides the want of opportunity detained him. Perhaps the dismal history of the previous attempts to reach the fatal city had come to his ears. He was not so mad as to walk deliberately into the jaws of death. Shannon's grave at Izabal was a warning symbol. Was it not possible to avoid the perils of this route? Assured by persons well acquainted with the country and the climate that the "safest, surest, and most prudent course" was around Cape Horn, he engaged passage on the ship *Leonidas* bound for "Valparaiso, Lima and Central America". Would not the president and secretary of state lend their approval?

DeWitt doubtless had not sufficiently pondered the effect his longest-way-round plan would have on the stern soldier who sat in the White House. Old Hickory's methods were direct. Dangers did not deter him. Safety and prudence were not in his vocabulary. Exactly what he said about DeWtt's proposal we do not know. Perhaps it would not be fit to print if we knew. The record we have is that softened paraphrase in a letter of Livingston's.

He [the President] directs me to inform you that he very much regrets that the circumstance of your lameness [for DeWitt was lame] will make it inconvenient for you to go to your destination by the usual route; but that he cannot by any means approve the project of making the voyage to the South

Seas, round Cape Horn, in order to get to Central America, a place almost at our doors.—You could not in framing the plan, have attended to the distance, and to other circumstances that would render it entirely inconvenient to you, and impossible to be sanctioned with propriety, by the government—You would have first, 170 Degrees of latitude to sail in a southern and a northern direction, and 70 or 80 of longitude in the different courses you will be obliged to pursue in order to arrive at a place to which you would arrive in the direct course, by going less than 30 degrees—Add to this, that when you arrive at Valparaiso you will be twice as far from your destination as you are now, and with infinitely fewer opportunities of reaching it.

This rebuke had a slight galvanic effect, and DeWitt engaged passage on a vessel soon to sail. But, detained by illness, he did not embark. In July, he wrote,

You shall hear from me as soon as my health is reestablished. In the meantime, in the name of humanity, do not hurry me off before I am fit to go.

In August, he gave details of his illness.

From the 2nd of May till the middle of June, I lay on my back, a mere lump of clay—a plague to myself, and I presume a greater plague to others.

Fortunately "by the blessings of God and the skill, care and attention" of his physician he survived. All of which left the obdurate president untouched. In September, another reprimand, more scathing than the last, was administered. The poor ailing man was reminded that the appointment, made long months ago, had been "dictated by the necessity of speedily renewing our intercourse with Central America", and he was given to understand that the sincerity of his desire to achieve that object was a matter of doubt in the mind of the president. This was effective. In October, the laggard agent, brow-beaten and abashed, set sail in a merchant vessel for Kingston, Jamaica, where he arrived after nineteen days of sufferings which he would not "undertake to describe". In November, a British packet took him to Belize, and in December he rode into the city of Guatemala.

Some incidents of his journey are worthy of remark. At Belize he met with a cordial reception from "His Excellency, Francis Cockburn, the Governor", who not only sheltered the forlorn traveler but offered a vessel and crew for the voyage to Izabal. "The impression which such godlike benevolence has imprinted in my mind," wrote DeWitt, "may be imagined but cannot be described." Poor fellow! He is never able to describe. He leaves so much for us to imagine. And we do imagine. Harsh words from Washington, whence kind words were due; friendliness at Belize, where animosity might have been expected. DeWitt wins our sympathy and then our admiration. He was not a robust, gallant, intrepid individual. He was on the contrary delicate of health, lame, shrinking, timid. He dreaded the hardships and dangers along the way. Yet, under pressure, he met them with fortitude. At Izabal he paid a visit to the last resting place of his lamented predecessor, Shannon, and, depressed by the wild appearance of the spot, procured a young orange tree and planted it at the head of the grave. This sacred duty performed he proceeded through tropical jungles and over difficult mountain trails to his destination. Every foot of the way was painful. Not only that, says DeWitt: "I was three times thrown from the mules—once at the hazard of my life."

Five long years DeWitt continued at his post. He did not run true to form and hasten back. Singularly, quirk, twist, aberration—something—marked him off from the common herd. It may have been nothing more than a desire of escape, of self effacement. It may have been inertia. It may have been a sense of duty. Or it may have been dread—dread of pain, dread of sickness, dread of death on land or sea. We cannot be sure, for DeWitt was strange. For a while his behavior seemed normal. He wrote regularly, giving the state department such information as he was able to gather. But he seemed not to be fully aware of his environment. He spoke too much of tranquility when there was none. His Central American view was limited by the mountains that surrounded Guatemala City. He did not sally forth. He was lame, and he shrank from the hazards of the road. He vegetated. After four years he wrote and meekly asked for leave to spend a few months in the United States. He was told in substance to come home and resign. This hurt. He had to explain that his object was serious, that he wanted "to visit a sick wife confined for months to her bed". Then Washington relented and granted him leave, which he would not for some time take advantage of. "The roads leading from the capital," he declared,

have for the last six weeks been so infested by armed bands of highwaymen, that no prudent traveller, and least of all a foreigner, will venture to set out for any distant point.

And prudence kept him on more than a year longer.

In DeWitt's absence changes had taken place at Washington. The old martinet who hated prudence had returned to Tennessee to spend his declining days at the Hermitage. Van Buren was in his place. Livingston had long since yielded his office to Louis McLane, and McLane had been succeeded by John Forsyth. But DeWitt reaped no profit from these changes. Scolding him had become a habit and he was welcomed with words of reprobation. He had been told not to leave his post until he had negotiated a renewal of the treaty which had been concluded with Central America in 1825 and which was now about to expire by its own limitations. He had violated his instructions. He had come home without the treaty. Disobedience so flagrant must be punished, and he was ordered to face again the perils of the road to Guatemala. He was to acknowledge his failure and do penance by going back to take proper leave of the Central American government and to bring the mission to a formal close. He could not make the state department understand that his failure was excusable; that he had done all anyone could do in the circumstances; that he had secured signatures to the renewal but could not get the document ratified, simply because the congress, the ratifying body, had ceased to function; that to incur all the risks involved in the return trip for the purpose of taking leave of a phantom government would be worse than useless. How disheartening! Forever driven, forever harassed, he had never received a word of kindness, of appreciation, or of commendation from his superiors. The world was cold, full of troubles and hazards and pain. And poor DeWitt chose to leave it by his own hand.

Four of the seven appointees thus far designated had been claimed by death. Still another, William Leggett, a native of New York City and sometime editor of the famous *Evening Post,* was to make the supreme sacrifice. He was appointed to do what DeWitt had rebelled against doing; that is, he was to go to Guatemala to close the luckless mission. Unfortunately he was already seriously ill, and his appointment appears to have hurried him on to his grave. Before the ink was fairly dry on his commission his earthly career came to an end. Whereupon, the government, nothing daunted, selected a new agent in the person of John L. Stephens. Though born in New Jersey, Stephens, like Rochester, DeWitt, and Leggett, was appointed from New York. But he was not like his confrères in any other respect. He was not a shirker to evade the task laid out before him; he was not an hypochondriac to nurse his ills; nor was he an invalid on the verge of the grave. He was indeed better equipped than any of his predecessors had been to undertake the mission. He was a man of superior intelligence; he had initiative; he knew men and affairs; and he was experienced in travel. Moreover, he was proficient in antiquarian studies, and this, together with his desire to explore the little known vestiges of the ancient civilizations of Central America, caused him to enter upon the enterprise with singular enthusiasm. Alas! he was to deal with ruins only; for the federation of Central America, like the Mayan régimes before it, had ceased to exist.

Within these limitations Stephens succeeded where others failed. That is, he reached Guatemala City, performed the last sad rites over the defunct mission, traveled widely over the country, made hasty but important archaeological investigations, and returned to the United States without succumbing to disease. Accompanied by an English artist, Frederick Catherwood, he sailed from New York in October, 1839, on a British vessel bound direct for Belize, and, meeting with no delays, landed there within the month. The new superintendent of the settlement, Colonel McDonald, received him with cordiality, and thus heaped up the debt of our gratitude to Belize. Nowhere else in this region were the British so amiably disposed toward the Americans. At Guatemala, indeed, the British consul general, Chatfield, sowed seeds of dislike toward us, and these seeds in the course of time germinated and grew and produced bitter fruit. Belize was a place of hospitality. The Shannons had been the recipients of its benefits, and Mrs. Shannon and her son who returned to it after the tragedy at Izabal, had cause to remember it with melancholy gratitude. DeWitt found its benevolence impossible to describe. Happily, Stephens suffered from no such disability. His account of the farewell dinner with which he and Catherwood were honored leaves us with a vivid sense of the reality of the settlement as a friendly haven for the American pilgrims who passed that way.

The large window of the dining room opened upon the harbour [says Stephens]; the steamboat lay in front of the Government House, and the black smoke, rising in columns from her pipe, gave notice that it was time to embark. Before rising Colonel McDonald, like a loyal subject, proposed the health of the Queen; after which he ordered the glasses to be filled to the brim, and, standing up, he gave, "The health of Mr. Van Buren, President of the United States," accompanying it with a warm and generous sentiment, and the earnest hope of strong and perpetual friendship between England and America. I felt at the moment, "Cursed be the hand that attempts to break it;" and albeit unused to taking the President and the people upon my shoulders, I answered as well as I could. Another toast followed to the health and successful journey of Mr. Catherwood and myself, and we rose from the table. The government dory lay at the foot of the lawn. Colonel McDonald put his arm through mine, and, walking away, told me that I was going into a distracted country; that Mr. Savage, the American consul at Guatemala, had, on a previous occasion, protected the property and lives of British subjects; and, if danger threatened me, I must assemble the Europeans, hang out my flag, and send word to him. I knew that these were not mere words of courtesy, and, in the state of the country to which I was going, felt the value of such a friend at hand.

Fortunately, Stephens had no occasion either to hang out his flag or to call for help; but he ran many risks and suffered hardships enough. At Izabal he saw the English engineer of the little steamer that had brought them into the Golfo Dulce, a man of Herculean frame, fall ill and lie helpless as a child. He remembered that he had been told that Izabal was a sickly place, and that it was running the gauntlet for life even to pass through it. He remembered, too, what he had strangely forgotten, that Shannon lay buried there; and he, like DeWitt, sought out the burial place, finding it on "a rising ground, open to the right, stretching way to the Golfo Dulce, and in front bounded by a gloomy forest". He also was depressed by the desolate spot, and ordered a fence to be built around the unmarked grave. Moreover, his friend "the padre promised to plant at its head a cocoa-nut tree". Cocoanuts and oranges! Whether DeWitt's young orange tree or the padre's cocoanut tree ever grew to drop their fruit in respectful homage on Shannon's grave, we do not know. Later passers-by tell us nothing. Rank tropical vegetation no doubt promptly claimed the lonely place and hid it forever from human view.

Stephens ran the gauntlet of fever at Izabal to encounter other hazards on the road. He and his party, mounted on mules and heavily armed, set out in the wake of a caravan of pack animals on the way to Guatemala. Passing a marshy plain, they soon entered an unbroken forest where the mules sank deep in puddles and mudholes. As they advanced the shade of the trees became thicker, the holes larger and deeper, and roots, rising two or three feet above the ground, crossed the path in every direction. At the foot of the Mico Mountains, over which they had to pass to enter the valley of the Motagua, the ascent began precipitously through a narrow gully, worn by the tracks of mules and the washing of mountain torrents. Beyond this defile they encountered still deeper mudholes and larger roots with the additional difficulty of a steep ascent. The woods were of impenetrable thickness, the rain poured, and there was no view except that of the detestable path before them. Stephens reflected that perhaps their inglorious epitaph might be, "tossed over the head of a mule, brained by the trunk of a mahogany tree, and buried in the mud of the Mico Mountain". Indeed all were tossed—Catherwood with such violence that Stephens, who witnessed his fall, was horrorstruck. The servant's mule fell backward, and then followed such a rolling and kicking on the part of man and beast that it seemed quite marvelous that nothing more serious resulted than a thorough plaster of mud for both. Stephens himself, when his turn came, by straining every nerve flung himself clear of roots and trees and barely missed impalement on his dagger, which had fallen from its sheath and stood with its foot of naked blade upright in the mud. Enough for one day—the first day—and enough to convince us that DeWitt could not have been guilty of exaggeration when he averred that he had been thrown three times on the whole journey. Indeed, in all the circumstances we are inclined to think that his "once at the hazard of my life" must have been a modest understatement of the facts in the case.

We cannot follow Stephens through all his adventures in Central America, for they were many and varied. At every turn he was exposed to perils. Not the least serious among them were those of which he had heard at Belize—the perils growing out of the distracted state of the country. On the way up to Guatemala, in spite of his official character, he was put under arrest and threatened with death by the ignorant and ruffianly alcalde of a wayside village; and at various points along the route he was saved from the violence of bandits by his own calm judgment and unflinching courage. Arriving at the capital he found the whole city in a state of awe. The term of the federal officers had expired some months before and no elections had been held to supply their places. Salvador and Quetzaltenango alone clung doubtfully to the federal idea, and Morazán, the champion of that cause, had abandoned the capital and now held momentary sway in Honduras. Carrera, an Indian, supported openly by a ragged and fanatical mob and covertly by the reactionary elements of the upper class, was master of Guatemala. The atmosphere was charged with hostility for foreigners. It had been some months before that the United States consul, Charles Savage, performed the act which won the admiration and gratitude of Colonel McDonald. On the occasion of an assault on the house of a British subject, one of the leading merchants of the place, Savage, as Stephens heard and related the incident

rushed down the street under a shower of bullets, knocking up bayonets and machetes, drove the mob back from the door, and, branding them as robbers and murderers, with his white hair streaming in the wind, poured out such a torrent of indignation and contempt, that the Indians, amazed at his audacity, desisted.

As yet there had been little change for the better. Only a few days before Stephens's arrival the British vice consul had been insulted and his flag fired upon. These acts seemed to be the expression of enmity not merely toward the British, but toward all foreigners. It was a dangerous state of affairs, yet the American representative passed through it all without suffering bodily harm.

Immediately after his arrival he took possession of DeWitt's house. On first viewing it he had been favorably impressed by its external appearance, and on entering he was charmed with its exterior. It was one of the finer residences of the city. Other houses of the capital were larger, "but mine", said Stephens, "combined more beauty and comfort than any habitation I ever saw". Yet ensconced in an official residence he had no official duties to perform. His credentials were addressed to a non-existent government, and unless Morazán, who still pursued the forlorn hope, should meet with success, it would become necessary to secure the archives, dispose of such property as could not be conveniently shipped to the United States, and close the legation. But Stephens did not sit in vain impatience awaiting developments. Central America lay before him with a thousand enticements, and he responded to its allurements. He traveled and observed, beginning with little journeys from Guatemala City as a base, and then extending his excursions to more distant parts of the country. From the Pacific coast of Guatemala, where he burned with fever and shook with ague, he embarked for Costa Rica, and on the voyage he lay in a hammock recuperating, an amusing himself by reading Gil Blas and Don Quixote. He traveled to the Costa Rican capital; ascended the volcano of Cartago, from which point he could view both the Atlantic and the Pacific; returned to the coast and journeyed northward on mule back; studied the Nicaragua Canal route in passing; visited old cities; climbed threatening volcanoes; rode through the whole length of Salvador; and, on his way to Guatemala met Morazán in utter rout before the fierce warriors of the Indian Carrera.

Convinced of the hopelessness of the federal cause, he put aside all idea of acting in an official capacity and devoted himself to archaeological investigations. He had already turned aside on his way up from Izabal to make a reconnaissance of Copán; and, during his absence in the south, Catherwood had descended the Motagua and examined the ruins of Quirigua. The two of them now set out along the great Guatemalan plateau, and entering the Mexican province of Chiapas, paused at Palenque to explore the highly interesting ruins in the neighborhood. Continuing their journey to the Gulf of Mexico, they went by water to the northern coast of Yucatán, and made a preliminary survey of a number of ruined cities there. They then set sail for New York. Rich in experience and laden with notes and drawings, the travelers returned to their starting point. They had been gone a little less than ten months, and within an even smaller space of time Stephens issued from the press, in two volumes, a fascinating account of their travels. Stephens's narrative, with its easy-flowing style, its vivid descriptions, and penetrating observations, together with Catherwood's excellent drawings portraying the little known monuments of a vanished civilization, gave the work an instant success. Edition after edition was called for, and thus the public as well as the department of state, acquired welcome, though belated, information about Central America.

What became of Stephens? The answer is that Central America enchanted him, and though it spared him for a time, at last it lured him to his death. As soon as his book was published he returned to Yucatán, accompanied as before by Catherwood, to carry forward his archaeological investigations. The fruit of the new expedition was another work no less felicitous than the first. After this he was elected a member of the New York State constitutional convention, and at about the same time he joined others in organizing the first American transatlantic steamship company. Then he became interested in the Panama Railroad Company and was successively its vice-president and president. This enterprise kept him for some time on the Isthmus, where his health, already undermined by his previous travels in Central America and Yucatán, at last gave way, and he passed to his reward at the untimely age of forty-seven.

The fragile and often broken thread must be taken up again. When Stephens disposed of DeWitt's paraphernalia and quit the Central American capital to wander among older and more interesting ruins, the break seemed to be final. But we never know what Washington will do. With William Henry Harrison in the White House and Daniel Webster at the state department it changed its mind. It heard rumors of a revival of the Central American federation, and, yearning for authentic information, designated William S. Murphy of Ohio as a "Special Confidential Agent" to go out and obtain it. Murphy's movements were relatively expeditious, and his sufferings, though great, were not beyond his power of description. Appointed in July, 1841, he reached Guatemala before the end of the year, "very sick of a fever taken on the road". Some weeks later he wrote: "I dislike apologies . . . but the chills and fever with which I have been afflicted . . . have greatly retarded my labors". These remarks were at the end of a thirty-five page legal cap letter. And he wrote other long reports. How much "authentic information" he might have provided if he had been at his best, is a subject upon which it would be futile to speculate.

Of one thing we may be certain: he could not have found any indication of a reviving federation, for there was none to find. On the contrary every sign pointed in the opposite direction. In the lucid intervals between his attacks of malaria, Murphy could see that. He could see too, that the reactionary elements in control were falling more and more under British influence, and that a corresponding sentiment of hostility toward the United States was being developed. He learned of the advantage the British were taking of the situation to make encroachments on the northern coasts of Honduras and Nicaragua, and of the tendency of those countries to look to the United States for protection against British aggression. In short, he saw and traced for the department of state the main outlines of the Central American question, now for the first time beginning to take definite form. Having done this—three months were required for the task—he escaped to the United States. But tropical disease apparently got him at last. He died during an epidemic of yellow fever in Galveston, a year or two later, while on a diplomatic mission the the Republic of Texas.

Six years passed before the United States called upon another of its sons to travel the dangerous road. Loath to admit the failure of the general government of Central America, the authorities at Washington were equally reluctant to recognize the existence of independent states within the territory once embraced in the single federation. Moreover, the energies of the northern republic, particularly in the Polk administration, were directed toward the acquisition of territory and the fixing of boundaries in the west. There were difficulties enough in that direction without rushing into new ones in the south. The British were free therefore to strengthen their hold on Guatemala, to ingratiate themselves with Costa Rica, and to seize such positions between these two states as were deemed essential for the control of interoceanic communication. As soon as the successful termination of the Mexican War seemed assured, however, the attention of the United States was turned once more toward the isthmian region. In March, 1848, Elijah Hise of Kentucky was commissioned as chargé d'affaires to Guatemala and empowered to conclude a treaty with Salvador. To this extent only was the dissolution of the federation acknowledged, no decision being made as to the status of the other countries formerly members of the union. Washington still hoped for the restoration of the federation, and if Hise found sentiment favorable he was to help bring it about. He was not, however, to challenge the British; for the treaty with Mexico not having been concluded, it was deemed unwise for the moment to bring the Central American question to an issue.

Hise chose the Panama route. The records do not show what considerations entered into his choice. It could hardly have escaped his notice that two good Kentuckians already lay mouldering in the ground at Izabal; and as he was to be accompanied by his wife, and a nephew—Kentuckians all—he may have been moved by the patriotic desire of conserving the noble strain to which he and they belonged. Unfortunately, he was not possessed of the pathfinding instincts of his forbears, and in his efforts to avoid a perilous road on the one hand he ran into a worse one on the other. On the voyage southward, early in the summer following his appointment, his ship was wrecked on one of the small islands of the Bahamas, and passengers and crew were forced to live for ten days on the barren spot in tents made of the sails of the disabled vessel. He had the good fortune, however, to find the means of continuing his voyage to the Isthmus. In three days, by the aid of canoe and the inevitable mule, he crossed with his suite to Panama; after which, he confessed, he and his family were indisposed. Weeks passed and no vessel sailed for the coast of Guatemala. In the meantime indisposition developed into serious illness, and as Hise's body suffered, his spirits sank. The Isthmus became a place of horror. Izabal could be no worse. In desperation he returned by a "dreadful and most hazardous" journey to Chagres, and sailed for Jamaica, where he expected to fall in with a vessel bound for the Bay of Honduras.

From Jamaica he wrote a doleful account of his sufferings; but he was not disposed to give up the mission. He had determined to send his wife and nephew back to the United States and then proceed by sea to the "Gulph of Dolce", from which, he declared, "I will if I live make my way by land to Guatemala." Yet he had the feeling that too much was expected of him. "If the mission is important," he complained, "the Govt. should enable me to get there or recall me." While waiting in Jamaica he was again prostrated with fever "and brought to the verge of the grave". Reduced to a mere skeleton, he "tottered on board" a vessel bound for Havana where he expected to find an opportunity to proceed on his journey; but he thought it was "due to truth and candour" to say that he almost despaired of reaching his destination alive. He expressed the hope that on account of the wretched state of his health the president would conceive it proper to recall him. Then, as if by magic and much to the credit of Havana, his health improved. He embarked for Omoa. On the way his health continued to improve and as his spirits rose correspondingly, he began to ponder on the destiny of his country. "By the by," he volunteered,

I should like to say something on the Cuba Question. A question upon which I think I am pretty well informed, but it would be out of place here; I would certainly give my support most cordially to an administration that should be in favor of—and knew how *to* EFFECT the ANNEXATION of Cuba to the United States.

It mattered little now that twenty days were required to sail from Omoa to the Golfo Dulce, and it mattered less that his vessel went on the rocks before it reached Izabal. The traveler was well, his wife and nephew were safe at home, and the dangers ahead seemed of little consequence. So they proved to be. After six months of wanderings and of torment our agent came happily to his destination.

He achieved little. While he peregrinated in the Caribbean the party in power at Washington went to the polls and lost. Three months after he reached Guatemala, the new administration took over the reins of government. Hise was then recalled; but as he did not for some time receive the letter communicating the fact, he remained at his post until the following summer. During his residence, which was thus extended to seven or eight months, he divided his time with perfect impartiality between the things he was authorized to do and the things he was not authorized to do. He concluded a commercial convention with Guatemala, in accordance with his instructions; and he tried to negotiate a similar convention with Salvador, also in accordance with his instructions. But this was dull work. What fascinated him was the forbidden challenge to England. He had not long been in Guatemala when he wrote the secretary of state:

It is clear to my mind that Great Britain designs to become the owner and occupant by force or stratagem of the ports on the Atlantic and Pacific coasts of Nicaragua which will be the points of termination of the canal communication between the two oceans.

Later he wrote:

English agents and influence under the experienced direction of the British Consul Genl. Fredk. Chatfield are alive and at work both in C. A. and at London to produce results most inimical to the U. S. and to embarrass and obstruct any negotiations here. I have reference to the Mosq. question.

Under conditions so provoking how could any chivalrous American refrain from throwing down the challenge to Great Britain? Hise could not. Authority or no authority he could not stand idly by and see weak nations overridden by a mighty power, and, incidentally, his own country deprived of a free crossing place to the Pacific. He entered into correspondence with the victims—inspirited them, urged them to resist the wicked designs of the British nation. Nicaragua being an especial object of his solicitude, he urged its government, with warm words of encouragement, to look to the great republic of the north for protection. "I say to you," he declared,

that the United States hopes and desires that the state of Nicaragua will stand on her rights, and that she may not for a moment consent to yield to the Diplomatic arts that may be practiced or the threats of hostility which may be uttered by Great Britain a single foot of her rights of Territory & Dominion in and upon the Mosquito Coast & Country and over the River and Port of San Juan de Nicaragua.

It so happened that Nicaragua was in the mood to throw itself into protecting arms. Accordingly, it sent a commissioner to negotiate with Hise. The result was a canal convention by the terms of which the United States was obligated to guarantee the sovereignty of Nicaragua over territory which the British stood ready to defend in the name of the Mosquito king. This was the challenge. But it never became effective. The new administration at Washington pursued a course of conciliation, not of challenge. Hise had his trouble for nothing.

In the best of circumstances, there was little that any United States agent could do; for Central America had fallen under the dominion of Britain. Though it was almost at our doors, its approaches were guarded by the British outposts of Jamaica and Belize. Its flanks—Guatemala and Costa Rica—while American forces slept, had surrendered to British direction and control. Its Atlantic shore line, embracing the eastern terminus of the Nicaraguan Canal route, had become in effect British territory under a thin Mosquito mask. Its Bay of Fonseca, dominating the western terminus of the route, lay under the guns of British warships. Its whole extent of land and waters was under the observation of British officials. Its very existence as a single state was subject to British whim. In the achievement of all this there had been no muddling through: no aimless, wanton aggression; no dying of agents *en route;* no floundering on the road. Everything had been done effectively and in proper season. Everything had been foreseen and prearranged. Every move in the north had been met by a countervailing move in the south. The field of battle had been prepared. The British were at their posts.

Such was the Central American situation in 1849; such the result of a quarter of a century of diplomatic preparation on the part of Great Britain; such the result of a quarter of a century of diplomatic futility on the part of the United States.

Other Articles of Interest

Griffith, William J. "The Historiography of Central America since 1830." XL (1960), 548-569.

————. "Juan Galindo, Central American Chauvinist." XL (1960), 25-52.

Kenyon, Gordon, "Mexican Influence in Central America, 1821–1823." XLI (1961), 175-205.

Naylor, Robert A. "The British Role in Central America Prior to the Clayton-Bulwer Treaty of 1850." XL (1960), 361-382.

Parker, Franklin D. "José Cecilio del Valle: Scholar and Patriot." XXXII (1952) 516-539.
José Cecilio del Valle, elected president of Central America, was accorded a considerable recognition by his own generation but has been relegated to comparative obscurity by later generations. Arce has come to be regarded as the greatest champion of Central American independence and Morazán is remembered as an outstanding advocate of Central American liberalism and federation. But Valle did more than Arce to win independence from Spain and Mexico, and if he had lived longer his plans and methods would have contributed more than Morazán's to preserve the

union and effect reform. Of the three only Valle understood the advantage of Central America's non-violent independence and sought to use this advantage to develop the peaceful and orderly progress of the nation. Valle was an early proponent of Pan-Americanism, vice-president of the Mexican congress, correspondent of European savants, member of the ruling triumvirate of Central America (1823), and member of the Central American congress. In presidential elections he won more electoral votes than Arce in 1825 and nearly as many as Morazán in 1830. In elections in 1834 Valle won by a clear majority only to die before the votes were counted.

Perry, Edward. "Central American Union." V (1922), 30–51.
A brief summary of the attempts at union by the Central American states, from their independence in 1821 until now. The few months of incorporation with Mexico under Iturbide and steps toward federation in 1842, 1845, 1847, 1852, 1862, 1876, 1885, 1887, 1890, 1895, and 1921 are discussed. The constitution of 1921, accepted by Guatemala, Honduras, and El Salvador, is described, as is also the prevention of Guatemala's participation because of revolution.

Scheips, Paul J. "Gabriel Lafond and Ambrose W. Thompson: Neglected Isthmian Promoters." XXXVI (1956), 211–228.

Selva, Salomón de la. "On the Proposed Union of Central America." III (1920), 566–570.
The need of the Central American states for United States support and encouragement in their movement toward union is emphasized. The desire for union has apparently existed since their independence. The only reasons for failure are the petty jealousies of dictators and military forces. Believing now that conditions favor union, Dr. Selva begs the United States to invite the delegates to Washington, to assist with advice, and to give them confidence through her own friendship in the movement.

Smith, Robert S. "Financing the Central American Federation, 1821–1838." XLIII (1963), 483–510.

Stanger, Francis Merriman. "National Origins in Central America." XII (1932), 18–45.
The five republics have developed nationally because of their isolation and their closer contact with outside powers than with one another. Furthermore, they differ in their relationship to native races. In the beginning they were willing to accept the Plan of Iguala, but the Mexican debacle left each a separate province; nevertheless, they desired centralization or annexation to a neighbor.

Valle, Rafael Heliodoro. "Dionisio de Herrera, 1783–1850: A Centennial Tribute." XXX (1950), 554–558.
Dionisio de Herrera lived through the most terrible years of Central American history. He wrote the declaration of political independence of Tegucigalpa (1821), served as elected representative to the Imperial Congress of Mexico (1822), and held many high offices, including that of chief of

state, in Honduras. He was a moral thinker, a believer in civil equity, and a practical statesman. He died in poverty and disillusionment.

Van Aken, Mark J. "British Policy Considerations in Central America before 1850." XLII (1962), 54–59.

Van Alstyne, Richard W. "The Central American Policy of Lord Palmerston, 1846–1848." XVI (1936), 339–359.

Williams, Mary Wilhelmine. "The Ecclesiastical Policy of Francisco Morazán and the Other Central American Liberals." III (1920), 119–143.

---

10. México y lo Mexicano

JOHN LEDDY PHELAN

Mexican historians have produced both solid volumes resulting from archival investigations and many lively essays that reflect their interest in philosophy and their concern to discover the true nature of their national culture. Leopoldo Zea, editor of the collection reviewed below, has provided stimulating leadership to Mexican writers in the latter approach. Anyone who would learn about the varieties of history cultivated in Mexico will discover much valuable material in this series. Professor Phelan, himself deeply concerned with intellectual history, teaches Latin American history at the University of Wisconsin.

A careful examination of this collection * illuminates many facets of the contemporary Mexican mind. This accomplishment in some substantial measure may be attributed to Leopoldo Zea's editorship of the series, for he formulated the philosophical framework that lends to its diverse com-

---

* The series is published in Mexico City by Porrúa y Obregón and Antigua Librería Robredo. The individual numbers are as follows: No. 1, *La X en la frente (Algunas páginas sobre México)*, by Alfonso Reyes. 1952. Pp. 93; No. 2, *Conciencia y posibilidad del mexicano*, by Leopoldo Zea. 1952. Pp. 110; No. 3, *Mito y magia del mexicano*, by Jorge Carrión. 1952. Pp. 104; No. 4, *Análisis del ser del mexicano*, by Emilio Uranga. 1952. Pp. 100; No. 5, *Cornucopia de México*, by José Moreno Villa. 1952. Pp. 149; No. 6, *El amor y la amistad en el mexicano*, by Salvador Reyes Nevárez. 1952. Pp. 93; Nos. 7 and 11, *En torno a la filosofía mexicana*, by José Gaos. 1952, 1953. Pp. 90, 83; No. 8, *Isagoge sobre lo mexicano*, by César Garizurieta. 1952. Pp. 93; No. 9, *Gusto de México*, by Mariano Picón-Salas. 1952. Pp. 98; No. 10, *Variaciones sobre tema mexi-*

ponents a coherent unity. The contributors to this series share a common objective: to discover the national ethos of Mexican culture.

Few of these volumes exceed one hundred pages, hence they are not intended to be works of exhaustive or original investigation. They are actually syntheses of prior monographic investigations, revisions of previously printed works, or hypotheses for future research. To reach the large audience of non-specialists is the announced objective. Many of the contributors bring to this task that high degree of literary excellence and that apparent, although sometimes deceptive, facility for discussing ideas that we in the Anglo-Saxon world have come to appreciate as a characteristic of the intellectual life of Latin cultures. In a collection of this size, the quality of the individual contributions is bound to be uneven. Yet none of these volumes lacks solid merit. Limitations of space, however, compel that the focus be placed on only those which seem to typify certain salient characteristics of the Mexican mind.

Specialists in a wide variety of disciplines are here represented, although the stress is on philosophy and history. The roster of contributors includes such distinguished names as Alfonso Reyes, Leopoldo Zea, Mariano Picón-Salas, Silvio Zavala, and José Gaos, as well as a host of younger scholars of promise and talent. Among the later, Ramón Xirau, José Durand, Francisco de la Maza, Juan Ortega y Medina, María Elvira Bermúdez, and Emilio Uranga deserve particular mention. There are some contributors who are non-residents of Mexico, including Mariano Picón-Salas, Paul Westheim, and José Moreno Villa.

The quest for knowledge about *homo mexicanus* owes its origins to the influence that the philosophy of the late Spaniard José Ortega y Gasset has been exercising over some of the keenest minds in contemporary Mexico. In the late 1920's, Samuel Ramos led his generation of *contemporáneos* from the French-inspired philosophical romanticism of Antonio Caso and José Vasconcelos to the German-oriented philosophy of Ortega.

In Ortega's "perspectivist" conception, philosophy is not a quest for certainty, but rather a search for a point of view on human existence. Ortega's celebrated postulate was: *Yo soy yo y mi circunstancia*. Historically speaking, the Orteguian philosophy replaced the *res cogitans* of Cartesian

---

cano, by Luís Cernuda. 1952. Pp. 81; Nos. 11 and 7, *En torno a la filosofía mexicana*, by José Gaos. 1953, 1952. Pp. 83, 90; No. 12, *Aproximaciones a la historia de México*, by Silvio Zavala. 1953. Pp. 160; Nos. 13 and 22, *México en la conciencia anglosajona*, by Juan A. Ortega y Medina. 2 vols. 1953, 1955. Pp. 120, 160; No. 14, *El occidente y la conciencia de México*, by Leopoldo Zea. 1953. Pp. 87; Nos. 15 and 16, *La transformación social del conquistador*, by José Durand. 2 vols. 1953. Pp. 87, 95; No. 17, *El guadalupanismo mexicano*, by Francisco de la Maza. 1953. Pp. 130; No. 18, *La calavera*, by Paul Westheim, Translated by Mariana Frenk. 1953. Pp. 123; No. 19, *Tres poetas de la soledad*, by Ramón Xirau. 1955. Pp. 73; No. 20, *La vida familiar del mexicano*, by María Elvira Bermúdez. 1955. Pp. 140; No. 21, *La emancipación literaria de México*, by José Luís Martínez. 1955. Pp. 88; Nos. 22 and 13, *México en la conciencia anglosajona*, by Juan A. Ortega y Medina. 2 vols. 1955, 1953. Pp. 160, 120; No. 23, *Crónica de México*, by Alfredo Cardona Peña. 1955. Pp. 115.

rationalism or the *ego cogitans* of post-Kantian idealism with the *ego circumstans*. Analytically, the proposition means that my ego, the second *yo*, is but one component of the total reality of my life, the first *yo*, whose other element is the world around me, *mi circunstancia*. From the onto-logical viewpoint, man neither makes himself in a vacuum nor does environment make him a victim. Man is free to determine what he is going to become, within the limitations imposed by the circumstances of his time, his place, and his history.

For Ortega there was no metaphysics, only metahistory, or better still, metaculture. The philosopher's task was not to learn the ways of nature, but the meaning of culture. As Patrick Romanell has already pointed out, Ortega attempted to do to metaphysics what Nietzsche previously had done to God. Both were expelled from philosophy.

Ortega's perspectivism coincides with the general trend in modern philosophy toward historical relativism and cultural pluralism. His outstanding contributions were in the nature of refinements. Perspectives are national and generational in character. Each nation as well as each generation develops a combination of fears, goals, and beliefs, a point of view toward the world which is unique. Samuel Ramos in the late 1920's found in Ortega's ideas an historical justification for a national Mexican philosophy. There is, Ramos argued, a Mexican point of view which is as fully justified as the European point of view. In his *El perfil del hombre y la cultura en México* (1931) he set out to explore the "circumstances" of Mexican culture with a method he borrowed from Alfred Adler's psycho-analysis. His diagnosis was that Mexican culture suffered from an "inferiority complex." Since independence, Mexico has copied indiscriminately American, French and British institutions and ideas without taking into account the Mexican circumstances of her mestizo culture. The national inferiority complex intensified as Mexicans became enviously aware of the wide chasm between the inferior copies of culture they had and the superior foreign models they never could have.

The full impact of Orteguian philosophy, however, was not felt until a gifted and diverse group of Spanish Republican exiles settled in Mexico after the end of the Spanish civil war. Spanish professors exposed a generation of Mexican students to modern German philosophy which Ortega a generation earlier had introduced into Spain both in his essays and in his editorial work in the *Revista de Occidente* and the publishing house of Espasa-Calpe. Thus, Mexican students were introduced to the existentialist wing of the phenomenological movement led by Edmund Husserl and Martin Heidegger and the historicism of Wilhelm Dilthey. Of all the Spanish *maestros*, José Gaos has exercised the most decisive influence on the present generation of Mexican students. A monument to his pedagogic labors is this series under review, for many of its contributors are his students.

Many of Gaos' students have set themselves apart as a "generation" distinct from the one whose spokesman was Ramos. The Orteguian-inspired intent of this collection under review is to spell out the "point of view" of this generation. Leopoldo Zea, Emilio Uranga, Edmundo O'Gorman, and Justino Fernández are just a few of the most articulate members of this group which has adopted the Greek myth of Hyperion as their symbol.

Basing themselves squarely on the cultural pluralism and the historical relativism of Ortega and Dilthey, the Hyperions have responded to the stimulus provided by the existentialist philosophy of Martin Heidegger. Ortega himself pointed the way in this direction, for he was among many other things an existentialist philosopher. The Mexicans, however, have a more direct contact with the primary sources of existentialism. José Gaos had translated into Spanish Heidegger's much discussed, but little read, *Sein und Zeit,* and the Mexican existentialists have chosen selectively some of Heidegger's concepts to describe Mexican culture.

Existentialism is not merely an exotic philosophical attitude applied to the social context of contemporary Mexico, for, in spite of its obscure and occult terminology, the philosophy of Heidegger responds to attitudes toward life that Hispanic peoples instinctively understand. This outlook can best be expressed by the much used phrase, the tragic sense of life. Heidegger conceived of human life as restlessness, preoccupation, and insecurity. Man is a transitional being, contradictory and mysterious, an idealist and a skeptic, a dreamer and a cynic, a mystic and a sensualist. Recognizing his tragic weakness as a finite and helpless being in a universe permeated with anguish, man achieves the realization of his selfhood by recognizing the temporality of human existence. Man is a being who exists in order to die. Heidegger's conception of man's restless search to achieve a fuller expression of his authentic selfhood in the face of endless obstacles strikes another responsive chord in Hispanic minds: the stoical wisdom of intellectual resignation.

The pivotal principles in Heidegger's thought are metaphysical despair, the necessity for human freedom, and the centrality of individual decision. For Heidegger, the essence of man emerges from the fortitude and the firmness with which he confronts his choices and takes his decisions. In an age in which a mass and mechanistic society has made aggressive inroads on the private domain of the individual, Heidegger's emphasis on the act of willing and the moral processes of self-fulfillment appear like a reformulation of the positive values of humanism. Heidegger's anthropocentrism in which there is no metaphysics for God or for nature is bound to appeal to a group of intellectuals such as the present generation in Mexico. They cherish a tradition of individual humanism, and they are genuinely alarmed that increasing industrialization threatens to dehumanize their culture. The Germanization of the modern Mexican mind, therefore, is not as radical a departure from tradition as might first appear. The Mexican existentialists are defending with Germanic weapons ideals and aspirations as old as Hispanic culture itself.

An ambitious attempt to apply Heideggerian concepts to Mexican conditions is Emilio Uranga's *Análisis del ser del mexicano*. Uranga subjects Ramos' hypothesis to a rigorous phenomenological scrutiny. The Mexican, he feels, is essentially sentimental. All his responses stem from a pathological fear of being harmed by the outside world that he instinctively views as hostile. Melancholy and lazy, he is insecure and oscillates between extremes. Uranga's ontology of *homo mexicanus* grows out of of his characterological analysis. He draws a sharp distinction between inferiority and insufficiency, as Ramos did not. Inferiority presupposes insufficiency, but the reverse does not apply, for inferiority is only one of the possibilities inherent in a situation of insufficiency. By no means is it the only one, and certainly it is not the choice that Heidegger regarded as the authentic one.

Like Ramos, Uranga believes that the national inferiority complex grew out of the conquest. The Indians deliberately placed themselves in the role of "children" toward their Spanish "fathers." The Aztecs mistakenly took Cortés' warriors for gods. The mestizo offspring of the Aztecs continued to hold the same attitude but in a less recognizable fashion. The mestizo endowed the Spaniard with God-like attributes of limitless perfection. Regarding himself as inferior to the Spaniard, the mestizo sought to model himself after the Spaniard. From the sixteenth century to the twentieth century, the mestizo has sought to mimic someone else whom he has elevated to a pedestal of superiority. In the sixteenth century the Spaniards played this role. In the nineteenth century, the English, the French, and the Americans merely replaced the Spaniards.

The existentialist interpretation of *indigenismo* is bound to cause a minor explosion, for existentialists regard that movement as the most recent expression of the imitative tendency that has dominated the Mexican mind since the conquest. In championing the cause of the Indian, the mestizo merely seeks to justify himself by projecting himself into another culture. So do the hispanophiles, the Europeanizers, and the Americanizers. Some measure of a fragile and false sense of security is found in imitating someone else. All these responses arose as a means of escaping from a world which to the mestizo seemed a Heideggerian universe of anguish and nothingness. To the existentialists, the Mexicans must seek their self-justification not through imitating other cultures, but by articulating from the chaos and the anguish of the world around them the authentic values of their own mestizo civilization. To this extent, Ramos' original hypothesis has been "existentialized" by the present generation.

Leopoldo Zea provides a historical complement to Uranga's ontological analysis. Reviewing the principal epochs of Mexico's development from the conquest to the Revolution of 1910, he diagnoses the root of all evil as the trend toward indiscriminate Europeanization. The early Christian missionaries, the creole leaders after independence, and the *científicos* of the Díaz regime, each with a different program, sought to Europeanize the natives without taking into account Mexican conditions. Each failed, and each failure intensified the national inferiority complex. Zea interprets the Revolution of 1910 as the first systematic attempt to reverse the trend from Europeanization to Mexicanization.

This new and highly articulate interpretation of Mexican history may be susceptible to revision in detail as well as in structure. Ultimately it may be repudiated. But today it represents the most evocative interpretation of Mexican history to emerge from contemporary Mexico.

Mexico's mission in this century, according to Zea, is to realize her cultural autonomy to complement the political emancipation she won in the last century. Although the whole emphasis in this collection is nationalistic, the spirit and the tone of its diverse components are scarcely parochial. All these writers demonstrate an acute sensitivity to Mexico's relations with other cultures; they are all poignantly aware of how those relations have shaped and often distorted Mexican development. Managing to strike a sound balance between cultural nationalism and cultural universalism, they argue that Mexico cannot make her unique contribution to other civilizations until the Mexicans discover the "Mexican."

Zea relates Mexico's declaration of cultural independence to contemporary world history. The people of Mexico, like the nations of Asia today, perhaps those of Africa tomorrow, are in revolt against the West. They are repudiating the Occident's claims to universality and cultural predominance. Now that Western civilization itself is in crisis, Zea suggests that the former colonial peoples of Asia and Hispanic America can offer something positive from their own indigenous cultures toward a new world civilization that will be more truly universal than that which the West previously offered.

In the existentialist frame of reference, the historian has a precise role to fill, for existentialists reject the idea that the past has no influence on the present. Man is an entity whose being consists not only in what he previously was but also in what he eventually may become; inherent in human existence is the possibility of choosing alternatives. Men's choices are limited, but not necessarily dominated, by the character of past events and by the concrete situation of the present. The past cannot be integrally restored, but certain historical traditions are apt to recur. The historian's task is to illustrate how the past conditions and delimits the range of alternatives for the future. Hence the existentialist historian orients himself toward the future.

The historian's point of departure is himself and the culture in which he lives. As a "cultural psychoanalyst" the Mexican historian must explore the origins and the development of those resentments and frustrations which caused the national inferiority complex. Only thus can future generations be liberated from those subconscious resentments which have thwarted Mexico's self-expression. The past must be relegated to the past by exposing it as such.

This conception of the role of the historian obviously has influenced the kind of topics that existentialist-minded scholars have chosen to investigate and the nature of the conclusions they have reached. In this collection there is a study by José Durand on the sociological adjustment of the conquistadores to the American scene. Francisco de la Maza illuminates how the cult of the Virgin of Guadalupe became a central focus around which some creole spokesmen sought to articulate the aspirations of their class through identifying the American creoles with the Indian Virgin of Guadalupe. Juan Ortega y Medina in studying the attitudes of Anglo-Saxon travelers to Mexican society points up the interrelations between foreign visitors' unsympathetic response to Mexican customs and the mania of the mestizos toward Europeanization. José Gaos' analysis of philosophical speculation in Mexico provides an historical framework for the emergence of a national Mexican philosophy. The same nationalist perspective conditions José Luis Martínez' account of Mexican literature. Even the professional historian Silvio Zavala, no existentialist himself, has chosen topics responsive to the aspirations of the present generation—the interaction of cultures in Mexican history and Mexico's contacts with other cultures. Each one of these studies is of undisputed merit, but they cannot be entirely understood except in relation to the climate of opinion they reflect and also attempt to formulate.

There are several lacunae. It is indeed ironic that an extensive series devoted to the history of Mexican culture contains no fresh interpretations of baroque architecture or the contemporary painting movement. Any formulation of the national ethos remains sorely incomplete without a consideration of these two artistic phenomena—preeminently Mexican in their expression and form and hence universal in their meaning.

Nor is this collection wholly representative of the present existentialist generation. Volumes by Justino Fernández and Edmundo O'Gorman have been promised, but have not yet appeared. A volume by Jorge Portilla, one of the founders of the Hyperion group, *La crisis norteamericana en la conciencia de México*, has long been delayed. Such a study is a must in view of their conviction that the United States is one cause of the national inferiority complex.

The present generation affectionately regards Samuel Ramos as its precursor. This collection affords ample evidence of how the disciples view their prophet. It is a pity that Ramos' promised contribution to the collection, *El mexicano del medio siglo*, has not yet appeared. It would be enlightening to learn how the prophet regards his disciples.

The fact that many of the announced volumes have not been published suggests the possibility that the future of the collection is uncertain. An exciting series of titles has been promised, but whether they will be published remains to be seen. One suspects that the initial enthusiasm animating the organizers of the project has diminished. What has been accomplished to date is an evocative achievement. The job ought to be finished.

The composite picture of Mexico that emerges from this collection is not pretty. Neither is it lurid. The self-analysis is candid, realistic, and mature. These writers avoid the extremes of either pessimism or optimism, self-pity or self-adulation. They all believe that the deficiencies in Mexican society that they have exposed are susceptible to remedy. At first glance it seems paradoxical that German existentialism with its essentially pessimistic view of human life has so deeply influenced a group of thinkers who are fundamentally optimistic about Mexico's chances for realizing a fuller cultural self-expression by means of a drastic revision of social and individual goals. This apparent anomaly suggests that the Mexicans have been selective in their response to the stimulus of existentialism.

Heideggerian pessimism permeates their description of Mexico's past. A kind of Orteguian optimism conditions their own outlook toward the future. Let there be no misunderstanding about their repudiation of the traditional idea of progress. They deny that change entails inevitable amelioration. Change also produces retrogression. Men can only choose for the better on the basis of authentic self-knowledge of the past in the Heideggerian sense.

What these Mexicans do not stress is a sociological approach to understanding Mexican culture. Some North American social scientists such as David Riesman, William F. Whyte, Margaret Mead, W. Lloyd Warner, and Robert and Helen Lynd have reinterpreted American society in an evocative fashion. These methods could fruitfully be applied to a study of Mexican society. Yet few contemporary Mexicans have done so. Studies on Mexico by Redfield, Parsons, Kelly, Brand, Foster, and Lewis have demonstrated the usefulness of this methodology. The ontological postulate of existentialism has led these Mexicans to ask the question: What is the Mexican man? They have seldom asked: How do Mexicans of different classes function in their society? The interaction of individuals to groups, of groups to classes, of class to class, the meaning of social status, and the operation of upward social mobility in a society undergoing change—all are sociological issues that seldom concern the contributors to this collection and might well engage their attention.

There is one notable exception to this tendency and that is María Elvira Bermúdez' *La vida familiar del mexicano*. Adopting the psychosociological methods of Adler and Fromm, the author first places family relations inside the class framework. Disdainful of womanhood and yet obsessed by his desire for women, the Mexican male in his attitude toward the other sex is a blend of pride and cruelty. He gives full reign to the *donjuanismo* to which he has been socially conditioned. The *machismo* of the males has created *hembrismo* in the women, an exaggerated intensification of certain feminine characteristics. Fatalistically and blindly submitting to the man's world in which she lives, the Mexican woman has traditionally sought in Roman Catholicism solace for her thwarted self-expression. Yet her much publicized Catholicism, the author suggests, may just be a façade behind which she conceals her real goal in life: not to live according to the lofty ethic of Christian morality, but rather to insure for herself a comfortable material existence as a compensation for her frustrations. Señorita Bermúdez sees in the *machismo-hembrismo* dichotomy the root of the civic irresponsibility and the lack of moral cohesiveness which Leopoldo Zea deplores. Her plea for a fuller and more interdependent role for the two sexes in Mexican society merits further attention. What should be stressed here, however, is that her sociological approach is one that could yield fruitful results if applied oftener by Mexican scholars.

Mexican society is undergoing a series of swift changes, whose total consequences are by no means apparent. Although industrialization is altering the social character of that land, few of the contributors to this series see fit to explore systematically the influence of these technological changes on the social structure. Many of the authors are eloquent spokesmen of the new cultural nationalism that dominates the intellectual landscape of contemporary Mexico. Yet it is no historical accident that the formulation of this goal of cultural autonomy coincides with the rise of the aspiration for economic autonomy through industrialization. Economic colonialism and cultural colonialism, which have plagued Mexico in the past, were not disconnected phenomena, and the relationship between the goals of economic sufficiency and cultural autonomy might well be explored.

It is apparent that the Mexican existentialists fear that industrialization will be superimposed indiscriminately, much in the same way that Anglo-Saxon political institutions were blindly imitated in the last century. Such a development could result in a dehumanization of Mexican culture as well as a further intensification of the national inferiority complex. These apprehensions are by no means groundless, but they cannot be dissipated by ignoring the existence of the issue. With a candor and fortitude of the type that Heidegger himself has outlined, the Mexican humanists must study systematically how a quasi-industrialized society can adjust to the circumstances of its mestizo culture.

If American scholars might examine with advantage the creative use that the present generation in Mexico is making of some concepts borrowed from Ortega and Heidegger, it is equally true that the Mexicans might profit from a more extensive use of some of the social science methods recently applied in the United States. Both peoples should become more aware of the differing climates of opinion prevailing in each culture, of which these two methodologies are but graphic reflections. Herein lies the basic significance for us of the collection under review. What these Mexican scholars are doing has a meaning that transcends the frontiers of Mexico. What they are thinking is of pertinence to the outside world. Their thoughts deserve to be pondered.

11. Dwight Morrow and the Mexican Revolution

STANLEY ROBERT ROSS

What caused the Mexican Revolution to slow down during the years 1928 to 1934? Were the cynicism and conservatism which overwhelmed the Revolutionary leaders in this period primarily a result of the "sinister" influence of U.S. Ambassador Dwight Morrow, as some writers have maintained? Dean Ross of the State University of New York at Stony Point here analyzes this controversial issue and assesses Morrow's relation to great issues of the period in Mexico: land, petroleum, and the Church.

When death came suddenly to Dwight Morrow in October, 1931, hardly more than a year after he had resigned his Mexican post, the eulogistic statements by Mexican officials and the editorial comment in the press went far beyond the requirements of international courtesy. Indeed, they tended to reflect a genuine affection for the man and a perception that his mission had signalized a new era in Mexican-American relations. In 1935 officials in the Secretaría de Relaciones Exteriores suggested to the Secretaría de Gobernación the appropriateness of naming the street in Cuernavaca on which the Morrow house was located after the former Ambassador. The Morrows had felt very much a part of Cuernavaca and had a strong attachment for their *Casa Mañana* on Calle Arteaga, the narrow, cobble-stoned street which the poetic Mrs. Morrow had described as an "unbroken line of painted adobe houses" running "from a pink church on a hill to a pink sunset on a mountain. . . ."

The Interior Department passed the recommendation along to the Governor of Morelos who, in turn, issued a directive to the *Ayuntamiento* of Cuernavaca. The city fathers obediently, but enthusiastically, complied. The following year, two bank clerks removed the plaques bearing Morrow's name on the street and replaced them with anti-American slogans. While the government ordered the plaques restored and those responsible for the vandalism punished, the incident suggests, perhaps, something more fundamental than the delinquency of a pair of *chamacos*. The recurrence of diplomatic tension between the two countries could have evoked the xenophobia or, more specifically, the anti-Americanism which strongly

From Volume XXXVIII (1958), pages 506–528.

colored the Mexican Revolution. More directly, the incident may have been symbolic of an underlying antagonism against the man who, it was alleged, had called a halt to that movement.

The charge that Mr. Morrow applied the brakes to the Mexican Revolution is understandable in terms of his background and of what apparently was happening between 1928 and 1934 in Mexico. Seductively appealing is the logic which ascribed to Morrow a role consistent with his antecedents as a corporation lawyer and Morgan partner. Also, it was convenient and satisfying to be able to blame the *yanqui* diplomat for the cynicism and conservatism which overwhelmed Mexican revolutionary leaders during those years.

This viewpoint, including the ridiculous explanation that Morrow had mesmerized Plutarco Elías Calles, was at first confined to gossip, private conversations, and extremist newspapers. A government official remarked to Commercial Attaché George Wythe that "Mr. Morrow is more dangerous to Mexico than was Ambassador Sheffield," implying that economic subordination and cultural infiltraton might be more threatening to Mexican nationality than military intervention. In more recent years this interpretation of the Morrow mission has been noted or espoused on both sides of the border.

Some have merely indicated that many Mexicans "believed . . . that [Morrow's] mission wrecked their Revolution." The author of a well-known history of Mexico asserts that Morrow played an important part in the "change of the *Callista* machine from an instrument of reform to one of reaction." Although this particular writer concedes that the desertion of the principles of the Revolution perhaps was inevitable, he contends that Morrow hastened the process by providing a rational justification. Eyler N. Simpson neatly summed up this attitude in the following appropriately cautious, but beguilingly suggestive, passage:

I simply note the fact that coincident with [Morrow's] residence the life went out of their revolution. . . . It may be that the revolutionary movement had already run its course. On the other hand, it may be that the kindly, sympathetic, well-intentioned, subtly flattering former Morgan partner by trying to help Mexico to put her house in order and to settle everything up in ship-shape, businesslike fashion succeeded in putting the brakes on the only real reform movement in the history of the country.

The Mexican Revolution, initiated as a political movement against the dictatorship of Porfirio Díaz, had evoked a response from the Mexican people suffering more direct grievances and aspiring to even more immediate, if less articulated, needs. The political breakthrough made possible the agrarian reform which answered the elemental cry for land. Agrarianism proved to be the keystone of a movement dominated by nationalism and directed toward the ordering of the Mexican household of which the Mexicans were to be the masters.

The state, controlled by nationals, was to be strengthened through positive delegations of authority and through the assertion of dominion over the subsoil resources. New pillars of governmental support were created by the extension and revitalization of the landowning peasant communities and by the creation of a privileged, government sustained labor movement which would provide leverage against foreign dominated capitalism. The revolutionary movement sought, indirectly, to assure the independence and strength of the Mexican state by attacking rival elements in the social structure: foreign capitalism, the hacienda system, and the Church.

These revolutionary aspirations were given legal form in the Constitution of 1917 and, during the following decade, received pragmatic, experimental application. Both in method and intent these reforms conflicted with American vested interests. The result was extended diplomatic controversy with overtones of intervention and conflict. The Morrow mission represented a turning point in the relations between the two countries and, at least, a temporary abatement of the tensions. The coincidence of this achievement with a noticeable retreat from revolutionary principles provide the circumstances for the allegation that Morrow had applied the brakes. While it can be established beyond question that due to the exigencies of the internal and external situation Mexican leaders had determined to abandon intransigence for conciliation before Morrow set foot in Mexico, the seriousness of the charge warrants detailed examination of what Ambassador Morrow was trying to do, what he did in respect to specific problems involving essential revolutionary principles, and where coincidence ends and causality begins.

Dwight Morrow, like his predecessors, went to Mexico to protect American interests. However, there was a significant contrast in his concept of the nature of those interests and the spirit in which he sought to defend them. Morrow rejected the use of force as well as the premise, assumed by Secretary Frank B. Kellogg, that vested property rights were superior under international law to sovereignty and could never be impaired. Morrow once remarked that

it is the duty of every one of our diplomatic representatives to a foreign nation to defend faithfully the proper interests of his country and of his countrymen. That is his legal . . . and . . . moral duty. If he fails in that duty, no other success can compensate for that failure. But it is also the duty of the representative of the foreign country to defend his country and his countrymen. We can best defend the rights of our own country when we understand the rights of other countries.

This was the key to Morrow's approach as well as the basis for his success. By charm, sincerity, and good will he cleared the atmosphere, dispelling the clouds of fear and distrust. The Mexicans were impressed by his intellectual ability, knowledge, and indefatigable application, charmed by his simplicity and informality, inspired by his trust, and bemused by his absent-mindedness and by his well-intentioned efforts to employ the few Spanish words he had acquired. Morrow had no ear for music or language, and the words "Sonora" and "Señora" were interchanged with happy abandon. More fundamental, however, were his efforts to understand Mexico and the Mexican point of view.

Through study and conversations with informed persons Morrow came to understand the revolutionary aims of the Mexican people. He recognized that these aspirations were the inevitable results of historical antecedents and that the Mexicans were trying to liquidate the consequences of a tragic past. He took the movement seriously and, while devoid of illusions as to the abuses which had cropped up in the administration and execution of the program, was most sympathetic to its fundamental principles. He was prepared to judge the Mexicans by their professed ideals as well as by their acts. Morrow concluded that there was nothing fundamental in the Mexican objectives which could not be reconciled with the larger interests of the United States. These did not include the trivial or unreasonable grievances or the selfish objectives of the American colony. The best policy, Morrow concluded, was that which in the shortest possible time would produce a contented, peaceful, and prosperous neighbor. The best way would be to help the Mexicans achieve their objectives, to take care of pressing needs that spelled survival and progress, and to put their house in order. The equity of incidental damage could be worked out afterwards. Mexico could be independent and still protect legitimate alien rights.

Morrow viewed each specific problem not only in the context of its historical background, but also in the light of his broad objective. He was more interested in effective agreements bearing on concrete problems than in the change of political or economic philosophies. In negotiation the Mexicans found Morrow always fair and reasonable, willing to go more than half way to achieve agreement. This, added to the diplomat's belief in the Mexicans and his efforts to understand their problems from their point of view, made the Mexicans anxious, once convinced that it was to their interests, to make their contribution to a pragmatic solution.

The question of American petroleum rights under the 1917 Constitution and subsequent regulatory legislation was the first problem to which Morrow turned his attention. The Mexican effort to break the control exercised by foreign interests over the oil industry and to vest control in Mexicans created an issue of the relative superiority of vested property rights and national sovereignty. A bitter diplomatic controversy with the United States ensued, and the petroleum companies were among the advocates of a more forceful policy. Because of the controversy and the refusal of the companies to apply for limited concessions, the petroleum industry was at a virtual standstill with deleterious effects for the economy in general and Mexican governmental revenues in particular.

Morrow studied the question with his customary thoroughness and recognized that the problem affected not only the claims and rights of the oil companies, but also the larger issue of the relations between the two countries. He concluded that two principles were involved: "a firm adherence to our rights" and "a scrupulous respect for the sovereignty of Mexico." Accordingly, the petroleum question was a legal, not a political or diplomatic, problem with its only possible solution within the area of Mexican law. Article XIV of the Mexican Constitution laid down the principle that legislation may not be retroactive, and the Mexican Supreme Court in the Texas Oil Case in 1921 had affirmed, and the Mexican Commissioners at the Bucareli Conference in 1921 had reaffirmed, that the performance of "positive acts" on preconstitutional grants vested ownership of the subsoil in the individuals or companies involved. While there were many possible courses of action, the practical question for Morrow was "what course we could get Mexico to pursue that would enable us to feel that the operation of the laws were not *per se* confiscatory?"

The Ambassador discussed the subject in a private conference with President Calles on November 8, 1927. In response to the Mexican executive's questions, the diplomat indicated that a judicial decision in one of the pending *amparo* (injunction) cases challenging the constitutionality of the 1925 law reaffirming the doctrines of the Texas case would go far toward solving the controversy. Nine days later the Mexican Supreme Court, in an amparo proceeding involving the Mexican Petroleum Company, declared that since the owner of the lands on which positive acts had been performed possessed oil rights and not mere expectancies, such rights could not be subjected to restriction or limitation. The majority decision also noted that the confirmation of these rights "did not modify them, but . . . recognizes them." In December President Calles recommended that the "anticonstitutional" articles of the petroleum legislation be amended to conform with the court decision.

Morrow took up the question with the petroleum representatives, but was unable to get from them any project which met with their combined approval. Calles sent his draft for amending the offending articles without consulting the Ambassador or the petroleum companies. On December 27 a committee of the Chamber of Deputies reported out a modified version of the amendments which included penalties for those failing to apply for confirmation of their rights and declared that the "confirmation of a right is its expressed recognition in its fullest extent . . . and no restriction can be established." The oil companies were not happy with either version. As a result of Morrow's representations, certain modifications were obtained before final passage. The word "confirmatory" was inserted to describe the "concession" which was to be authorized without the descriptive phrase "under the law."

A further question arose as to whether Americans applying for confirmatory concessions in prohibited maritime zones would forfeit their rights to such lands. Morrow called to the attention of Calles that the foreign companies "might fear to seek confirmation of their old rights under the new law if there was any question that such a course might involve a surrender of their old rights." Since it was too late to make further changes in the legislation, the Mexican officials agreed to an exchange of letters covering this point between the Huasteca Petroleum Company and Secretary Morones.

The drafting of new regulations for the amended law was hampered by suspicion on both sides. When it became increasingly apparent that the petroleum representatives and Mexican officials would be unable to reach agreement, Morrow had J. Reuben Clark prepare a suggested draft including the minimum number of amendments regarded as necessary. In each instance where changes were suggested the language was taken, so far as possible, from the actual expressions of Mexican officials or of decisions by the Mexican Supreme Court. The source of each suggestion was noted in the margin of the draft. By March 15, through informal conferences of Morrow and his representatives and Secretary Morones and his, agreement had been reached except as to the inclusion of the exact definition of positive acts as given by the Mexican commissioners at the Bucareli Conference. This matter was resolved at a luncheon between Morrow and Morones at San Angel Inn. Article 152 of the amended regulations was to include the exact definition of positive acts from the Bucareli meeting, but the word "or" in the last clause was to be omitted to avoid the possibility of anyone contending that a mere abstract intention to exploit property for oil constituted a "positive act" within the meaning of the regulations.

To permit the companies to know what kind of a concession to expect, a draft concession was included in the amended regulation. The Foreign Office wanted to include a waiver of nationality (Calvo) clause, but Morrow, in a series of conferences, obtained the substitution of a less harsh prohibition against the transfer of rights to another alien or to a foreign government.

When the amended petroleum regulations were promulgated, Morrow and the State Department issued statements indicating acceptance of the steps voluntarily taken by the different branches of the Mexican government as a practical conclusion of the governmental controversy and relegating to the operation of Mexican administrative and judicial agencies such further questions as might arise. The settlement was hailed as a great achievement for Morrow. However, the *Nation* contended that Mexico had conceded exactly what the United States could have obtained at any time. In contrast, *The New Republic* concluded that the Mexicans had surrendered their social program. Morrow good-naturedly observed that the two viewpoints "seem to wash each other."

The unhappy reaction of the New York oil men should give pause to those who contend that the settlement was unfavorable to Mexico. The petroleum magnates wanted nothing less than a complete victory in Mexico as well as to avoid a precedent which would affect their interests in other countries. Morrow, recognizing that the Mexicans had gone as far as they could, refused to support the extreme demands. He stated point blank that he did not go along with the contentions that "no course short of an absolute confirmation of rights, or alleged rights, would be satisfactory" and that "the Mexican Government has no right through proper processes to review the validity of title held within her territory."

Morrow had not expected the New York oil people to be satisfied, but he was surprised at the "extent to which responsible oil companies seem to believe that it is the duty of the State Department to run their business in foreign lands." With unusual vehemence he wrote Undersecretary Olds that he "would like to be present when somebody tells these people their real name!" Morrow was confident that the oil people "will be satisfied ultimately with the adjustment if they will only go back into the oil business instead of trying to teach international law to all Latin America." Eventually all of the companies, with no alternative, accepted the situation, and the settlement lasted until the oil expropriation of 1938.

The petroleum settlement was a compromise which represented a victory for both governments. The United States had maintained the principle of vested property rights. Recognizing such rights when acquired through positive acts, Mexico formally renounced retroactive action, including the intention to place a time limit on the enjoyment of such rights. However, Mexican officials had declared repeatedly and publicly that Article 27 would not be given retroactive application. Mexico also accepted a much less harsh provision for the Calvo clause. However, Calvo clauses have not proved an effective device to forestall diplomatic interposition or intervention, and Mexican officials had conceded previously the American contention that such a waiver could not extinguish the obligation of a government to protect a national in the event of a denial of justice. Lastly, it must be remembered that under the Morrow settlement differences between the foreign companies and the Mexican government were to be resolved through the due operation of Mexican administrative and judicial agencies. The explicit inclusion of a Calvo clause in the confirmatory concessions would not have guaranteed more.

The United States, in turn, accepted the Mexican insistence on a confirmatory concession changing the form of title as well as the contention that vested rights in the subsoil existed only when positive acts, broadly defined, had been performed. There was no provision covering the rights of owners of "untagged" lands. The United States had recognized the sovereign right of Mexico to legislate regarding property within her jurisdiction as long as such legislation was neither retroactive nor confiscatory. In fact, the settlement was effected within the framework of Mexican law and, in the process, Mexico had maintained the revolutionary principle that the subsoil was the property of the nation.

The petroleum settlement altered the mood of the Mexican government and established confidence in Morrow. It made it possible for him, in an unofficial capacity, to seek a settlement of the religious controversy. The Mexican leaders believed that restrictions on the Church subjecting it to civil control were essential for the survival of their revolution. Efforts to enforce this control resulted in Catholic resistance which ran the gamut from a religious strike terminating public services to an economic boycott and armed rebellion. While Morrow was distressed to see the Mexican people denied their religion, he also was interested in the conflict as a threat to Mexican stability and progress.

Study of the nature and the historical development of the problem convinced the diplomat that it could be resolved, if at all, only through a common-sense adjustment on the basis of the actual facts. "It cannot be settled in principle. . . . What must be sought is a practical *modus vivendi*" whereby both sides retain dignity. Discussion of specific laws also had to be avoided. Morrow was convinced that "when you get into the discussion of particular laws you are lost. The letter killeth. Perhaps it can be brought about that the spirit will give life."

Accordingly, Morrow's aim was to displace distrust with confidence on both sides. He had to convince the clergy that the restoration of historic privilege was impossible and that if they would accept the Revolution as an accomplished fact, the Church would recover its essential liberties and be able to proceed to its spiritual mission. The government had to be convinced that the clergy had made such an acceptance and would dissociate themselves from counterrevolutions and foreign interventions. To avoid continuation of the controversy the Church would have to accommodate itself to the laws which the government would have to be prepared to apply in a spirit of reasonableness.

The key to unlocking the door to a modus vivendi was to be found in the abortive efforts to mediate the conflict in 1926. At that time members of the hierarchy had disavowed any revolutionary intent, and Calles had declared that the registration of clergymen was merely an administrative measure. Morrow took the question up with Calles as a personal friend and as a friend of Mexico. The President assured him that he had no desire to control the spiritual life of the Church or to destroy its identity, but that it was his duty to enforce the laws. However, they would be applied reasonably if the clergy kept out of politics. These statements made possible the meetings with Father John J. Burke whose negotiations were based on the premises that the revolutionary government was strong and that Calles' assurances could be relied upon. However, the opposition of intransigents delayed matters, and the assassination of President-Elect Álvaro Obregón by a religious fanatic prevented completion of the arrangement.

As a result of the failure of this early effort to reach fruition, Morrow was wary regarding a revival of negotiations with Provisional President Emilio Portes Gil. He made his position quite clear to Catholic leaders. The diplomat was willing to use whatever good will he had acquired in an effort to adjust the "distressing religious question," but he was not prepared to run the risk of interrupting other important questions "unless the Church really desires to consider an adjustment . . . along the lines already discussed." Salutary press releases by Portes Gil and Archbishop Leopoldo Ruíz y Flores set the stage for a settlement on this basis.

Nevertheless, Dr. Walsh of Georgetown University presented Morrow with the conditions of the more intransigent prelates. The Ambassador told him that it was impractical to talk to the President about changes in the Constitution or the laws. In contrast, Morrow wrote to Archbishop Ruíz, with the expressed approval of Portes Gil, that the government would issue a declaration regarding the scope and interpretation of the laws to include: a disavowal of any intention to destroy the identity of the Church; an assurance that the administrative registration requirement did not contemplate the registration of persons other than those designated by the hierarchy; permission for religious instruction within the confines of any church; the expressed willingness of the government to confer with the authorized head of the Catholic Church in Mexico to avoid unreasonable application of the law; and the right of Catholics to seek modification of the laws through constitutional channels. Shortly thereafter negotiations were begun between Archbishop Ruíz and Bishop Pascual Díaz and President Portes Gil.

When the negotiations reached the stage of preparing the respective public declarations, difficulties arose. The wording of the President's proposed statement seemed brusque to the clerics, and the prelates brought up questions of the details of existing laws. To avoid another breakdown, Morrow stepped in, prepared the statements for both sides, and achieved agreement in advance of the next meeting.

The Church agreed to resume its religious functions in exchange for the assurances indicated. As a result of the settlement the three year old "Cristero" rebellion was terminated, ending a state of anarchy in five states. The Church had been assured of its spiritual independence and control of its own establishment, and, most significantly, accorded quasi-recognition of its juridical entity. This alone represented a major departure from revolutionary concepts, but it was the only possible basis for rapprochement. This concession was not only necessary, but was justified in a settlement premised on clerical realization that the restoration of the old social order was impossible and acceptance that the new revolutionary regime was likely to endure. A significant by-product of the settlement, facilitating subsequent consultation within constitutional lines, was the designation of a Mexican, Archbishop Ruíz y Flores, as Apostolic Delegate and of a Mexican of Indian extraction, Bishop Díaz, as Archbishop of Mexico and titular head of the Catholic Church in that country. The revolutionary laws remained unchanged, although moderated in interpretation and subject, as all legislation, to the will of the Mexican people.

Morrow recognized that the religious problem had not been solved.

What he had achieved was a modus vivendi which would require considerable self-restraint and good will on both sides. He hoped that the arrangement would mean the beginning of a real peace. While the presence of cynical revolutionaries, for whom anticlericalism was the sole point of contact with their former ideals, and religious extremists, who dreamed of past glories, meant continuing strife, the Morrow settlement ended a crisis and indicated the direction of a real solution.

The program intended to answer the agrarian aspirations of the Mexican people constituted the most complex problem for Morrow. Since agrarian reform was regarded as the cornerstone of the Revolution, and understanding of the diplomat's attitude and activity in this connection is fundamental to an accurate appraisal of Morrow's relationship to that movement.

While Morrow had serious reservations about the efficacy of solving problems by governmental interposition, he conscientiously sought to understand the land reform program. He recognized that land reform was an essential part of the revolutionary movement and frequently expressed his sympathy for the necessity of stabilizing the peon on the land. In his view the revolution was neither all black nor all white. The truth lay somewhere in between the claim that the movement had transformed the country and the contrary contention that it had brought nothing but ruin and suffering. "This revolution, like all revolutions, has been frightfully costly. It has started some new things which ultimately may be of great value to the people. These new things are experimental institutions. Some of them may grow into permanent institutions."

American property rights were affected by the land program, but Morrow's attitude was that the Mexican land legislation was valid and that Mexico had the right to expropriate private holdings to effect land reform so long as such action was neither discriminatory nor confiscatory. Since President Calles had offered to consider with equity and justice any concrete cases, Morrow pursued a policy of handling claims on an individual basis seeking to prevent or void injustices. Formal notewriting was abandoned in favor of personal investigation by Embassy staff members, often accompanied by Mexican officials, followed by informal discussion. Whenever investigation revealed the impropriety of a particular claim, Morrow refused to press the matter. In other instances he worked for a satisfactory settlement whereby the essential elements of Mexican policy would be fulfilled while limiting American losses. By this procedure friction in the application of the agrarian laws was minimized and some flagrant seizures were reversed. In some cases it was possible to obtain the return of the lands, to effect settlements satisfactory to the owners, or to reduce the amount of land expropriated. Where agrarian cases involved violations of the provisions of the agrarian laws, Morrow's policy was to aid and encourage claimants to bring action in Mexican courts. Where expropriation was in accordance with the law except regarding payment, submission to the Claims Commission was recommended.

While handling individual cases, Morrow hoped to achieve a general solution of the agrarian problem not only in the interest of American property owners, but also in the interest of the recovery of Mexican agriculture and the financial stability of the Mexican nation. To meet the majority of abuses encountered he recommended that provisional occupation of the land be eliminated and that all petitions must be approved by the National Agrarian Commission. It was anticipated that owners then would enjoy greater security and that expropriations would be based on utility rather than on political consideration. Regarding illegal trespasses, Morrow felt that the only solution was "to help the Mexican Government to acquire the strength to keep domestic order."

However, to achieve the aforementioned general objectives Morrow believed that agrarian expropriations should be slowed down. On the one hand, he endeavored to persuade Calles that the Mexican government, without definitely changing its policy, could limit the taking of new lands and devote its energy and resources to improving the land already taken. Scientific agriculture, irrigation, education, and credit were to be emphasized. On the other hand, he consistently recommended that the agrarian program be put on a "pay as you go" basis with budgetary provision for current expropriations. Morrow anticipated that "when the Government came to spend real money for the taking of lands, it would necessarily balance the utility of that expenditure against the utility of new roads or new schools."

Under the terms of the Warren-Payne agreement at Bucareli the United States government had agreed to the acceptance of agrarian bonds for expropriations of less than 1755 hectares. However, the bonds represented questionable compensation in the light of the unlimited policy of taking land which undermined the value of the securities and threatened the whole financial structure of Mexico. Thus, the question of adequate compensation for American property owners was intertwined with the question of Mexican stability.

The method of financing the agrarian program was the great weakness in the budget system. New obligations were continuously being created without Treasury control over the amount or rate at which they were incurred. Here was an item which could destroy the entire financial program. Morrow explained his position as follows:

My attitude has been that to the end of bringing about economic and financial improvement in Mexico, the Government should adopt as soon as possible the practise of paying for the lands that it takes, placing in the annual budget the amount which it can afford to dedicate to land distribution in the succeeding year. Until Mexico does this, it cannot be said that she has a completely balanced budget. . . . This reform, however desirable it may be, is hardly one upon which foreigners can strongly insist. . . . It should be noted that the suggestion that I have made does not contemplate a change in the land program. It does contemplate, however, a change in the financial administration of the land program.

The Ambassador consistently advocated this reform as the basis of a general solution with the President, Secretary of Agriculture, and Secretary of the Treasury of three successive administrations. During the early months of 1928 he endeavored to bring the Mexican officials to a realization of the fact that "however important the agrarian problem might be from a social or political standpoint, no sound solution of the problem might be reached without taking into full account the economic factors involved ... and without making adequate provision for payment for lands taken." It was estimated that about five million pesos would be needed, and Morrow hoped that funds could be designated for the second half of 1928 or the first half of 1929. By April the diplomat felt that Montes de Oca (Treasury), Dr. Parres (Agriculture) and President Calles favored his plan, although they were not convinced it was politically opportune.

Mexican public opinion was not ready for a change, and the assassination of President-Elect Obregón and the assumption of the provisional presidency by Portes Gil forestalled any attempt to implement Morrow's recommendation. In his inaugural address Portes Gil, a known *agrarista*, defined his task as the "carrying on" of the revolutionary program of his predecessors. This he proceeded to do by speeding up land distribution so that 1929 represented the high point of assignment of lands to *ejidos*. Calles and Montes de Oca had suggested the inclusion in the budget of ten millions for indemnification for lands expropriated during 1929, but Portes Gil rejected the suggestion on the grounds that cash compensation was not required under the law, that the sum proposed would be inadequate, and that the support of the peasants would be essential when the government was challenged, as he felt sure it would be, during the election year. In a public interview Portes Gil declared that the government could not introduce any modification of the law regarding payment for lands and that bonds would continue to be issued.

For the American Embassy the agrarian problem became more acute during 1929. Because of the manifest impossibility of accomplishing anything in the way of an immediate general solution of the problem, efforts were largely directed toward defending American properties. However, toward the end of the year the prospects brightened for the adoption of Morrow's key proposal. The platform of the newly created official party, the *Partido Nacional Revolucionario* (PNR), contained a plank which proposed that as soon as possible lands should be paid for in cash. The party's candidate, Ortiz Rubio, spoke of the inviolability of private property and the obligation of the state to idemnify the owner for any loss.

It can hardly be contended that Ortiz Rubio's campaign utterances were characterized by clarity or consistency of ideas. Indeed, his announced intention to protect everybody—*ejidatario, ranchero,* and *hacendado*—would have given the famed Mr. Dooley reason to pause. However, the general tone was conservative and revealed little understanding of agrarian reform. The reconstruction of *ejido,* according to one student of the subject, was neither an act of justice nor of social reform, but a transitory phase in the process of developing a class of small property owners. In late December it was reported that General Calles, returning from a trip to France, had given an interview in New York in which he expressed doubts about the agrarian program. Alluding to his observations abroad, Calles reportedly expressed the belief that Mexico ought to proceed more slowly and, in consideration of her credit, as soon as possible begin to pay cash for lands taken. Ortiz Rubio, in an interview that was more like an echo than a coincidence, pledged that future land takings would be paid in cash.

However, the National Chamber of Agriculture caused difficulties for Calles and Ortiz Rubio. The conservative landowners' group, taking advantage of the Calles-Ortiz Rubio declarations, voted to petition the President to suspend "the application of the agrarian law." Calles advised Morrow that he did not propose to be grouped with the old *hacendados* and, despite his understanding with the diplomat and his own convictions, it was impossible to go forward as planned.

A few months later Calles was again quoted on the agrarian question. He was reported to have expressed the view that the agrarian program had failed, that it had created a tremendous financial burden for the nation, and that it must be brought to an end. This report was the signal for attack on the agrarian program from all quarters. The administration responded by slowing down land distribution, by the issuance of legislation designed to shackle the program, and by decreeing "stop laws" which set a time limit for submitting petitions for lands in five states. The revolutionary express had slowed perceptively and seemed about to be thrown into reverse.

The shortcomings of the agrarian program itself and the pressure of economic conditions were the justifications most frequently offered. Agricultural production had declined and imports had risen sharply. At the very time when there was a growing awareness of the extent of the financial burden of the agrarian reform and its repercussions on the nation's credit and financial stability, the effects of the depression and of the high tariff policy of the United States began to be felt. Some Mexican officials began to doubt the wisdom of a thoroughgoing agrarian program. Of equal importance was the wave of complacency and cynicism which overwhelmed some of the older revolutionaries. Conservatism replaced revolutionary enthusiasm as leadership, entrenched in power and enjoying its attributes, became remote in time and space from the needs and aspirations of the rural masses.

The crucial figure in this reversal was Calles. The influence both of his trip abroad and of Morrow on his thinking can be minimized. Long

before Morrow arrived in Mexico Calles revealed himself as basically conservative in regard to agrarian matters. It is true that during his presidency
the rate of land distribution was accelerated and other aspects of the program were amplified. However, emphasis was placed on conformity to the
law, on discouraging supplementary grants in favor of making the utiliza-
tion of assigned lands more successful, and in the creation of a middle class
of independent farmers. He regarded the *ejido* as a training school in a
transition to private property. Once the threat of American intervention
was removed, Calles was prepared to follow a more conservative approach
consistent with these ideas.

Morrow's contribution consisted in clarifying the financial difficulties
involved. The diplomat's role will not be exaggerated when it is realized
that his most fundamental recommendation—the allocation of current
funds to cover expropriations—was not implemented except in regard to
amplifications, an infinitesimal part of the program. The measures actually
taken went far beyond Morrow's recommendations and, in large measure,
were effected after he had resigned his post. The conservative viewpoint
persisted long after his departure, and its explanation is to be sought principally in the circumstances of the times and the psychology of the Mexican
leaders.

The resultant slowdown in agrarian reform provided a needed breath-
ing spell while Mexico and the rest of the world rocked under the impact
of the depression. Most significantly, the agrarian reform was not nullified
nor was the program ended. An effort to make the stop laws general was
defeated in Congress, and agrarianism won a major victory with the approval of a decree ending judicial review in agrarian cases. The agrarian
legislation, modified to be sure, remained on the statute books facilitating
a revitalization of agrarian reform in 1934.

After the agrarians, the labor movement represented the most important new element of governmental support. Indeed, during the early years
of the Calles administration the *Confederación Regional Obrera Mexicana*
(CROM), backed by the government, organized practically everyone and
enjoyed almost absolute power. Morrow studied the Mexican labor movement and its program and welcomed contact with its leaders. Early in his
mission he lunched at San Angel Inn with half a dozen top labor officials.

Mr. Morrow arrived wearing a mismatched suit, one shoe unlaced, and
his tie a bit awry. The general impression added to his agreeable manner
was a distinct surprise to the labor leaders. Morrow told them that usually
neighbors whose backyards touched view each other's premises from the
most unimpressive angle and were most likely to have quarrels across the
back fence. He noted that he was very glad to meet the labor group of
whom he had heard such unfavorable reports as they had, of course, heard
unfavorable reports of him.

The favorable impression Morrow created on that occasion was maintained throughout his mission, and his relations with Mexican labor officials

remained amicable. However, as the fortunes of the CROM and the Mexican Labor Party declined from 1928 on, there were those who tried to connect these developments with the arrival of Dwight Morrow. The connection was more one of coincidence than of causality. The eclipse of the CROM was partly of its own making. From a pinnacle of power, particularly when its exercise is abused, there is only one direction to go. There were indications that the CROM's "hegemony could not endure indefinitely." The organization had been guilty of autocratic and arbitrary conduct towards unorganized labor and the independent unions. Graft and corruption undermined the leadership and sapped the moral strength of the movement.

Before Morrow came to Mexico there were several conflicts between CROM leaders and Calles and a noticeable decline in the favor with which the movement was regarded by his government. In addition, there was a long smouldering rivalry between the *agraristas* and the *laboristas*. The struggle was most pronounced in the provinces, and the labor group had never been able to control a majority of the state governments. The latent conflict was brought into the open by the issue of the reelection of Obregón. The Labor Party withdrew its reluctant support of the hero of Celaya, and its eclipse gathered momentum.

The assassination of Obregón hastened the inevitable as the Obregonistas and *agraristas* turned their ire against the CROM and its political affiliate. Portes Gil moved energetically to weaken the CROM and to destroy its power. At its annual convention in December, 1928, the CROM, either from desperation or from an exaggerated estimate of its strength, forced the issue with General Calles. Spurned by its old protector, the CROM survived as a second-rate organization, alternately attacked and ignored by successive administrations.

Coincidence works two ways. Morrow's mission coincided with the initial steps toward the enactment of a uniform labor code. The diplomat recognized that the confusion and uncertainty of the state laws were handicapping industrial revival. While he favored uniform legislation, he was concerned lest haste produce a measure which would deter new investments in Mexico. Nevertheless, when Portes Gil convoked an employer-employee convention to discuss a federal labor law and took the necessary steps to clear the way constitutionally to enact such legislation, Morrow wisely refrained from taking any position or formal action.

Morrow did hold an informal conversation with President Calles. The diplomat noted that many employers were much exercised as to the effect of the labor law on economic conditions in Mexico, but added that he "felt that a law of this general type was apt to do neither the good to the laboring men that was expected nor the harm to the employers that was feared." He expressed the hope that there would be no hasty decision, but that a small committee would give the projected law careful study after the convention. Calles indicated that he understood that such a procedure was contemplated, and Portes Gil's subsequent action confirmed this impression.

When a commission of the American Chamber of Commerce in Mexico came to the Embassy to protest the proposed labor law, Morrow pointed out that he was the Ambassador to the Mexican people and not to special interests. Among the code's articles which the delegation regarded as most objectionable and dangerous was one dealing with the employer's liability. The Ambassador pointed out that, in this regard, the proposed Mexican legislation was no more radical than English law. Portes Gil's proposal formed the basis of the Federal Labor Code passed almost two years later. Constitutional Article 123, the Magna Carta of the Mexican labor movement, had been given national legislative expression.

The Mexican Revolution was colored strongly by nationalism, and one of its major objectives was the strengthening of the state. In this area Dwight Morrow made a very real contribution. At the presentation of his credentials he indicated the need for mutual respect and explicitly recognized the sovereignty and independence of Mexico. His subsequent action, always predicated on a respect for Mexican law, was faithful to these words.

By clearing the atmosphere of distrust and fear and by restoring Mexican-American relations to a peaceful path Dwight Morrow helped to strengthen the Mexican government and insure its survival. Motivated by a desire to see Mexico as a peaceful, prosperous neighbor, Morrow interested himself in anything that affected the stability and progress of the country. Whenever a military, political, or economic problem arose, he was to be found supporting the established regime and willing to place the prestige of his position on the scales in its behalf. His financial views brought the diplomat into conflict with his former banking associates who were seeking a new agreement with Mexico relative to the external debt. Morrow recognized the validity of the viewpoint expressed by an associate that "it would be a shortsighted policy for the creditors to insist that they be paid at whatever the cost to the people of Mexico."

Dwight Morrow did not stop the Mexican Revolution. His role in the slowing down of the revolutionary process must be interpreted in the light of his motivation and weighed against the powerful forces represented by the growing disillusionment and cynicism of Mexican leaders and the economic pressures of the depression. Under the circumstances a digestive period was more than justified. The Mexican people retained their revolutionary principles intact, and the Mexican government emerged stronger and more stable. Under Cárdenas it was possible to resume the revolutionary policy in all its aspects and to an unprecedented extent. The fortuitous confluence of the Good Neighbor policy, the lowering clouds of World War II, and the skillful application by Josephus Daniels of the diplomatic tradition initiated by Dwight Morrow enabled Mexican-American relations to survive the revitalization and extension of the Mexican Revolution.

Other Articles of Interest

Ellis, L. Ethan. "Dwight Morrow and the Church-State Controversy in Mexico." XXXVIII (1958), 482–505.

Ross, Stanley Robert. "Bibliography of Sources for Contemporary Mexican History." XXXIX (1959), 234–238.

SPANISH SOUTH AMERICA

12. The Image of a Dictator:
Gabriel García Moreno

PETER H. SMITH

Much has been published by dictators and about dictators, but relatively few writers have analyzed how the changes in popular conceptions of dictators reflect basic political points of view in Latin America. The following study presents the "image" of one dictator—Gabriel García Moreno of Ecuador—as both conservatives and liberals have delineated it since his death in 1875. Edward Freeman's dictum "History is past politics" might be revised, in the light of this article, to read "History is often present politics," although of course historians are, in all countries, men writing with certain contemporary predispositions that cannot fail to affect their views of the past. Mr. Smith, a doctoral candidate at Columbia University, based this essay on his Master's thesis.

Most of the literature about *Caudillismo* in Latin America places great stress upon the question of charisma—that is, the extent to which a leader's "spiritual qualities" or sense of mission embodies the aspiration of his followers and thereby serves as a basis of popular support. The emphasis seems proper, since there can be no doubting the importance of any dictator's charismatic qualities. At the same time, little attention has been paid to the fact that popular conceptions of dictatorial legitimacy (and illegitimacy) have undergone a number of significant changes since the early 19th century. Since they reveal important shifts in the bases of power for authoritarian regimes, an understanding of these trends is fundamental to a thorough comprehension of charisma and caudillismo. In an attempt to trace some of these changes, the following essay will explore the Latin American "image" of Ecuador's Gabriel García Moreno as it has evolved from his own lifetime to the present.

The methodology is simple. The major works about García Moreno have been placed in their historical context, and then analyzed according to the way in which they justify or dismiss the legitimacy of the *morenista* dictatorship. Most of the writings are by Ecuadorans, although some other Latin American works have been included. Through its emphasis on the background of each book, this technique provides some insight into the political mentality of the Ecuadoran intelligentsia as it has shifted with cultural circumstances. Thus by concentrating on the image of a single dictator this essay employs the tools of historiography to analyze the development of political attitudes in Ecuador over the last hundred years.

The facts of García Moreno's life are generally well known. Born in Guayaquil in 1821, he married a middle-aged aristocratic *quiteña* after a brilliant academic career. Named to the presidency by a conservative junta in 1859, when the country was ravaged by anarchy, García Moreno tried to consolidate his power through an abortive agreement with General Ramón Castilla of Peru (then at war with Ecuador), and then he wrote some letters to chargé d'affaires Émile Trinité which suggested that the country should become a protectorate of France. He finally resorted to a military campaign whose victory was climaxed by the convocation of a national assembly which, in 1861, drew up a new constitution and elected García Moreno president. It was during this administration that he executed a number of famous political prisoners, and led Ecuadoran troops to humiliating defeats at the hands of Colombia. He also replaced the traditional Patronato with the Concordat of 1862—thus surrendering the State's time-honored control over the ecclesiastical business of the Church—and started an ambitious program of public works.

After resigning from office in 1865, García Moreno accepted a short diplomatic assignment to Chile, but a barracks revolt lifted him to the head of another provisional regime in 1869. Once again he called a convention that passed a new constitution and elected him president of Ecuador. While the construction of roads, schools, and hospitals was continued, the most outstanding feature of this regime was its ecclesiastical policies: the constitution stipulated that a person had to be a Catholic in order to be a citizen of Ecuador, missionaries (notably Jesuits) were invited to run the nation's schools, García Moreno publicly protested Victor Immanuel's seizure of the Vatican City in 1870, and the republic was dedicated to the Sacred Heart of Jesus in 1873. Exasperated by his almost theocratic rule, liberals assassinated García Moreno on August 6, 1875.

I. The Contemporary Controversy

It comes as no surprise that García Moreno—as a dictator—meant different things to different people. Particularly during the second administration, his strongest pillar of support was the Roman Catholic Church. Clerics generally regard him as a gallant champion of justice and virtue. "What a heroic spectacle he made," marvelled one priest, "detested by scoundrels ['*los malos*'], worshipped by the people, denounced by the enemies of good and defended by all men of good will: the beloved son of the Great Pontiff, the only supporter of justice in this world." In the Catholic view, García Moreno's dictatorship was practically synonymous with the City of God. But his unique ecclesiastical policies not only lent prestige to the Church; they also altered the balance of political power in Ecuador by securing its almost unqualified support for the president himself.

The upper classes also approved of the morenista regime. Generally Catholic and jealously proud of its relative *limpieza de sangre*, the land-owning oligarchy supported García Moreno's administration because it combined political stability with economic progress. The Sociedad Patriótica de Quito, for example, proclaimed that the president was "the first to establish the foundations of national prosperity," and pointed to the highways and new schools. Similarly, the *Manifiesto del Azuay* endorsed his candidacy for reelection in 1875 by rejecting the clerical notion that García Moreno was some kind of evangelical administrator, and concentrated on his merits as a gentleman, scholar, and patriot. He had married into an aristocratic family, balanced the national budget, and stimulated material progress. Property was secure and order was enforced. In terms like these, the morenista dictatorship was exalted because it stood for both peace and prosperity.

Though he has been widely regarded as a "civilian" caudillo, García Moreno also counted heavily on the military. Administrative reforms and changes in personnel did not constitute a wholesale rejection of the army, only a readjustment that suited the president's personal and political needs. Both of his presidential coups, in 1859–1860 and 1869, succeeded because of military support. Throughout both administrations, García Moreno's most trusted aide was General Juan José Flores. His only nominee for the presidency during the convention of 1869 was General Secundino Darquea. The presidential message of 1871 conspicuously praised "the loyalty and valor of the army and the national guard." Military expenditures also increased: in 1862, when the country was at war with Colombia, 333,000 pesos were spent on the army; in 1873, when the country was at peace, 381,383 pesos were assigned to the "national defense." While the military expressed no clear-cut opinions of García Moreno, it seems probable that it supported his policies largely because he satisfied at least part of the army's own desire for influence and power.

A group of liberals, on the other hand, were outspokenly discontended. Deeply influenced by the writers of the European Enlightenment, for example, Juan Montalvo wrote a famous pamphlet called "La dictadura perpetua," which bitterly assaulted the morenista regime for its ineptness and moral turpitude. Under García Moreno's leadership, said Montalvo, the entire society was sick: "The soldier over the civilian, the friar over the soldier, the executioner over the friar, the tyrant over the executioner, the demon over the tyrant, all floundering in a sea of evil darkness!" Fanaticism bred intolerance and ignorance led to crime. There was no progress at all.

Furthermore, Montalvo objected to the existence of dictatorship on any basis whatsoever. Scoffing at the contention that "circumstances" required the perpetuation of García Moreno's authoritarian rule, he went on to assert that no conceivable amount of material progress could justify dictatorship. To prove his point he offered the fictitious example of a benevolent despot in the Americas:

> Once upon a time, in the new world, there was a people whose king was the sovereign, the judge, the father of the family: nothing was done without his approval: he controlled the nation, preached in the temple, made decisions in the courts, and guided domestic life. He knew everything and he criticized everything. The king was not a tyrant, and the nation underwent *a great amount of material progress*. There was a highway, for instance, the likes of which Rome had never seen, and which connected the two capitals of the empire: historians called it another wonder of the world. And with all this, the people lived in sadness, because they were not free, and because happiness is not compatible with despotism. How could it be that such a great amount of material progress was not enough to satisfy the people, and bring them out of barbarity? [Because] the people had not made any moral progress, and for this reason they were barbarians in the midst of material greatness.

Though a dictator was not necessarily a "tyrant," he could never propagate moral progress. To Montalvo, occupied with questions of virtue and morality, dictatorship itself was thoroughly intolerable. Democracy was the only legitimate form of government. Not surprisingly, the pamphlet concluded with a call for revolution. This was the message, apparently, that inspired a group of young citizens to assassinate García Moreno in August of 1875.

II. The Liberal Perspective

The liberals were delighted by the news of the dictator's death. In exile when he heard of the event, Montalvo was exultant: "my pen," he cried, "has killed him!" Even after the flush of excitement had passed, he continued to praise the conspiracy. To his mind, the assassination had saved the national honor. "If García Moreno had died in his bed, the Ecuadoran people would have always been stamped with the mark of a slave; now that he's been killed, the country that he victimized can become one of the free nations of the world." Having undergone a political catharsis, Ecuador could finally assume her rightful place as a republic among the Americas. García Moreno's death had opened the way for democracy.

Montalvo's prophecy was not borne out by the course of events. Most of the dictator's personal supporters were removed from positions of power, but it was doubtful if the country's political climate had changed a great deal. The new president, Antonio Borrero (whose newspaper, *El Centinela*, had strongly opposed the morenista regime), did nothing to change the constitution of 1869: the State, as Montalvo saw it, was still the slave of the Church. As Montalvo complained in *El Regenerador*, Ecuador needed an entirely new constitution; otherwise there might just as well have been no assassination at all.

Then in September of 1876 Ignacio Veintimilla launched a barracks revolt that swept him into the presidency. He promptly abolished the Concordat and reinstated the Patronato, but soon abandoned all pretensions of popular legitimacy by suspending the constitution and proclaiming himself "dictator" of Ecuador. Clericalism, it seemed, had given way to militarism, and Montalvo was driven to fury. Though he made passing references to García Moreno in *Las catilinarias*, the brunt of his attack was directed against Veintimilla. In fact this new dictator was so inept, wrote Montalvo, that he could not even be a genuine tyrant. "Ignacio Veintimilla neither has been nor will ever be a tyrant: his mind is virtually that of a beast. His heart doesn't throb, it grovels in piles of slime. His passions are primitive and insane; his motives are inspired either by greed or by the devil." Such criticism found fault with the dictator himself, rather than with the authoritarian structure of his government. Previously, Montalvo had objected to the mere fact that García Moreno was a dictator. Now he was taunting Veintimilla because he lacked the strength to maintain a strict rule.

This change in emphasis revealed a subtle (though incomplete) shift in Montalvo's attitude towards dictatorship in general. For in the midst of his despair, he began to exhort "a man" (*'un hombre'*) to lead the way from chaos to liberty. Under present conditions Rousseau's General Will could never assert itself; the people needed a leader, a charismatic figure who could embody their hopes and their needs. Anarchy was not democracy, and a strong government—even some kind of benevolent dictatorship—might pave the way to order and freedom. At any rate, Montalvo had some nagging second thoughts about García Moreno's assassination. "In view of what has happened in Ecuador since the death of García Moreno," he confessed, "I would gladly have let the great tyrant live."

One of Montalvo's most intimate companions during these years was Roberto Andrade, who had taken part in the assassination. At first Andrade gloried in the praises of Montalvo, but he was soon upset by widespread indignation against the conspiracy and bewildered by the nation's failure to press for a program of democratic reform. Feeling partly responsible for the brutality of the Veintimilla regime, Andrade then attempted to prove to the world (and probably to himself) that the murder had been justified in a book entitled *Seis de agosto*, written in the 1880's.

This book opened with the declaration that the assassins had intended to "crush tyranny in the person of the tyrant, in the name and under the authority of the Fatherland." Their only purpose had been to make it possible for the people to establish their own government. Given the circumstances in 1875, Andrade argued, García Moreno's death was indispensable. He had betrayed the country in his dealings with Castilla, in the letters to Trinité, and in the Colombian wars. He had humiliated the nation by placing it under the control of the Pope. He had suppressed all opposition with inhuman brutality. All Ecuadorans hated him. There was no other choice but to kill him.

Having linked the conspiracy to the popular will, Andrade then pin-pointed the reason for the absence of a democratic revolution after the dictator's death: General Francisco Javier Salazar, García Moreno's Min-ister of War, who ran the government in the months immediately after the murder. According to Andrade, Salazar had secretly agreed with Colonel Sánchez (one of the members of the conspiracy) to keep the army loyal to the government during the assassination. García Moreno would be killed, Salazar would come into power, and Sánchez would get control of the army. In this way Salazar used the liberal plot for the sake of his own designs: the army followed his orders, the president was killed, and Sánchez was shunted off to obscurity. Salazar thus betrayed the revolution, and anyone could see the disastrous results: "Ecuador is dying," muttered Andrade, "smothered in excrement."

In 1895, however, the liberal Eloy Alfaro won the presidency from Luis Cordero in a brutal military campaign. A new constitution banished all religious orders and drastically curtailed the privileges of the Church. To Andrade this meant the end of García Moreno's oppressive "Jesuitism" and the beginning of a new era for Ecuador. "The inchoate revolution of August 6, 1875, in Quito," he wrote, "has just been consummated on June 5, 1895, in Guayaquil." History had vindicated the assassination of García Moreno.

Yet the political malaise that followed the Alfaro revolution left Andrade uncomfortable, and in 1922 he published an article which disclosed a "hitherto unknown" crime of García Moreno's. The story maintained that the dictator had poisoned his first wife, Rosa Ascásubi, with an overdose of laudanum. The motive was provided by García Moreno's incestuous love for Rosa's niece, Marianita, whom he married after the funeral. In a proper tone of shock, Andrade concluded that such a nefarious act could only have been conceived by a perverse criminal mind. "His features weren't those of a man of the world, or those of a thinker or philosopher; they were those of a practised criminal. . . ." The man was practically insane. By im-plication, of course, this warped psychology had much to do with the evils of the morenista dictatorship.

Throughout his writings, Andrade referred to García Moreno's po-litical rule as a "tyranny." Though he never clearly defined the term, it is evident that he first identified it with the formal structure of an authoritarian government. At the time of the assassination, his justification for tyrannicide was essentially the same as Montalvo's: by overthrowing the dictatorship, it would unleash the pent-up forces of democracy and lead to the establish-ment of a free republic like the United States. In time, however, Andrade came to see the impracticality of pure democracy in Ecuador and began to espouse the leadership of a junta run by the intelligentsia ('*la clase sana*'). As he lost his preoccupations about the notion of centralist government, he started to associate "tyranny" with García Moreno's person and his policies rather than with the fact of one-man rule. It was not so much the concentration of power that bothered Andrade, it was the arbitrary use of that power.

García Moreno not only silenced the press; he prohibited any free thinking; he converted colleges into convents; he turned soldiers into petty monarchs; he corrupted the nation by placing its education in the hands of corrupt people; he systematized robbery by calling it confiscation; he and his men were bandits, but they went unpunished and even paid; he cursed the enemies of tyranny by calling them pagans, and persecuted them, executed them, exiled them, tormented them, and confined them to pestilent deserts; he quaffed down the blood and tears [of his victims]: such was the government of García Moreno in the fifteen years that he ruled Ecuador.

In this case "tyranny" was identified with the ruler himself, not the dictatorial structure of his government.

In a similar manner, Pedro Moncayo—who had been one of García Moreno's most obstinate opponents in Congress—became increasingly indifferent to personalistic rule itself. In his *Historia del Ecuador de 1825 a 1875*, for instance, he simply accepted dictatorship as a fact of the national life. The chief significance of García Moreno's rule was that it only consummated the nation's political ills. "A frenetic and bloodthirsty tyrant," he had ushered in a new era of violence and oppression: "To speak of independence was ironic, to speak of liberty a crime." García Moreno's worst sin had been the negotiation of the Concordat, whose hypocritical piety lent a semblance of method to despotic madness. Vengeance hid behind sanctity, tyranny was practised in the name of God: surely, said Moncayo, this was the beginning of the end.

All in all, Moncayo's attitude towards the illegitimacy of García Moreno's dictatorship was ambivalent. He undoubtedly felt that the sheer brutality of the man disqualified him from the right to rule. But to some extent Moncayo was also concerned with questions of constitutional procedure, and seemed to feel that a proper respect for the distribution of authority might well have avoided some of the national pitfalls. Looking back on his days as a senator, for example, he suggested that a strong congress might have stilled the chaos of 1859. Thus a non-dictatorial government would have been more effective than the authoritarian regime of García Moreno. As Moncayo saw it in the early 1890's, the morenista dictatorship was illegitimate not only because of its inherent injustice, but also because of its inefficiency.

The liberals' growing tendency to identify the evils of this dictatorship with the leader himself instead of with the structure of his government was also revealed by Jacinto López' "La muerte de García Moreno," an article which appeared in 1922. In general the essay praised the assassins and their deed, but it also disclosed another "hitherto unknown" episode which accounted for Faustino Rayo's eager participation in the murder. García Moreno, went the story, had tried to seduce Rayo's wife. The good lady resisted and told her husband all about it when he returned from the Oriente. The men then became deadly enemies. Rayo leaped at the chance to join the plot, and was the first to take a hatchet to the tyrant's head.

In spite of his thesis that García Moreno was the author of his own undoing, López also maintained that the very fact of dictatorship merited his assassination. The mere concentration of power in the hands of a single person—apart from his use of it—seems to have constituted oppression. "If there had never been any desperate ferocity, unbridled and insatiable as it was; if there had only been pure and simple oppression, a bloodless tyranny without any savage atrocities, [García Moreno] would have deserved to die as he did. . . ." Dictatorship, in this case, was synonymous with tyranny. López took the same kind of stand that Moncayo did: dictatorship was a bad thing, and García Moreno made it worse.

Up to this point liberal thinkers revealed an essentially dualistic conception of the morenista dictatorship. At first the whole idea of one-man government was so thoroughly abhorrent that authoritarianism of any kind was illegitimate *ipso facto*. After García Moreno's death, however, his rule became increasingly identified with himself, instead of with the structure of his government. This shift in emphasis was incomplete, and by the turn of the century the illegitimacy of García Moreno's rule was determined by varying combinations of these two factors. Part of this ambivalence was no doubt due to the difficulty of distinguishing between dictators and dictatorships: since the political form of such a government was defined by the existence of an omnipotent leader at the top, a discussion of either was bound to lead to a discussion of the other. Men like Montalvo, Andrade, Moncayo, and López, furthermore, had grown up under the influence of the Enlightenment. They were not likely to ignore the admonitions of Locke and Rousseau about the evils of centralized government: form, as well as function, was important.

The tendency to identify oppression with the person instead of the political structure was clear, nevertheless, and was partly due to the workings of historical perspective. As Moncayo's *Historia* . . . showed, the basic task of the historian was to expose and assess the facts of the past rather than to speculate about alternative possibilities. The fact of dictatorship was a given quantity: thus liberals were drawn away from posthumous questions about political structure, and forced into an evaluation of García Moreno's government as it actually was. A discussion of the relative merits of democracy and authoritarianism would only have involved these writers in endless and pointless polemics.

Another explanation for this trend lies in the declining influence of the Enlightenment and nineteenth-century European liberalism. To many people, the confusion that reigned after Alfaro came to power in 1895 demonstrated that the General Will (if such a thing existed) was not the only key to political progress. Locke's notion that men were instinctively peaceful also lost relevance in a country where ruler after ruler bulled his way into the presidency at the point of a bayonet. Positivism began to encroach on idealism, and men began to think about governments in decidedly unromantic terms: anything, they said, for order and peace. Furthermore, a national self-consciousness grew up, hand-in-hand with a disillusionment about the United States. Ecuadorans no longer wanted a polity that would be only a pale imitation of the American model, they wanted one that was their own. It might not be a dictatorship (or it might), but at least it would be different. For these reasons, liberals became increasingly unconcerned about the injustices inherent in dictatorship.

The debunking of García Moreno's personality reached its peak in Roberto Agramonte's *Biografía del dictator García Moreno,* published in 1935. The book's avowed purpose was to interpret the dictator's career from a psychoanalytical point of view, and the Cuban doctor (who later became one of Fulgencio Batista's most prominent opponents) managed to discover that García Moreno had almost every mental disease available. Great emphasis was placed upon his boyhood life: fear of thunderstorms reflected his latent neuroses, and parental beatings led him to a precocious sadism. From his mother García Moreno inherited "hyperthyroidism, vitality, nervous energy, epileptiform tendencies and certain traces of schizophrenia, with exaggerated impulsiveness and irritability." Poverty had left him in an ambivalent world, one of harsh reality and another of far-flung dreams. Since he had never had any real childhood, his entire life had been abnormal.

Agramonte used this same method to explain the facts of García Moreno's political life. Peace and stability were totally incompatible with a mentality of this kind, since "the schizoid is the perpetual hero of a continuous conflict; his life is an assortment of tragedies, motivated by a sense of danger." Such tendencies also accounted for his clerical reforms, as the only reason that García Moreno promulgated such a program was that "he wanted to convert his individual condition into a general law, a categorical imperative." The dictator's fanatical piety was due only to the fact that he regarded himself as another Christ, destined by God to redeem mankind. By the same token, public works were interpreted as self-idolatry, a kind of vicarious narcissism.

According to Agramonte, it was the uncontrollable urge for domination that accounted for García Moreno's dictatorship. He first pointed out that any political leader was affected by power, and could be seduced by its temptations. If this was the case with normal men, an eccentric would be driven to insanity: "sensuality leads to orgy, coldness to crime, mysticism to fanaticism; adulation becomes narcissism, and pride becomes megalomania." Though it is evident that Agramonte disapproved of dictatorship, he never really treated it as a political phenomenon. His conclusions were exaggerated, but his approach was clinical and apolitical. Dictatorship was not so much a means of government as a mental disease.

Part of the reason for Agramonte's failure to consider the strictly political aspects of the morenista dictatorship lay in the fact that he was a Cuban, and therefore somewhat detached from issues and events in Ecuador. Benjamín Carrión, on the other hand, has always been deeply involved in the problems of his country. One of the nation's leading intellectuals, and a flaming liberal, he was undoubtedly dismayed when the conservatives made deep inroads into liberal strongholds in the elections of 1944 and 1948. From that time on, the traditional doctrinal difference between the two parties took on renewed importance: liberals continued to insist on the complete separation of Church and State, while the conservatives stoutly held out for an accommodation of interests. The bitterness increased until Camilo Ponce Enríquez, a clerical rightist, won the presidential election in 1956. Partly in response to these events, no doubt, Carrión came out in 1959 with one of the most scathing attacks on García Moreno since the era of Montalvo: *García Moreno, el santo del patíbulo.*

In this book Carrión adopted many of the techniques that Agramonte had used some twenty years before. Amid lengthy discussions of the dictator's personal character, special attention was paid to García Moreno's isolation from the busy life of Guayaquil, where he grew up as a child. While the streets of Guayaquil were bubbling with the spirit of independence from Spain, said Carrión, the boy was sheltered inside his mother's sad and impoverished home. Thus Gabriel never had any contact with the common people of Ecuador or with the ideology of revolution. "Here," claimed Carrión, "was the first contradiction in the life of Gabriel García Moreno. Between his house and the street. Between his mother and the masses. Between himself and the rest of the world."

In this way the author established one of the principal points of his book: that, in spite of his influence on the country, García Moreno was by no means typical of Ecuador. This idea was closely linked to Carrión's own sense of nationalism. As he pointed out in the prologue, the genuine founders of Ecuador were great Indian chieftains like Atahuallpa and the rebels of August 10, 1809. For Carrión, it was imperative to assert that García Moreno was not one of the great heroes of Ecuadoran history, but a villain of the national past. For the central theme in García Moreno's political life, he maintained, was treason. The accession to power in 1859-1860, for instance, was marked by a series of betrayals, including the agreement with Castilla and the letters to Trinité. Once in office, too, the dictator promptly "delivered the national spirit to a group that was foreign, totally foreign [notably the Jesuits]." In modern parlance, García Moreno was simply un-Ecuadoran.

Carrión also argued that García Moreno's influence accounted for many of the country's contemporary problems, since he had left the people with the obstacles of ignorance, feelings of inferiority and a legacy of shame. But the worst heritage of all was tyranny. For the dictator's executions of political prisoners marked the beginning of a tradition of brutality that had continued practically down to the present. These actions also revealed García Moreno's persistent disregard for constitutional procedure, since they indicated that his fundamental purpose was not to maintain public order but to consolidate his personal power. Unfeigned nepotism, pseudo-religious fanaticism, and terroristic methods all betrayed the dimensions of García Moreno's egotistical ambitions. This lust for power, said Carrión, explained the *cuartelazo* of 1869. The ensuing constitution was even worse, since it made García Moreno "a dictator *de jure*" as well as *de facto*.

Yet Carrión made no explicit statements about the illegitimacy of dictatorship itself. He denied that García Moreno's programs for reform and public works could justify his rule, since they never gave him the right "to tyrannize the people and deprive them of their essential liberties." But the basis for this opinion was the contention that García Moreno's projects were neither effective nor progressive, and that his policies were treasonous besides. For in the prologue, Carrión seemed to concede that beneficial programs might justify dictatorship. Though "harsh and dictatorial," for example, "Pericles liberated the people and spirit of Hellas." Therefore not all authoritarian governments were necessarily bad. Carrión seemed to object to García Moreno more because of his tyranny and lack of patriotism than because of the fact that he was a dictator.

Thus the liberal attitude towards García Moreno and his dictatorship underwent a significant evolution. Most nineteenth-century observers, especially before the assassination in 1875, objected to the whole idea of dictatorship. Tempered by historical perspective and nationalism, this view gradually gave way to the feeling that authoritarianism itself might not be inherently evil. Then Agramonte totally ignored the political implications of personalistic rule, and Benjamín Carrión seemed to admit that dictatorship could be beneficial in disinterested hands. In spite of this change, liberals were steadfast in their opposition to García Moreno. Their invective was always harsh: its emphasis was simply shifted from the formal centralization of power to the person who employed it. As time passed, the liberal image of García Moreno evolved from the conviction that he was bad because he was a dictator to the observation that he was just a bad dictator.

III. The Conservative Reaction

Conservatives were shocked by the news of García Moreno's death, and hastily set about to glorify their hero. The afternoon of August 6, 1875, a pamphlet entitled "Día nefasto" spread throughout Quito, mournfully announcing that "the noble blood of the Regenerator of the Fatherland has just been shed by miserable and faithless assassins. . . ." The paper vowed that García Moreno's death would not bring a revolution, and that his martyrdom would perpetuate the conservative order: inspired by his memory, responsible citizens would strive to maintain "the reign of true progress, which his wise and indefatigable spirit has founded in this country." Ennobled by his death, the dictator had journeyed directly to Heaven. By killing García Moreno, the assassins had only martyred him.

As praise was heaped upon the president's memory from all corners of the nation, it became apparent that some conservatives regarded the assassination as a liberal attempt to seize control of the government—a misguided political coup that could only unleash the forces of chaos. Dictatorship, they felt, was necessary for the preservation of civic order. But the majority felt that the issue had been joined in a very different way. In their view the assassination did not represent any popular distaste for the political aspects of García Moreno's rule, but an impious scheme to overthrow his Catholic and apostolic polity. The question was not dictatorship or republicanism, but piety or heresy. It is within this dualistic value framework that most of the conservative images of García Moreno have been conceived.

R. P. A. Berthe's *García Moreno: presidente de la república del Ecuador, vengador y mártir del derecho cristiano*, published in 1887, was the first full-length biography of the dictator. It was also the most ecstatic. In the French Redemptorist's view, García Moreno's private virtues were impeccable, a shining demonstration of the Christian spirit. The letters to Trinité were no real cause for consternation (especially in a Frenchman's opinion!), and political executions were simply matters of national urgency. But the padre's greatest praise was reserved for García Moreno's establishment of a Catholic state, founded upon the principle that the Church should control the government. The Concordat of 1862 made García Moreno the greatest statesman since St. Louis, and the constitution of 1869 gave ample proof that there was at least one dedicated Christian ruler in the nineteenth-century world. In order to exhalt his subject, Berthe also emphasized the backwardness in Ecuador's national past: Simón Bolívar, Juan José Flores, Vicente Rocafuerte, and José María Urvina had only retarded the country's development. Into the midst of this corruption and decay charged the resplendent figure of García Moreno: alone, "a Christian Hercules," he struggled against the forces of chaos and impiety.

This book also argued that García Moreno had acquired a popular mandate for his authoritarian rule. Berthe carefully described the dictator's election to the presidency in the convention of 1860, and then pointed out that he had accepted a second term—after the barracks revolt of 1869— only because of popular demand and "the imperative duty of defending his religion and his country." An even more important sanction, however, was provided by the idea that García had come into power through the special guidance of God. Implicit throughout the whole biography was the notion that providential design had selected García Moreno to propagate the message of Christ on earth. Thus he had not seized power for personal reasons, but because of a sacred mission. In this case questions about the authoritarian structure of his government were irrelevant, since it was impossible for a near-saint to be a tyrant.

Berthe's eulogistic biography touched off a heated controversy in Ecuador. Liberals charged that he had glorified a despot at the expense of an entire people, and Antonio Borrero rattled off a massive *Refutación . . . del libro titulado: García Moreno, presidente . . . del Ecuador, vengador y mártir del derecho cristiano* (1889) in an effort to salvage the national honor. In a posthumous volume published in 1904, Juan León Mera—who had been one of the dictator's closest associates—countered Borrero's argument with the contention that liberals were actually debunking Ecuador's reputation whenever they berated García Moreno. Borrero might have corrected some factual inaccuracies in Berthe's work, said Mera, "but patriotism . . . has not altered the essential fact that the refutation has done much more to harm the name of the country than the [original] book in question." In this view, García Moreno's personal image was so closely identified with that of the nation in general that praise of the ex-dictator was practically synonymous with praise of the country itself.

Though it objected to the portrait of the dictator as a demigod, Mera's *García Moreno* was similar to Berthe's biography in many ways. He maintained that the president had died a martyr to his faith, and insisted that other national leaders—mainly Flores, Rocafuerte, and Urvina—were either unscrupulous or inept. Yet the conclusion that he drew from this material was more political than that of the French Redemptorist, since Mera claimed that the answer to demagoguery and dissension lay in dictatorship as well as in the Gospel. "What could the remedy possibly be," he asked, "other than energetic and persistent action, inspired by an enlightened patriotism, free judgment . . . and a solid morality which does not waver one iota from Christian doctrine?" These were the convictions behind García Moreno's policies: therefore the regime was both an historical and a moral necessity.

Mera's chief addition to the conservative logic was an explicit refutation of the liberal doctrine of popular sovereignty. In the conventional Thomist manner, he postulated the existence of an eternal divine law, expressed in reality through natural law and finally interpreted by mankind as human law. Government existed as an instrument of God, not of the people, and political structure (as conceived by the mortal minds of Locke and Rousseau) should never be regarded as an end in itself. It was not the democratic or dictatorial shape of a polity that mattered, it was the actual moral content:

Therefore the forms of government, the manners of exercising sovereignty, are variable; but the divine principle or moral law respecting order, harmony, control and conservation is not subject to change in the slightest bit: the principle of sovereignty emanates from God and for that reason is unchangeable. Man, individually or collectively, only puts this principle into practice, in the manner that seems most convenient; and here lies the danger of error, since the attempt to implement this principle on the basis of liberty becomes subject to the passions and caprice of mankind.

In this sense García Moreno's dictatorship was absolutely justified, since the unpredictability of the General Will suggested that the centralization of power was necessary to good government. Even so, a ruler's legitimacy was ultimately determined by the consistency of his policies with the moral laws of God: if anyone had met that test, said Mera, García Moreno had.

The year 1921, the centennial of García Moreno's birth, ushered in a predictable amount of praise. Tracts and sermons were dedicated to the memory of "The Catholic Regenerator," and poets addressed the erstwhile president in a number of passionate odes:

> The eternal passage of time
> Has not dimmed the greatness that is thine,
> And never will, in all surety,
> Leave in darkened obscurity
> The brilliant glory of your life sublime!

Most of these writings simply versified Berthe's image of García Moreno as an impeccable demigod. Written almost exclusively by Catholic priests, these eulogies never really dealt with the question of García Moreno's political legitimacy. Generally speaking, in fact, Catholic authors responded to the centennial in terms of religious dogma. They favored his government because of his allegiance to the papacy and canonical law, rather than because of its efficiency and justice. Very little attention was paid to the question of governmental structure: as Mera had shown, the mechanics for the distribution of authority made little difference, since it was morality that really mattered. Besides, men who were subject to the rigid hierarchy of the Mother Church, and who recognized the spiritual infallibility of the Pope, were unlikely to dispute the secular legitimacy of one-man rule.

In keeping with these ideas, the Rev. Tomás Alvarado wrote a pamphlet entitled "García Moreno, heraldo del reinado social de Jesucristo," in 1921. Its basic purpose was simply to praise the martyred hero for his private and public virtues. Like Moses *('el caudillo de Israel')*, the Eucadoran president had liberated an entire people from pagan ignorance, anarchy, and destruction. Passing reference was made to the impious doctrine of the separation of the Church from the State, and the dutiful priest assured his readers that García Moreno's dictatorship was absolutely necessary "for the social reign of Christ to be impressed upon a people subjugated by liberalism." Yet his primary attention was not devoted to the political legitimacy of such rule, but to its Catholic principles.

In the same vein José Le Góuhir y Rodas' elegy of *Un gran americano* (1921) praised the dictator for his piety. One of the most interesting aspects of Le Góuhir's book, though, was its distinction beween the forces of good and evil. In his view a worldwide struggle was taking place between the "Revolution" (which included socialism, as well as the liberal doctrines of the French Revolution) and the "Reaction" (which advocated the

Thomist notion of Catholic order). Inspired by the writings of Rousseau and Voltaire, the Revolution was attempting to establish political justice without any regard for moral justice: under universal suffrage, a faithless social order would be governed by the laws of arithmetic rather than by the laws of God. The Reaction, of course, stood for moral justice and divine authority. Thus García Moreno derived his chief importance from being the champion of the nobler cause. By mere definition, therefore, anything *"antigarciana"* was necessarily *"anticristiana."* Again, his legitimacy as a dictator was provided by divine rather than popular sanction.

Paradoxically enough, however, Le Góuhir also made a guarded attempt to point out that a Catholic polity actually incorporated all the noble precepts of the misguided Revolution. Liberty, fraternity, and equality were in fact "the very pillars of the Christian state, which itself is based upon the double foundation of authority and faith." Freedom was meaningless without order, he argued, and order demanded religion. In this manner, the ecclesiastically oriented morenista regime pointed the way to the goals of revolutionary democracy.

This attempt to identify García Moreno's dictatorship with liberal doctrine was undoubtedly a response to the politics of Ecuador. Eloy Alfaro's military coup in 1895 had given the liberals a virtual monopoly on governmental power, and the conservatives were defeated at the polls for decades on end. Yet it was clear to most observers that the liberals' popularity was due to their promises rather than to their performance. Public works were faltering, Brazil and Colombia both won control over disputed border territories, and the mighty crash of a cacao boom left the economy at a standstill. Presidential successions were still punctuated by violence, and in the early 1920's the executive mansion was occupied by the undistinguished José Luis Tamayo. These tumultuous circumstances clearly defined the conservative's political strategy: if they could identify themselves with the grandiose goals of the liberals, then the superiority of their governmental policies as a means to reach those ends would readily assert itself.

In this context, Pablo Herrera's *Apuntes biográficos del . . . Señor Gabriel García Moreno* (1921) was calculated to make one point: that the conservative morenista regime had actually been more progressive than any of the so-called "liberal" administrations. In calling the convention of 1860, said Herrera, the dictator had established the principle of representation by population rather than by district. This change, along with the convocation of such an assembly in the first place, represented "two liberal innovations" that were promulgated "not by the *liberal* school but by those who upheld the principle of liberty based on justice, religion and morality." Significantly, the writer did not mention the fact that García Moreno reverted to the principle of geographical representation in the elections for the assembly of 1869.

Herrera envisioned two kinds of "liberalism": one, as preached by Montalvo and practised by Alfaro, was utopian and anarchic; the other, as executed by García Moreno, was just and realistic. In this view the self-styled "liberals" represented the essence of impiety, since their opposition to García Moreno emanated from their hatred of the Church and not from any genuine objection to his political actions. The morenistas, on the other hand, were dedicated to the cause of order and progress; violence was only a natural part of the struggle against the forces of evil and reaction. In these terms, authoritarian rule should be regarded not as oppressive reaction, but as a rational approach to change. It was out of sheer embarrassment, Herrera concluded, that "secret societies" began to plot the president's death. "For they could not tolerate the existence of any government which inspired prosperity, civilization and progress, not on the basis of impious liberalism but *on the hardened rock of the Church*, in the shade of Catholic principles and under the sanction of God's law." García Moreno had simply out-liberalized the liberals themselves.

Although Alfaro's party was still in power some twenty years later, the nation was far from stable: between 1931 and 1941, for instance, four-teen presidents shuffled in and out of office. Economic and social crises multiplied, as the presence of foreign investment capital sparked chauvinistic demonstrations of protest, and anti-Semitic riots broke out in 1938. Carlos Arroyo del Río ushered in a period of relative peace in 1940, but the nation was still split between Quito and Guayaquil, the Indians and the whites, the rich and the poor. As Gabriel Cevallos García maintained in *Entonces fué el Ecuador*, published in 1942, the country's history was one of con-tinuing "folly" *('erranza')*. He also predicted that this situation would persist until the Ecuadoran people had become integrated into a single na-tional entity. In this way, Cevallos García revealed the purpose in his study of García Moreno: "to derive lessons of nationalism from the life of an Ecuadoran, the supreme Ecuadoran. . . ."

In sharp contrast to previous eulogistic works about García Moreno, this book did not praise the dictator for his sense of piety and order. As Cevallos saw it, García Moreno's most distinguishing characteristic was "violence." By this term the author did not mean brute force or passionate vengeance, but a capacity for action. It belonged only to heroes, men of will and determination: he frequently compared his subject to Prometheus, de-fying the gods of anarchy and decay. Violence opposed all the habitual evils of the common man: by its very nature, it waged a continual war against bureaucracy, ineptitude, laziness, prejudice, and immorality. It was essen-tially a cathartic agent. "Ecuador will be saved," warned Cevallos, "only when it can commit violence."

Thus García Moreno was neither a conservative nor a counterrevolu-tionary, but a full-fledged revolutionary. The essence of his revolution lay in the fact that he had imposed a political and social system on Ecuador that fitted the traditions and needs of the country. Under his rule, Ecuador had thrived as a unified nation from 1861 to 1875. Implicit in this analysis, of course, was the idea that García Moreno's charismatic qualities had entitled him to rule as a dictator. On one level, the problem of political legitimacy was solved by the mere fact of personal superiority, since García Moreno was an exceptional individual who had succeeded in creating a national entity out of chaos. It would have been ridiculous (if possible) to dilute this powerful influence with the circuitous processes of representative democracy. The dictator's unique relationship with the people and the country, in fact, transcended all the customary norms of political procedure. In this sense there was simply no question of legitimacy.

At the same time, Cevallos took special pains to assert the relative merits of dictatorship and democracy. As he put it, strong government was not necessarily despotic. History had shown that, despite occasional bloodshed, "one-man governments have been good governments." Democratically elected leaders, on the other hand, have hidden their failures under the mantle of popular sovereignty: they were not so completely responsible for their policies as dictators were. Thus dictatorships were generally more efficient (and probably less corrupt) than democracies, and the form of a government did not matter nearly so much as its policies. "If García Moreno ruled as a tyrant," wrote Cevallos, "history has absolved him."

In the meantime, Manuel Gálvez' intense Argentine nationalism was leading him to seek a solution to his country's problems in authoritarian government. In 1942 he discovered the archetype for political leadership in *La vida de Don Gabriel García Moreno*. Indeed, the Ecuadoran dictator had embodied an heroic sense of life. Though Gálvez made no attempt to portray García Moreno as an impeccable individual, he regarded the ex-president as a consummate patriot—and this was his dominant virtue. From his boyhood days, supposedly, his only mission had been that of saving the nation. Furthermore, his ultimate goal was a moral one, since Catholicism would be the basis of a spiritual regeneration. Because of the specific exigencies in Ecuador, therefore, García Moreno had drafted an essentially Catholic constitution.

But for Gálvez as for Cevallos García, the virtue of this action was derived not so much from its compatibility with the teachings of Holy Mother Church as from the fact that he had erected a polity that was indigenous to his homeland. In spite of all the references to sanctification, García Moreno was praised more as a patriot than as a Catholic. Thus the problems of nineteenth-century Ecuador justified the *morenista* dictatorship. "Despotism was exercised in matters of morality," admitted Gálvez, but "the despotism of Don Gabriel, fatherly and sympathetic to the people, was intended to impose virtue and religion. For this sacred end he was not afraid to resort to violence and threats: he was a terrorist for God." As a means, therefore, dictatorship (even a violent one) was justified by the nobility of its ends.

Ecuador underwent a number of significant changes in the years that followed Gálvez' work. As a member of the postwar world she became conscious of the problems of economic development. Improved communications brought part of the Oriente into contact with Quito and Guayaquil, and students started to clamor for wholesale social reform. These fundamental changes were reflected by a gradual shift in the balance of political power. Led by Jacinto Jijón y Caamaño, conservatives made steady gains in the election of 1944 and 1948. Even after Galo Plaza's highly successful term, Camilo Ponce Enríquez was elected to the presidency in 1956. Now confident, conservatives began to boast of their hero—Gabriel García Moreno.

Writing in the early 1950's Severo Gomezjurado, a Jesuit, boldly announced his intention to defend the dictator in ¡ ¿*Mártir García Moreno?* ! (1952). The book justified political executions, exalted García Moreno's role in the wars against Colombia, and even argued in favor of the French protectorate. In short, Gomezjurado resorted to the same line of reasoning that Berthe had employed three generations before: García Moreno had never done anything wrong. Somewhat as Herrera had done, the Jesuit argued that material progress under the morenista regime had so mortified liberals all over the world that they started an international conspiracy against him (led by none other than Otto von Bismarck). The victim of this dastardly plot, García Moreno sacrificed his life in defense of the Holy Church. He was undoubtedly a martyr, and the only valid question was whether or not he should be canonized. As though to still his own doubts, Gomezjurado concluded his book with an account of some twenty miracles that had been attributed to García Moreno.

In the midst of these ecclesiastical concerns, Gomezjurado dealt quite specifically with the issue of dictatorship. He flatly stated that governmental structure must be defined by the political and cultural needs of the country. "In effect, the government is for the nation, and the nation is not for the government. As a result, the governmental form must be adapted to the cultural state of the country, with regard to religion, civics, economics, international affairs, in order to acquire the most benefits and to avoid as many evils as possible." National demands could make no concessions to political purism. Late nineteenth-century Ecuador needed a strong and Catholic government, and García Moreno provided it in the form of a dictatorship. In this view there was nothing inherently wrong with dictatorship or any other form of government. Gomezjurado's only stipulation was that it should come in the right place at the right time.

From its stunned horror in 1875 to its measured opinion of the 1950's, therefore, the conservative image of García Moreno changed in significant ways. While there was never any serious question about the political legitimacy of his government, the grounds upon which it was justified varied a good deal. Secular writers like Cevallos García argued that one-man rule was demanded by the political conditions of the time; Catholics generally agreed, but many priests maintained that the erection of a Catholic state would have justified dictatorship under any circumstances. During the 1920's, too, some nimble minds went so far as to identify the morenista means with the liberal ends. But in general, no one disguised the fact that García Moreno had been a dictator. On both ecclesiastical and temporal grounds, however, conservatives forcefully maintained that he had been a good one.

IV. Conclusion

Probably the most striking aspect of this entire controversy is the absolute and continuing irreconcilability of the liberal and conservative attitudes towards García Moreno. In the course of its development the debate took on varied forms: "patriotism" was a rhetorical device employed by both sides, which steadfastly insisted that their respective arguments led the only possible way to national salvation. Questions of historiography were also raised: conservatives exalted their hero by disparaging Ecuadoran life before and after García Moreno's reign, and liberals turned this interpretation upside down by praising Rocafuerte and Alfaro at the expense of García Moreno. Occasionally, someone like Luis Robalino Dávila chose to regard the dictator as a vital force in the national past which deserved as much praise as the writings of Juan Montalvo. But such exceptions were rare. For the most part, Ecuadoran and other Latin American writers who have dealt with García Moreno fell into one of two categories: either they worshipped him or they hated him.

One reason for the intensity of this controversy lies in the absolute difference in the values and perspectives of the two sides. Liberals thought in essentially political terms, as their principal goal was the equitable distribution of justice and civil liberty. Catholic conservatives, on the other hand, praised García Moreno not so much as a president as a messenger of Christ, the founder of the City of God: his opponents were not rivals or rebels, but sinners and heretics. In this sense, liberals and conservatives were speaking entirely different languages. There could be no meaningful dialogue when objections to dictatorial legitimacy were answered in terms of providential design.

Nor have the lines of political opposition in Ecuador changed a great deal. Ever since García Moreno's lifetime, the major doctrinal difference between liberals and conservatives has been the relationship between Church and State. The former group has constantly advocated the complete separation of spiritual and temporal powers, while the conservatives have persistently argued that the Church should have some voice in governmental affairs. Because of his ecclesiastical policies, García Moreno has always been the symbolic figurehead of the conservative cause. Thus any discussion of his own merits becomes immediately involved in the contemporary politics of Ecuador; to some extent his memory is an issue in itself.

In sum, this analysis strongly suggests that the popular "image" of a dictator—that is, both the basis and the content of his charismatic appeal —varies according to the political circumstances of the time. When liberals were out of power, they tended to object to dictatorship as a governmental form; after years of near-chaos under their own presidents, they started to shy away from that conviction. Similarly, when the conservative party had reached its nadir in the early part of this century, its members made noticeable attempts to associate themselves with the goals of liberalism; during the rise of conservative power after the Second World War, Catholics proudly reasserted the supremacy of the morenista polity. By the same token, the wide divergence between the two parties' views of García Moreno is an indication of the deep fissures in recent Ecuadoran politics. For this reason, of course, this study of Ecuador does not pretend to be a "model" for the evolution of the dictatorial image in other Latin American countries—where specific circumstances are naturally different—but it does yield two conclusions. First, in historiographical terms, a dictator's memory is only a function of the existing political situation. Second, any analysis of a caudillo's popular or charismatic appeal must consider its particular context, since the recognized bases of dictatorial legitimacy are subject to significant change.

---

13. The Introduction of
Classical Economics into Chile

ROBERT M. WILL

Economic history and the development of economic ideas in Latin America have rarely received the attention they deserve. Some of the more dramatic events and outstanding figures have been studied, but much remains unknown. The article below describes the introduction into Chile of the doctrines of Adam Smith and J. B. Say in the period from 1819 until 1856, when Courcelle-Seneuil began his famous lectures in Santiago. Classical economics did not triumph, a circumstance that Dr. Will, professor of economics at the University of British Columbia, explains by reference to conditions in Chile.

The French economist Jean Gustave Courcelle-Seneuil is generally recognized as being the founder of classical economics and economic liberalism in Chile. Historians would have us believe that the ideas of the great classical economists—Smith, J. B. Say, and Ricardo, in particular—were virtually

From Volume XLIV (1964), pages 1–21.

unknown to Chileans before Courcelle-Seneuil inaugurated his immensely popular lectures on political economy at Chile's Instituto Nacional in 1856.

The fact is, however, that there was always, at least from 1819 onward, a small group of Chileans acquainted with classical economics and aware of what the classical economists had to say on such matters as tariffs, money, and the role of the state. Classical ideas had a negligible impact on Chilean economic policy during this early period, however, primarily because Chileans rejected the idea that economic laws were universal in their application and that what was ideal for a country such as Great Britain, from a policy point of view, was bound to be ideal for Chile. Such doctrines as free trade and *laissez-faire*, Chileans thought, were products of mature and already industrialized countries, and that for this reason were unsuited to conditions found in countries that had yet to develop an incipient industry. The predilection was for a national system of political economy which took into account a country's state of economic development, and which prescribed means by which a higher state of development could be achieved. Even those Chileans who accepted classical doctrines as being valid did not recommend that they be implemented without modification or restraint in Chile.

Chilean economic thought at the close of the colonial era (circa 1810) was rooted firmly in the neo-mercantilism which dominated late eighteenth-century economic thinking in Spain, and which formed the basis of that country's commercial and colonial policy during most of the eighteenth century. The few colonials who gave any thought to economic questions were, on the whole, orthodox in their thinking; their views differed little from those held by the majority of Spanish economists and writers on economic subjects. Like his counterpart in Spain, the Chilean intellectual looked to the neo-mercantilists Campomanes, Ward, and Campillo y Cosío for guidance in economic matters, and continued to do so for at least a decade after independence from Spain was finally won in 1819.

The impact which these three economists and statesmen (all three held responsible posts in the Spanish government) had on economic thinking and policy in Spain and Hispanic America was phenomenal. References to their major works are to be found in colonial manuscripts preserved in the Chilean National Archives, as well as in the country's early periodical literature. Campomanes' views on *educación popular*, for example, were the chief inspiration behind the Instituto Nacional, founded in Santiago in 1813. Ideas of these and other economists whose works were read in Spain at the close of the eighteenth century spread quickly to the New World, despite what appears to have been a serious scarcity of books in at least some of the colonies.

The claim made by Chilean historian Barros Arana that Manuel de Salas, the most distinguished and able economic thinker in Chile at the close of the colonial period, had studied and was influenced by Smith's *Wealth of Nations* appears to have been based on error. Salas' economic ideas were formed during a six-year residence in Spain (1777-1783) and during the years immediately following his return to Chile, at which time it would have been almost impossible for him to have come into direct contact with Smith's ideas. Smith was known to only a handful of Spanish intellectuals before 1790, and the first Spanish edition of *The Wealth of Nations* did not appear until 1794. It was probably several years after this before the first copy of Smith's work reached Chile. Even in his later writings, some of which are dated as late as 1824, Salas showed little indication of having been influenced by Smith or any other classical economist. The neo-mercantilist bent of Salas' economic thinking is evident in the numerous reports and memoranda he wrote as syndic of the Royal Consulado of Santiago, in which he urged the establishment of new industries in the colony and the dissemination of useful knowledge, especially the industrial arts, as a means of achieving this end. Like Campillo y Cosío and other neo-mercantilists, he advocated greater freedom of commerce between Chile and Spain as being in the interests of both colony and mother country. Economic liberalism as conceived by Smith and other classical economists was, however, alien to Salas' way of thinking; the state, he believed, must play a positive role in the development of a national economy through aid to education, assistance to incipient industries, including tariff protection, and public care for the poor and indolent.

The first reference to Smith or any other classical economist in Chile appeared in 1813 in a plan of studies drawn up for a national academy or center of higher learning. The plan, submitted to the government by the Rector of the Colegio Carolino, caller for the teaching of political economy according to "Genovesi, Smith and Say." Earlier plans for a national academy included political economy among the subjects to be taught, but said nothing about the texts or reference books to be used. The Rector's plan was adopted, with few modifications, as a blueprint for the Instituto Nacional which opened its doors to the public in 1813, but which was forced to close early the following year when Santiago was reoccupied by Spanish forces: Political economy was on the curriculum of the Instituto in 1813, but no evidence can be found to suggest that it was among the subjects taught during the first brief period of the institution's history. When the Instituto Nacional reopened in 1819, a course in political economy based on Say's *Traité d'économie politique* was offered, and was compulsory for all students enrolled in law.

II

Several Chileans, some of whom held high positions in the government, had come into contact with classical economics by the early 1820's. This was so, despite the difficulty experienced in obtaining books, especially in Spanish, after normal relations with Spain were ruptured in 1810. Only French editions of Say's *Traité d'économie politique* seem to have been available in Chile as late as 1820, although the first Spanish edition of this work appeared in 1804. Both Smith and Say were quoted in 1819 by Chileans protesting a government proposal to abolish the export duty on specie as a means of putting an end to the illegal export of the precious metals. José Santiago Portales, superintendent of the government mint in 1819, not only objected to the abolition of all export duties on specie, but also was critical of the means the government proposed to recoup the revenue lost by such an expedient—an increase in the seignorage charge collected at the mint. This latter measure, Portales maintained, was tantamount to altering the value of the country's currency, the dangers of which had been clearly pointed out by Say. The remedy which Portales prescribed for ending the clandestine export of specie was typically Smithian: existing export duties should be lowered, not abolished. The contraband trade, Portales rightly observed, was encouraged by the high duties then in effect, with the result that little was collected by the government in the way of revenue.

Very similar views were expressed in a letter which appeared in *El Telégrafo*, one of the first periodicals to be published in Chile. *El Telégrafo's* correspondent, identified only as "the economist," first made the point that the precious metals differed little from other articles of commerce, and for this reason their exportation should not be obstructed. "I shall deny with Say and the best political economists," he wrote, "that the exportation of money in coin causes injury to the country from which it is extracted." This anti-mercantilist dictum was not all that this self-styled economist had to say about the proposed abolition of export duties on specie and an increase in seignorage charges. He also claimed that governments have a special responsibility to preserve the value of the currency, since any alteration in the value of money results in a concomitant change in the value of "land, houses, and of all articles of prime necessity and of luxury." Like Portales, *El Telégrafo's* correspondent blamed the clandestine trade in specie on the height of existing duties. Smith, he pointed out, had demonstrated clearly that the contraband trade would thrive whenever the payment of duties was more burdensome than the consequences of being caught smuggling.

The first major policy test for economic liberalism in Chile came during the 1820's and 1830's, when the new nation was faced with the problem of deciding the type of commercial policy it would follow. Contrary to popular opinion, the Decree of Free Commerce of 1811, which was the first act dealing with an economic matter passed by Chile's first revolutionary junta, was not a product of Smithian liberalism, or a document which was influenced by the doctrine of free trade. Its chief purpose was to free Chileans from the clutches of a commercial policy which had given Spain a virtual monopoly of all trade with foreigners and had subordinated the interests of Chileans to those of the mother country. The Decree opened Chile's ports to foreign vessels and gave to Chile for the first time the right to trade directly with foreigners; it also placed a duty of 30 per cent on all imports and authorized whatever prohibitions on imports "that are considered suitable to the development of the country's industry." The intent of the decree was to establish "freedom of trade" and not "free trade," a subtlety of meaning frequently overlooked by students of early commercial policy. It is doubtful whether a single member of the junta of 1811 had ever heard of free trade, let alone believed that it was a doctrine that might be applied with advantage in Chile at that time.

By the early 1820's this situation had changed insofar as free trade and the doctrine of economic liberalism had become known to a small group of influential Chileans. However, no one in a position to influence or determine policy seriously advocated a lowering of tariffs or suggested that the country should abandon the protectionist course it had embarked upon in 1811. During the last year of the O'Higgins administration (1817–1822), protectionist sentiment within the government reached an apogee in the form of legislation raising the duty on imports considered detrimental to local industry, and of a new and highly protectionist tariff schedule which was presented to the Preparatory Convention of 1822 for approval. The proposed tariff schedule was so severely criticized by the Convention that it was never put into effect, but opposition to it was not on grounds of the high degree of protection it would have afforded domestic industry. Instead, controversy over the tariff of 1822 centered around the person of the Minister of Hacienda, José A. Rodríguez, who, rumor had it, stood to profit by an increase in the price of certain imported goods that he and a business partner had acquired. Of interest here is not so much the fate of the tariff bill or of the minister who conceived it, but of what the latter said in its defense. Rodríguez, who professed to be an ardent student of political economy, admitted that the tariff schedule he presented to the Convention was not in strict accordance with the views of Smith and other economists, but he defended it on the grounds that the high duties proposed were needed to develop new industries in Chile. "We are all liberals," the Minister of Hacienda told his critics, "in all that does not tend to ruin us."

When it came to formulating economic policy, neither O'Higgins nor his ministers, nor their successors, showed any predilection to cast off economic ideas in vogue at the end of the colonial period. There persisted the belief, firmly imbedded in neo-mercantilist literature and associated in Chile with the activities of the Royal Consulado, that industry could be developed only with the assistance of, and encouragement from, the State. And by no means was the tariff the only instrument of policy employed to achieve this end. Special tax concessions were granted in 1824 to nationals and foreigners establishing factories for the manufacture of hemp, linen, copper-goods, and other products which could be made from Chilean raw materials. To the extent that Chile's early independent governments addressed themselves to economic, in contrast to purely financial issues, the emphasis was clearly on economic development or *fomento*—to use a word popular in Spanish economic literature at the end of the eighteenth century. In the realm of economic policy, the link with the past was, if anything, strengthened under the aegis of self rule and as a result of the optimism with which Chileans viewed the economic future of their country.

Another influential Chilean who displayed a knowledge of classical economics during the early post-independence period was Camilo Henríquez, churchman, revolutionary, and founder in 1812 of Chile's first newspaper, the *Aurora de Chile*. Henríquez became interested in classical economics while living as an exile in Buenos Aires between 1814 and 1822. While in Buenos Aires, Henríquez devoted many hours to the study of political economy and to the reading of books which he had not been able to obtain in Chile or in Lima, where he had studied as a youth and where he had been incarcerated by the Inquisition for reading Voltaire and other prohibited books. He was particularly impressed by the progress which the study of political economy had made in Buenos Aires compared to Chile, and by the influence which he thought the ideas of the great economists had on government policy in Buenos Aires. "Here," Henríquez wrote to Manuel de Salas in 1822, "it is known from experience that political economy and statistics are as necessary to the government as mathematics to physics." A neo-mercantilist in his early days, Henríquez returned to Chile in 1822, a firm believer in, and popularizer of, the new economics of Smith and the English classical economists.

This popularization Henríquez undertook by founding the *Mercurio de Chile*, a political and literary review modeled after the best English journals of the day. Such a periodical, he hoped, would help remedy his countrymen's lack of sophistication in political and economic matters—a deficiency which he considered especially serious since they now had the responsibility of managing their own affairs. During its brief existence (1822–1823), the *Mercurio de Chile* instructed its readers on such subjects as public finance and debt management, topics which should have interested Chileans at the time, since the country was in the process of contracting its first foreign loan in London. In fact, Henríquez seems to have regarded himself as something of a specialist on public finance. He wrote at length on the subject in the *Mercurio*, and recommended to his readers long lists of books on public finance and debt management. His chief objective as a publicist in economic matters was the establishment in Chile of a judicious system of public credit similar to that which existed in England. Of the various features of the English system of credit, it was the provision of a sinking fund for the prompt retirement of public debt which caught his eye, and which he urged be adopted in Chile as quickly as possible.

Henríquez also put to good use his knowledge of political economy by serving in a number of official capacities, including as a member of Chile's first Congress. As a member of a three-man treasury commission appointed in 1823 to inquire into means of managing Chile's newly acquired external loan, he presented one of the first plans for establishing a bank in

Chile. Henríquez was unaware of the deep-rooted suspicion of banks which existed in Chile at that time, and which prevented any type of bank being established permanently in the country until after 1850.

A fourth influential Chilean who was acquainted with classical economics during the first years of independence was Diego José Benavente, Rodríguez's successor in the Ministry of Hacienda. Benavente was also editor of *El Liberal* and of other periodicals to which he regularly contributed articles on economic subjects. Benavente had read and studied Smith's *Wealth of Nations*, as well as the works of such French popularizers of Smithian ideas as Ganilh and Garnier. As a journalist, Benavente was critical of tariffs as a means of developing national industry and as a source of government revenue, but as Minister of Hacienda he developed a fairly tolerant attitude toward the country's protectionist commercial policy. Like many other Chileans, he believed, when faced with the responsibilities of office, that conditions in Chile called for other policies than those which were likely to produce the best results in economically more advanced countries. For example, he denied that the doctrine of laissez-faire could be made to work in new and undeveloped countries such as Chile, contending that the scope of government activity must be wider in these countries than in more advanced societies. "It is not the same in a new [society]," he wrote in reference to Chile, "with virgin soil, a robust population which has lived three generations in ignorance. . . ." Although he cautioned against unnecessary governmental intervention in the economy, Benavente was nevertheless willing to assign to the state a much more important role that was Smith and the proponents of laissez-faire. "Although the father of political economy classifies as only three the duties of the sovereign or the government which must be supported out of general taxation," Benavente wrote, "we believe that there must be many more. . . ." The government, he maintained, should assume responsibility for (1) the defense of society against violence, whether inflicted by its own members or by foreigners; (2) the support of public worship; (3) the administration of justice; (4) education; (5) the maintenance of diplomatic relations with foreign powers; (6) the maintenance of public officials; and (7) the collection and administration of public revenue.

Benavente agreed with Smith that the cost of certain government services or functions should not be met out of general revenue, but should be defrayed by those persons benefiting directly from them. Yet he believed that taxes on the whole should conform to the ability-to-pay principle. He reminded the Senate in 1824 that "every Chilean must contribute to the support of the Republic in proportion to his ability." The most equitable tax from this point of view, Benavente suggested, was a direct tax on capital invested in real estate and other forms of tangible property. Such a direct tax on rural property, as well as a tax on the incomes of public employees, had been decreed by O'Higgins in 1817, although no record exists of these taxes ever having been collected. Little did O'Higgins or Benavente anticipate the struggle that all Latin American governments were to experience in reforming the tax system, especially in replacing regressive indirect taxes by direct taxes on property and income.

III

Something of an intellectual giant appeared on the Chilean scene in 1828 in the person of José Joaquín de Mora, a well known Spanish journalist, poet, and politico. Exiled from Spain in 1823 on account of his liberalism, Mora settled in London, where he became best known for his association with the *Mensajero de Londres* and the *Correo Literario i Político de Londres*, papers dedicated to the cause of Latin American independence and the diffusion of liberal ideas in Latin America. While in London, Mora added to his many talents an understanding of political economy, which he acquired through extensive reading of the English classical economists and through personal contact with such distinguished economists as J. R. MacCulloch. Mora was invited to Buenos Aires in 1827 by President Rivadavia to edit *La Crónica Política y Literaria de Buenos Aires*, the official newspaper of the River Plate government, and from there moved on to Chile the following year.

Mora arrived in Chile at the invitation of the Chilean government, which at that time was struggling for survival against mounting opposition from the conservatives. The government hoped to make use of Mora's powerful pen and prestige to strengthen its political position, and with this in mind lent substantial financial support to two Mora enterprises— *El Mercurio Chileno,* a political and literary review which began publication in 1828, and the Liceo de Chile, a secondary school which the government expected would replace the Instituto Nacional as Chile's institution of higher learning. The Instituto was under the control and influence of the Conservative Party and for this reason the government was anxious to withdraw official support from it. Mora served the liberal Pinto administration in other capacities as well: he was the author of the ill-fated Constitution of 1828; and in 1829 was a member of a government commission set up to study the question of banks. However, his influence in official circles was short-lived, being brought to an abrupt end by the revolution of 1829 and the ascendancy of the Portales dictatorship. Mora was finally forced into exile by Portales in 1831. His economic views, discussed below, were made known to Chileans in a series of articles which appeared in *El Mercurio Chileno* in 1828.

Mora was an uncompromising liberal. He believed that only through the adoption of a liberal economic policy based upon the teachings of Smith and his leading disciples would the newly independent countries of Latin America be able to develop economically. Like Henríquez, Mora also tried to impress upon Chileans the need to establish in Chile a system of public credit similar to that of the English. He saw in public credit the means by which the small and scattered savings of individuals could be mobilized and used for the financing of social capital (public works), thereby increasing the productive capacity of society. Public credit was to Mora something that creates "wealth which did not before exist," for in the absence of a well developed system of credit, a certain proportion of total savings would always remain unutilized, and therefore lost to society. The fruits of government borrowing, however, could not be enjoyed by every country, since not every government enjoyed the reputation of solvency and integrity in financial matters needed to make a system of public credit work. Confidence in the government's ability to handle its finances and honor its debts could best be obtained, Mora claimed, by keeping the public informed about government finances, and by letting government creditors know to what uses their funds were being put.

Two articles in Mora's *El Mercurio Chileno* were devoted to the subject of taxation. He accepted Smith's four canons of taxation, but thought it necessary to add to them four "no less just" canons suggested by Sismondi. These additional criteria of a good tax system were (1) a tax must fall on income and not on capital, since a tax on the latter would destroy the very source of all wealth; (2) for purposes of taxation, a clear distinction must be made between income and gross receipts, for only income is a net concept in the sense that it does not include elements of cost such as depreciation and maintenance of fixed capital, replenishment of inventories, and maintenance of labor; (3) a tax is a payment for benefits received from the government, and for this reason individuals who do not benefit from a government service should not be taxed to defray its cost; and (4) the greater the ease of avoiding paying a tax by shifting or moving the tax base, the lower should be the tax. Mora warned against taxes which prove unduly burdensome to production, or which violate the principle of laissez-faire, a principle which he insisted "must be the ideal of our economic legislation." His faith in laissez-faire, however, was a qualified one. Governments, Mora believed, should help, not hinder, private enterprise, especially enterprises considered essential to the economic development of the country. With this role of the government in mind, he advocated special tax concessions to industries which were unlikely to be established in Chile without some such encouragement or stimulus.

Mora disagreed with economists who maintained that indirect taxes are superior to direct forms of taxation insofar as they (1) are more convenient to pay; (2) conform more closely to the ability-to-pay principle of taxation; and (3) are more universal in their application since they tend to be paid by all consumers. These advantages of indirect taxes Mora considered to be largely illusory. The burden of an indirect tax does not fall on all persons in relation to their ability to pay, with the result that an equal sacrifice is not demanded of everyone. An indirect tax, Mora pointed out, might well be regarded as a "minor nuisance" by the rich, while constituting a "painful cause of privation" for the poor. An import tax on tea, coffee and sugar he cited as an example of an indirect tax which bears heavily on the poorer classes but which is scarcely felt by the better-to-do consumers of these commodities. Indirect taxes were also condemned on the grounds that they were costly to collect, and that they give rise to fraudulent and deceitful practices devised to avoid paying them. Mora believed the advantages of direct taxes to be threefold. First, the collection of taxes on property and other forms of wealth does not require the multitude of collectors and inspectors needed to collect indirect taxes; secondly, revenue from direct taxes is fairly certain while that from indirect taxes, especially taxes on consumer goods, tends to be uncertain, depending on tastes, the availability of credit, and many other eventualities; and thirdly, direct taxes lend fewer opportunities for evasion and dishonesty in collection.

IV

No topic of political economy evoked more interest and led to more discussion in Chile in the years immediately following independence than the question of free trade and what was the best commercial policy for a country in Chile's position. Articles on commercial policy began to appear in the Chilean press in 1827, the first and most noteworthy of which was a three-instalment article written by Mora, and reprinted from his *La Crónica Política y Literaria de Buenos Aires*. Mora was outright in his condemnation of protective tariffs as a means of achieving industrialization in America. "The idea of obstructing foreign importations in order to give rise to national industry," he wrote, "seems to us to be the most absurd of all the ideas capable of entering the mind of an economist." Prohibitions and duties on imports, he noted, do not result in benefits for the entire nation, but only for a small group of producers which is protected from the competition of foreigners. For the greater part of the population, tariffs mean higher prices "for what could have been had at a moderate price."

However, neither Mora's eloquence nor the logic of his argument had much impact in a country which, as far as economic philosophy was concerned, still looked to the colonial past and which had pursued a protectionist course since the days of the revolutionary junta of 1811. Free trade as a tenet of economic liberalism became known to an increasing number of Chileans during the 1820's, but a majority of those familiar with classical economics held firmly to the view that conditions in Chile called for the adopttion of policies different from those that might be expected to produce results in Europe. The theories of Smith and his disciples, it was pointed out in 1827, had been conceived and nurtured in countries which had already attained a high level of economic development and national wealth, a fact which did not mean, however, that these same theories were applicable in Chile. Free trade might well be the appropriate policy for industrially advanced countries such as England, but prove disastrous for a young country such as Chile. A few Chileans expressed utter contempt for "beautiful systems of political economy" which were without application in their country and which succeeded in proving "on paper only" how a country can achieve prosperity. Another group justified a protectionist policy on the grounds that Chileans on the whole would be better off employed in producing many of the manufactured commodities then imported than in mining the precious metals needed to pay foreigners for imports. This same group, however, noted that the gain to be derived from a high tariff could not be realized immediately, and that initially, or in the period immediately following the imposition of a protective tariff, certain "sacrifices" and inconveniences would be required on the part of the public, including the putting up with "the imperfection of manufactured commodities and the higher price to those who consume them." Eventually, these initial costs of protection would be more than offset by gains in employment, higher wages, and greater wealth generally.

A second article by Mora on tariffs and commercial policy appeared in his *El Mercurio Chileno* in 1828. On this occasion Mora chose to defend the doctrine of free trade by appealing to natural law. He quoted Grotius to the effect that nations have a "natural right" to trade with each other, and maintained that the imposition of tariffs or other obstacles to trade constituted a violation of this right. No one, Mora claimed, except the Supreme Power itself has the right to interfere with the free movement of commodities between countries.

Mora also questioned the efficacy of the tariff as a means of raising government revenue, especially in those cases where an increase in the price of imports results in a sizable reduction in their consumption. If the demand for imports were elastic, Mora was astute enough to observe, higher tariffs, instead of increasing government revenue, may well result in a diminution of revenue. A purely revenue tariff, to be productive of revenue, must of necessity be low. But Mora had other objections to customs duties as a form of taxation than the fact that, if set too high, they tend to restrict consumption and yield negligible amounts of revenue. First, customs duties are expensive to administer compared to other forms of taxation, requiring the erection of customs-houses and the employment of an excessive number of administrators, collectors, guards, inspectors, etc.; secondly, they violate Smith's third canon of taxation which states that a tax should be levied at a time convenient for the taxpayer; and thirdly, customs duties are subject to greater fraud in collection than most other forms of taxation.

Twenty years later the pros and cons of free trade were still being debated in the press and in learned circles, but the balance of the argument, as earlier, weighed heavily in favor of protection and against any suggestion that Chile should adopt a more liberal commercial policy. An attack on the doctrine of free trade was the subject of a thesis submitted in 1847 in the University of Chile's Faculty of Law and Political Science. The thesis, published in the University's *Anales*, consisted primarily of a refutation of the following arguments which had been put forth in defense of a liberal commercial policy: (1) free trade influences favorably the accumulation of capital and the growth of population; (2) free trade and the closer commercial relations which it brings about improves international relations and hence lessens the chances of war; (3) a protective tariff designed to stimulate the production of a particular commodity tends to discourage the production of commodities normally exported; (4) increased consumption of foreign goods, made possible by free trade, acts as a stimulus to the production of national goods exchanged for them; and (5) import duties do not constitute an equitable means of raising government revenue. Industrialization and a high level of economic development were only possible in Chile, the student maintained to the satisfaction of his examiners, if the government pursues a rigorous system of protection.

A more eloquent plea for protection was made the following year by Cristóbal Valdés, a Santiago lawyer who fancied himself as an amateur economist as well. Valdés renewed discussion concerning the applicability of classical economics in Chile, especially the suitability of the doctrine of free trade in new and undeveloped countries. "The greatest questions of economic science, those which are in the Old World the order of the day," he wrote, "cannot for the time being have either application or influence among us. . . ." With the comment that "what is an absurdity there [Europe] can be a useful institution among us," Valdés argued that only a high tariff wall was capable of establishing in Chile the factories and industry needed to achieve national prosperity. Protection to domestic industry is necessary, he noted, on account of the higher costs of production which are usually found in new and undeveloped countries. The United States was cited as an example of a young country which owed its prosperity and power in a large measure to its factories and industries which, Valdés was quick to relate, had been "established contrary to the principles of the immortal Say and the predictions of Europe."

Equally strong support for a protectionist policy came from official circles during the administrations of Joaquín Prieto (1831–41) and Manuel Bulnes (1841–51)—support which on the whole was translated into legislation whenever the tariff came up for revision. The Tariff Ordinance of 1834 is a case in point. This legislation, despite the fact that it placed a number of articles on the free list, thus giving it the semblance of a free-trade document, established *ad valorem* duties of up to 35 per cent on other imported articles "according as they are more or less favorable to the development of our wealth." More than a decade later, the Minister of Hacienda repeated the government's intention to lend, by means of the tariff, as much assistance as possible to any new industry that might be established in the country. "Industry in America," the Minister remarked in his annual report to Congress in 1848, "cannot be born or flourish on its own account. . . . When a country possesses or can easily obtain the raw materials which are used in the manufacture of an article, appropriate means must be taken to establish an industry, and to promote its growth by sheltering it from competition. . . ." Like Valdés, the Minister pointed to the United States as a country which had done well under the regime of a protective tariff, and as a country whose policies could be imitated with advantage in Chile. But he was not without regard for the criticism that government endorsement of a protective policy was bound to arouse among advocates of free trade. What was wrong with such critics, the Minister remarked in his report of 1849, was that they "forget that principles are modified by time and various other circumstances. . . ."

V

As mentioned earlier, the first course in political economy was probably offered at the Instituto Nacional in the year 1819. In 1827 a government commission appointed to investigate the caliber of instruction at the Instituto reported without further comment that political economy was being taught "according to Say." And two years before that a resolution was passed in Congress directing the students of political economy at the Instituto Nacional to write a report for Congress on the subject of the single tax. All evidence suggests that political economy was firmly established in the Instituto's curriculum during the 1820's, years, even decades, before the subject was taught as a separate discipline in the colleges and universities of the English speaking world. Twenty-one students attended classes in political economy at the Instituto in 1827, and by 1845 this number had increased to seventy, a figure which cannot be taken, however, as a true indication of the subject's popularity, since students were required to take it in order to graduate in law.

Instruction in political economy at the Instituto Nacional before 1856, the year in which the French economist Courcelle-Seneuil began his lectures, was invariably poor. Taught by professors whose prime interest and responsibility were the teaching of law, the subject failed to arouse the interest of more than a handful of students. At least one professor had the misfortune of being accused of being uninspiring, largely because he delivered his lectures by rote, and of refusing to present his students for examinations as required by the regulations of the Instituto. Students who did sit for examinations in political economy apparently were required to do little more than repeat stock answers to questions taken straight from Say's *Traité d'économie politique.*

It was not until the middle of the century that real concern was shown over the poor quality of instruction in political economy at the Instituto

Nacional. The Rector of the University of Chile, under whose jurisdiction the teaching of political economy at the Instituto fell, lamented in 1848 the fact that students did not have a text in political economy which was "adapted to Chile." "Who does not appreciate," he stated, "how indispensable it is that a text in this science takes into consideration the particular needs and resources of the country?" The teaching of political economy in Chile was also criticized on the grounds that no attempt was made to relate theory to the economic situation in Chile, or to discuss problems or questions of particular interest to Chileans. "Of what value is it to us, . . ." the lawyer-economist Cristóbal Valdés asked in 1850, "to know if machines are useful, and if they have produced benefits or evils to the countries which have adopted them when we do not have even a textile factory? . . ." In place of this type of inquiry, Valdés suggested that professor and students discuss such questions as the means of introducing industries into Chile, the efficiency of the country's tax system, and the advisability of monetary reform—topics which he felt would lend prestige to political economy and make its study worthwhile.

Valdés also criticized the continued use of Say's *Traité* as a text, and recommended in its stead Garnier's recently published *Élements de l'économie politique*, largely on the grounds that the latter book was more up to date, was briefer and less difficult to read, and could be easily adapted to conditions in Chile. A proposal to adopt Garnier's *Élements* as a text was also brought before the Council of the University of Chile in 1850. The book probably was used as a text between 1852 and 1856, i.e., during the years immediately preceding Courcelle-Seneuil's installation as professor of political economy.

Chileans also had the opportunity to learn about classical economics from the increasing number of books on the subject which became available after 1820. Most of these books were to be found in private rather than public libraries, or in the libraries of schools or other institutions. The library of the Instituto Nacional, for example, possessed only two books on political economy as late as 1853, and one of these was Say's *Traité*. Private libraries were of two classes: magnificent libraries which had been collected in Europe and brought to Chile intact, of which the 9,000-volume library of Mariano Egaña was the outstanding example, and much smaller and less pretentious libraries which were gradually built up from a growing list of books which became available in Santiago bookstores. The Egaña library contained the principal works of Lauderdale, Steuart, Smith, Malthus (both his *Essay on Population* and *Principles of Political Economy*), Ricardo, James Mill, Say, and Sismondi. Books on political economy were always more abundant for the fortunate few with a reading knowledge of French. A majority of the books on this subject advertised by a Santiago bookstore in 1848 were in French, as was the case with most of the books available at the Biblioteca Nacional after its opening in 1854.

VI

Although the names of Smith and Say were known in Chile prior to 1819—the year of independence—few opportunities existed for the dissemination of classical doctrines in the country until after independence, and even then many Chileans learned about classical economics secondhand and under circumstances scarcely conducive to a deep understanding of the subject. Books, the periodical press, and the classroom served as the principal means by which the new economics was introduced into Chile, but at no time before Courcelle-Seneuil's appointment at the Instituto Nacional in 1856 could it be said that classical economics was in vogue in that small circle of Chileans who comprised the country's educated and ruling class. Those who openly associated themselves with classical economics and defended such policies as free trade and laissez-faire were dissenters from the main stream of Chilean economic thought. Significantly, the two individuals who were most knowledgeable about classical economics, and who did more than anyone else to educate Chileans in economic matters—Camilo Henríquez and José Joaquín de Mora—had learned their economics outside Chile.

Classical economics did not become better known in Chile before 1856 and was not accepted as a basis for policy making for at least three distinct reasons. First, the teachings of the classical economists and proponents of economic liberalism lacked a champion in Chile of sufficient eloquence and persuasiveness to convince Chileans to change their way of thinking about such matters as what was the appropriate commercial policy for Chile to follow and what should be the role of the state in the country's economic life. Secondly, the media or vehicles through which classical economics reached the educated Chilean were inadequate to effect a revolution in economic thinking or to exercise any substantial influence over the actions of those responsible for formulating economic policy. Books, especially the original works of the classical economists, were scarce and frequently were available only in French; periodicals which sometimes carried articles on political economy were sporadic, short-lived, and always restricted in circulation. Furthermore, the teaching of political economy at the Instituto Nacional, while based on Say's *Traité*, was of low caliber and succeeded in stimulating little, if any, interest in the subject. Chileans, through these media, learned only enough about classical economics to associate it with the doctrines of free trade and laissez-faire and with other ideas considered to be inapplicable or lacking in relevancy in Chile.

The third factor responsible for the retarded acceptance of classical economics in Chile was the heritage of the past. The specter of neo-mercantilism, with its emphasis on protection and encouragement of domestic industry and on state intervention in the economy, hung heavily over

Chile at the dawn of independence and continued as the dominant influence on economic policy for nearly a quarter of a century. Chileans were not disposed to cast off the economic ideas in vogue at the end of the colonial period, but wished to put these ideas and the policies they supported to work in the service of Chile and Chileans. Closely related to this affinity with Spanish neo-mercantilist thought was the feeling, held by many Chileans between 1820 and the mid-1850's, that such doctrines as free trade and laissez-faire were not absolute truths which have equal validity and applicability in all countries. There was a tendency to view economic theory as being something relative—as guides to policy which had to be modified and adapted to the economic situation (state of economic development) found in each country. It was the emphasis that late eighteenth-century Spanish economic thought placed on economic development, education, and improvement of the arts that attracted the attention of newly independent Chileans and contributed to the durability of this body of thought long after the teachings of the classical economists and the champions of economic liberalism were known in Chile.

Another Article of Interest

Kinsbruner, Jay. "A Comment on the Exclusiveness of Protection in Chilean Economics at Mid-Nineteenth Century." XLV (1965), 591–594.

CHAPTER FIVE

BRAZIL

14. Social Life in Brazil
in the Middle of the Nineteenth Century

GILBERTO FREYRE

Professor Freyre has become the most popular and widely read historian of Brazil, and his views have roused much discussion in his own country and elsewhere. The present study was his Master's thesis at Columbia University, and reveals his abiding interest in "l'histoire intime." He wanted to know, as did Walter Pater, "how people lived, what they wore, and what they looked like." Students who may be daunted by the many pages and voluminous footnotes of his later works will find in this article a most engaging story, a sort of family portrait, for which he used personal sources and a wide variety of printed materials. This thoroughly enjoyable account is, in fact, an excellent introduction to his method and style. An expanded, definitive version of this study has appeared in Portuguese.

*　　*　　*

... l'histoire intime; c'est ce roman vrai que la posterité appelera peut-être un jour l'histoire humaine.—*Les Goncourts.*

The following essay is an attempt to make clear to myself what the Brazil of the middle of the nineteenth century was like or, to use Walter Pater's words when asked what he studied history for, to know "how people lived, what they wore and what they looked like". In a way, the preparation for it was unconsciously begun years ago when, as a child, I used to ask questions of my grandmother about the "good old days". She was then the only one in our family to admit that the old days had been good; the others seemed to be all "futurists" and "post-impressionists" of some kind or other. But in studying, more recently, my grandmother's days, I have approached them neither to praise nor to blame—only to taste the joy of understanding the old social order.

To do this was even a more difficult task than I had imagined it to be. I had to fight my way through the accounts of prejudiced, uncritical, and superficial minds—through periodicals, lithogravures, manuscripts, books of travel, and diaries. I turned to foreigners as the most dependable of all the social critics of the period—a period about which Brazilian writers have written either to glorify or to blame, never with a fair spirit of criticism. I found my material in the Hispano-americana of Dr. Oliveira Lima in the Catholic University, Washington, D. C., the New York Public Library, and the Library of Congress. Dr. Oliveira Lima's Library—probably the most select of its kind in America or Europe—has not yet been opened to the public and I owe to his kindness the honor of having been the first investigator to use it.

Some of the facts inserted in this essay were gathered from survivors of the old order, among them Mrs. Richard Rundle, of New York and formerly of Rio de Janeiro. The description of student life in Pernambuco is based on what I heard from Dr. João Vicente Costa, of Pernambuco.

It is a commonplace that the years 1848–1864 mark, in the history of Brazil, an era of peace, conformity, and decorum in public affairs. The student of the period is impressed by other less obvious features: the sound condition of public finance; the slow but definite material progress; the crude technique of production; the important part played by religion in practically every phase of social life; the disregard in all parts of the Empire, even in Rio de Janeiro, for the commonplaces of public hygiene; the attachment to traditions of which the Brazilian had not learned to be ashamed; the corruption among the clergy; the lack of sap in literature; and the almost total absence of critical thought.

From 1848 to 1856 the Empire increased in economic well being. The "Codigo Commercial", put into effect in 1850, was a good stimulant for business; so was the law authorizing the Bank of Brazil to issue circulating notes, thus extending facilities for credit. Statistics show that foreign commerce—the export of coffee, sugar, cotton, hides, rum, rosewood, and cattle horns—more than doubled between 1849 and 1856. According to a foreign observer "from 1850 to 1860, inclusive, the great tropical staples of coffee, sugar, cotton, and tobacco, actually increased more than thirty per cent". Budgetary conditions of the period—so fully described by the Count Auguste van der Straten-Ponthoz in his work *Le Budget du Brésil*—reflect the sanity of the general economic situation, though the mode of taxation was anything but perfect. Oliveira Lima says that by 1860 the Empire "had acquired its full vigor", after a decade of domestic peace, and of increase in agricultural production and foreign trade.

In their material environment and, to a certain extent, in their social life, the majority of Brazilians of the fifties were in the Middle Ages: the élite only was living in the eighteenth century. Only a few men, such as the emperor himself, and a few women, such as Nisia Floresta, were conscious of the Europe of John Stuart Mill, hoop-skirts, Sir Charles Lyell, George Sand, four-wheeled English carriages, and Pius IX. Politically the English type of government was the model after which a sensible, and even sophisticated, oligarchy, in whose power the stern emperor often intruded like a big moral policeman, governed the country. Among some of those oligarchs such subteties and nuances of political theory as "what is the nature and what are the limits of the moderating power in a parliamentary monarchy?" were often discussed. But more practical subjects occupied their attention: the better administration of civil justice, the building of railways, the relations with the boisterous republics to the south, the slave trade. They were studious and took their responsibilities seriously. The imperial senate was, during the fifties and early sixties, an assembly of brilliant minds. Machado de Assis has left us a graphic description of the senate he knew in 1860—the senate of the old Marquis of Itanhaem, of Rio Branco, Nabuco de Araujo, Zacarias de Goes—a place where public affairs were discussed in an able, entertaining, sometimes caustic, but always dignified, way.

As in the *ante-bellum* South of the United States, the best intelligences of Brazil in the fifties and sixties were engaged in politics. Literature, sand-wiched between politics and journalism, was a very watery and thin filler; no pungency, no original flavor. It is true that in the late fifties, Indianism began to appear in the poems of Consalves Dias and the novels of Alençar; but most of it was insincere and full of false notes. As to critical thought there was none in philosophy, literature, or religion; there was some in political writers: Zacarias de Goes, Viscount de Uruguay and, in the late sixties, Tavares Bastos. But it was only in the seventies that a restless group of "young intellectuals" was to rise in Pernambuco, under the shadow of its law school, to color Brazilian life with an infusion of their own youth mixed with much of ill-digested European influences.

In an examination of the economic structure of Brazilian society in the middle of the nineteenth century we find on one side a class of landown-ers and slaveholders; on the other, the mass of slaves, and between the two a few "petits bourgeois" and small farmers, not counting the bureaucracy and leaving out the mercantile interests—the bulk of which was foreign. A sort of medieval landlordism prevailed. Land was owned by coffee planters in the south, cattle-proprietors in the inland provinces and Rio Grande do Sul, by *senhores de engenho* (sugar planters) in the Northeast, especially in Pernambuco. Along the coast and in scattered points of the interior were extensive monastic estates. The class of small farmers were the *"roceiros"*, not a few of whom were colored freedmen. Most of the *petit bourgeoisie* was composed of *marinheiros*, or newly arrived Portuguese. Some of these were able to rise, by their perseverance, from being keepers of kiosks or small grocershops, and *mascates*, or peddlers, to the comfortable merchant class—the fathers of future statesmen, diplomats, and judges. The liberal-ism of the empire, so eager to recognize individual merit, was favorable to newcomers.

By the middle of the nineteenth century the population of Brazil was, roughly speaking, seven millions. J. L. Maré, in his book *Le Brésil en 1852 et sa colonization future*, estimated it as six to seven millions. In an article published in *O Diario* (Rio de Janeiro), on December 11, 1847, F. Nunes de Souza, a Brazilian statistician, assumed the population of the country to be, then, 7,360,000. Of these he classed 2,120,000 as whites: 1,100,000 as free colored, 3,120,000 as negro slaves, 180,000 as free native African, and 800,000 as Indians. Miscegenation was going on freely. As early as 1818 or 1819 the French naturalist Auguste de Saint-Hilaire found such a mixture of races in São Paulo that he described it as an "étrange bigarrure d'où resultent des complications également embarrassantes pour l'administration et dangereuses pour la morale publique". Alfred R. Wallace found in Para "a most varied and interesting mixture of races".

"There is," he writes, "the fresh-colored Englishman, who seems to thrive as well here as in the cooler climates of his country, the sallow American, the swarthy Portuguese, the more corpulent Brazilian, the merry Negro and the apathetic but finely formed Indian; and between these a hundred shades and mixtures which it requires an experienced eye to detect." The American, C. S. Stewart, U. S. N., who visited Brazil in the early fifties, was surprised at "the fearfully mongrel aspect of the population".

The bulk of the population lived on the coast, but one inland province, Minas Geraes, had become very populous since the eighteenth century. In Nunes de Souza's statistics, Minas Geraes is given 1,130,000 inhabitants. That vast province had been settled by *garimpereiros*, or gold-hunters—men from São Paulo, restless and virile. Saint-Hilaire calls them "une nuée d'aventuriers". By the middle of the nineteenth century the once active towns of Minas Geraes were declining or, at least, stagnant. Villa Rica was but the shadow of what it had been. The province was becoming agricultural and its moral conditions, which had been so bad during the gold fever and in the early part of the century, were now improving. The Catholic Church, extending from Mariana the tentacles of its moral discipline, was softening the rough-mannered pioneer, who now said the *Benedicite* before his meals.

São Paulo was perhaps the most prosperous province during the decade 1850–1860. Its population reached in 1847, 800,000—as much as Pernambuco. Its capital had become, as far as material progress goes, one of the best cities in the empire. Its houses were attractive and its streets wide and straight. Around the city there were the *chacaras*, or country-houses, surrounded by *jabuticabeiras* and other fruit trees and farther inland, the *fazendas*, or coffee estates, where symmetrical rows of coffee trees extended for miles. The prosperity of São Paulo during the fifties is explained by the increase in the exports of coffee. In June of 1855, 206,002 bags of coffee were exported from Rio de Janeiro; in June of 1856, 178,444. As to its intellectual activity, which centered in the Law School, São Paulo was inferior to Pernambuco: it was inferior to Pernambuco, to Bahia, and of course to the metropolis, in social life.

The agricultural progress of Pernambuco during the fifties was also marked. Its production of sugar increased from 10,000 tons, in 1821, to 70,000, in 1853, making Recife the greatest sugarmart in the empire. The bulk of the sugar came from those *engenhos*, or sugar-estates, around the Villa das Floes, in the region known as *matta*. From Recife to the river Una there were, by 1855, some three hundred large sugar-plantations. The owners of those estates lived in a sort of baronial style, forming a homogeneous class in respect to their economic interests, social life, and politics. They ruled over their estates, and over the small towns, in a true feudal way. Were not they the descendants of those arrogant planters who expelled to Bahia, in 1666, a captain-general, or colonial governor, sent by the metropolis? With them the aristocratic manner and manners went back for generations. They were descended from some of the best blood of Portugal and it was through their ancestors that the vague thing we call culture first reached Portuguese America. During the forties, fifties, and early sixties the refinement of life and manners came to flower once more in Pernambuco, thanks to that gentleman-scholar, Governor Baron da Boa Vista. The women dressed well; the receptions in the governor's palace were brilliant, and brilliant were the performances in the theater of Santa Isabel, and the ceremonies in the church of Espirito Santo. A writer of the period calls attention to "le luxe, qui commence à prendre un certain developpement à Pernambouc."

Bahia was, economically, the rival of Pernambuco. It had some sugar-estates but was more important as a center of cotton and tobacco culture. Manufactures were developing there and an American traveler describes a cotton factory that he visited in Valença—probably the best one then existing in Brazil. In 1851 the revenue of Bahia was 4,784,600 milreis while that of Pernambuco was 4,639,427 milreis. But later on the cholera epidemic made itself felt in Bahia in a more deadly way than anywhere else in Brazil. Many slaves died in the years of 1855 and 1856; hence the economic crisis that followed and affected not only Bahia exports but coffee as well.

To the Brazilian of the fifties the country to the west of Minas Geraes, Pernambuco and Bahia—the *sertão*—was a region of even greater mystery and fear than to the later-day Brazilian. It was free from any policing: law and even Dom Pedro meant nothing to its inhabitants. Taxation among them, for instance, was impossible in those days: no system of tax-gathering was suave enough for their scruples of independence. We are told by an English observer, writing in 1860, of an experiment at collecting duties on hides in the *sertão* of Pernambuco. "The sertanejos caught the miserable tax-gatherer with the same glee that a Galway mob would seize a process-server, tripped him, killed a bullock, sewed him up in it with his head protruding, and sent him back with the Spartan message 'If the emperor wants beef, let his man take it with him' ".

The *sertanejo* of the fifties was even more picturesque than the *sertanejo* of today, whom Euclydes da Cunha has so vividly described in *O Sertão*. In the fifties he wore an enormous stock of hair", a "battered steeple-

crowned hat", and a cotton shirt and breeches. The Reverend Doctor
Fletcher describes the entering of a family of "sertanejos" into Recife,
where they came to sell their cotton and hides, having to travel from fifteen
to twenty days before reaching the coast. The man rode "perched upon a
couple of oblong cotton-bags strapped parallel to his horse's sides, followed
by his train of a dozen horses or mules, loaded, in the same way, with cotton
or sugar. A monkey, with a clog tied to his waist, surmounts one in place
of the driver; parrot and his wife another: and a large brass-throated macaw
with a stiff blue coat of feathers another." These caravans were a sight that
city children enjoyed watching: I remember having heard my grandmother
refer to them as one of the colorful memories of her childhood.

Mention must be made, of course, of Rio de Janeiro. By the middle of
the nineteenth century that province was the first in population with
1,500,000 inhabitants. Scattered in it there were foreign colonies, some of
which were prospering. They were composed of Germans and German
Swiss. That of Petropolis counted 2,565 members. Its condition was good,
the colonists specializing in the cultivation of corn and potatoes and in the
manufacture of butter and cream cheese. So did the colonists of Nova
Friburgo, who were 2,000 in number.

Manufacturing interests were concentrated in Rio de Janeiro, around
the *corte*, or the capital of the empire. Of the seventy-two factories that
existed in Brazil, for the manufacture of hats, candle, soap, beer, cigars, and
cotton, fifty-two were located in the province of Rio de Janeiro. The remaining were distributed as follows: in Bahia ten, Pernambuco four, Ma-
ranhao two, and São Paulo, Minas Geraes, Parana, and São Pedro, one each.
These manufacturing interests were mostly in the hands of aliens. The labor
itself was partly foreign. The porcelain factory in Minas Geraes had expert
workers brought from the famous establishments of Saxony. But free
negroes and mulattoes were often employed. Fletcher saw in a cotton-
factory in Valença, Bahia, "the whole operation of modeling, and finishing,
performed by negroes". Even the foreman of the foundry was a Brazilian
negro. Negroes became skilful in more delicate industries such as the making
of artificial flowers with feathers—an industry of which the French traveler
Max Radiguet wrote that it "semble avoir atteint son apogée à Rio Janeiro".
Mme. Ida Pfeiffer was surprised to find in the "ateliers" of Rio de Janeiro,
"les plus distingués des noirs occupés a confectionner des habits, des souliers,
des ouvrages de tapisseries, des broderies d'or et d'argent. Plus d'une
negresse assez bien habillée travaillait aux toilettes de femmes les plus ele-
gants et aux broderies les plus delicates."

It was in the fifties that the first railways were built in Brazil but only
in the seventies did they become a serious factor in the economic and social
life of the country. By 1858 the Dom Pedro Railway had only extended
twenty-seven miles. Railways were in construction in São Paulo, Bahia, and
Pernambuco. But most of the traveling was still done by water, or, when
this was impossible, on horse and mule back or by ox cart. Count van der

Straten-Ponthoz writing in 1854 remarked that "au Brésil tous les trans-ports s'executent peniblement a dos de mulet". The president of the prov-ince of Goyaz—we are told by the same author—had to travel for three months to arrive from Rio de Janeiro at the capital of his province. Caravans of goods traveled for five months before reaching the capital of Matto Grosso from Rio de Janeiro.

Steam navigation made notable progress in Brazil during the fifties. It was followed by improvements in the towns it touched. Para, for instance, gained much from the line of regular steamers on the Amazon, inaugurated in 1854. Such luxuries as camphene lights and macadam generally followed steam-navigation. Hence the progress noted by foreign observers in coast and riverside towns. The others were hardly affected by any touch of progress until railways penetrated the country. They remained truly medi-eval—no public lighting, no street cleaning, no macadam. And medieval they were in their customs and in their relations to the great landowners around whose estates the towns and villages were scattered.

The power of the great planters was indeed feudalistic, their patriar-chalism being hardly restricted by civil laws. Fletcher, who traveled through the interior of Brazil, wrote: "The proprietor of a sugar or cattle estate is, practically, an absolute lord." And he adds: "The community that lives in the shadow of so great a man is his feudal retinue: and, by the conspiracy of a few such men, who are thus able to bring scores of lieges and partisans into the field, the quiet of the province was formerly more than disturbed by revolts which gave the government much trouble." Oliveira Lima says that those communities living in the shadow of the great planters were very heterogeneous: he compares them to the army of lieges that the Portuguese nobles of the eighteenth century kept in their states: *bravi* or rascals, bull fighters, friars, guitarrists, etc. The large Brazilian estate was a self-sustain-ing unit—economically and socially—depending little on the world outside its large wood gates. It had its cane-fields or its coffee-plantations, and plan-tations of mandioc, black beans, and other produce, for its own consumption. Its population included, besides the owner and his family, *feitores*, or over-seers, *vaqueiros*, or shepherds, sometimes a chaplain and a tutor, carpenters, smiths, masons, and a multitude of slaves. Fletcher visited a coffee estate in Minas Geraes which contained an area of sixty-four square miles. Besides the rows of coffee trees he noticed large tracts of mandioc, cotton and sugar, an abundance of cattle, and one hundred and fifty hives with bees. "Of all the articles mentioned above," Doctor Fletcher informs us, "not one finds its way to the market. They are for the sustenance and clothing of the slaves, of whom the Commendador formerly had seven hundred." In the large sugar estates of Pernambuco, scattered between Recife and the Una river, and against whose feudalistic powers the revolution of 1848 is said to have been a protest, certain domestic industries developed along with agricultural activities, among them the making of wines from *genipapo*, the making of charqui, or jerked beef, cream cheese, and, of course, all sorts of sweetmeats and cakes. These activities were superintended by the "old missus" herself.

The work people of the plantations were well-fed, and attended to by their master and mistress as a "large family of children". They had three meals a day and a little rum (*caxaca*) in the morning. Their breakfast consisted of farina or *pirão*, with fruits and rum; at midday they were given a very substantial meal of meat or fish; in the evening, black beans, rice, and vegetables. On holidays it was customary on certain estates to have an ox killed for the slaves and a quantity of rum was given to make them merry. Then they would dance the sensuous measures of the *batuque* or other African dances or sing or play the *marimba*.

As a rule the slaves were not overworked in the households either in the plantations or in the city. It is true that much was being said in the fifties, of cruel treatment of slaves in Brazil, by the British anti-slavery propaganda. Later on the British dark account of conditions was to be repeated in Brazil by Brazilian anti-slavery orators such as the young Nabuco and Sr. Ruy Barbosa—men inflamed by the bourgeois idealism of Wilberforce as well as by a very human desire for personal glory—and they did it in so emphatic a language that the average Brazilian believes today that slavery was really cruel in his country. The powerful fancy won over reality. For, as a matter of fact, slavery in Brazil was anything but cruel. The Brazilian slave lived the life of a cherub if we contrast his lot with that of the English and other European factory-workers in the middle of the last century. Alfred R. Wallace—an abolitionist—found the slaves in a sugar plantation he visited in North Brazil "as happy as children". He adds: "They have no care and no wants, they are provided for in sickness and old age, their children are never separated from their wives, except under such circumstances as would render them liable to the same separation, were they free, by the laws of the country." As to conditions in the south of the Empire, an American observer, unsympathetic and even hostile towards the Brazilians, gives the following account: "As a rule, in the Southern part of Brazil, slaves were fairly treated and generally had much more liberty than was compatible with very efficient service though I have known cases of individual cruelty which have made my blood boil with indignation." Doctor Rendu wrote that "en général les Brésiliens ne surchargent pas leurs esclaves de travail". The Reverend Walter Colton, U. S. N., found the slaves in Brazil "generally treated with kindness and humanity by their masters". Mme. Ida Pfeiffer, who visited Brazil in the late forties, writes in her famous book: "I am almost convinced that, on the whole, the lot of these slaves is less wretched than that of the peasants of Russia, Poland or Egypt, who are not called slaves." But it is an English clergyman—the Reverend Hamlet Clark, M.A., who strikes the most radical note: "Nay indeed, we need not go far to find in free England the absolute counterpart of slavery: Manighew's London Labour, and London Poor, Dicken's Oliver Twist, Hood's Song of the Shirt and many other revelations tell of a grinding, flinty-hearted despotism that

Brazilian slaveowners never can approach." As Professor Hayes points out, in England, "audiences wept at hearing how cruel masters licked their cowering slaves in Jamaica: but in their own England little Englishmen and Englishwomen ten years old were being whipped to their work," sometimes "in the factories of some of the anti-slavery orators".

At sunset the whistle of the sugar-mill closed the day's work on the Brazilian plantation. The workpeople came then for their last meal, after which they went to bed. But first they came to ask their master's and mistress' blessing: "Benção, nhonho!" Benção Nhanha!" holding out their right hand. Then the master and the mistress would say: "Deus te abençoe" (God bless you), making at the same time the sign of the cross.

In a typical Brazilian city-home of the higher class—say, the home of a custom-house officer—slaves numbered on the average fifteen or twenty. Since slaves were plentiful, certain necessities, and even luxuries, were produced at home, under the careful oversight of the mistress; cloth was cut and made into dresses, towels and undergarments; wine was distilled; lace and crivo (a sort of embroidery) were manufactured. Besides this the housewife superintended the cooking, the preserving, the baking of cakes, the care of the sick; taught her children and their black playmates the Lord's Prayer, the Apostles' Creed, and the Ave Maria; kept them from mischief and pathological abnormalities—such as eating clay—against which the "log" or the "tin mask" were sometimes employed as punishments.

Slaves were plentiful. The staff of a large city-house included cooks, those trained to serve in the dining room, wet-nurses, water carriers, footmen, chambermaids—the latter sleeping in their mistresses' rooms and assisting them in the minutest details of their toilette, such as picking lice, for instance. Sometimes there were too many slaves. A lady told Doctor Fletcher that she "had nine lazy servants at home for whom there was not employment" and another one that she could not find enough work to keep her slaves out of idleness and mischief. It is easy to imagine how some housewives became pampered idlers, spending their days languidly in gossiping, or at the balcony, or reading some new novel of Macedo or Alencar. Doctor Rendu had such in mind when he unjustly generalized about the Brazilian women: ". . . . elles passent des journées entières à leur fenêtre". Nor had F. Dabadie seen a Brazilian interior when he stated that the Brazilian ladies were lazy—"si indolentes", he says, "pour la plupart, qu'elles aimeraient mieux renoncer a toute parure et se condamner a vieillir en chemise sur une natte ou dans un hamac que d'aller acheter dans un magasin les afflutiaux dont elles raffolent". It is true that the Brazilian lady of the fifties did not go out for her shopping. She was a house prisoner. Moorish prejudices kept her from those pretty shops of fancy goods, bonnets, jewelry, *bijouterie*, which travelers admired so much in Rio de Janeiro, the Italian naval officer Eugenio Rodriguez describing them as "elegantissimi magazini." But at home she did not stay in her hammock. In a typical home works of all kinds went on during the day. Linen, silk, millinery, fancy goods, were bought from samples and pattern-books, after much running of negro boys from shop to the house: or, in many cases, from the peddler who came once or twice a week, making a noise with his yardstick. It was not necessary to go to the market to buy vegetables, fruit, or eggs since venders of these rural products, as well as of milk, meat, and fish, came to the home. There were itinerant coppersmiths who announced themselves by hitting some old stewpan with a hammer. Even novels were sold at the door. Paulo Barreto tells that Alencar and Macedo—"the best sellers" of the period—had negroes go from house to house, selling their novels in baskets. Therefore, the fact that the Brazilian woman did not go to the shops does not mean that she was too lazy to do her own shopping. She did it. And after the shopping was done in the morning it was she who superintended the various kinds of work going on in the household. The Count de Suzannet, who was anything but pleased with the Brazilian women, remarks that "elles président aux soins du ménage donnant leurs ordres aux negresses ou veillant elles-mêmes à la préparation des mets". Fletcher who, though a Protestant clergyman, enjoyed the intimacy of many a home in Brazil, thought that the Brazilian housewife answered to the description of the "good woman" in the last chapter of Proverbs: "she looketh well to the ways of her household and eateth not the bread of idleness." Carlos de Laet—the last brilliant mind of a departed order—tells us that "to accuse a lady of not knowing how to manage her household was then the most unpleasant offence to her". Oliveira Lima characterizes the Brazilian housewife of this period as possessing "ability to manage" (*capacidade administrativa*), without which it was impossible to keep such large households going. Others might be quoted to show that in this matter the weighing of evidences reveals an active, rather than an idle woman, as the typical Brazilian housewife in slavery days.

The double standard of morality prevailed in the fifties: the lily-like woman was idolized while incontinence in the man was slightly regarded. It is true that the Emperor Dom Pedro II. made the standards of sexual morality stricter for those who were around him or who aspired to political eminence. He was a sort of Queen Victoria in breeches—only more powerful—and watched the statesmen like a moral detective. It is commonplace that he refused to appoint men to eminent positions on account of irregularities in their private life—a tradition which the Republican leaders found too foolish to maintain. But the emperor's influence was only felt in the high spheres of officialdom. In the large country estates irregularities went on freely, the colored girls constituting a disguised harem where either the master or his sons satisfied their exotic sexual tastes. Doctor Rendu remarked of the Brazilians that "leur passion pour les femmes ne connait point de frein; ils s'y abandonnent sans retenue et ne reculent devant aucune tentative pour la satisfaire". From these relations with slave girls resulted a substantial increase in the number of slaves—an improved slave breed since, in many cases, the male parent was a Portuguese—I mean ethnically, not civilly—of the best blood. From such unions of first-rate men—the gentry—and their slave women sprang those able halfbreeds who, even during the Empire, rose to prominence and have given the Republic some of its best leaders.

In the cities of Brazil of 1850, bachelorhood did not offer the charms it offers in sophisticated centers. But bachelors enjoyed certain licences. Social legislation did not disturb them; neither did the priests who, being bachelors themselves, must have felt an acute "consciousness of kind". Bachelors and widowers even advertised for mistresses, in a suavely disguised way. This sort of publicity shocked an American Puritan, a Doctor Creary. He quotes some of the advertisements in the papers of Rio de Janeiro, one of which is from a "young single Englishman" who wishes "a colored girl to take charge of his house"—a colored girl "who is poor and to whom everything will be given to make her happy".

In his attitude towards his wife the Brazilian of the fifties was a true patriarch of the Roman type. She was given authority in the household, but not outside. Outside she was to be, legally and socially, the shadow of her husband. "A promenade below, with the chance of a flirtation, is denied her," the American C. S. Stewart remarks in his book. Pointing out the virtues of the Brazilian matron in the *ancien régime*, of which he is the most eminent survivor, the Count Carlos de Laet says that "she knew how to obey her husband". Monsieur Expilly, a French feminist who visited Brazil in the fifties, was indignant at what he calls "le despotisme paternel" and "la politique conjugale". "La broderie", he writes, "la confection des doces (confitures), le bavardage des negresses, le gaffoune, le maniament de la chicote et, le dimanche, une visite aux églises, voilà les seules distractions que le despotisme paternel et la politique conjungale permettaient aux juenes moças et aux inquietes senhoras".

While the woman spent most of her time indoors, the man—the city man—spent most of his, out—in the street, in the plaza, at the door of some French hotel or in his office or warehouse. The condition was much like that in ancient Greece where people thought, with the wise old Xenophon, that "it is not so good for a woman to be out-of-doors as in, and it is more dishonourable for a man to stay in than to attend to his affairs outside". Brazilian men, like the Greeks, enjoyed the easy fellowship of the street and the plaza—and in the street and the plaza they discussed politics, Donizetti, the Aberdeen Bill, and transacted business. We are told by Sampaio Ferraz, in his excellent work "O Molhe de Olinda", that in Pernambuco, during the last half of the nineteenth century, the most important business was transacted outdoors, under the trees of Lingoeta. Lithogravures of the period, which I examined in Oliveira Lima's collection, show the streets—Rua Direita and Largo da Alfandega in Rio, Lingoeta in Pernambuco, and so on—full of groups of men, talking, smoking, taking snuff, while coffee or sugar carriers run with their cargoes, their half-naked bodies shining with oily sweat. The sentiment of home was not strong among the Brazilian men when the patriarchal family was in its full vigor. Nor did they have mundane clubs—unless if we accept as such the Masonic lodges. The street was their club.

This may serve as an explanation of the fact that the city Brazilians of the fifties did not seem to have attractive homes. Twenty years before a French traveler, Louis De Freycinet, had observed that the Brazilians spent most of their time sleeping, or outdoors, or, sometimes, receiving their friends: therefore they only needed—the Frenchman thought—a reception room and the bedrooms. In the fifties the city houses were practically the same that De Freycinet had seen. They were heavy and solid, like those fat Moorish towers that nothing seems to uproot; their walls were thick, made of bits of stone mixed with mortar. Ewbanks informs us that they were "mostly two stories". As to the walls he writes that they "are of rough stone coated with a stucco of lime and loam, which makes them appear as if white-washed". "Some owners"—I am still quoting from Ewbanks— "show their taste by coloring the stucco in panels or otherwise; light blue and pink are favorite tints". In those old houses, a few of which survive, there were big spouts at the eaves of the roofs, where the rain was *shooted* in the narrow streets.

The plan of the old Brazilian house was the poorest that one can imagine. Indeed, in this respect, it was a masterpiece of architectural stupidity. Doctor Kidder, an American, was entertained in a house in Pernambuco where "the first or ground floor was denominated the armazem and was occupied by male servants at night; the second furnished apartments for the counting room, etc.; the third and fourth for parlours and lodging rooms; the fifth for dining-rooms; and the sixth for a kitchen". Of course such a skyscraper was not the typical residence. But one wonders why the houses were built as if space was scarce and looked gloomy, heavy, fat. Most of the houses of the well-to-do had a carriage-house and a stable on the ground floor, for in the forties and fifties, at least in Rio and Pernambuco, carriages with luxuriously cushioned seats and gorgeously dressed negro postilions, took the place of the old *cadeirinhas*, or palanquins. I have the photogravure of the carriage which belonged to a wealthy coffee-trader of Rio de Janeiro—a carriage drawn by four white horses, with a black coachman in the box and a postilion. In Bahia the steepness of the streets prevented the introduction of wheeled-carriages and as late as the seventies palanquins were used there.

As to the furniture of the household—tables, sofas, chairs, marquises, bedsteads—they too were heavy, solid, made of rosewood, *oleo, vinhatico*, and other indigenous woods. Each reception-room had a large sofa at one end and rows of chairs, one from each end of the sofa. They were arranged with a childlike idea of symmetry—I mean as a child places his toy-soldiers in line for a battle—in straight, regular rows. In some houses the sofa and the chairs were adorned with laces and colorful ribbons. A piano was seldom lacking, for as Francis de Castelnau observed in Brazil "dans presque toutes les maisons l'on voit ou l'on entend un piano, souvent même dans les plus chétives". When visitors came not only were games of romps, such as *pilha tres*, enjoyed, but a sonata or a polka was played at the piano by a lady. It was also *accompanied at the piano* that the young men recited "Oh, guerreiros da taba sagrada!" or "Waterloo, Waterloo, lição sublime!" or "Se eu morresse amanha"—poems from the favorite bards of the period. Sometimes the master of the house, being a flute or a violin virtuoso, would entertain his visitors. Most of the men in those days played the piano or the violin or the flute. My paternal grandfather—a sugar planter—was a violin virtuoso. The keen taste for music was perhaps what made Brazilian slaveholders kind and gentle.

De Freycinet forgot that Brazilians needed, besides a parlor and many bedrooms, a large dining hall. They had large families and liked to have their friends for dinner. It was on the tables, over the large dishes of fat pork and black beans, of pirão, a sort of unctuous pudding which Arthur de Oliveira has celebrated in his colorful prose, of *cangica*, fancy breads, sweetmeats, cakes, and frozen desserts, that the Brazilians showed the best of their patriarchal hospitality. Foreigners were delighted at the delicacies with which the Brazilians loaded their tables, specially the *doces* and creams of indigenous fruits like oranges, *maracujas*, *goiabas*, mangoes. The most epicurean of them, Max Radiguet, explains that "les fruits les plus exquis et les plus parfumés, savamment combinés avec les ingrédients ordinaires flattent le palais et l'odorat". In most of the houses the desserts were prepared by the mistress herself; she also served the dishes with her own hands.

A very apt custom followed in regard to the dinner guest was to offer him, soon after his arrival, a light coat of linen, silk, or alpaca. A traveler informs us that "whenever a person is invited to a select dinner party it is always expected that he should make his appearance in a coat of sable cloth; but immediately on his arrival he is invited to "take it off" and offered one of fine linen as substitute". This custom is still followed by a few intelligent Brazilians.

In most of the homes the "Benedicite" was said before the meal and "Gratias" after it, the slaves joining in the brief ceremony. After "Gratias" was said, all made the sign of the cross.

Religion played an important part in the family life of Brazil in the middle of the nineteenth century. The home-education, that is, the early training of boys and girls, was very religious. Children were piously taught by their mothers to fear the Almighty Man-God, who watches all that we do and marks in a huge notebook all our sins for future punishment. They were told also stories of the Virgin Mary and her little, plump, rosy baby —the Divine Infant—who grew into the Man of Sorrow and our Savior. They were taught to say the Lord's Prayer, the Apostles' Creed, the Ave Maria, the Salve Regina, and the cathechism. They said their prayers on rising in the morning and on retiring at night. On retiring they went to their parents and all elders present to receive their blessing. At least once during the year the parents took their children to the altar of Holy Communion and to confession. The most religious parents sent their sons to the parish church to serve the mass as altar-boys. Most of the *engenhos* had their own chapels, where the family's beloved dead were buried, instead of being taken to the cemetery. Practically every city-house had its *oratorio* with the images in a glassed case, before which the family gathered for worship in a sweet atmosphere of incense and scent of roses.

Home discipline was based on the fear of the Lord, but when this failed a whip was vigorously used. It was often too severe. Boys of fifteen were chastised for offenses that a latter-day parent would regard slightly. An unmarried son of twenty odd years would not dare to smoke in the presence of his father. As to the girls they never joined their elders in conversation unless specially invited to do so. The slaves were beaten when found in mischief, and punished with the "log" or the "thin mask" when caught in injurious vices. The mistress of the house always kept a whip. The French feminist Expilly placed the handling of the whip (*le management de la chicote*) among the occupations of a Brazilian matron.

At eight or nine the girl was sent to a religious boarding school and kept there until she was thirteen or fourteen. There her training, begun at home, was continued. She was trained in that fine art—the art of being a woman. Music, dancing, embroidery, prayers, French, and sometimes English, a thin layer of literature—such were the elements of a girl's education in the boarding school. She came back a very romantic, and sometimes bewitching, little creature, reading Sue, Dumas, and George Sand, besides the gossiping *pacotilhas* such as *A Marmota* and Alencar's saccharine, but often erotic, *folhetins*. And how she could pray! And how she could dance! The dances of the period were the quadrille, the lanciers, and the polka; to dance them well, to be light as a feather and tiny as a piece of lace, was the highest ideal of a girl—I was told by a lady who took dancing lessons from the same teacher as Princess Isabel.

Ladies bloomed early. The years of giddy childhood were short. At fourteen or fifteen the girl dressed like a lady. Docility, and even timidity, was considered a grace. The girl was trained to be timid or, at least, to look timid before people—as timid as a little boy before the circus elephant. The Brazilian girl of the fifties was everything that the so called "very modern" girl is not. "Perhaps they were too timid"—Carlos de Laet writes of the girls of that period—"but they were adorable in their timidity". Those very timid girls were playful and talkative when given a chance. Max Radiguet tells of the custom of the Brazilian society girls going to the imperial chapel in Rio de Janeiro, where an excellent orchestra assisted by a choir of Italian soprani played every Friday evening. There "pendant toute la durée de ce concert religieux les femmes accroupées sur leur caire de tapisserie prenaient sans scruple des sorbets et des glaces avec les jeunes gens qui venaient converser avec elles dans le lieu saint". When such merry rendezvous, in the shadow of the church, were not possible—and the cus-

tom was discontinued just as dances in the churches were discontinued—
love-making had to be even more platonic. There was, for instance, love-
making by means of a fan—that is, girls could make their fans speak a
particular language of love which all lovers were supposed to understand.
"It all depended on how the fan was held", an old lady explained to me
while her tapering, white fingers handled a delicate fan in a thousand and
one ways.

But as a rule marriage did not result from romantic lovemaking. The
man whom the girl married in her early teens was seldom her own choice.
He was her parents', or her father's, choice. An English traveler describes
how betrothals were made: "Some day the father walks into the drawing
room, accompanied by a strange gentleman, elderly or otherwise. 'Minha
Filha', he remarks, 'this is your future husband'." Sometimes the "future
husband" was a pleasant surprise—a pale youth of twenty-three or twenty-
five, a ruby or an emerald sparkling from his forefinger, his moustaches
perfumed, his hair smooth, oily . . . a hero who had escaped from some
bright German oleogravure or from the pages of a novel. And romantic
love developed between the contracting parties. But other times the "future
husband" was some fat, solid, newly-rich Portuguese, middle-aged, his neck
short and his hands coarse. Perhaps a very fine person—inside; but what a
death-blow for a sentimental girl of the fifties. And yet she often accepted
him—the potbellied one—such a marriage being nothing more than a
business partnership. Unfortunate marriages of the latter type became a
favorite theme with Brazilian writers of fiction in the sixties and seventies,
Guimaraes' *Historia de Uma Moça Rica* being typical of that literature.
But one should be discriminating in the matter: some marriages arranged
by the girl's parents were as happy as marriages ordinarily are.

Early marriages meant early procreation. At fifteen a girl was generally a mother. Sometimes she was a mother at fourteen and even thirteen.
The Reverend Walter Colton wrote in his diary: "A Brazilian lady was
pointed out to me to-day who is but twelve years of age, and who has two
children, who were frolicking around her steps. . . ." And he adds: ". . . ladies
here marry extremely young. They have hardly done with their fictitious
babies, when they have the smiles and tears of real ones." As a consequence,
girls faded early, having tasted in a hurry the joy of careless youth.

The boy, too, was born middle-aged. Dom Pedro's prematurity may
be taken as typical. He was made an emperor at fifteen, and he was then
very thoughtful and serious; at twenty he was an old man. Youth flew
from him in a gallop. Brazilian education favored then, more than in a later
day, the prematurity of the boy. Very early he was sent to the *collegio*,
where he lived and boarded. Though his home might be a street or two off,
very seldom—usually once a month—was he allowed to go there. He often
got from home boxes of cakes and bon-bons, but no such things as toys.
Toys were for little boys; he was nine or ten, nearly a man. As a rule he
studied hard his Latin grammar, his rhetoric, his French classics, his sacred

history, his geography. When that big occasion—the final examinations—came, he shone, answering well all that Padre So-and-So asked about Horace, Noah, Rebecca, rules of punctuation, the verb *amare;* and all that some other teacher asked about Racine, Vesuvius, and what not. Then his father sent him a present: *The Luziadas* or Milton's *Paradise Lost.* He went to mass on Sundays, sometimes acting as altar-boy dressed in a scarlet cloak, and though he was little more than kneehigh, he wore in the street a "stiff black hat" and carried a cane. Doctor Fletcher writes of the Brazilian boy of the fifties: ". . . he is made a little old man before he is twelve years of age, having his stiff black hat, standing collar and cane; and in the city he walks along as if everybody were looking at him, and as if he were encased in corsets. He does not run, or jump, or trundle hoops, or throw stones, as boys in Europe and North America." In the *collegio,* besides "the ordinary rudiments of education", he learns, Doctor Fletcher writes "to write a 'good hand', which is a universal accomplishment among the Brazilians; and most of the boys of the higher classes are good musicians. . . ." The French physician, Doctor Rendu, vents upon the Brazilian boy his caustic humor: "A sept ans", he writes, "le jeune Brésilien a deja la gravité d'un adulte, il se promene majestueusement, une badine a la main, fier d'une toilette que le fait plutôt ressembler aux marionnettes de nos foires qu'à un être humain". I have seen photographs of Brazilian boys in the sixties: sweet, seraphic-looking creatures, curled, oiled, dressed like grown-ups, trying to look like old men.

At fifteen or sixteen the boy finished his studies in the *collegio.* It was time to go to the professional school. Here, as in the girls' betrothal, it was the father's or family's choice that generally prevailed. The tendency was to scatter the boys in different schools, so that the family would be represented in different professions. One was picked to go to Pernambuco or São Paulo to study law or diplomacy; another to enter the medical school; a third to be a cadet in the military school; a fourth to go to the seminary. Among the most pious families it was considered a social, as well as a moral, failure not to have a son studying for the priesthood. Sometimes the youngest son, though of no churchly turn of mind, was the scapegoat. The family simply had to have a *padre.* As to the stupid son, who could not make good anywhere, the sensible parents sent him to business, which was looked down upon by gentlemen.

The flower of the family was picked for the law school—the law school being the training-ground, not for magistracy only, but for the parliament and the cabinet also, and for diplomacy. There were two law schools—that of Olinda, in Pernambuco, and that of São Paulo. Writing from São Paulo in 1855 Doctor Kidder said of its law school: "It is here and at the Pernambuco Law School (which contains three hundred students in the regular course) that the statesmen of Brazil receive that education which so much better fits them for the Imperial Parliament and the various legislative assemblies of their land than any preparatories that exist in the Spanish-American countries".

The "regular course", to which Doctor Kidder refers, came after a sort of pre-law course which included Latin, geometry, rational and moral philosophy, and other subjects. The "regular course" extended over a period of five years, the following subjects being studied: philosophy of law, public law, analysis of the imperial constitution, Roman law, diplomacy, ecclesiastical law, civil law, mercantile and maritime law, political economy, and theory and practice of general law.

Some of the professorships were occupied by men of notable talent, such as Paula Baptista and Aprigio Guimaraes—the latter a Christian Socialist. Others were notable for their excesses of Catholic piety rather than for sound scholarship and sheer love of truth. In the law school of Pernambuco, Trigo de Loureiro and Braz Florentino—who wrote a book against civil marriage—represented the latter. Religious piety—not always the excess of it—permeated the life of faculty and student body alike, making it colorful and even hieratic. Grave professors and students trying to look as grave as possible took part in the big processions, all bearing candles and shuffling, hieratically. Frock-coated professors, dressed in their *opas*, went to hear the sermons in the Church of the Espirito Santo. The late Professor Camara, of the Pernambuco law school, in his very entertaining chronicle for 1904, which smells so little of the official and so much of the literary, summarizes the description he found in the school's archives of a procession in 1854, promoted by the students, who had organized themselves into a brotherhood—*Irmandade do Bom Conselho*. In this solemn procession, among the kneeling people, the young men carried an image to the Church of the Third Order of São Francisco, preceded by the Bishop of Olinda in gorgeous purple satin, by the president of the school, and the professors, also members of a brotherhood.

But this churchly atmosphere in the day time did not prevent most of the students from being merry, boisterous, and even wicked, after sunset. They did not care a rap for rowing or any ball game—not even for cock-fighting, which some of their elders enjoyed. Making love to actresses was their favorite sport. There were generally two rival actresses, like Candiani and Delmatro, in São Paulo, and Eugenia Camara and Adelaide do Amaral, in Pernambuco, and surrounding each, a fervent group of admirers—some platonic, some not. Each group had a "poet" instead of a "cheer leader", and oratorical duels were fought in the theaters. Tobias Barretto and Castro Alves excelled, in the sixties, in that sort of mental sport. Tobias made probably the strongest impression, with his crashing hand as if ready for a blow, his white teeth flashing, his eyes inflamed. He headed the group of the actress Adelaide do Amaral; Castro Alves, that of Eugenia Castro. Eugenia soon became the student's mistress and on her "he spent on two or three nights his monthly allowance".

Skip to 234

It was in the shadow of the theater that the young men enjoyed themselves, writing verses to actresses, fighting for actresses, spending money on merry suppers with actresses. For their elders, also, the theater was the center of amusement—the theater and the church. Rio de Janeiro had three fairly good theaters, with which such sophisticated Europeans as Radiguet were not at all displeased. Dabadie wrote in 1858 that "l'art dramatique et l'art lyrique sont dignement encouragés a Rio", describing the São Pedro Theater as "un des plus vastes et plus beaux que nous ayons vu". The operas of Meyerbeer, Verdi, Donizetti, and other composers were sung and performed there, in the presence of the emperor. In Pernambuco, the opera house had found an excellent patron, in the forties, in the governor Baron da Boa Vista. Doctor Fletcher points out in his book that "the first musicians go to Brazil". "Thalberg", he adds, "triumphed at Rio de Janeiro before he came to New York".

The *entrudo*—the ancestor of the modern carnival—was an occasion of great joy, being a festival of all classes. It consisted, then, in throwing at each other "limas de cheiro", or small, colored waxen balls filled with perfumed water. In Rio there were masquerade balls in the theaters: São Januario, Lyrico, São Pedro, Gymnasio. The Paraizo Theater opened its doors for all the people. So brutal was then the *entrudo* that basins and tubes of water were used, besides the *limas*.

Most of the religious festivals and processions were marked by the note of joy. Ewbanks remarks in his journal that the religious festivals "constitute the chief amusement of the masses—are their principal sports and pastimes, during which the saints themselves come out of their sanctuaries and, with padres and people, take part in the general frolic". The "general frolic" was carrying the saints in procession—processions that shuffled through the streets from one church to another: a fat bishop crowned with a miter under his canopy, blessing people to the left and the right: priests, friars; little girls dressed as cherubs or *anginhos;* a band that suddenly played a martial tune while, moved by the music, negro rascals danced in front of the procession, sometimes also quarreling and cutting each other with knives. The procession of Saint George—the patron saint of Brazil—was followed by dances and all sorts of merrymaking. The days of Saint John, Saint Peter, and Saint Anthony—the latter a full colonel in the Brazilian Army—were celebrated with outbursts of popular joy. So was Christmas, when presents of turkeys, pigs, cakes, and slaves were exchanged. The festival of Saint Ephigenia, a sort of black Madonna, was enjoyed to the utmost by the colored folks, whose "consciousness of kind" was ably aroused by the priests.

Besides the procession of the "Dead Lord", when the image of Jesus as a corpse was carried among the silent kneeling of all, the fanatics, wearing crowns of thorns, maltreated their half-naked bodies, the only sad procession was that of "Encommendação das Almas". It had even a touch of *macabrezza*—of pathological delight in grief and suffering. It took place at midnight. Men dressed in somewhat the same manner as the knights of the American Ku Klux Klan and carrying paper lanterns went through the shadowy, silent streets, serenading people. One of them went ahead bearing aloft a large cross. In that macabre serenade they chanted prayers for the souls suffering in purgatory—the souls of dead prisoners and of men dead in the sea.

In the towns of the interior there were certain crude attempts to perform mystery plays. The personages in those plays were the Devil, the Capital Sins, the Holy Father, the Virgin Mary, Saint Peter, Judas, etc. A contemporary writer says of those rustic plays, that they lacked any literary form but sometimes one would find in them "very amusing scenes" and "expressions full of wit and humor".

Religion played, as these hints have probably indicated, a prominent part in the amusements of the rustics and, to a certain extent, of all classes. It was also the backbone of organised charities. By tolerating and even encouraging superstitions, it did harm to the physical as well as the moral health of the people; it was through its hospitals, agencies of social charity, and the devotion of its nuns that it redeemed itself. Among the masses the most superstitious ideas concerning disease—its prevention and treatment —prevailed. A foreign observer writes: "Ancient cures—worthy of Pliny —are still in vogue. Earthworms fried alive in olive oil, and applied warm as a poultice, remove *whilows*, which are common among blacks and whites". The same author remarks: "I suppose there is hardly a Roman Catholic female in Brazil, from the Empress to a negress, who does not guard against invisible foes by wearing in contact with her person a coup of diminutive shields". Bone *figas* and pieces of "holy rock" were also used against "evil eye" and diseases. Superstitions penetrated within the walls of hospitals and killed their inmates. Both Ewbanks and Radiguet tell the story of an inmate of the Lazaros Hospital—an institution in Rio de Janeiro for the treatment of diseases of the leprous type—who submitted to the experiment of being cured of his leprosy by the bite of a poisonous snake. The snake was brought but so repulsive were the gangrened parts of the man that the reptile shrank from the contact. The man then squeezed the snake, was bitten and died in twenty-four hours. But while superstitions were rampant there were institutions, under Catholic control, where good care was taken of the sick and unfortunate. They were not sectarian, but open to all. The following description, by a Protestant, of the Misericordia Hospital in Rio de Janeiro reminds one of a propaganda pamphlet of the Y. M. C. A. "Its doors are open at all hours, night and day, to the sick of both sexes, of all religions and of every country and color, without any forms or condition of admittance: all receive gratuitously the ablest medical attendance and the best nursing and care." Most of the religious brotherhoods provided for social assistance and charity, maintaining hospitals, old people's homes, and distributing money to distressed families. The Brazil of the fifties was full of beggars—beggars in the streets. Some of them were old negro slaves, suffering from leprosy who were sent out by their masters to excite the pity of the charitable with their putrid, gangrened wounds. There were also beggars who had nothing on earth the matter with them—except laziness. Radiguet met one of these parasites in Rio, who was taken through the streets in a hammock, hung from a bamboo which two negro slaves supported on their shoulders. The French traveler asked him why he did not sell his two slaves to which the beggar replied, his dignity offended: "Senhor, I am asking you for money, not for advice."

It is amazing how the Brazilians of the fifties managed to live in such miserable conditions of dirt and bad smell as they did. There was practically no public hygiene to speak of. It is in a semi-official outline of the history of public health services in Brazil that the following description appears, of Rio de Janeiro in the middle of the nineteenth century: "A filthy city, in which, it may be said, there was no air, no light, no sewers, no street cleaning; a city built upon bogs where mosquitoes freely multiplied". Mme. Ida Pfeiffer saw, as she walked through the streets of Rio, carcasses of dogs, cats, and even a mule, rotting. She also refers to "le manque complet d'egouts"—the complete lack of sewers. This condition was common to the other cities of the empire—even to Pernambuco, where the Dutch had left a touch of their cleanliness. Charles Darwin, who was there in the thirties, writes of its filthy streets and offensive smells, comparing it to oriental towns. In all the towns of the empire the removal of garbage, ashes, decaying matter, and vegetables, and human excrements was made in the crudest and also the most picturesque way. Those wastes were put in pipes or barrels, nicknamed *tigres,* and carried on the heads of slaves who dumped them into rivers, the seashore, and alleys. Sometimes as a witness referred to a later-day Brazilian hygienist, "the bottom of the barrel would cast off, the contents soiling both the carrier and the streets". The decaying material was left near the bridges or on the seashores, flocks of carrion crows being depended upon to do the work of scavengers. The removal of the garbage and human waste was generally made after the church bells rang "ten o'clock". In Pernambuco the *tigres* were emptied from the bridges into the rivers Capibaribe and Beberibe: in Rio they were taken on the heads of slaves to be emptied "into certain parts of the bay every night, so that walking in the streets after 10 o'clock is neither safe nor pleasant". This quotation is from Ewbanks who adds: "In this matter Rio is what Libon is and what Edinburg used to be".

As there were no sewers to carry off the drainage there was no plumbing in the houses. The system of water supply was that of the *chafariz,* or public fountain. There was a constant dashing to and fro of big negro water carriers, taking water for the houses, sometimes to the third or fourth floor, where the kitchen was located. Those water carriers worked harder, perhaps, than any other class of slaves; for Brazilians made free use of water, thus making up in personal cleanliness what was lacking so painfully in public hygiene. Next to his hot coffee and his snuff, a Brazilian loved a hot bath best of all. Everywhere—in cities and in the great as well as the humble houses of the interior—water, soap, and a large clean towel welcomed a guest. On examining statistics of the period, I found that more than one third of the seventy-two factories then existing in the empire were soap factories.

Though there was no plumbing in the houses and bathtubs were unknown, rich and poor took a sheer joy in bathing. Poor people bathed in rivers, under the public eye. Landing in Para, the American, John Esaias Warren, was attracted to the freedom with which people bathed and swam in the river. "The first spectacle which arrested our attention", he writes, "was that of a number of persons of both sexes and all ages, bathing indiscriminately together in the waters of the river, in a state of entire nudity." And his comment is: "The natives of Para are very cleanly and indulge in daily ablutions; nor do they confine their baths to the dusky hours of the evening but may be seen swimming about the public wharfs at all hours of the day." While the well-to-do in the cities used "gamellas" or large wooden bowls for their ablutions those in the country states— gentlemen and ladies alike—went to the nearest stream where they could also enjoy a good swim. The suburban *chacaras* in Pernambuco, along the Capibaribe river, had crude bathhouses made of coconut palms. There the ladies undressed and then dipt into the water in free, white, nakedness, like happy mermaids.

It was customary to wash one's hands before and after a meal, the slaves bringing bowls with beautifully embroidered towels. Doctor Fletcher noticed this in Rio as well as in the interior of Minas, where he traveled in an oxcart. Not many years before Saint-Hilaire had been delighted at the apostolic simplicity with which the small farmers in Minas Geraes came themselves with a basin and a towel to wash their guest's feet before he went to bed. Children had their feet washed by their mothers or negro nurses before going to bed. On this occasion their feet were also examined, so that *bichos de pe* might be extracted with a pin, if found.

But all this free use of water and soap did not mean that personal cleanliness was absolute. The gentlemen, for instance, were given to excesses in the taking of snuff. They took a pinch of it every ten minutes or so. As to the ladies, most of them had lice in their hair. There is hardly a Brazilian whose grandmother was free from lice. To have them picked by the deft fingers of their maids was even a pleasure which some of the most fashionable ladies enjoyed. This sort of tolerance towards lice among the Brazilian ladies was inherited from their Portuguese grandmothers, Portugal being—according to an English traveler who visited that country in the latter part of the eighteenth century—"perhaps the richest country in lice".

The fifties were in Brazil a period of great mortality. There were two epidemics—yellow fever and cholera. The yellow fever was very deadly, specially among foreigners, in 1850, 1852, 1853, and 1854. The cholera epidemic reached its zenith in 1856. During it slaves died like flies. The terrible pest scattered grief throughout the country and among all classes. Sylvio Romero, who was then a child, has written a short but vivid account of the effect of the cholera upon a plantation in the north.

Religion, which helped Brazilians to laugh, to go through sickness, even to flirt, also helped them to die. Good Catholics, they passed away holding a candle and murmuring the names of Jesus and the Virgin Mary. When one became desperately ill his or her family sent for the priest, who came in white lace, followed by his acolyte and by friends of the dying one and pious persons—all chanting dismally through the streets. Funerals were pompous but with a touch of humorous—I am using the adjective in its most refined sense—grotesqueness. Children's corpses were buried in scarlet or blue coffins, and dressed as cherubs or angels, with wings and their hair arranged in locks. When supplementary locks were required the undertaker supplied them—"locks as well as rouge for the cheeks and pearl-powders for the neck and arms". Ewbanks remarked: "Fond of dress while living, Brazilians are buried in their best, except when from religious motives other vestments are preferred. Punctilious to the last degree, they enforce etiquette on the dead." Yes, they enforced etiquette on the dead, and vanity besides etiquette. Generals were gorgeously dressed in their full uniforms, still with embroideries of gold; statesmen, in full dress, with all sorts of glittering stars, crosses, and ribbons of orders of nobility; priests, in their magnificent silk robes; maids, in white dresses; with green chaplets of white flowers and blue ribbons. Members of religious brotherhoods dressed as saints—Saint Francis, for instance. Before the coffin was closed, prayers were said by the priest; then—a shuffling of feet, hysterical cries of distressed women, the shrill laments of slaves, and the dead was taken to the cemetery or the church.

---

15. A New Portrait of Mauá the Banker: A Man of Business in Nineteenth-Century Brazil

ANYDA MARCHANT

Economic history and the story of business in Latin America have attracted few historians, although masses of archival material exist and the answers to many challenging questions must eventually be sought there. Miss Marchant, a member of the bar of Virginia and of the Supreme Court

From Volume XXX (1950), pages 411–431.

who has for some time cultivated the field of Brazilian history, here gives a brief account of Baron Mauá, an outstanding banker and entrepreneur of nineteenth-century Brazil. He was greatly influenced by his extensive experience with British merchants: he carried on his business correspondence and on provocation swore, in English. His far-flung enterprises collapsed in 1875, but he was one of the boldest and most prominent Latin American businessmen of his century whose career still causes discussion among historians.

Brazilian historians have never paid much attention to the economic history of Brazil, and, indeed, have generally maintained a deprecatory attitude toward the businessman and his effect on the country. Involved in this neglect is the figure of Ireneô Evangelista de Souza, Baron and Viscount Mauá (1813-1889), still an almost unknown and little-studied man, even though he was Brazil's pioneer railroad builder and industrialist, an imaginative entrepreneur, and a daring innovator in investment banking.

Mauá's business life began when he was an orphan at the age of nine, in the shop of a Portuguese merchant in Rio de Janeiro in 1822. By the time he was sixteen, he had become the confidential clerk of Richard Carruthers, an English merchant and importer of English manufactured goods. Carruthers taught him the English language and English business methods, and introduced him to the variety of industry and the concepts of credit that were commonplace then in England but unknown in Brazil. When Carruthers retired to England in the late 1830's, he left his favorite clerk as managing partner of his business in Rio. By 1840, Ireneô was an important member of the business community of Rio—"Senhor Iréneo," as his English acquaintances seem characteristically to have mispronounced his name. By 1850, he was an industrialist as well as a merchant and ready to embark on investment banking in a large way.

One of the things that the boy Ireneô had learned in Carruther's firm was the idea of financial credit as a basis for industrial expansion. The most important practical result of his first trip to England in 1840 had undoubtedly been the founding, in Manchester, of the firm of Carruthers, De Castro and Company, because Carruthers' name was invaluable when his protegé needed to raise capital in England to float many of his early enterprises. Mauá's banking career was based on Carruthers' international connections, for Carruthers had his own web of international credit: his firm in London, a branch of the Manchester house; Carruthers, Souza and Company in Buenos Aires; Carruthers, Dixon and Company in New York. As the old man withdrew more and more from an active part in these businesses, Joseph Reynell de Castro, who was linked to Ireneô by boyhood friendship as well as by business partnership, took over the direction of these English affairs.

Mauá's financial network in Brazil grew so quickly that when he had decided by 1850 to have his own banking house in Rio he easily connected

it intimately with the Manchester firm. In July, 1851, he founded the
Banco Mauá e Companhia with a capital of ten thousand *contos*. It did not
have the power to issue notes, but in heated debates over its charter in the
Chamber of Deputies it had won the right to issue drafts and bills of exchange. These drafts and bills were for a term of five days with a value
of not less than two hundred *milreis* (about $100 or £25) and their total
at any time could not be more than one third of the bank's actual funds.

Mauá had not hesitated after he had the head office going and the
business sprang at once into busy life. In 1853, he established branches in
São Paulo and in Rio Grande do Sul. In 1851, the bank's deposits had been
valued at 214 contos, and by March, 1854, had grown to 950 contos. In
1851, it had held discounted bills for over one thousand contos; in 1854,
for over nine thousand. Only the Banco Commercial, with a total sum of
over ten thousand contos in discounted bills in 1853 could equal it in
volume of business.

Indeed, this very prosperity precipitated Mauá's first conflict with
the Emperor and those who advised him on the financial policy of the
Empire.

II

Banking in Brazil had had a slow start. The paper money of Dom
João VI's first Bank of Brazil had been a new thing to Brazilians. Public
confidence was not increased by the easy way in which Dom João treated
the Bank as his private fund of ready money and, taking the gold and silver
back to Portugal with him, left Brazil with a plague of copper money and
counterfeit paper. The first bank was liquidated in 1829. A scheme to
create a second in 1833 failed for want of subscribers. Only in 1838 was
the Banco Commercial do Rio de Janeiro founded, with the power, which
it never used, to issue paper money.

In the period between 1851 and 1856, Brazil was enjoying exceptional
prosperity. There was plenty of gold in the country. But the businessmen
complained of only one unfavorable element: there was not enough paper
money to keep pace with the demands of business. Caught up in the rapidly
developing modern methods of business, they were fast leaving behind the
idea that the only real money was specie or cash in hand.

The Minister of the Treasury in 1853, however, was more conservative. The political life of Joaquim José Rodrigues Torres, Viscount Itaboraí,
dated from the days of the Regency, and he was therefore a man who carried considerable weight with the Emperor, whose favorite financial ad-
viser he was until his death in 1872. He believed that paper money was
a snare and a delusion and that real money was specie. It took much persuasion to make him concede that a bank with the right to issue paper
money was a boon to the country, and he certainly did not believe that
such a bank should be a private concern.

The result of the constant pressure from businessmen was the reluctant giving of his approval to the creation of the third Bank of Brazil as a bank of issue, to be formed from the forced merger of the Banco Commercial with Mauá's bank. Eighty thousand shares were distributed to the shareholders of the two banks. Thirty thousand were offered for public sale in Rio itself, and when more than three thousand eager buyers presented themselves for this lot, offering 10 per cent above the nominal price, the Treasury made a profit of six hundred contos. The new bank finally began operations on August 10, 1854, under the direction of Viscount Paraná.

The fifty thousand shares that Mauá and his shareholders received for their share in the merger did not reconcile Mauá to the high-handed destruction of his house. At first he could not believe that the government really intended to drive his bank out of business, or, rather, absorb it, but Itaboraí soon made it plain that such was the case. Convinced, he desisted from actively opposing the government's plan, he said,

... nourishing the hope that I could coöperate with the great credit institution that was to be created to introduce a new era of development and progress in the economic and financial life of the country.

Therefore, I took an active part in the organization of the present Bank of Brazil, being elected as one of its directors. Nevertheless, manipulation of the election of members of the board of directors resulted in the inclusion of some men who were hostile to me and the exclusion of others who would have been on my side in the voting. In such circumstances, I refused the office, in spite of the insistence of the Minister of the Treasury that I should accept it.

He then tried to create a company which in structure imitated the French *société en commandite par actions*. The Brazilian law did not mention such an organization and Mauá sought to interpret its silence as tacit permission. But the government thought otherwise and Viscount Itaboraí's opinion triumphed in the form of a decree issued on December 13, 1854, declaring such companies null and acting retroactively to dissolve Mauá's new enterprise.

Mauá, seeing the situation as hopeless, now created Mauá, MacGregor and Company, with an English partner and a branch in London, as a simple partnership. In spite of the insecurity of such a form of company, of which he remained acutely aware, the firm flourished. He had no difficulty in accumulating a large sum of capital, for, he said, "it was my intention to do what the Bank of Brazil refused to do."

The official bank, in the meantime, while Mauá, MacGregor and Company, more resilient than most (its drafts and bills were worth more than the paper money issued by the bank), was enjoying a solid prosperity, had turned itself into a factory to make paper money. It had encountered, too, the world crisis of 1857, precipitated by the troubles of the cotton market in the United States and the threat of war in Napoleon III's Europe. The price of coffee, now Brazil's great staple export, fluctuated violently in the consuming markets. The Bank of Brazil's paper money was depreciated, specie was driven out of the country, the exchange declined, and the cost of living shot up.

That crisis [said Mauá] soon made obvious how weak was the prop upon which the men of the specie-money school relied to prove their golden dream of converting paper money into specie, something I had always considered impracticable, except during rare periods. . . . Gold, which for the moment served the purpose of a circulating medium in competition with paper money, was rapidly converted into merchandise, which had at once to be exported to supply the deficit which the fall in the value of products brought about.

In 1857, changes in the cabinet made a friend of his the minister of the treasury—Bernardo de Souza Franco (later Viscount Souza Franco), a vigorous opponent of the theories of Viscount Itboraí. The period when Souza Franco took office was at the worst moment for Brazil in the contemporary world crisis. His first action to rescue the official bank was to call upon Mauá, MacGregor and Company to help it maintain the exchange rate at 25½ English pence to the milreis (the exchange rate had fallen as low as 22 pence) and thus prevent the silver money from following the gold out of the country. At his request, Mauá, MacGregor and Company drew on its London branch on March 12, 1858, for the sum of £400,000; in April, it drew again for £200,000; in May, for £150,000; and in June, for another £60,000.

Though these maneuvers were successful, they did not meet with the approval of Souza Franco's political opponents, because his ideas on the best financial policy for the Empire were diametrically opposed to those of both Viscount Itaboraí and Viscount Inhomerim (Francesco de Salles Torres Homen), another convinced opponent of paper money who was shortly to succeed Souza Franco in the Treasury. To these conservative men, the issuance of paper money by six banks was nothing short of a "financial carnival." It was madeness and, they believed, it had been inspired by Souza Franco's close friend Mauá. To them, the only way to create capital was to work and save money, by which they meant specie. Capital could not be created by banks of issue. Souza Franco's time in office was brief. Inevitably, Itaboraí and Inhomerim won the day, for their views, the reflection of the slowly accumulating and familiar type of wealth represented by a *fazenda*, a plantation, and slaves, were more acceptable to the Emperor.

III

In the late 1850's and early 1860's, as a man in his forties, Mauá was in his prime. He was a man of average height, with brown hair, a fair skin, penetrating dark eyes under straight eyebrows, a long nose and a firmly closed mouth. His very attitude in standing for his portrait distinguished him from the typical Brazilian public man of his day, the inheritor and perpetuator of traditional gestures. He stood straight, energy apparent in every line of his figure, as if he had only paused for a moment to interrupt his all-absorbing affairs, with a trace of preoccupation still in his expressive yet reserved glance.

In private life, he was a family man of very simple tastes, a devoted husband and father. He never went on his frequent long journeys without taking his wife and some of the older children with him. When he was in Rio and came home in the evening preoccupied with financial affairs, he would walk up and down in his wife's sitting room, thinking aloud in English, for one result of his early training was that English had become his personal language, the language in which he thought, preferred to write his letters and, on provocation, swore.

His working day ended late, in the office he kept next to his bedroom, where he sat and wrote letters for half the night. He began a new day sharp at nine o'clock, reaching his downtown office before the clerks, and often in the press of business he forgot to eat. Especially on the days when the steam packets left for Europe, when he had long letters, full of detailed instructions and advice, to prepare for his partners, MacGregor in London and De Castro in Manchester, he stayed at his desk and the porter brought him food from the nearest hotel.

His memory was prodigious, for he could carry in his head the balance sheets and business details of all his enterprises, which at one time numbered twenty or more. He paid good wages and was liberal with bonuses. The old business habits he had learned with Carruthers remained with him, with the concept that a well-paid employee was worth the money in the loyalty and willingness thus obtained. His manner with his employees was a part of his art of managing his affairs. He never shouted at them, even when work was badly done, but instead questioned and advised, and, if he gave orders, gave them in a low voice. If he was dealing with a man expert in some technical field, like metallurgy or shipbuilding, in which he had only his own practical genius to guide him, he never presumed to give orders. In a subject in which he was really a master, like accountancy, he always had a reasonable explanation and the patience to present it in persuading those who worked under him to do as he said. But in spite of these soft manners, there was never any doubt when he had made up his mind.

A delicate, cheerful courtesy was a part of his nature, and he made no distinction between high and low concerning whom should receive such treatment from him. Intrigue, bad faith, personal attack could make him angry and even violent and abusive, but mistakes and a lack of understanding in those under his orders never awoke in him anything but a tolerant patience. His confidence in himself gave him a steadiness and optimism in dealing with other people that overcame all but his most implacable enemies. Unlike the typical public man of his day, raised in the enervating climate of slavery and a society of manners and privilege, he was not touchy, arrogant, autocratic. He was vain of only one thing: his own abilities to solve financial and economic problems.

Such was the man seen from the outside and seldom does a man of this character provide an opportunity for the student to meet him face to face. And yet it is from some of his few surviving business letters that the student may form his own judgment of Mauá. In January, 1861, Mauá wrote a letter to his old friend and patron, Richard Carruthers, which synthesizes the man in the heyday of his physical and mental powers. He wrote in English, an English that, with all its personal touches and idiosyncrasies of style, was obviously the language of his private thoughts, his ambitions, his deepest feelings.

Dear Mr. Carruthers: Being aware that my correspondence with De Castro is constantly laid before you and from him getting also, regularly, accounts of your health, I have not thought it advisable to send a duplicate of what I write to him. At the commencement of a new year I cannot, however, allow the first Packet to leave without directly expressing my heartfelt pleasure at the continuance of your health and well-being at the lovely spot you picked for your residence, where I conceive you enjoy as much of happiness as can be hoped for in this earthly habitation. It is indeed singular that, with minds equally disposed to enjoy quiet and home happiness and all that is good in me arising from the lesson inspired into my youthful mind thirty years ago by you, we should have adopted such widely different means of life to arrive at the same end. The facts, however, can be explained with greater ease than would appear at first sight, for, amongst the lessons imbibed in my mind by the friendly or rather father like advice given me by you at that early period of my life, the love of one's country was a theme very frequently touched upon in our conversations, and the seed existing, it could hardly fail to grow up and engross my ideas as with the hope of being useful to my country, at all events in the sphere of life which fate has destined for me. Believe me, the idea of doing good, both to my country, and as extensively as my means would allow, privately, to those who need it, has been the groundwork of my apparent ambition, and I cannot help thinking that this honesty of purpose has merited the approval of Providence, on reflecting that more than once I have been saved by an almost miraculous interference. I refer to the support obtained at the close of 1857 from a perfect stranger, who advanced two hundred thousand pounds at a critical period, which saved my firm from liquidation. And as regards my pocket, the past year has been a brilliant one and every succeeding one henceforward will show increased profits, as the vast accumulation of capital in my establishments at a low rate of interest must become of great profit; and confidence is daily strengthening on the part of the public. As regards my mercantile position, a number of envious wretches have repeatedly tried to do me harm. Last year they redoubled their efforts to succeed at a moment when the Banking house met with hard times. My calmness and firm bearing brought the plot to the ground. Now they appear to have given up as a bad job such attempts, and the establishment is getting stronger than ever with the public. By the end of the present year its position *will leave nothing to wish for*. Early next year, God willing, I shall have no impediment to realise my long protracted voyage to Europe, leaving everything on this side in perfect order, and after eighteen months' residence abroad, I hope on my return to have silenced for ever the gratuitous enemies I have had. The Government and the Conservative party, so called, lost the elections entirely—this party from an anxiety to govern *too much*, meddling with all the dealings of trade and have alienated all tradesmen from them, their main support before. On the other hand, the Liberals have entirely changed their ideas, being now men of order, aspiring to get into power only by legitimate constitutional means, and as they promise to meddle but little with the working of industry and trade, their attainment of power is hail'd with hope. In fact, my dear Mr. Carruthers, I fully expect that my troubles are now over—*mais vale tarde do que nunca.*

On March 10, 1861, Maúa wrote to his partner De Castro in Manchester:

The market is working under a great pressure for money, since the screw is being tightened by the Bank of Brazil to an almost unbearable extent, they say, with a view of permitting a rise in the Exchange to enable them to pay in gold without danger. The everyday experience is, however, showing the Directors, who are about the most stupid men we have in the trade, that the means they adopt are not the right ones, for in this respect, Brazil is not in the least affected by the markets around it, as occurs everywhere in Europe. We have no other means to support the value of our currency except the *value of exports.* This has been proved over and over again. Before the crisis of 1857–1858 the issue of the Brazil Bank exceeded thirty thousand contos. It was thirty-four thousand contos when the crisis was announced and the exchange rule up to the very eve of the bad news at twenty-six and a quarter to twenty-seven. The cry out of the Midas Brazileiros (as I called them in my written opinion) against the issue was heard, the Bank went on restricting the issue ever since. Yesterday it was reduced to seventeen thousand contos and nine thousand contos of government paper have been withdrawn from circulation, so that if we take into account, as of course must be done, the ten thousand contos of money, gold and government notes, which the Bank has in its coffers, the circulating medium is just two thousand contos less than it was when the Bank was established! ... Thus when the paper in circulation was in fact a hundred and fifty per cent more than at present, the Exchange was higher than it is now, and yet our great *economists* talk about restricting the *Bank circulation* that gold may flow into the country! as if the gold could be imported without being paid for! By adopting entirely the ideas of our pretended economists the Bank has done a great deal of harm.

It is obvious from this letter that Maúa's position was in the midst of the theories hotly debated in Brazil at the time. His views were based on a simple idea: one does not develop a vast, wild country, full of natural resources but needing an immense amount of initial outlay, with gold that one carries about in one's pocket.

The financial crisis of which he treated did not get better. It grew worse. In the United States appeared the menace of the Civil War. Europe was in the throes of financial troubles. Brazilian coffee was unsteady. In

1860, there had been deluges of rain in São Paulo, so that the trains of mules could not bring the sacks of the precious bean to market. In 1861, there was a drought in Rio Grande do Sul and in Uruguay that affected the cattle and hide markets. Farther south still, in the Argentine Confederation, a civil war threatened between the Confederated Provinces under Urquiza and the province of Buenos Aires.

In Mauá's commercial correspondence during the first half of 1861, anxiety over these disquieting factors appears again and again. MacGregor, his partner and the manager of the London branch of Mauá, MacGregor and Company, was frightened and angry at the threat to the stability of the firm, aggravated, he thought, by Mauá's own daring methods of confronting the danger. He was a far more cautious man, less confident of finding ways out of difficulties as they arose, nervous about the least irregularity in the arrival of remittances from the head office in Rio or the branch offices in the River Plate. The failure of one packet to bring the sum he expected threw him into a panic and he wrote to Mauá with more frankness than discretion.

His letter pained Mauá. MacGregor's health, the thought,

. . . must be indeed shaken, and to an extent seriously depressing your mind, for to observe your writing (it would appear, *in earnest*) about having been prevented from taking the necessary steps to place your family comfortably, for fear of seeing them turned *into the street!* *!* in consequence of the fear of funds not being forwarded to meet the obligations of the firm, must be indeed painful to me. . . . The remarks made by you under such circumstances, I say, are calculated to establish the conviction in my mind, either that you are a sufferer in health, which causes me heartfelt pain, being sincerely your friend, or that you are so utterly disgusted with the business in consequence of the misfortunes we have had to contend against, that you are looking for a pretext to withdraw your responsibility from such an ill-managed concern, which keeps you in constant dread of seeing your name in the gazette and your family in the street! On pondering over such grave assertions, and being well satisfied that you are a kindhearted man and therefore not likely to write in such terms merely to create annoyance and pain in an equally kindhearted man and *friend*, I became convinced that I have no right to exact from you the painful sacrifice you evidently make in continuing my partner.

Instead, he suggested that they close the London branch office, which they could do at any moment, and "avert the danger which haunts your imagination and which makes you so miserable." In its place, a new London firm of Mauá and Company was to be created, with De Castro as managing partner.

De Castro, he told MacGregor, was

a man of great business knowledge, who has also got experience in the school of adversity on one occasion, his mind is the very soul of honor, and his intellectual powers inferior to few in his class. . . . If you prefer it and your health requires it . . . he can take charge of the firm in London whilst you get abroad to refresh your health, and the change above referred to may be brought about later on, or not at all, just as you desire or wish, for nothing is further from my mind than any idea of inducing you to retire—my object is merely to leave you *perfect freedom*, having your well-being and happiness *to heart*, for I am one of those who is always ready to make any kind of sacrifice for my friends but who never desires that my friends make any sacrifice to serve me. . . . With De Castro the case is different. He knows that I would strip myself of my last shirt to save him and I know he would unhesitatingly do the same for me. We are attached to each other from *boyhood*. We have *both* a right to expect that each of us will do what the other desires; consequently I do not look forward to any refusal from him, and you have therefore only to tell him what you wish to be done and I am sure he will agree to everything for my sake.

Seeing things from the Rio office and full of the exhilaration that came from the successful management of something of which he was thoroughly the master, he still could not understand MacGregor's fears and recriminations. Certainly, there seemed to be no reason for lack of confidence.

The capital of the concern [Mauá, MacGregor and Company] has remained and remains *untouched*. How can you talk of our losses absorbing one third of our capital? And remember, we have just been robbed by a most unjust sentence on the part of the Tribunaes [the Brazilian courts] of a very large sum advanced against first-rate securities which if fully recovered (as it ought to be) would have exempted us from more than one third of the entire losses we have sustained, and the accumulated losses were written off in one balance sheet, altho' they belong to four years—take all these things into consideration and remember that we were caught with all sails set during the greatest commercial crisis on record, and you will be disposed to do justice to your efforts. Without the efforts and the influence displayed, our firm would certainly have gone into forced liquidation. Instead of complaining, I am, therefore, most thankful to Providence that nothing worse occurred. As regards the partners, none of us (thank God) are working for daily bread, and the experience acquired is a large capital for future business, and in two or three years, I am quite certain, we will bring up the average of our earnings from so much labor, anxiety, and care.

MacGregor had been hasty and now he made plain that he had no idea of leaving Mauá, MacGregor and Company. Mauá, in a letter that was a skillful mixture of exhortation, friendly advice, and cheerful remonstrance, was glad he had decided to stay.

Allow me to repeat my request and recommendation that you take the necessary steps conducing to health, comfort and welfare and happiness, for being a man who finds so much happiness as can be hoped for in this world of cares, in the bosom of my family, I cannot but sympathise, deeply, with you, when you tell me you have been eight months away from your family without seeing them once! No wonder you felt annoyed and disgusted with the cares and weight of duties which involved the necessity of so unbearable a sacrifice! I cannot but imagine, however, that within thirty or fifty miles in the suburbs of London, where Railway trains are seen moving in all directions, there will not be many a nice, well-situated country place which you might hire or purchase, to place your family and go every day to enjoy a quiet homely rest after the labor and care of the day's work; pray do so by all means, and you will soon see the agreeable change in the state of your mind which this modification in your mode of living will work.

MacGregor he could manage and persuade, but it was always De Castro to whom he opened his mind, complaining, sometimes, in a tone of reasonable regret, about MacGregor's limitations; and to De Castro he always signed himself simply "Mauá," without the "Baron" with which at this time all his other letters concluded.

The misunderstanding with MacGregor blew over, but, in spite of the prosperity of Mauá, MacGregor and Company in Rio, he remained somewhat chagrined at the failure of the London branch to shine with the splendor due a firm bearing his name. He told MacGregor that

. . . two partners are required in London; one remains in the counting house, whilst the other moves about and is seen wherever other bankers and respectable merchants are to be seen. I am convinced that the firm in London stands inconceivably below its due position in London.

It was De Castro he wanted for the second partner in the London house, and by the same packet (January 7, 1861), he wrote to him:

In London, from what I have observed, and am informed, if the firm is conducted with greater energy by a man who strives to become popular and does not waste away time in the counting house and makes a better use of it, the business doing with Brazil, the Plate and other European correspondence, embracing operations to the extent of three hundred thousand pounds per month, ought surely to raise the house to a proper standing in London in a very short period, instead of its being slighted by people who are as distant from us in character and means as darkness is to light.

He had reason to be touchy. Mauá, MacGregor and Company had branches in Buenos Aires, Montevideo, the city of Rio Grande do Sul, Pelotas, Porto Alegre, Santos, São Paulo, Campinas and Pará. For a firm only seven years old it was doing marvelously well. Including De Castro, he had at this time four partners: MacGregor in London; Ricardo José Ribeiro, in charge of the office in Montevideo; and a young Englishman named Leslie, manager of the office in Buenos Aires, to whom he frequently wrote letters full of the advice of an old hand to a beginner in the financial game. The head office in Rio was under his own eye. Ever watchful for the possibility of expansion, he had instructed Ribeiro, in Rio Grande do Sul, that he wanted his own economic ideas and the financial policies of his house advertised by means of circulars and other printed notices, so as, in time, to establish a branch or agency of Mauá and Company in every town or city of the province with a population of three thousand or more people. And in every office they must always have two or three promising young men who would learn to work in the bank and would be suitable material for advancement when the opportunity came.

But if the fortunes of the house remained bright, the general economic scene became darker. Three great international firms with important Brazilian holdings—Baring Brothers, Peabody and Company, and Brown, Shipley and Company—were badly affected by the approaching Civil War in the United States. The Brazilian government also felt the repercussions of bad news nearer at hand. To the south, across the border in the old Banda Oriental, trouble was brewing that was to culminate in 1865 in the Paraguayan War. But, despite every sign of approaching danger, most people in Brazil who had put their money in banks were caught without warning by the sudden financial collapse of 1864—the "September crisis." It was the most extraordinary monetary crisis, said William Scully, the editor of the *Anglo-Brazilian Times*, that had occurred since the days of Law and the South Sea Bubble. The great firm of Souto and Company closed its doors on September 10, 1864. Its bankruptcy was a signal for runs on all the banking houses. The streets were full of people trying to withdraw their money. The police was called out to control the mobs. So great was the effect of the panic that the Bank of Brazil lost its right to issue paper money, which henceforth became a function exclusively of the Treasury.

Mauá, MacGregor and Company was not spared from the run on the banks, yet, with other houses crashing all around, it weathered the storm. In fact, the firm flourished. Perhaps Mauá saw a grim retribution in the panic, for, as he wrote to Ribeiro, unhappily there "did not exist a public spirit sufficiently energetic, on the part of the governed, to require the governors to march in accordance with public opinion." The governors could therefore go on with their own ideas until the results, which were sometimes catastrophic, as in the case of the September Crisis, convinced them of their mistakes.

Ribeiro was in a position to know how Mauá regarded the inflexible and anachronistic financial policy of "the governors," because as early as 1860 Mauá had thus written to him:

In place of the ranch-owner, the husbandman, the landowner, the lawyer, and all others keeping what they own unproductively in money in their houses, we must induce them to bring these sums, great and little, and deposit them in the Mauá firm and its branches. When the masses understand the immense advantage of drawing credit from their money, what great sums may accumulate in our branches, to be newly employed with advantage, aiding labor and industry, producing conditions of prosperity in different localities, and what benefits will result from this impetus, and how much faster will march the creation of wealth in our country! In the United States there is a branch bank or agency in all localities where more than fifty houses are built. In England, despite the small size of the country and because of the denser population, there are three thousand seven hundred banks, banking houses and their agencies!

which occupy themselves exclusively in concentrating the money capital for useful employment, and from this fact arises the amazing creation of wealth that thus operates to transform these countries day by day.

IV

His partner MacGregor once voiced the opinion that Mauá always looked too much on the bright side of things. It was an accusation he good-naturedly repelled with the reply that "I generally look to all points, altho' I am not one of those who fly *sem ver segue*."

Optimist as he often appeared to be, he never deceived himself about his Brazil or his place in it. His financial successes in the 1850's and 1860's left him little to desire, but he knew that money alone and the power it gave him were not enough to make for him a comfortable place in the Empire. In Dom Pedro II's Brazil, there was really no place for the combination of gifts and disadvantages that he possessed. To the Emperor himself, Mauá was always a suspect person, a dangerous man because he was powerful and not thoroughly subordinate to the dictates of the Emperor's court. Dom Pedro did not care for moneyed men whose wealth was not tied up in *fazendas* and slaves and who had sources of influence and strength outside the Emperor's sphere of control. Mauá could at times be irritated at the Emperor's coldness and indirectly expressed distrust, but to him the main complaint was the time and energy he had to spend in managing public men, from the Emperor down, whose grasp of finance and whose theories of economic development he thought both rudimentary and out of key with the times and the needs of the country. He summed up his feelings in a letter of May 8, 1861, to his old friend and patron, Richard Carruthers:

I am happy to be able to inform you that all my business and public undertakings are at this moment in a flourishing condition, Ponta d'Areia [his iron foundry across the bay from Rio] alone excepted. Experience, aided by indefatigable exertions, have enabled me to correct and put to rights all the working parts of the machinery which now performs its duty in perfect order, so much so that I can now contemplate, with comfort, a visit to Europe next year, taking with me all my family, with a view of remaining there for at least eighteen months, as it is my intention to see all that may be worth seeing from Portugal to Constantinople, remaining half of the time in London to get thoroughly initiated in the doings of the great Metropolis. I am anxious in fact for the moment of leaving Rio, for, with my feelings and hot temper, I cannot contemplate the *misgovernment* which is going on in Brazil in our days, without opposing the nonsensical proceedings of the Executive, which has been gradually absorbing all the power. To take an active part, in contending against such ideas, would oblige me to come out of my obscurity, which I cannot think of, and consequently to withdraw for a period from the scene of action is my best course. On my return I hope to see better ideas prevailing, and not having done much in the past, I can readily excuse myself from taking a prominent part in the direction of the government in the new order of things.

With such an attitude, it is not surprising that his greatest successes in creating a banking system based on the deposits of middle-class people were achieved outside Brazil. In Brazil, such a success was necessarily limited, for the middle class was still negligible. In the River Plate countries, however, free of the incubus of slavery, there was more opportunity, and the House of Mauá had never neglected opportunity.

Though doing business in Brazil in spite of the Emperor was a problem large enough to try the patience and exercise the ingenuity of the cleverest banker, Mauá never lacked boldness in looking for money from people who wished speculative profits from what he considered first-rate securities. He wanted capital for investment and he raised it in banking transactions. The loans for his railroads were particularly involved and difficult to manage. The money had to be raised in London for such enterprises; there was not nearly enough capital to be found in Brazil, or at least it was unwilling to come forward. But English investors, putting money into South American railways, were speculating. They did not consider such uses for their money as sound long-term investment and they naturally expected speculative profits. Seen from the other side of the Atlantic, Brazil was a place to make a fortune quickly. Mauá, on the other hand, his head full of the immense economic possibilities of the New World, insisted that such investment could be first-rate and comparable to the best to be found anywhere else in the world. He was aware of the problems presented by slavery, governmental inertia, and a sparse, thinly spread population, but he was also aware of the dangers to sound credit that arose from too much of the get-rich-quick mentality among many of his shareholders.

The wish that he had expressed to Carruthers for leisure for recreation and European travel could not be fulfilled for several years. His manifold interests in the River Plate and, indeed, all his financial affairs were now gradually being drawn into the involvement of the Empire and the whole River Plate region in the preliminaries of the Paraguayan War. In 1864, he apparently saw no fruitful continuation of the existing situation, and, no longer postponing action every few months as each new crisis arose, broke off his affairs abruptly. He had a new scheme in mind—the merger of his house with the London and Brazilian Bank.

Much to the surprise of the international money market, he arranged the merger in London to create a new company to be known as the London, Brazilian and Mauá Bank. It was to be an international house, with branches in Portugal, Argentina, and Uruguay. For Mauá, the merger with one of the most solid banking houses of the period would have consolidated all his banking operations in Argentina, Uruguay, and Brazil. Each of the countries except Brazil approved the charter within a few days, but for effectiveness in Brazil approval by the Emperor's government was also needed.

Perhaps it was the very fact of the merger's concentrating tremendous power in the River Plate countries in Mauá's hands that frightened the Emperor's government. And that government was easily alarmed at this period as it found itself with fewer and fewer ways of escape from the events that were leading it into its first foreign war. The Emperor's Council of State thought about the matter for two months. In the end, the Council, ignoring the considerable strength that the new company would have given the Empire at a time when it needed aid in international affairs, rejected the charter.

It was the final triumph of the men of conservative beliefs in regard to banking who were in the Emperor's government. The subsequent history of Mauá's banking schemes, especially in the River Plate, merely emphasized this rejection by the Brazilian government of his theories of banking practice. Yet his banking house, in spite of consistent official disfavor and because of the vigor and ingenuity that he brought to its management, only collapsed, in 1875, after a long struggle and as a result of the disastrous effects on the Empire itself of the Paraguayan War and the disintegration of the slave-based economy. When that collapse came, there was then left, not merely the debris of Mauá's financial structure but of an epoch in the history of Brazil.

Another Article of Interest

Graham, Richard. "Mauá and Anglo-Brazilian Diplomacy 1862–1863." XLII (1962), 199–211.

---

16. Causes of the Collapse of the Brazilian Empire

PERCY ALVIN MARTIN

Professor Martin of Stanford University made an important contribution to the development of Latin American history in the United States by his concern with the history of Brazil. The present article examines and interprets the various reasons historians have advanced to explain the fall

From Volume IV (1921), pages 4–48.

of the empire in 1889. Today, after the passage of almost half a century since the article appeared, and the growth of a school of Brazilian historians more critical than this author of Pedro II and the empire over which he presided, Professor Martin's presentation needs to be supplemented by additional viewpoints. But anyone who would undertake a study of the demise of the only empire firmly established in the Americas could do no better than to begin with this article.

To ex-President Roosevelt has been attributed the statement that there were two revolutions whose motives he had never been able to fathom— the February Revolution which overthrew the government of Louis-Philippe and the Brazilian Revolution of 1889 which brought to an end the only empire in the new world if we except the shortlived monarchy of Maximilian in Mexico. And in truth the causes of the collapse of the imperial regime in Brazil seem at first sight inexplicable. When on November 15, 1889, the world learned that the venerable Emperor Dom Pedro II. had been deposed and a republic declared the news was received with incredulity coupled with a feeling akin to indignation. Outside of South America at least the feeling was all but universal that the Braganza dynasty had become thoroughly acclimated in Brazil; that it was largely due to the wisdom and statemanship of her ruler that Brazil had enjoyed a half century of almost unbroken peace, accompanied by a material progress which was the admiration and envy of her South American neighbors. Under the liberal and enlightened rule of her emperor, Brazil, the "crowned democracy of America" had apparently solved the difficult problem of wedding the principles of an hereditary monarchy with the political and personal freedom assumed to exist only in a republic. To depose and banish the kindly and genial old emperor, the "grand-son of Marcus Aurelius" as he was somewhat whimsically called by Victor Hugo; to send into exile the aged ruler whose every thought was directed to the welfare of his country, seemed not only unwise but ungrateful. It is the object of this paper to submit to a brief scrutiny the causes of one of the most striking and momentous political transformations in the history of Hispanic America.

It is a historical commonplace that the causes of the great crises in a nation's history, whether it be a civil or foreign war, or as in the case of Brazil, a bloodless revolution, are apt to be complex and strike their roots deep into the nation's past. The explanation ordinarily given for the overthrow of the Braganza dynasty, namely the resentment of the army at the alleged ill-treatment it had suffered at the hands of the imperial government, a resentment culminating in a barrack-room conspiracy and a military pronunciamento of the traditional Spanish American type, is much too simple. If the monarchy tottered and fell at a blow leveled by a few disgruntled regiments garrisoned at Rio de Janeiro, it was because the supports on which the monarchy might be expected to rely were lacking. By 1889, the Brazilian Empire, which to the world at large presented such an imposing front, had in reality become a hollow shell, ready to collapse at the first assault. One by one the foundations on which the stability and persistance of the Empire were based had crumbled.

As a preliminary to our analysis of the causes of the downfall of the Empire stress should be laid on certain peculiar characteristics of the Brazilian monarchy. The history of continenal Europe would lead us to believe that if the cause of a monarchy is to become identified with that of the nation certain indispensable conditions must be fulfilled. A monarchy must derive its vitality, and to a certain extent, its sanction, from a national and warlike tradition, a hereditary nobility of which the reigning prince is the chief, a military spirit, incorporated in the prince and finding in him its highest expression, a clergy whose interests are closely identified with those of the crown, and finally a profound conviction in the popular mind of the legitimacy of the privileges and authority claimed by the ruling dynasty. Such a conviction would of course be greatly reënforced by the belief that the sovereign was invested with certain mystical attributes, emanating from the doctrine of the divine right of kings.

In the case of Brazil under Dom Pedro II. these conditions were in considerable part lacking. The Empire possessed a titled aristocracy, to be sure, but it was not hereditary; it enjoyed no political privileges, and the mere possession of a title did not of itself assure any great social prestige. In other words the titles of the swarm of barons, counts, and viscounts whose sonorous names were supplied by the rivers and other geographical features of the Empire were largely honorific distinctions, bestowed by the emperor as a recognition of public service, or for the establishment of a school, hospital, or insane asylum. They were also used, as in England, by the prime minister to pay political debts or to win over possible political opponents. There was little in common, however, between the nobles of Brazil and the aristocracy of England or the noblesse of France under the ancient regime; nor did the court of Rio de Janeiro reflect the pomp and splendor of St. James or Versailles.

As for the emperor himself he was too all outward seeming the exact antithesis of the crowned heads of the late empires of continental Europe. Of the conventional trappings of royalty, he had few if any. Simple, democratic in his tastes, hating all display and ostentation, accessible to even the humblest of his subjects, caring nothing for military pomp, he might inspire respect and esteem, but seldom veneration or awe. By no stretch of the imagination could this kindly, genial, scholarly ruler be regarded as an exemplar of the divine right of kings.

Yet it would be idle to deny that during the greater part of the nineteenth century the Empire enjoyed a real popularity and could count on the support of almost every element of the population. Especially was this true in the '50's, '60's, and '70's, when the influence and prestige of Dom Pedro II. were at their height. The army, the great landowners, the professional classes, the clergy, were all regarded as pillars of the throne. But as the century began to draw to its close one by one these props fell away; the last agony of the Empire found the logical defenders of the dynasty either apathetic or actively hostile. How is this waning of the star of the monarchy to be reconciled with the real and indisputable benefits which the Empire had brought to Brazil?

This change in popular attitude is to be seen most clearly perhaps in the case of the large landowners. This class, comparatively small in number but great in wealth and influence, he had always been regarded as one of the pillars of the monarchy. They formed the nearest approach to a landed aristocracy to be found anywhere in South America outside the Republic of Chile. From the great *fazendeiros*, the coffee kings of São Paulo; from the ranchers of Minas Geraes; from the old families of sugar and cotton planters in Bahia and Pernambuco, had been recruited many of the staunchest supporters of the Empire. It was the irony of fate that the loyalty to the throne of this influential class was converted over night into an indifference or hostility as a direct result of the greatest social and humanitarian reform ever consummated in Brazil. On May 13, 1888, Princess Isabella, acting as regent for Dom Pedro who was then in Europe, signed the bill definitely extinguishing slavery in the Empire. That slavery was destined to disappear; that its existence was a standing reproach to the fair name of Brazil, no one undertook to deny. Unlike slavery in the United States, slavery in Brazil, at least in its latter days, had as an institution no defenders. The cleavage in public opinion came between those who favored gradual emancipation and the champions of immediate liberation. Up until 1888 the former had been in the ascendant. In 1871 the Rio Branco bill was passed which, among other provisions, declared that henceforth all children born of slave mothers should be free. In 1885 freedom was granted to all slaves over 60. But the abolitionists were not satisfied. Led by a phalanx of able and enthusiastic young men, of whom the most noted was Joaquim Nabuco, later appointed the first Brazilian ambassador to the United States, they kept up a ceaseless agitation in press and Parliament and prepared the ground for the final act of 1888. Princess Isabella had become an ardent convert to the abolition cause and threw into the scale all the influence of the monarchy.

The most anomalous and unfortunate aspect of the problem was the question of indemnity. It is probable that the planters would have acquiesced in the situation, even with a certain cheerfulness, had they received some compensation for their slaves. But the abolitionists, who now found themselves in a strategic position, were opposed on principle to any indemnity. This attitude reflected on their part little political acumen or sagacity. The chief wealth of many of the planters was confined to their slaves; to these men emancipation without indemnity seemed to spell financial ruin. Especially was this true in the north where it was hopeless to expect to substitute for slave labor that of European immigrants. But when it became clear that a bill for complete emancipation was certain to be voted by Parliament a curious situation developed. Though the hope of some compensation had in the past been held out to the planters, at the present juncture no one apparently dared to incur the charge or even the odium of pronouncing the word indemnity; this despite the excellent precedent established by England and France in the case of their slaveholding colonies in the Antilles and the Guianas. Even the Brazilian slaveowners themselves, with a delicacy little short of quixotic, seemed loath to mention the fatal word. They feared apparently that they would be accused of placing their opposition on too sordid a basis. The prime-minister, João Alfredo, seemed to have been laboring under the same generous obsession. He made the mistake of assuming that emancipation had become such a national ideal or aspiration that it would be unseemly to tarnish it with financial considerations.

It is true that Princess Isabella had received intimations that abolition, immediate and without compensation, might be fraught with grave consequences for the Braganza dynasty. Yet some of the most experienced of Isabella's advisors deprecated any such peril. Dantas, the ex-prime minister in reply to Senator Cotegipe who was opposing the act as being too drastic declared: "It were better only to wear the crown a few hours and enjoy the immense happiness of being a fellowworker with a whole people in such a law as this, than to wear the same crown year upon year on the condition of keeping up the accursed institution of slavery. No, there is no danger. From my experience and on my political responsibility I declare from my seat in this house that today we have a new country, that this law is a new constitution."

The popular rejoicings which followed the passage of the emancipation bill awoke few echoes among the great landowners. Following a natural reaction, this influential class ceased to regard its interests as identified with those of the monarchy. While little if any overt opposition was manifest there were evidences of a strong undercurrent of revulsion, to those who could look beneath the surface. It is significant for instance that within a month after the passage of the act of May 13 a number of the larger municipalities of the provinces of Rio de Janeiro, São Paulo and Minas Geraes addressed themselves directly to Parliament demanding not only indemnities for the loss of the former slaves, but what was more ominous, the calling of a constituent assembly to discuss the whole problem of the future government of Brazil. Small wonder therefore that many of the planters joined the ranks of the Republicans or at least looked with complacency or open approval upon their anti-dynastic propaganda. The number of converts to the republican cause was especially strong in the provinces of Rio de Janeiro where the saying was current that since the blacks had been freed it was time the whites should be emancipated likewise.

The defection of the great landowners and those financially interested in the maintenance of slavery had been preceded by the loss of another element in the population to which the monarchy should logically have looked for support. Through a chain of mistakes and errors which should never have arisen the Empire had aroused the hostility of the clergy even as it had that of the former slaveowners.

The limits of this article naturally preclude any detailed account of the relations of the church and state under the Braganza dynasty. It may merely be noted that, when Brazil separated from Portugal, the new Empire continued to exercise the jealous and petty supervision over the church that had characterized the Portuguese government since the dignities and prerogatives of the great military orders had been attached to the crown in 1551. This tendency towards an exaggerated regalism was of course accentuated during the despotic rule of Pombal. Of the various prerogatives bequeathed by the mother country to her trans-Atlantic offspring, the most important was perhaps the *patronato*, or right of patronage, a right tolerated, but never recognized by the Holy See. As the nineteenth century wore on the supervision of the state over the church became more minute and vexatious; every important act of the ecclesiastical authorities was subject to inspection and revision.

For a full half century after Brazilian independence this system had evoked no serious opposition from the clergy. The clerical question, in the sense it is understood in Catholic Europe or in such South American countries as Chile had never arisen in Brazil. From the first the Empire had recruited many of its staunchest supporters from the ranks of the clergy. The most striking instance was of course Padre Diogo Feijó who acted as regent of the Empire during the troublous years 1835–1837. The clergy had full liberty to enter politics and there were repeatedly to be found a number of able and patriotic priests in the Imperial Parliament. If, as has been frequently alleged, the tutelage of the state was but a veiled form of slavery the clergy had willingly acquiesced in this servitude.

In 1873 a change came. The cordial relations hitherto existing between the Empire and the Church were suddenly interrupted by a quarrel of extreme bitterness. The contest which has sometimes, though with scant justification, been styled the Brazilian *Kulturkampf*, was in part but a repercussion of those ultramontane tendencies which during the preceding decade had made such headway in Catholic Europe, particularly in France. As was to be expected the movement was signalized in Brazil by a revival of certain Catholic practices and teachings which had gradually fallen into abeyance.

The relation of the Church to the Masonic Order was the storm-center about which the conflict revolved. It should be kept clearly in mind that the masonic lodges in Brazil had up to this time evinced no antagonism to the Church. Representatives of the clergy were frequently counted among their members. Moreover the lodges had entrenched themselves solidly in public esteem through the conspicuous service many of their members had rendered in public life. A number of the protagonists of Independence had been masons. Dom Pedro himself was a mason; the prime minister, the Baron of Rio Branco was a Grand-Master of the Orient. In many communities the lodge had become a common stamping-ground for monarchists, republicans, Catholics, and free-thinkers.

An institution enjoying wide popularity at this time in Brazil was a kind of religious and benevolent association known as the *irmandade* or brotherhood. Though the members of this organization were almost exclusively laymen it was conducted to a large extent under church auspices and was supposed to be amenable to church discipline. Up until 1873 masons had been freely admitted to membership; their presence in the brotherhoods had not only occasioned no scandal but was regarded as proper and fitting. It was not unusual to find influential Catholics members of both the masonic orders and the *irmandades*.

On which side rests the responsibility for the interruption of these harmonious relations is still a matter of controversy. Certain it is, however, that to the exalted, ultramontane elements among the Brazilian clergy such a situation was regarded as scandalous. The opposition to the masons was led by the Bishop of Olinda, Mgr. Vital de Oliveira, a young, hot-headed prelate, who had been educated in Rome and had been swept into the current of Catholic reaction associated with Pius IX. In December, 1872, Dom Vital, as he was generally called, ordered the *irmandades* of Pernambuco to expel from their organizations all members who were masons unless they should withdraw from this order, "which had repeatedly been the object of condemnation by the Church."

In issuing this command Dom Vital ran directly counter to the laws of the Empire, as the order condemning masonry had been promulgated without the sanction of the government. The *irmandades*, moreover were not only religious but also civil corporations and in the latter capacity did not come under the authority of the Church. The bishop none the less persisted in his course and when the *irmandades* refused to expel the masons their chapels and churches were placed under an interdict.

The *irmandades* in their distress appealed to the imperial government, which in turn laid the matter before the Council of State. In a famous *paracer* or decision, signed by the distinguished Minister of Justice, Nabuco de Araujo, this body declared that the bishop had exceeded his authority in demanding the expulsion of the masons from the *irmandades*. In pursuance of this decision the government ordered the bishop to withdraw within a month the sentence of interdiction. Dom Vital not only refused to obey this injunction but enjoined refusal on his vicars under threat of suspension *ex informata conscientia*. He publicly declared that he refused to abide by the constitution as he recognized no higher authority than that of the Church. The remaining members of the Brazilian episcopate, with the exception of Dom Antonio de Macedo Costa, Bishop of Pará, took no active part in the controversy. Dom Antonio, however, late in 1873, endeavored to subject the *irmandades* of Pará to the same discipline as had been applied by Dom Vital in Pernambuco.

The imperial government took vigorous action to bring to an end a controversy which was filling northern Brazil with dissension and threatening to envenom the relations between the Empire and the Church. It determined to attack the Bishop of Olinda in the most vulnerable point of his defense. In the early autumn of 1873, it sent a special mission to Rome under Baron Penedo to secure an official disapproval of his acts. Penedo carried out his instructions with tact and success. Pius IX., through the Secretary of State, Antonelli, wrote a famous letter to the Bishop of Olinda, formally disapproving his conduct and containing, according to Penedo, the phrase *gesta tua non laudantur*. The refractory bishop was ordered to restore the brotherhoods to their former state and to reestablish peace in the Church.

It would have been well for the prestige of the monarchy had the government been content to let this diplomatic triumph close the incident. But in spite of the success of the Penedo mission the government determined to prosecute not only the Bishop of Olinda, but also the Bishop of Pará, who as we have seen had entered the lists in defense of his colleague. Both men were tried and convicted by the Supreme Court at Rio and sentenced to four years of hard labor; Dom Pedro commuted the hard labor and after two years granted pardon to both of the bishops.

It is beyond cavil that the religious controversy of the seventies seriously impaired the prestige of the Empire. The prosecution of the bishops and their four years' sentence won them much sympathy not only in Brazil but also in Europe. Among ultramontane circles they were naturally regarded as martyrs. The Brazilian clergy, though for the most part holding aloof from the controversy, felt keenly the affront suffered by their bishops. This grievance against the Empire, harbored in secret, found passionate expression upon the advent of the Republic. The collective pastoral letter of March 19, 1890, written by the former Bishop of Pará, now Archbishop of Bahia, and signed by the entire Brazilian episcopate declared: "We have just witnessed a spectacle which filled the universe with astonishment; one of those events by which the Almighty, when it is pleasing unto Him, teaches tremendous lessons to peoples and kings; a throne suddenly precipitated into the abyss which dissolvent principles, flourishing in its very shadow, had during a few years dug for it."

One of the prime factors in the collapse of the Empire was of course the growing sentiment in favor of a republic as the ideal type of government. The very name republic had a certain magical appeal among a people whose political thinking was for the most part immature. That the free soil of America, the continent of liberty, should be the seat of an empire ruled over by the scion of an old world dynasty seemed to such Brazilians illogical and absurd. *O Imperio è planta exotica no continente americano* was a phrase which steadily gained currency in the press and finally was heard even in Parliament. Such ideas found most ready lodgement among the professional classes, especially the lawyers and journalists. Towards the end the officers of the army became inoculated with the republican virus and, for reasons which have already been noted, republican propaganda in the last days of the Empire made rapid headway among the planters and the clergy.

A clear distinction is of course to be made between the republican ideal on the one hand, and the Republican Party, fostered by republican propaganda on the other. While the latter did not make its appearance until 1870 the former antedated the independence of Brazil and harks back in fact to the period of the French Revolution. It is a fact worthy of note that almost every political upheaval in France has had its reverberation in Brazil. In 1789 broke out the ill-starred revolution in Minas Geraes headed by Tiradentes. The July Revolution which brought Louis Philippe to the French throne was not unrelated to the forced abdication and banishment of the dictatorial Dom Pedro I in 1831. While the Brazilian Empire had by the middle of the century struck its roots too deep to be seriously affected by the proclamation of the Second Republic in France in 1848, the republican spirit was by no means extinct.

It was not until 1870, however, that these vague republican aspirations crystallized into a definite political organization, with a program and plan of campaign. Once more the direct impetus came from abroad. The establishment of the Third Republic in France and the temporary overthrow of the Bourbon monarchy in Spain awoke powerful echoes in the only monarchy in the new world. On December 3, 1870, a number of the most enthusiastic of the Brazilian Republicans put forth a Manifesto destined to become famous, as it marked the beginning of a political agitation which finished only with the collapse of the Empire. This document, which was published in the first number of *A Republica*, the official organ of the new party, consists of a "Statement of Motives", followed by an "Historical Retrospect". In the latter we are informed that "the Empire has filched from the Brazilians the glorious conquests sought for by the Wars of Independence in 1822 and 1831. Liberty in appearance, despotism in reality —the form disguising the substance—such is the characteristic of our constitutional system". After a lengthy arraignment of both the spirit and organization of the Empire the Manifesto closes with an eloquent appeal to "American ideals". This document was signed by 57 Brazilians, among whom were a number who sprang into prominence in the overthrow of the Empire.

The extravagant hopes of the signers of the Manifesto proved to be premature and with little foundation in fact. The new party, after being a nine days' wonder, caused scarcely a ripple of excitement on the placid current of Brazilian political life. The people as a whole were indifferent, the paper *A Republica*, launched with such a flourish of trumpets, died of inanition after a precarious existence of barely four years.

For the next decade and a half the movement grew slowly and adhesions were comparatively few. Its greatest vitality was to be found not in the Capital but in the provinces, particularly in São Paulo and Rio Grande do Sul. Small but active clubs sprang into existence and in São Paulo a number of Republican Congresses were held. In this province the movement was largely under the guidance of two young and able lawyers, Manuel de Campos Salles and Prudente de Moraes Barros, both of whom became presidents of the Republic. It was not until 1884 that the Republican Party entered its candidates for election to Parliament. Although they gained three seats in the parliamentary session of 1885, their candidates were defeated in subsequent elections and it was not until the last year of the Empire that republican deputies were again returned.

The abolition of slavery in 1888 was a turning point in the history of the Republican Party. We have seen that many of the slaveowners, as well as brokers and others identified with agricultural interests, enrolled in the new party or gave it their moral support. The Republicans in turn were quick to seize upon the occasion and proceeded to capitalize their advantage to the full. Hitherto republican agitation had been carried on sporadically and without system. It was now determined to launch an unremitting propaganda through the length and breadth of the Empire. The number of republican papers, especially in the provinces increased by leaps and bounds until in 1889 they amounted to 88. While few of the metropolitan dailies adopted republicanism as their credo a number were of immense indirect assistance through their unsparing attacks on the government. The Republicans also exploited for their own interest a section of the papers, particularly in the case of the great *Jornal do Commercio*, called publicações a pedidos, open to any type or class contribution on the payment of a relatively small sum.

Republican agitation was by no means confined to the press. In the last years of the monarchy apostles of the new faith went up and down the land, holding public meetings, and winning proselytes to the cause. Of these itinerant propagandists the most picturesque and important was a young man named Silva Jardim, whose tragic death shortly after the advent of the Republic helped to invest his exploits with a legendary and heroic character having little warrant in cold fact. This remarkable man, of whose ability and intellectual endowments differing views are held by his own countrymen, seems to have had little appreciation of the common proprieties of life. But he was enflamed with the zeal of a fanatic and possessed a certain magnetism which carried his audiences with him. Within a period of little less than two years—from January, 1888, to November 15, 1889—he passed through entire provinces, speaking in hundreds of towns and cities, heartening his coreligionists, converting the undecided and even the hostile. His tour through North Brazil in 1889 when he dogged the heels of the Prince Consort, Count d'Eu, who had undertaken this journey to revive the prestige of the monarchy, is regarded by his admirers as his greatest triumph.

It is difficult accurately to appraise the results of this republican propaganda. While converts were undoubtedly made, their number and importance may easily be exaggerated. Aside from a few zealots like Jardim and a group of able journalists and politicians in the provincial capitals the number of avowed Republicans was comparatively small. Perhaps their most striking success—if success it may be called—was to lower the prestige of the monarchy. The evidence seems to be overwhelming that in political matters the great bulk of the Brazilians were inclined to be apathetic; nowhere, outside of certain restricted circles, was there any insistent or overwhelming demand for the abolition, much less the violent overthrow, of the existing regime.

But the Republicans, even had they been much more numerous, would have been incapable of consummating the overthrow of the monarchy had its supporters rallied vigorously to its defense. Unfortunately many of this class had grown lukewarm in their devotion and loyalty to the Empire; others played directly into the hands of the Republicans through their intemperate, and ofttimes venomous, attacks on the monarchy, attacks frequently motivated by personal pique, thwarted ambition, or merely by the spirit of the *frondeur*. Certain it is that in the late seventies and eighties the star of the monarchy began to wane. There was a growing conviction that the golden days of the Empire were over. Many Brazilians looked back with longing to a generation or even a decade earlier when under the guidance of a galaxy of able and patriotic statesmen chosen by the emperor, Brazil reaped the benefits of what was in many respects a model constitutional government. In the great days of Olinda, Paraná, Zacharias, the Elder Rio Branco, and Nabuco de Araujo, Brazil was a standing refutation of the jibes of such foreign critics as Lastarria and Alberdi that the only American empire had as the maxims of its policy internal despotism and unscrupulous foreign aggression.

One of the most striking indications of the decline of the Empire was the increasing sterility with which the two great political parties seemed to be afflicted, a sterility which was naturally reflected in the labors of Parliament. There was gradually forced home to the thoughtful Brazilian the conviction that the Liberals and Conservatives had abandoned their earlier ideas in favor of a sordid opportunism. The complete volte-face of the Conservative Party in 1888 when it espoused the cause of emancipation, a question whose solution logically developed upon the Liberals, gave rise to the most cynical commentaries.

Justly or unjustly the emperor was also taxed with the responsibility for the political disintegration which appeared towards the end of his reign. There is reason to believe that the charge harbors at least a kernel of truth. During the waning of the Empire, Dom Pedro was a weary, and for months at a time, a sick man. Towards the end his attitude in regard to public affairs was colored with a certain scepticism merging into fatalism. He made little effort to stave off the catastrophe with which he must have seen his dynasty was menaced.

The attacks on the emperor which did so much to impair the prestige of the monarchy had as their chief burden the abuse of those prerogatives granted him by the constitution under the designation of the Moderative Power. Under cover of this authority, the emperor was accused of having set up a kind of veiled and irresponsible despotism to which the name of *poder pessoal* was loosely applied. In the appointment of his prime ministers he constantly aimed, it was charged, at maintaining a certain equilibrium between the two political parties in order that the balance of power might always remain in his hands. Though nominally responsible to Parliament, the ministry, critics declared, was really under the control of the emperor. Confronted with a hostile Chamber of Deputies, the ministry was more apt to dissolve Parliament than to go out of office. The electoral system was such that any ministry following dissolution was able to secure a unanimous Chamber and thus remain in office at the good pleasure of the emperor. Dom Pedro was furthermore accused of never allowing his ministers to rise in popular estimation beyond a certain level; nor did he ever accord them his full confidence.

These accusations were by no means confided to zealous Republicans whose stock in trade consisted in disparagement of the Empire. The utterances of a number of Dom Pedro's distinguished ex-ministers have become almost classic. Eusebio de Queiroz, after having been minister for a little over two years, said to his friends: "Who has once been minister of Dom Pedro must put aside all sense of shame to occupy such a post a second time". Senator Silveira Martins stated in Parliament: "The Government is bad; the system is bad. We are living under a disguised absolutism; it is necessary to end it". Ferreira Vianna, speaking of the emperor declared: "Forty years of falsehoods, perfidy, domination, usurpation; a caricature of a Caesar; a prince who is a conspirator." But the most celebrated of these indictments was that of the famous novelist José de Alencar. In 1870, possibly as a result of the emperor's refusal to appoint him a member of the Senate, he violently broke with Dom Pedro and in a series of articles contributed to the press of Rio de Janeiro subjected both the emperor and the *poder pessoal* to a scathing arraignment. The sensation caused by these attacks of Alencar was heightened by the fact that less than a decade earlier in a widely-read work entitled "Letters to the Emperor" and signed by "Erasmus" he had depicted Dom Pedro as a model constitutional monarch whose excellent intentions were frequently thwarted by an oligarchy of self-seeking politicians. But in 1870 Alcencar entirely recanted his earlier beliefs; the emperor has become a despot while the *poder pessoal* "like a monstrous octopus invades everything from the transcendent questions of high politics to the trifles *(nugas)* of petty administration."

It is now recognized that these attacks on the alleged exercise of despotic power by the emperor are somewhat wide of the mark. Under the social and political conditions then prevailing in Brazil the emperor could hardly have avoided the exercise of the *poder pessoal*, which was thrust upon him by the force of circumstances. There did not exist that indispensable prerequisite to a genuinely representative government—the expression of national opinion by means of a popular vote. We can clearly see now—a fact necessarily obscure to contemporaries—that the smooth functioning of the machinery of government year after year without a serious breakdown was due in large measure to this tireless vigilance of the emperor. Despotic Dom Pedro may have been at times. Not always were the susceptibilities of his ministers duly safeguarded. But above the interest of parties, of cabinets, of the dynasty itself, was the higher interest of the nation; this was the lodestar by which the actions of the emperor were guided; this the touchstone by which he judged both men and events. In the phrase of the Brazilian historian, Oliveira Lima, "if there was any despotism, it was the despotism of morality."

If despite these attacks the emperor was to the very end of his reign the object of affection and esteem by large classes of the Brazilians, the same could not be said of his daughter Princess Isabella, and the Prince Consort, Count d'Eu. Both were unpopular; both were the victims of charges and calumnies having little basis in fact. More specifically, the princess was accused of being under the control of the church; it was freely declared that on the death of her father the policy of the government would be amenable to clerical influences. As for the prince consort nothing could be alleged against him save his reserved, somewhat formal bearing and the fact that he was a foreigner.

In spite of the alienation of the planters and the clergy; in spite of the inroads made by republican propaganda in the ranks of intellectuals and to a certain extent among the mass of the people; in spite of the waning prestige of the dynasty, the Empire might have lasted many years longer had it been able to count on the loyalty of the army. Without the active participation of certain military elements the Republic would not have been declared on November 15, 1889. What were the causes of the disaffection in the army? What plausible reasons could the military leaders advance for their abandonment of the emperor?

The whole subject of the rôle of the army in the collapse of the Empire is both complicated and controversial. Even now, over a quarter of a century after the event, there exist the sharpest divisions of opinion as to the motives and even honesty of the leaders of the revolt.

Broadly speaking Brazil had been free from the blight of militarism so typical of certain of her Spanish American neighbors. Military dictatorships had been unknown. The higher positions in the government had been filled almost entirely by civilians; it is significant that of the fifty-four ministers of war in the thirty-six cabinets under Dom Pedro II., only eighteen had been officers in the army. While the well-known pacifist leanings of the emperor were partly responsible for this situation the Brazilian people as a whole were strongly averse to militarism.

The Brazilian army had given a good account of itself in the few foreign conflicts in which the nation had been involved; especially was this true of the Paraguayan War in which both the army and navy added heroic chapters to the annals of Brazilian history. Yet the army, especially in times of peace, had never been a model of discipline. The civil wars and revolutions which had characterized the period of the Regency (1831–1840) and the early years of Dom Pedro's reign had bred a feeling of recklessness and even insolence among the army chiefs. The contact with the Platine Republics during the conflict with the tyrant Rosas and during the Paraguayan War had a deleterious effect. Despite the efforts of President Mitre of Argentina to infuse a new spirit into Argentine institutions only too often the Brazilians found in their southern neighbors a school of despotism and all the evils of *caudillismo*. The chronic disturbance in the Province of Rio Grande do Sul, necessitating the presence of large forces on the Uruguayan frontier, aggravated these evils. Finally the imagination of certain of the Brazilian chieftains was captivated by the sinister but dynamic personalities of Rosas, Rivera, and the younger López.

During the decade of peace following the Paraguayan War the army became increasingly lax in discipline and morale. The type of instruction given in the military schools indirectly fostered this tendency. As a result of a series of reforms in higher education, science, and mathematics were given the places of honor in the curricula. The result was that instruction became theoretical rather than practical; purely military subjects were relegated to a secondary place. Many young officers prized the degree of *bacharel* (bachelor) and *doutor* (doctor) more than their military patents. The lower officers began to find vent for their energies in political discussion in which the terms freedom and equality figured prominently; the higher officers were often more concerned with literature and the vogue of the Positivistic philosophy of Auguste Comte than with military tactics or discipline. The privates, recruited almost exclusively from the lower classes, prone to regard their officers as they would plantation overseers with the additions of gold braid and trappings, were so much malleable material in the hands of their leaders.

All public agitators at the time, republican or otherwise, upheld the doctrine that the members of the army were subject to military discipline only when on duty or in action. At other times they might freely participate in public affairs as "citizens in uniform."

In a country like Brazil, in which military discipline is not reenforced by long tradition and in which politics is one of the dominant passions of the race, such a doctrine was especially seductive to those unfamiliar with the problems of government.

Under these circumstances many of the officers began to aspire to a brilliant rôle in politics. This tendency was increased through the absence of any law debarring members of the army from a political career. A number of officers were elected to the Chamber of Deputies and were appointed to life membership in the Senate. Protected by their parliamentary immunities they did not hesitate to attack members of the cabinet including the minister of war. Further possibilities of tension between the military and the government were always present owing to insistence of certain of the officers on their alleged right to ventilate their grievances through the medium of the press.

The historians of the revolt of 1889 have succeeded in creating the legend that the army during the last years of the monarchy was the victim of intolerable injustice and vindictive persecution on the part of the government and that it was only when all other means of redress were exhausted that recourse was had to armed rebellion. But when the specific grievances of the army are subjected to a close scrutiny they shrink to pitiable dimensions. For the most part they are either frivolous or based on a palpable misunderstanding. It is possible that the imperial government treated the army with neglect but there is no evidence that this neglect was studied or due to any animus. The unprejudiced investigator is forced to the conclusion that in the final instance the real grievance of the military was the refusal of the government to grant the army a privileged position in the state. Had Brazil possessed a strong military tradition; had the army been content to eschew politics and confine itself purely to its proper rôle of providing for national defense and internal security, it is improbable that any serious issue would ever have arisen.

The first serious clash between the army and the government occurred in 1883. Under the belief that a bill fathered by Senator Paranaguá was a covert attack on the army, a large number of officers of the Military School of Rio de Janeiro formed a *Directorio* whose chief object was to launch a press campaign against the measure. Adhesions from higher officials including a number of generals, and even from students of the Military School poured in. A certain Lieutenant Colonel Senna Madureira, whom we shall meet later, wrote a series of articles for the *Jornal do Commercio* vigorously attacking the bill. Partly as a result of this agitation the obnoxious measure was thrown out by the Senate; at the same time the government called attention to the ministerial *avisos*, repeatedly issued, prohibiting officers of the army from having recourse to the public press without the previous consent of the minister of war.

The year 1883 also witnessed an event which filled the supporters of the monarchy with the gloomiest forebodings and served as a direct encouragement to the unbridled pretension of the army. As is well known the press under the Empire enjoyed a freedom frequently degenerating into a license which did not spare the imperial family itself. Under cover of this toleration a number of disreputable and scurrilous sheets were published in Rio de Janeiro. Such a paper was *O Corsario (The Corsair)*, edited by one Apulcho de Castro. In the fall of 1883 appeared a series of vicious attacks on the reputation and honor of a cavalry officer stationed in the Capital. Rumor had it that the victim of these attacks, together with certain of his brother officers, was plotting vengeance on the editor of the offensive sheet. Fearing the worst Castro appealed to the police for protection. The chief of police sought the cooperation of the ministry of war. The decision was reached to remove Castro in broad daylight to a distant part of the city where he might be safe from his enemies. To assure him protection a certain Captain Avila was detailed by the ministry of war to accompany him. But the carriage had hardly left the police station before it was beset by a mob in which a number of officers, dressed as civilians, figured prominently. Castro was stabbed to death despite the protests of his escort. In the official investigation which followed no serious effort was made to apprehend or punish the perpetrators of this crime. Both the police department and the ministry of war were held in popular opinion to have been derelict in their duty. The painful impression caused by this outrage was deepened by the fact that while the investigation was still pending the emperor saw fit to visit the quarters of the regiment to which the suspected assassins belonged. Possibly no single event in the later days of the Empire did more to bring the monarchy into disrepute than the unpunished assassination of an obscure and wretched journalist.

The order issued by the minister of war, forbidding officers from ventilating their grievances in the press, was soon disregarded. In 1886 Colonel Cunha Mattos published an attack on one of the deputies who had accused him in the Chamber of conduct in the Paraguayan War unbecoming an officer. The dispute became so acrimonious that the government felt constrained to act. In July, Minister of War Alfredo Chaves formally censured Cunha Mattos, pointing out that he had not only disregarded various ministerial *avisos* but also the order of the adjutant general, which under date of December 20, 1884, had forbidden any officer from carrying on a discussion in the press, even to vindicate himself from unjust accusations. He was sentenced to a nominal imprisonment of eight hours in the headquarters of the general staff.

As Cunha Mattos received both the censure and punishment without protest the incident might soon have been forgotten but for the unexpected and intemperate action of Senator Pelotas. The Viscount of Pelotas, General Camara, as one of the heroes of the Paraguayan War, enjoyed general esteem and wielded great influence in military circles. As a friend and fellow officer of Cunha Mattos he felt called upon to take up his defense. In a lengthy speech, vibrant with suppressed emotion, delivered in the Senate on August 2, 1886, he expressed amazement at the severe punishment inflicted upon the offending officer and declared that the other officers of the army would see in the sufferings of their comrade an offense committed against them all. "The official who is wounded in his military honor has the imprescriptible right to avenge himself." When one of the Senators interjected, "if the law permits it", Pelotas replied: "I do not say that our laws permit it; I am informing the noble minister of war of what I understand a soldier should do when he is wounded in his honor . . . and he who is speaking will thus proceed whether or not there is a law to prevent him. I place my honor above all else". The effects of this tirade, uttered by an old soldier, a veteran of the Paraguayan War, on the younger officers needs no comment. The following year when the military question had reached an acute stage the prime minister rightly charged Pelotas with the major responsibility for the crisis.

Meanwhile the government, hoping to strengthen the hands of the minister of war, submitted the whole question of the use of the press by the army to the Supreme Military Council. This body handed down a decision to the effect that the members of the army, like all other citizens, might according to the constitution, freely have recourse to the public press. The only exception was questions exclusively between members of the military; these should be forbidden lest discipline suffer. This decision, which played directly into the hands of the radical elements of the army, was naturally regarded as a severe blow to the government. Had it been wise it would have at once recognized that its position in regard to the censures based on the ministerial *avisos*, or even on the order of the adjutant general, was no longer tenable. This it refused to do and as a result soon found itself in a false and even ridiculous position.

While the tension created by the Cunha Mattos episode was still acute, fresh fuel was added to the fire. On August 16, 1886, Lieutenant Colonel Senna Madureira published in a paper in Rio Grande do Sul an article intended to vindicate himself against a slight which he alleged had been cast upon him by a member of the Senate. The article, widely copied in the metropolitan press, aroused much comment. When reprimanded by Minister Alfredo Chaves, unlike Cunha Mattos he refused to accept the rebuke in silence. In November, 1886, he published a vigorous memorial in which he took the ground that no law forbade an officer from defending himself in the press, adding that he for one would refuse to recognize the competency of the minister of war in such matters. He wound up his memorial with the demand that he be granted a trial before a council of war.

This protest of Madureira, coupled with the refusal of Alfredo Chaves to remove the censure or permit a trial before a council of war, caused great resentment among the military and won for Madureira much sympathy and admiration among the various elements opposed to the government. The fact that he was known to possess strong republican leanings was an added circumstance in his favor. A new and ominous factor was suddenly injected into the controversy when there rallied to his support perhaps the most popular official in the entire army, General Deodoro da Fonseca, destined to be the outstanding personality in the Revolution of 1889, the Chief of the Provisional Government, and first President of the Republic. At this time he was the chief military authority in Rio Grande do Sul and was also vice-president of the province. Possessed of but moderate intellectual gifts, headstrong and impulsive, passionately convinced of the justice of any cause he espoused, he was only too often the pliant tool of men more clever or less scrupulous than himself. At the present critical juncture he took up the cause of Madureira and granted permission to a large number of officers stationed at Porto Alegre to hold a meeting of protest against the acts of the minister of war.

The prime minister, Baron Cotegipe, whose cabinet (conservative) had held office since August 20, 1885 fully realized the importance of having Deodoro as a friend rather than an enemy. But when both persuasions and blandishments proved unavailing, he relieved Deodoro from his duties in Rio Grande do Sul and summoned him to Rio de Janeiro. With his own and his brother officers' grievances rankling in his breast the disgruntled general was willing to go to any length to humiliate the cabinet and render its position untenable. On February 2, 1887, was held under his patronage a great meeting of protest in one of the largest theatres of the Capital. Over two hundred officers were present and the public was admitted to the galleries. From the first it was evident that the purpose of the meeting was to bring pressure to bear upon the government. To the accompaniment of tremendous applause a motion was carried investing Deodoro with full authority to defend before both the government and the emperor the rights of his comrades and his class. In pursuance of this mandate, on February 5, Deodoro sent an open letter to Dom Pedro. Although the writer professed loyalty to the monarchy the burden of the letter was a recital of bitter accusations against the government and insistent demands for justice to the army. It was a frank effort to override and break down the constitutional powers of the government.

In the face of this assault the ministry fell a victim to divided counsels. When energy and unity were essential the cabinet temporized and fell back upon half measures which tended only to aggravate the seriousness of the crisis. There is evidence that the minister of war favored drastic action: Deodoro should be retired from the army and the Military School—rapidly becoming a hotbed of anti-dynastic intrigue—should be closed. But Cotegipe and possibly the emperor opposed these measures and on February 12 Alfredo Chaves tendered his resignation. Once again the belief gained currency that the government had been worsted by the army.

On the very day that the minister of war left the cabinet Deodoro wrote another open letter to the emperor in which references to the government were couched in even more violent and minatory terms than in its predecessor. To neither of these letters did Dom Pedro vouchsafe either acknowledgment or reply. Cotegipe declared in this connection that "the cabinet would not remain in power a single hour if it ceased to be the channel through which all communications should pass to his Majesty".

Although Cotegipe had refused to support the minister of war his own course of action was little calculated to allay the growing resentment of the army. On the burning question of the rights of the two officers, Cunha Mattos and Madureira—nominally the pivot about which the whole controversy turned—he yielded to the extent of offering to remove the censures if this were asked for as a favor and not demanded as a right. This compromise the leaders of the army indignantly rejected and on May 14, 1887, was given to the press an energetic and vigorously worded manifesto addressed "to Parliament and to the Nation", and signed by both Deodoro and Pelotas. The gist of this document was the necessity of appealing to the Brazilian people and their representatives for the justice denied the army by the ministry. At the same time Pelotas delivered a speech in the Senate in which he warned the ministry of its dangerous course, ending his address with the covert threat that unless the cabinet reconsidered its action the army might be forced to take independent measures to defend its own interests.

A way out of the impasse into which the ministry and army chiefs had drifted was at length suggested by Senator Silveira Martins on May 20. The government was invited to declare null and void the censures directed against the two officers, thus bringing the whole episode to a close. After some hesitation this solution was accepted by the cabinet; Cotegipe recognized that it emerged from the controversy "with its dignity somewhat scratched" (*cum alguns arranhões na dignidade*) a phrase which became celebrated.

The heavy atmosphere of suspicion and distrust was only partly clarified by these eleventh hour concessions wrung from the ministry. The military question was suddenly complicated by the emancipation movement, which as we have seen, came to a head in 1888. During the summer and fall of 1887, the slaves, especially in the Province of São Paulo, began to abandon their plantations *en masse*. As the local authorities were quite unable to cope with the situation recourse was had to the army. But the task of chasing run-away slaves was exceedingly repugnant to the soldiery. This sentiment was shared by Deodoro and the powerful Military Club of Rio de Janeiro. In October, 1887, the club sent a petition to Princess Isabella, who was then acting as regent, begging in the name of humanity, that the army be relieved of this odious task. Isabella ignored the petition, while Cotegipe, who was generally regarded as hostile to the abolition movement, refused to act. In practice, however, the soldiery proved a broken reed to the planters, as they rarely if ever captured the slaves whom they were supposed to pursue. None the less the whole episode tended still further to estrange the army from the government.

The Cotegipe cabinet, after having weathered so many storms, was fated to go down to defeat before the pressure from the army, which on this particular occasion had joined hands with the navy. In the spring of 1888, an officer of the navy, Captain Leite Lobo, while dressed as a civilian, was apprehended by the police on pretexts which he regarded as frivolous and subjected to various indignities before his release was effected. The influential Naval Club, vigorously supported by the disaffected elements in the army, raised a great hue and cry, demanding the resignation of the chief of police. Cotegipe refused to yield to this clamor and when Princess Isabella acceded to the demands of the Naval Club and the army, the prime minister resigned (March, 1888). Still another triumph was added to the laurels of the army in its conflict with the government.

The Cotegipe ministry was followed by that of João Alfredo (March 10, 1888), likewise conservative. We have already noted that the energies of the new cabinet were largely absorbed by the solution of the emancipation problem and the great act of May 13. Partly on this account the military question was temporarily relegated to the background. The cabinet showed, however, that it could act with vigor and firmness when occasion demanded. When, at the beginning of 1889, rumor reached Brazil that a conflict was impending between Paraguay and Bolivia the government adopted the bold course of sending to the frontier in distant Matto Grosso two battalions from the Capital under the command of Deodoro, thus removing from Rio de Janeiro the most important leader of the dangerous faction in the army. Had João Alfredo's successor persisted in this course of action the next decade of Brazilian history would have been quite a different story.

On June 7, 1889, came into office the last cabinet of the Empire. It was recruited from the Liberal party and was presided over by Affonso Celso de Assis Figueiredo, Viscount of Ouro Preto. The new prime minister was a man of ripe experience in public affairs. He had held the portfolios of finance and war in 1879 and 1882 respectively and had also served a long apprenticeship in both houses of Parliament and in the Council of State. He was a brilliant lawyer, a formidable debater, and a sincere and devoted supporter of the Empire and the reigning dynasty. As a close student of political and economic problems he fully realized that the maladies from which the Empire was suffering were amenable only to the most drastic and thorough-going remedies. The program which he submitted to Parliament embodied the most comprehensive series of reforms ever sponsored by any of Dom Pedro's ministers. These reforms included extension of the suffrage through the removal of property qualifications, full autonomy of the provinces and the municipalities, election of the presidents of the provinces instead of their appointment, abolition of the life Senate, reorganization of the Council of State, freedom of education and its improvement, reform in agrarian legislation, reduction of export duties, and promotion of credit establishments designed especially to aid the agricultural interests in tiding over the crisis caused by emancipation.

There is some warrant for the belief that Ouro Preto's heroic measures to inject new life into the decrepit institutions of the Empire would have attained a measure of success had they been granted a fair trial. Early in his ministry he won the full confidence of the business circles of the capital; by a stroke of brilliant financiering he converted a portion of Brazil's foreign debt on very favorable terms; foreign exchange, always a barometer of the prosperity of the country for the first time in the history of the Empire went above par. His political reforms, could they have been carried out, would showing that the monarchy was quite capable of meeting the demands of have gone far towards neutralizing the propaganda of the Republicans by the Brazilian people for a fuller participation in public affairs. The large measure of autonomy granted the provinces would have met the justifiable charge that the Empire had fallen victim to an excessive centralization. There were not lacking impartial observers who predicted that under the guidance of Ouro Preto the Empire was about to take on a new lease of life.

Unfortunately the new cabinet in its laudable desire to quicken the economic and political currents of the nation failed to attach sufficient weight to what was after all the gravest menace to the Empire: the grievances and pretensions of the military. To be sure, Ouro Preto had some reason to depreciate the importance of the military question. The army, it would seem, had won all its contentions. The honor of the two aggrieved officers had been fully vindicated; the right of the army to ventilate its grievances in the press had been recognized; the ministry, which had attempted to thwart the wishes of the military, had gone down to defeat. Moreover, the first acts of the Ouro Preto cabinet presaged a policy of conciliation. Probably at the instance of the emperor, two high military and naval officers, Viscount of Maracajú and Baron Ladario were assigned the portfolios of war and marine respectively, thus breaking a long tradition of civilian appointments. The object was probably to allay discontent among the officers by placing them under control of men of their own profession. As a further concession, Ouro Preto recalled from Matto Grosso General Deodoro da Fonseca. The future was soon to reveal that the prime minister could hardly have committed a worse blunder.

It soon appeared that all attempts on the part of Ouro Preto to bridge the ever-widening breach between the government and the army were fruitless. Of actual grievances against the new cabinet the army leaders had few and these were almost too trivial to merit serious discussion. The punishment of the officer in charge of the treasury guard for a minor dereliction; a clash between the soldiery and police in Minas Geraes; the failure of Ouro Preto to accede to the wishes of the Director of the Military School of Ceará in regard to an appointment: such were the acts of the cabinet, for the most part purely disciplinary in character, which were seized upon by the opposition press and enemies of the Empire as proofs of the injustice of the government towards the military. In the absence of fact the most extravagant rumors were pressed into service. It was declared that the prime minister had nothing less in mind than the total dissolution of the army; as a step in this direction certain of the regiments which were the object of Ouro Preto's special dislike were to be sent to the most distant provinces. The place of the army was to be taken by the police force of the Capital and the National Guard; the latter body according to a plot revealed by the *Diario de Noticias*, was to be armed and placed under the command of the unpopular Count d'Eu. It was even alleged that the government was contemplating the creation of a "Negro Guard" (*Duarda Negra*) to whose special protection the dynasty was to be committed. These charges, capitalized by the hostile press and disseminated by Republican agitators acted as a powerful solvent to undermine the loyalty of the army and to weaken the monarchical sentiments of the people.

Thus far the disaffected elements in the army, with occasional exceptions, had not made common cause with the Republicans. Opposition had been directed against the government and particularly the ministry in office and not against the dynasty. In this regard the attitude of General Camara, Viscount of Pelotas, one of the signers of the famous Manifesto of May 14, 1887, was typical of that of his class. In a letter written to Ouro Preto in 1890 he declared that he had not considered the possibility of the Republic during the lifetime of the emperor. That the plans and purposes of certain of the recalcitrant officers were directed into frankly revolutionary channels was due in large part to the teachings and machinations of a single individual, Lieutenant-Colonel Benjamin Constant de Botelho Magalhães.

This official, whom the more ardent of the Brazilian Republicans have regarded as not unworthy of the honors of an apotheosis, had for a number of years been professor of mathematics in the Military School of Rio de Janeiro. He was a thorough exponent of that theoretical type of education which, as we have seen, had, in the latter days of the monarchy, made such headway in the Brazilian military academies. The decisive event in his intellectual development was his discovery of the philosophical system of Auguste Comte known as Positivism. The young professor was fascinated with the seductive theories of Comte which seemingly represented the definite integration of all human knowledge; during the remainder of his life he was one of the most ardent champions of Positivism in Brazil. The movement for a time made considerable headway and is regarded by some as one of the factors in the collapse of the Empire. Through the misinterpretation, wilful or otherwise, of Comte's system, the Brazilian Positivists claimed that they found in their master's teaching warrant for the belief that a republic was the ideal type of government. In any event, Benjamin Constant, partly as an outgrowth of his philosophical speculation, became an enthusiastic convert to the republican cause. Inspired with the zeal of a fanatic he did not scruple to inculcate in his students doctrines subversive of their loyalty to the Empire and to Dom Pedro. His keen intelligence, persuasive oratory, and sympathetic personality caused the young officers and cadets to become pliant instruments in his hands. As a consequence the Military School became a veritable hotbed of republican propaganda. It followed as a matter of course that in the controversy between the army and the government he threw the full weight of his influence into the scale in favor of the military. One incident became famous. On October 22, 1889, a group of Chilean naval officers visited the Military School. In the presence of the minister of war and the foreign guests, Benjamin Constant made an impassioned plea in favor of his comrades in arms, protesting against the "charge of indiscipline, disorder and insubordination leveled by the government", adding that "they would always be armed citizens but never *janizaries*". On the following day his students greeted him with vociferous applause accompanied by a shower of flowers.

The preliminaries of the conspiracy of which Benjamin Constant was the guiding spirit may be passed over rapidly. Unlike the other aggrieved military leaders he was held in check by no dynastic scruples or loyalty to Dom Pedro; to postpone the establishment of the Republic until the death of the emperor would in his opinion play directly into the hands of Ouro Preto and his plan for a monarchical reaction; moreover Princess Isabella and the Count d'Eu, once they were enthroned, might be much more difficult to brush aside than the kindly and peace-loving old emperor. In fine, it was Benjamin Constant's self appointed task to forge the accumulated grievances against the government and more particularly the cabinet of Ouro Preto into a weapon capable of demolishing the monarchy.

Secure in the support of the cadets of the Military School he turned to the powerful Military Club to which many of the prominent officers stationed at Rio de Janeiro belonged. At a secret meeting, held on November 9, and attended by one hundred and fifty-three officers, he was given *carte blanche* to make a final effort to obtain a cessation of the alleged persecutions to which the army was being subjected. Entrusted with this commission he called upon General Deodoro da Fonseca, who, as we have just seen, had been recalled from Matto Grosso, and proposed to him a plan of action not only against the ministry but also against the monarchy. The old soldier was not immediately won over. For a time his loyalty to the emperor, from whom he had received nothing but favors, struggled hard against the passionate pleadings of Benjamin Constant. He finally capitulated: "The Old Emperor (*o Velho*) is no longer the ruler, for if he were there would not be this persecution of the army; nevertheless, now that there is no other remedy, *carry the monarchy by assault*. There is nothing more to be hoped from it. Let the Republic come."

From this moment both set feverishly to work to prepare for the advent of the Republic. Up to this time, with the exception of the editor of the *Diario de Noticias*, Ruy Barbosa, no civilian had been initiated into the plot. On November 11 was held a meeting at Deodoro's house at which in addition to the general and Benjamin Constant were present Ruy Barbosa, Quintino Bocayuva, Artistides Lobo, Francisco Glycerio—all prominent civilian leaders of the Republican party and later members of the provisional government. At this meeting the overthrow of the monarchy was definitely decided upon, in the words of one of the conspirators, "as a measure of urgent necessity for the salvation of the country and the only possible means of restoring the army". The details of the revolt were then worked out; the uprising was scheduled for the evening of November 16 when the emperor would be holding a conference with his ministry. On the 13th the conspirators won another prominent military chieftain to their cause, namely, the adjutant-general of the army, Floriano Peixoto, a warm personal friend of

Deodoro, and in due time destined to be the second president of the Republic. The adhesion of Floriano was regarded as an especial piece of good fortune as he enjoyed the entire confidence of the prime minister and the minister of war.

It does not fall within the scope of this article to discuss in detail the actual events of November 15. The military and republican plotters had things practically their own way. Up until almost the last moment the government was strangely blind to the imminence of the catastrophe. To be sure the prime minister was beset by rumors and anonymous denunciations but he refused to accord them any credence. His suspicions were first aroused when he learned something of the decisions reached at the Military Club on November 9. On November 12, he held a cabinet meeting in which he discussed with the ministers of war and justice the need of precautionary measures. But Minister of War Maracajú scouted even the possibility of a military revolt. "Have no anxiety", he stated to Ouro Preto; "we are on the watch, Floriano and I; nothing will happen". And on the following day this same Floriano Peixoto, who, as we have just seen, was adjutant-general of the army and the recipient of the full confidence of the prime minister wrote to Ouro Preto: "At this hour your Excellency must have observed that plotting is taking place in certain quarters. Attach no importance to it. . . . Trust the loyalty of the military leaders who are on the alert. I thank you once more for the favors you have deigned to bestow upon me."

Despite these assertions Ouro Preto took such eleventh hour precautions as seemed possible. On the 14th, the minister of war was requested to summon Deodoro and if his explanation of his recent conduct was unsatisfactory to remove him from the army; the president of the Province of Rio de Janeiro was ordered to concentrate such troops in the Capital as he had under his command. Finally the minister of justice was instructed to have the police force and national guard ready for any emergency.

The military uprising, scheduled as we have seen for the 16th of November, took place a day earlier as the result of widely scattered rumors, launched on the 14th, to the effect that the government had ordered the imprisonment of Deodoro and Benjamin Constant and the embarcation for the provinces of a battalion of infantry and a regiment of cavalry whose loyalty was suspected. These rumors, utterly without basis of fact, were invented by a certain Major Frederico Solon "as a patriotic stratagem of war" to exacerbate the feelings of the soldiers of the Second Brigade and cause them to precipitate the revolt by taking matters into their own hands. The stratagem was successful. On the night of the 14th, the troops stationed at the imperial palace at Boa Vista in the suburbs of the Capital decided to leave their garrison and fully armed, to march to the Campo da Acclamação, a great park or square in the centre of the city where was located the office of the ministry of war. Learning of this move through Benjamin Constant, General Deodoro rose from his sick bed and hurrying to Boa Vista put himself at the head of the revolting troops.

Through the vigilance of the chief of police, the news of the uprising of the Second Brigade reached the prime minister immediately after the soldiers had left their barracks. At this crisis Ouro Preto displayed both coolness and energy. He sent word to the members of his cabinet to meet him at the marine arsenal, which was immediately placed in a state of defense to repel all attacks. The police force and the municipal firemen were ordered to be ready to march at a moment's notice. The regiments stationed on the Island of Bom Jesus and at the Fortress of Santa Cruz were summoned to the city.

But Ouro Preto was now guilty of a blunder which made the success of the revolt all but inevitable. On his arrival at the marine arsenal, Viscount Maracajú declared that he would return to the war office, which was his post in time of danger. Ouro Preto strongly urged that the entire ministry remain at the marine arsenal, which in case of attack, could be much more easily defended than the war office; moreover, owing to its location on the edge of the harbor, aid and reënforcements could easily be summoned. Maracajú not only did not yield to these arguments but seconded by Floriano Peixoto persuaded the prime minister against his better judgment to accompany him. "The presence of your Excellency," he observed, "is necessary to encourage resistance." This was the type of appeal Ouro Preto found difficult to resist. After receiving assurances from Floriano that everything possible would be done to put down the revolt the prime minister accompanied by several members of his cabinet repaired to the war office.

Here Ouro Preto beheld evidences of both incompetency and treachery. Nothing had been done to put the large fortress-like building with its spacious courtyard in a state of defense nor had any effort been made to intercept the Second Brigade during its long march from Boa Vista to the heart of the city. Surrounded by treacherous friends and evil counsellors the prime minister was caught in a trap from which no escape was possible. Shortly before daylight the revolting brigade with Deodoro da Fonseca at its head reached the park in front of the ministry of war. Orders issued by Ouro Preto and repeated by Maracajú to attack the rebellious troops fell upon deaf ears. When the prime minister reproached Floriano that such a refusal to obey orders hardly became a veteran of the Paraguayan War the adjutant general replied: "Yes, but there we were confronted by enemies; here we are all Brazilians." Shortly afterwards Deodoro rode into the great court yard of the war office amid the *vivas* and acclamations of the troops. The revolt had triumphed.

The immediate results of the pronunciamento whose antecedents and character we have endeavored to sketch are well known. The emperor, summoned by telegraph from his summer residence at Petropolis, made futile efforts on the afternoon of the 15th to form a new cabinet. But even while these deliberations were taking place at the Boa Vista palace the Republic was proclaimed at the Muncipality and the provisional government was organized with Deodoro da Fonseca as its chief and Benjamin

Constant as minister of war. At the same time troops were thrown about the palace and the emperor and his family made prisoners. On the 16th, Deodoro formally notified Dom Pedro of his deposition, and banishment from the country within a space of twenty-four hours. The reply of the aged emperor may be quoted:

In view of the representation delivered to me to-day at three o'clock in the afternoon, I resolve, yielding to the force of circumstances, to depart with all my family for Europe to-morrow leaving this country beloved by us all and to which I have striven to give constant proofs of deepseated devotion during almost half a century when I filled the position of chief of the state. In departing therefore I with all my family shall always retain the most tender remembrances of Brazil and offer ardent prayers for her greatness and pros- perity.

Before daylight on the morning of November 17, the imperial family was forced to embark on the *Alagoas*, which under convoy of a Brazilian man-of-war set sail directly for Europe. The emperor, already in failing health, died less than two years later in Paris, at the modest Hotel Bedford.

The proximate cause of the collapse of the imperial regime was a barrack-room conspiracy participated in by only a fraction of the Brazilian army whose grievances were skillfully exploited by a small group of deter- mined men bent on the establishment of the Republic. The ultimate cause, as we have endeavored to show, was the slow crumbling of the foundations on which the stability of the Empire depended. We have seen that the monarchy had gradually ceased to be identified with the nation in the minds of the majority of the Brazilians. It had become a thing apart, encompassed with a growing isolation, an object of respect but incapable of arousing, save in a small restricted class, any feeling of self-sacrifice or devotion.

Yet the Brazilian people as a whole had neither part nor lot in the Revolution of 1889. Utterly fallacious is the view, assiduously fostered by certain apologists of the revolt, that the overthrow of the Empire repre- sented a great popular reaction against an intolerable despotism. The re- joicings with which the advent of the Republic was hailed were shortlived and in many cases artificial. The populace at large, after the first exuberance had cooled, was almost completely apathetic and regarded the new regime with a mixture of indifference and cynicism. The true character of the re- volution was candidly admitted by one of the leading republican propa- gandists, Aristides Lobo, minister of the interior under the Provisional Government. "I should like to call November 15 the first day of the Repub- lic," he wrote, "but unhappily I cannot do so. What has taken place is one step—perhaps not even that—towards the advent of a great era. What has been done may mean much if the men who are about to assume power possess judgment, patriotism, and a sincere love of liberty. But at present the stamp of the new government is purely that of the military. This is logical. The work was theirs and theirs alone, for the collaboration of the civilian element was almost *nil*. And the people stood by stupefied, dumbfounded, without an inkling of what it all meant. Many honestly believed they were beholding a parade."

Whatever may be the verdict of history on the motives and ideals behind the Revolution of 1889 it is even now reasonably clear that sooner or later the coming of the Republic was inevitable. The Empire touching elbows so to speak with all but one of the Republics of South America was inexorably fated to become more and more of an anachronism. Yet he would be quite wanting in historical perspective who with his eyes fixed only on the remarkable progress and achievements of the Republic would ignore or minimize the beneficent rôle which the Empire played in the national evolution of Brazil. Thanks in large part to the ability, patriotism, and rugged honesty of Dom Pedro II. the monarchy rendered the nation inestimable services. It supplied the cohesive force which prevented Brazil from falling a prey to anarchy and possible dismemberment. Under its aegis Brazil took her place among the most liberal and enlightened countries of Hispanic America. A half century of almost unbroken internal peace made possible a material prosperity which until the spectacular rise of Argentina was unique in South America. Through its intervention in the Platine Republics to aid in the overthrow of the odious tyranny of Rosas and López the Empire won for itself the political preponderance of the continent. Yet after all perhaps the greatest service rendered by the Empire was to afford the Brazilian people, decade after decade, a large and fruitful apprenticeship in the practice of self-government within the spacious confines of a liberal constitutional monarchy. Thus were laid, solid and enduring, the foundations on which the success and prosperity of the Republic had ultimately to depend.

Another Article of Interest

Cleary, R. "Brazil under the Monarchy." II (1919), 600–610.
> An excerpt from an undated manuscript work in the Library of Congress by a long-time resident of Brazil which discusses the unpopularity of non-Portuguese emigration to Brazil, the work of German colonizing companies who sent immigrants from lower classes, persons who were not received with favor by native Brazilians. Yet Brazil, the author admits, owes a great deal to a few prosperous German industrialists, though in 1889 it was no place for foreigners of any nationality.

17. Rubber River: An Account of the Rise and Collapse of the Amazon Boom

JOHN MELBY

The Brazilian economy has for centuries been characterized by a boom—due to the sale of one product for the international market, such as sugar, gold, diamonds, or coffee—followed by a "bust." The history of rubber was perhaps the most spectacular. The following article recounts the rise of the wild rubber-gathering industry in the Amazon from about 1879, when the drought in Ceará forced Brazilians of the dry northeast to emigrate or starve and thus provided a cheap labor supply, until competition from plantation rubber in the Far East in the early 1900's broke the virtual world monopoly of the Amazon rubber barons.

The peak period (1890–1910) witnessed an implacable exploitation of the laborers, who died in great numbers in the unfamiliar jungle environment, and produced a spendthrift society which indulged in extraordinary luxuries. An imposing opera house was built at enormous expense in Manaus, a thousand miles up the Amazon, and whole companies of Italian singers were imported. It was even alleged that the wives of the rubber barons sent their soiled linens back to Europe for proper laundering.

Dr. Melby, who carried on research on this subject as a part of his preparation for the doctorate at the University of Chicago, describes this boom period well, in all its human and international complications.

Francisco de Orellana's voyage down the Amazon in the middle of the sixteenth century was the prelude to a long and exciting period of South American history culminating in the feverish seventy-five years of the great rubber boom that finally collapsed in 1910. The first three hundred years of this history were adventurous ones; intrepid Jesuit and Carmelite fathers penetrated the farthest recesses of the Amazon valley in pursuit of their missionary objectives. The expulsion of the Black Robes from all the Portuguese colonies by the Marquis of Pombal in 1757 ended the firm but gentle sway which they had exercised over the scattered Indian tribes. They had, in addition, made another contribution to Portuguese power. By their assistance in consolidating far to the west the domains of Lisbon, they had balked Spain in her desire to move as deep into the heart of the continent as possible. The century following the departure of the Jesuits witnessed an

Volume XXII (1942), pages 452–469.

orderly, if comparatively uneventful, development of agriculture. The chief features of this period were the transition from a colonial to an independent status, and the ensuing decade of violence and disorder.

I

Until the discovery by Charles Goodyear that rubber could be made useful by means of vulcanization, the sticky substance had been largely a curiosity. The Indians of the Amazon had long been familiar with it and used it for waterproofing and to make primitive playthings. A few efforts had also been made to export it in the form of rubber shoes, but progress along commercial lines was limited because the natural product was too easily affected by weather conditions. Vulcanization opened a new era for rubber; and life began to stir in the valley after 1850.

The first sign of activity was the organization of the Companhia de Navegação do Amazonas, holding a monopolistic charter from the Brazilian government to exploit steam navigation throughout the Amazon and its tributaries. Distance and difficulty of transportation have always been inexorable facts in the history of the river. The Companhia do Amazonas, as it was known, was an encouraging step in the solution of the problem. The service which the company provided was both good and extensive. Through its facilities alone could rubber be transported expeditiously, and in large quantities, to the great markets at Belém and Manáus.

Financially, the company was profitable. Its charter provided for a substantial subsidy from the federal government with the qualification that it would be paid as long as dividends did not exceed twelve per cent. It was not long before profits went beyond this limit. In order to retain the subsidy, the company proceeded to increase the face value of the original stock so that, within a dozen years, actual dividends on this stock amounted to some thirty and forty per cent annually. Thus it was possible for the original shareholders to take all the profits and at the same time continue to receive an unneeded subsidy. Such practices were at times criticized by conscientious officers of the government, but the attack against them was never carried out successfully.

In 1874 the entire assets were bought by an English group which reorganized the concern as the Amazon Steam Navigation Company, capitalized at six hundred and twenty-five thousand pounds. The British had now only to sit back and enjoy the profits since the real pioneering work and development had been done by the Brazilians. The British firm did nothing more than maintain and expand the existing shipping facilities, but it should be added that the furnishing of good river transportation was in itself a vital contribution to the growth of the rubber industry.

The second sign of changing times was the effort to attract immigration. Rubber required large quantities of cheap and hardy labor. All that was available was the native Indian whose numbers were altogether too small to furnish what was demanded. Furthermore, the Indian in his docility was not sturdy enough to withstand the monotony of regular employment, the physical hardships of rubber gathering, or the brutality of forced labor. Consequently, he either perished in his work or retired into unused lands in order to escape servitude. The only solution to the problem was the importation of labor.

During the course of rubber prosperity numerous attempts were made to attract settlers on a large scale. All schemes ended in failure. Several efforts were designed to secure Japanese labor, but few Japanese appeared. Others involved were Europeans, yet the vast majority of the few who actually reached the valley died from the ravages of disease and malnutrition.

One of the extremely interesting experiments concerned Confederate exiles. These were Southerners ruined by the Civil War and disgusted with the Reconstruction. Rather than continue to live under such conditions, several thousands of them made plans to start life anew in other parts of the world. The majority of those who went to Brazil established themselves in the southern part of the country, but one group settled at Santarém, on the Tapajoz River. Matters went badly from the start. The settlers at Santarém arrived without adequate knowledge of the country to which they had come. Moreover, they possessed no money and little equipment, and spoke no Portuguese. Few of them had ever done any actual physical labor, and many in the group were too old to begin life in the tropics. Before long, most of the colonists were clamoring to return to the United States, convinced that the Reconstruction was preferable to the hardships of a pioneering experience. And despite their total lack of resources, many of the dissatisfied exiles managed to be repatriated.

On the other hand, some Americans did remain; and their descendents are still to be found, though they seldom speak English or have more than a hazy recollection of their background. Some have prospered, and the two sons of an original settler have one of the few successful rubber plantations in the valley. The general failure, however, was a source of great disappointment to those who had hoped that the venture might be the beginning of a large-scale white immigration from the United States that would provide the hands needed for the rubber industry.

The labor situation appeared hopeless until Nature interposed her solution by bringing drought to Ceará. This northeast corner of Brazil had long been noted for its droughts, but none was more severe than the celebrated one of 1879. The inhabitants were faced with the choice of death or emigration, and, as a result, tens of thousands of people left for the Amazon. The *Cearenses* died almost as fast as they arrived, but the recruiters of labor were persuasive, and each cessation of the rains in Ceará was followed by a new exodus to the Amazon to take the place of those who had perished. This rapid and disastrous turnover in workers was a perennial source of concern, but as long as some sort of help was available the gathering of rubber in large quantities was possible. Rubber had at last secured its labor.

The third indication of new life was the controversy over the opening of the Amazon to world traffic. The great Brazilian waterway was the last of the principal rivers of the world to remain closed. Even after the opening of the Río de la Plata prior to 1850, an event which might have served as a precedent, Brazil resolutely refused to follow the example of her southern neighbors. Thanks to the persuasiveness of Lieutenant Matthew Fontaine Maury, the United States played a leading rôle in the movement to internationalize the Amazon. Maury was a hydrographer of solid reputation, and his efforts were brought to the attention of, and commended by, the American Congress.

The American public was also greatly intrigued by the possibilities of the Amazon valley, especially in the South, where southern ports looked forward to the expansion of their shipping trade. For all these reasons, therefore, the Navy Department ordered Lieutenants William L. Herndon and Lardner Gibbon to enter the Amazon region from the Pacific side of the continent, to follow the course of the river to its mouth, and to report their findings. The results of the undertaking convinced the proponents of the opening of the river that their dreams of the wealth of the valley were true.

Possibly alarmed at the exuberant manifestations of interest on the part of the American public, Brazil continued to be wary. Despite all diplomatic urgings, she steadfastly refused to yield. On the other hand, during the latter part of the 1850's, with the opening of the West to colonization and the brewing of those difficulties which form the background to the Civil War, the interest of the United States in the Amazon began to lag. As a consequence, the question was held in abeyance until 1864. By this time there had been a shift in Brazilian opinion which the visit of Professor Louis Agassiz and the concern of the emperor in his work powerfully aided. The result was the decree of December 7, 1866, opening the river and certain tributaries to the merchant shipping of the world. The third element vital to the full expansion of the rubber industry had thus been provided.

II

Until the overthrow of the monarchy in 1889, the rubber trade was characterized by a steady and reasonable growth. Production continued to increase in volume, and prices tended to follow suit. Prosperity seemed a normal condition of life for the great centers of Belém and Manáus and their environs. Prices of commodities rose and some men waxed wealthy, but the boom had hardly begun. Rubber was not yet sufficiently in demand; the consumption of the product in Europe was still limited. A sharp economic rise in the valley first became apparent with the sudden emergence of the bicycle craze in the United States in the 1890's and the consequent demand for rubber tires. This coincided with a great increase in the use of rubber for many other articles. The final touch came with the invention of the automobile.

The great boom years may be said to have extended from 1890 to 1910. It cannot, however, be asserted that these two decades witnessed an uninterrupted progression to the high level of three-dollar rubber in the early months of the latter year. Rather was the process a succession of waves which took prices to new levels, each rise being preceded by a sudden drop that brought the market to the brink of ruin. Such declines should have showed the rubber industry that a stabilizing factor was lacking in its economic organization. Each period provoked outbursts among those affected, but there was never at any time any recognition of the basic problems involved.

The first serious decline coincided with the panic of 1893 in the United States and created considerable uneasiness. Subsequently there were several minor declines. Yet all of them were no more than a prelude to the sharp drop of 1907–1908. The mid-months of 1907 had seen the rise of the price of rubber to such a height that many dealers expected to receive as much as two dollars per pound for their product. Hopes were dashed when prices were cut in half in the latter part of the year. This condition lasted until the early months of 1908 and gave rise to endless remorse for past sins. Before anything constructive could be done, the tide turned again, and pious resolutions gave way to boundless optimism. This marked the beginning of the dizzy spiral which culminated in 1910. In the frenzy which continuing strong prices created; all else was forgotten; and there were those who were heard to have expressed the belief that prices would continue to rise forever. In May, 1910, the top price passed three dollars, and the tension became well-nigh unbearable. Then, with a sudden crash, the flimsy structure collapsed. In one desperate dive prices were cut in half and thereafter continued to fall. Unfortunately, all future efforts at reconstruction were to be balked by the spectacular growth of Asiatic plantations which had played a conspicuous rôle in ending the hegemony of the Amazon.

III

Not the least interesting aspect of the period of boom and collapse was the life of the men who lived in the valley and stood to profit or lose by market fluctuations. The personnel of the rubber industry was organized into a pyramid at the base of which were the *seringueiros*, or workers, who actually went out into the forests to gather the latex. They were very largely drawn from Ceará, and, in the isolation of the jungle, they were never free from disease, starvation, and exploitation. Their life was a closely controlled one. They brought their stocks of rubber to the *patrão*—the lessee of the area worked by *seringueiros*—and received credit from him, not money, which was used against needed supplies. Since the *seringueiro* could in no other way satisfy his wants, these supplies were sold to him at prices which barely allowed him enough for subsistence.

In return for supplies, the *patrão* disposed of his stocks of rubber through *aviadores*, or agents who made periodic visits to production centers. The former was subjected to much the same vicious system as the *seringueiro*. The agent took his rubber to the merchant princes in the great centers of Belém, Manáus, and Iquitos, whence it found its way to the principal consumption markets of the world. In the end the leading firms and the government, which levied ad valorem taxes that averaged twenty per cent, drew the major share of the profits.

Money was spent recklessly. Broad avenues began to grace colonial cities, and huge government buildings, waterworks, parks, docks, and theatres were built. The wealthy lived in splendor, importing a wide variety of luxuries. Even in Iquitos, two thousand miles up the Amazon, manufactured articles from abroad could be had in abundance.

When rubber prices dropped from three dollars to one, the economic life of the valley was not able to support the shock. Buildings were deserted, elaborate mansions were left vacant, parks and avenues were abandoned, and grass again grew in many streets. Needless to say, the plight of the *seringueiro* was especially bad. No longer able to buy even the most meager supplies, he had no alternative but to stay in the jungle and rely on his own initiative. Other classes of society were also affected by the *débâcle*. Unfortunately, no significant part of the profits which had been made in the rubber trade was put to productive uses in the valley itself. In the last analysis, the real profits were made by manufacturers, although the work of the *seringueiro* was largely responsible for the prosperity of the rubber industry.

One of the little-known aspects of life in the Amazon during the heyday of rubber concerns the several outstanding pioneers who, with a dogged determination, sought the farthest reaches of the valley in the quest for the precious latex. Among the most famous of their number were Funes at San Fernando de Atabapo, Julio César Araña in the Putumayo, and Nicolás Suárez of the Beni River.

In essence, the story of Suárez was the story of seven brothers who crossed the Andes in 1872 from the western part of the continent to see what lay on the other side of the mountains. But Nicolás was the unquestioned leader of the family, and he had the foresight to appreciate the future importance of rubber. He first secured a monopoly of the carrying trade on the Madeira River; then he supplied the local population with provisions. His rubber operations soon began to prosper. At one time he carried more than ten thousand employees on his payroll, including four hundred who devoted themselves exclusively to portage work around the falls of the Madeira.

His headquarters were at Cachuela Esperanza, but he maintained branches throughout the Amazon valley, the Acre, at Manáus, Belém, and London. The business details of the firm were left to his brothers; Nicolás himself was always to be found in the forests, supervising the actual labor. With a nominal capital of four million *bolivianos*, he controlled at least five million hectares of rubber lands, ranges on which grazed a quarter of a million head of his own cattle, a sugarmill producing ten thousand arrobas of sugar annually, a power plant, an ice plant, and all the provision business of a vast area. His holdings were at one time probably worth between ninety and a hundred million *bolivianos*. In 1912 he refused twelve million pounds offered by an English company for his rubber holdings alone.

Ten years later, rubber in the Beni was practically worthless, but Suárez was far from destitute. He had had the foresight to vary his enterprises. Despite the crash in the rubber market, he was able to maintain his predominant position in the area.

IV

It would indeed have been surprising if, at some time during the course of the rubber boom, there had not arisen a conflict between the Amazon nations, especially in view of the indeterminate status of many boundaries. The rubber man was no respecter of imaginary lines, and where he could find the coveted product thither he went regardless of political sovereignty.

The most notable controversy of the period involved the Acre territory. Long practically uninhabited and subject to the control of Bolivia, the Acre came into prominence when immigrants from Ceará finally penetrated the area and discovered enormous reserves of rubber. By 1900 the Brazilian settlers, who formed the greater part of the population, felt strong enough to contest Bolivian authority, but the rebellion, lacking support, was promptly suppressed.

Anxious to prevent a recurrence of violence, and conscious of her weak position, Bolivia thereupon leased the entire area to an international syndicate to which she granted monopolistic privileges and rights of sovereignty, including the power to police the Acre and collect revenues. The reaction in Brazil was instantaneous and brought a strong protest from the government. Rio de Janeiro insisted that Bolivia had committed an illegal act by surrendering her sovereignty over the region to a private company, and felt that the undertaking constituted a menace to Brazil. Bolivia, however, refused to revoke the concession.

When, in 1902, Brazilians in the disputed territory again rose in revolt, they declared the independence of the region and petitioned for union with Brazil. When the Rio government now threatened to occupy the territory by force of arms if Bolivia should refuse to sell it, Bolivia chose the latter alternative. By the Treaty of Petrópolis of November 17, 1903, the Acre was ceded to Brazil in return for the sum of two million pounds.

Ironically enough, the collapse of rubber deprived the Brazilian victory of much economic meaning, and after 1910, Brazil lost much of her interest in developing the area.

V

During the years of rubber pre-eminence, and especially during periods of depression, the charge was frequently made that the Brazilian government took no constructive steps to ameliorate the conditions of the rubber industry. Official interest in the new source of wealth was early limited to the levying of taxes. Throughout the empire, the provincial and central governments shared the revenues. With the promulgation of the republican constitution of 1890, state and municipal authorities were given the exclusive use of the levy on rubber. Taxes were promptly increased; over a period of years they averaged roughly twenty per cent ad valorem, a considerable burden, indeed, on the industry and a perennial source of complaint. There was seldom a year when taxes on rubber did not constitute at least three fourths of all state revenues in the Amazon area.

Prior to 1907 government interest in the industry centered mainly on taxation. Some individuals in high places, to be sure, were aware that unhealthy conditions of a dangerous nature existed, but their words of admonition passed unheeded. A few isolated attempts were made to introduce mildly remedial legislation, but here again all efforts proved abortive. Popular sentiment was in the main indifferent as long as prices continued to rise; periodic drops did not last long enough to make people vitally conscious of evils. From time to time legislation was passed to encourage plantation rubber or stimulate improvements in the technique of handling the wild variety. These efforts failed to secure results, and the old method of wild-rubber gathering continued. In fact, the complaint was usually made that if the government was really interested in the industry, it would lower taxes and stop giving advice.

The sharp decline of 1907–1908 created serious alarm in the market and led to several unsuccessful valorization schemes. The real rush of legislation came after 1910, when it was apparent that a definitive change had taken place in the rubber industry. Imploring appeals were made to Rio, resulting in the rubber defense law of 1912, one of the finest pieces of rubber legislation ever drafted. The drafters of the law realized that the only solution for the Amazon was to compete effectively with Asiatic plantation rubber.

A few voices had long attempted to call the attention of Brazil to the dangers of foreign competition, but the majority of rubber men refused to believe that the plantation method could lower the costs of production or supply the market with sufficient stocks. The realization that this could be done finally produced the Brazilian collapse. The country, however, woke up too late.

The defense law of 1912, in the attempt to make the Amazon a plantation center, offered advantageous concessions to planters, encouraged agriculture, specified improvements in transportation, provided for the organization of hospitals and medical facilities, and sought to attract immigrants. A fifty per cent reduction in export taxes was conceded on planted rubber. Excellent though the measure was, it obtained no results. Adequate appropriations were withheld, and management did not fully understand the opportunities within its reach. Moreover, the Far East enjoyed the great advantage of two decades of preliminary activity. Before the Amazon could be in a position to compete on the market, the British plantations would have successfully controlled consumption. In the face of these handicaps, no concerted planting was undertaken.

Meanwhile, valorization schemes were tried. The Bank of Brazil brought itself to the verge of bankruptcy by buying rubber and holding it for a rise in prices which never occurred. Several other banks were organized for the same purpose with the assistance of foreign capital. Organizations of producers agreed to withhold stocks from the market. It was even proposed seriously that the government, because of its superior resources, should acquire the entire crop and hold it until the consumer could meet Brazilian demands. What the rubber men apparently did not realize was that the Amazon no longer controlled a sufficiently large proportion of the world crop to make the slightest impression on prices.

VI

The Far Eastern rubber industry owes its beginnings to Henry A. Wickam, a British planter from Santarém. In 1876 he smuggled several thousand rubber seeds from Brazil and sowed them in Kew Gardens in London. From there the young plants were sent to Ceylon, where they soon began to thrive. For a long time, the interest of Far Eastern planters in rubber was slight, but reverses in the tea market, the profits from the new product, and the dissatisfaction of manufacturers with natural rubber encouraged a number of individuals to persist in the growing of latex trees. In 1900 a small shipment of plantation sheet rubber from Malaya was offered for auction in London. In 1905 it began to appear regularly; after 1910 the supply from the Orient increased with fantastic rapidity.

In the futile effort to meet foreign competition, large-scale corporations were organized in Brazil for the growing of plantation rubber. The record of failures was disheartening. The Orton Rubber Company, established about the year 1897, eventually found it impossible to continue. Of some two hundred Basque settlers expressively brought over by the concern to Brazil, only six reached the company's property alive. The Amazon Rubber Estates, Limited, found its entire capital of three hundred thousand pounds gone before a single pound of rubber had been collected. The Comptoir Colonial Français, which took over a Brazilian property, lost one million dollars.

The most ambitious attempt was that of the Rubber Estates of Pará, Limited, formed in 1898 with a capital of three hundred and fifty thousand pounds to work an estate on Marajó Island with an estimated one million three hundred thousand trees. Despite a previous record of production, the new company, during the first year of operation, collected exactly eighty and three-quarters tons of rubber; during the second, fifty-eight. A reorganization of the concern was agreed upon, but the venture did not prosper. On the contrary, the Rubber Estates reached the extreme of offering its properties for an annual rental of two hundred and fifty pounds.

A number of frankly promotional schemes were also offered to the gullible public. Typical of the hoaxes was the Peru Pará Rubber Company, with a reputed capital of three million dollars and an unlimited number of latex trees in some undisclosed part of South America, which advertised for investors in the Chicago newspapers of 1905. Contributors were promised dividends of seventy-five per cent for life. Obviously, such shams by foreign promoters were not encouraging to those who wished to invest in legitimate enterprises.

The real obstacles in the way of plantation rubber in the Amazon were far more formidable than many people supposed. The greatest problem was labor, for the profitable gathering of latex depended on a large supply of fairly efficient and cheap hands. To be sure, the utilizable population of the valley amounted to about a million persons, but most of them were Indians who found it impossible to adjust themselves to the exigencies of the rubber industry. *Cearenses*, on the other hand, were much more satisfactory, but they perished in great numbers. Again, the government frowned on Oriental and African labor; and Europeans did not arrive in appreciable numbers. No practical solution was found then for the labor problem, nor has it been found today.

The second obstacle was the decay of native agriculture. In colonial times Pará had been self-sufficient in articles of basic consumption and had, in fact, produced an exportable surplus. The concentration on rubber forced dependence on imported foodstuffs which were eventually sold for three to six times their normal price. This was the unfortunate result of the irresistible lure of a cash crop of high value. The *seringueiro* thus found it more profitable to abandon his small garden plot and rely solely on imported articles. Such a supply of labor could hardly have been cheap. Indeed, a respectable share of the profits from the rubber trade probably was devoted to the support of workers who nevertheless lived perilously close to subsistence.

The problem of sanitation was equally important. *Seringueiros* were scattered, for the most part, over areas where sanitation was entirely unknown, and were thus exposed to the ravages of jungle fevers and intestinal infections. In many areas, productivity was lowered at least one third through disease. The Brazilian commission that surveyed the state of Pará reported that conditions were bad except in parts of Belém. Moreover, medical facilities were to be found only in urban areas. In his survey made in accordance with the defense law of 1912, Dr. Oswaldo Cruz was shocked by the conditions he saw, but he did not look at the future with pessimism. Though the work would involve a tremendous outlay of money and effort, he believed that the sanitation of the valley was not impracticable.

The problem of diet was the natural outcome of the decay of agriculture. The native settler of the Amazon had originally developed a diet which furnished him with the basic elements needed for health. With the development of the rubber industry, the dependence on importations led, in many instances, to disastrous consequences. Owing to high prices, the quantity of food the average *seringueiro* consumed was drastically reduced to an amount barely enough to maintain actual existence. Beri-beri, for example, became a terrible scourge. The effects of malnutrition not only told appallingly on the individual but also constituted a heavy drain on the rubber industry.

The cost of transportation was also a heavy burden. Distances were enormous. Some two thousand miles of river separated Belém and Iquitos. The Putumayo was still farther away. Another factor in the Amazon rubber trade was the speculative character of the industry. The boom may be said to have been a vast speculation in rubber, foodstuffs, labor, and foreign exchange. Part of the uncertainty may be readily understood. Rubber stocks came from wide and oftentimes unknown regions. Furthermore, the flow of latex varied with the rainfall. It was, therefore, impossible to foretell with any reasonable degree of accuracy what the yield in a given year would be.

The several obstacles touched on in the preceding paragraphs combined to make it impossible for the Amazon to compete with the Far East in the rubber trade. At no time did there seem to exist in Brazil a genuine effort to find a hopeful solution to the many problems which confronted the industry. Perhaps Brazilians realized that the Amazon hardly offered the necessary conditions for plantation rubber.

In this connection, it may be well to observe that the best example of the opportunities to be found in the production of plantation rubber, and also of the great difficulties involved, is the Henry Ford experiment in Brazil. Consisting of two and a half million acres one hundred and ten miles up the Tapajoz from its junction with the Amazon, the Ford property was originally obtained in 1927. Production on the plantations at Fordlândia and Belterra is even now beginning on a fair scale. To achieve his ends, Ford was obliged to build a modern town and undertake other extensive improvements. He has not been able to solve the labor problem satisfactorily; he has only with difficulty secured sufficient man-power for the needs of his projects; yet Ford has demonstrated the possibility of eradicating the various diseases which attack the planted tree in the Amazon and of producing a latex that can compete with Asiatic rubber in quality and cost. He has also shown that obstacles to healthful living and sanitation in the valley are by no means insuperable.

VII

The practicability of plantations and the immediate prospect for wild rubber in the Amazon assume a great importance today. The loss of Asiatic sources of supply has, of course, turned the attention of the United States to the potentialities of Brazil's rich valley; and rubber merchants there are endeavoring to satisfy as large a part of the demand as possible. In the main, wild rubber will be involved, since plantations require years of care and preparation before they reach a stage of satisfactory productivity. It is unlikely, however, that the rejuvenation of the wild rubber industry will be accompanied by the mistakes of the past. The bitter lessons of fomer days have been learned too well to give rise to a false optimism. Present indications are that the new phase of the trade will follow along economic and constructive lines.

To be sure, due recognition is being given to the problems which the possible widespread development of synthetic rubber will create. There seems to be no doubt that the synthetic product is in many respects comparable to the natural one. If the former can be manufactured at a reasonable price, the demand for natural rubber will be considerably reduced, although a certain amount of latex will very likely continue to be used.

Even in the event of the complete success of synthetic rubber, the economic life of the Amazon need not suffer. Outside of rubber, the natural resources of the valley have scarcely been touched. A sound course of action would seem to be the exploitation of tropical forest products, drugs, nuts, timber, and plants. A beginning has already been made in such things as the cultivation of *timbó*, a weed used in the manufacture of insecticide. Various rapid investigations have shown that possibilities along similar lines are great and only need further study to grow into positive results. Undoubtedly, a diversified extractive economy, resting on a solid agricultural foundation, would provide for the Amazon a far more reasonable development than would be possible under the sole rule of rubber.

Other Articles of Interest

Martin, Percy Alvin. "Slavery and Abolition in Brazil." XIII (1933), 151–196. A brief survey of the origin of Negro slavery in Brazil, its gradual extension, the place which it occupied in the social, economic, and political fabric of the state, and the successful efforts of the Brazilian people to free themselves from this incubus without bloodshed or serious economic dislocation. The tension over the slave trade between Great Britain and Brazil overshadowed the whole period from 1807 to 1888.

Stein, Stanley J. "The Passing of the Coffee Plantation in the Paraiba Valley." XXXIII (1953), 331–364.

The Paraiba Valley, the most productive coffee area in Brazil in the middle nineteenth century, suffered decline as a result of soil impoverishment, aging coffee trees, sluggish agricultural methods, the instability of the slave labor force, and other causes. The real decline, which was well advanced by 1888, belies the view of planters and later interpreters that a flourishing coffee economy was wiped out by the abolition of slavery. The process of gradual decay in all its detailed aspects is traced in the conditions of Vassouras, a *municipio* typical of the coffee counties of the Paraiba.

18. São Paulo Since Independence:
A Cultural Interpretation

RICHARD M. MORSE

The years since World War II have seen in the United States a steady increase in the attention paid to Brazil. Today its history is recognized as an integral and important part of general courses on Latin America, and numerous specialized courses are offered on the development of the largest and most populous country of Latin America. Professor Morse of Yale University has been a leader in this movement, and the article below represents a fusion of his Brazilian interests with his more recent concern with urban history.

The city of São Paulo has today an estimated population of 2,700,000. This figure represents a hundred-fold increase during the past eighty years, and makes São Paulo the most spectacular example of metropolitan growth in Latin America. The purpose of this essay is to convey something of the city's history in the nineteenth and twentieth centuries through a selective examination of its cultural expression. Of central interest are the implications of São Paulo's emergence from the parochialism of a rural, creole community into the cosmopolitanism of an industrial metropolis. These implications are of course relevant to the histories of many other Latin American cities, but São Paulo, because of its long colonial isolation and the abruptness of its transformation, reveals them in singularly dramatic fashion.

São Paulo's artists, thinkers and men of action of the past century have, in their confrontation with the modern world, been tempted to neglect their elusive creole, hinterland heritage, which enshrines neither viceregal

From Volume XXXIV (1954), pages 419-444.

panoply nor dominant Indian or African culture patterns. They have been more inclined than most other Latin Americans to deny their history, to grasp at ready-made and, in the new context, precarious solutions and ideals from abroad. In this study, therefore, mid-nineteenth-century romanticism and the *modernista* movement inaugurated in 1922 are of particular concern; for these two movements fruitfully assimilated foreign cultural influences and at the same time gave expression to special characteristics of the *paulista* milieu.

At the time of Brazilian independence in 1822 São Paulo was a town of some 20,000 souls. To an approaching traveler it would have been visible from a distance, clustered on its hilltop. It presented a comely appearance with the proportioned silhouette of its religious buildings and the plain white, and sometimes pink or straw yellow, walls of its two-story residences. The encircling plain was enhanced by palms and araucarias and by handsome country houses *(chácaras)*, whose owners challenged the inferior soil with gardens and orchards. Only on ascending the central rise would the traveler have trodden the streets of the city proper. For a Brazilian town these were surprisingly clean, if allowance were made for open sewers, an anti-social shopkeeper who was thoughtless with his rubbish, and the mongrel pup indecorous enough to expire in a gutter. And, though irregularly paved, they were of sufficient width to accommodate the screeching ox-carts, burdened mules and loquacious slaves bearing jugs to and from the public fountains.

The community commanded no abundant sources of wealth and subsisted largely by a modest polyculture. Connected to the port of Santos and the outside world by a tortuous road over the coastal range—the *Serra do Mar*—São Paulo's was an austere, introverted society, dominated by patriarchal customs and church ceremonial—though not untempered by social warmth and graces. Its pressing concerns were local ones, customarily addressed in spontaneous and communal rather than formal and bureaucratic fashion.

São Paulo's provincialism was clearly reflected in its cultural expression. From the Indians the town had inherited no advanced arts; moreover, it lacked the wherewithal to import European ones, and the outlook or disposition to develop them to any extent locally. Within these limitations, the most noteworthy achievement was perhaps the architecture of the patriarchal dwellings: the *sobrados* within the town and the *chácaras* on its outskirts. These houses were of *taipa*, or rammed earth, and never of the granite which gave Rio de Janeiro, Recife, Salvador and even Santos an urban, European complexion. They were also truly functional, if by that term is meant the unpretentious comeliness arising from rational use of local materials and from cognizance of social patterns and tradition. A characteristic feature of the *sobrado* was the *rótula*—a type of jalousie, though with close-laid diagonal strips of wood instead of louvers—which formalized the flirtations of sequestered daughters. Inside, the receiving-rooms (*alpendres*) were cheerfully painted, the older ones with arabesques, and tastefully though simply furnished. An occasional framed engraving that had been dumped from the European market for its ugliness merely emphasized the *paulista*'s innocence of citified artistic canons. The modern metropolis has consigned the *sobrados* and their way of life to oblivion, but their grace and dignity may still be confirmed in early photographs of São Paulo and in quiescent towns of the present-day interior, such as Itu and those along the Paraíba valley.

Occasional pictorial expression was inspired by the vigorous scenes of daily life. Miguel Arcanjo Benício da Assunção Dutra (1810–1875) recorded in ingenuous but convincing watercolors the inebriate or balmy street-wanderers, with their trains of mocking ragamuffins, known as *tipos populares*. An earlier painter, Padre Jesuíno do Monte Carmelo (1764–1819), is remembered for his religious canvases and murals. In a study of Padre Jesuíno, Mário de Andrade pointed out a strain attributable to much of São Paulo's formal culture of the era:

> Jesuíno resides in that uneasy middleground between legitimate folkloric art and legitimate erudite art. There is a touch of irregularity, of—yes, of commonness in his work which has nothing of the forces, forms and fatalities of folkloric art. But Jesuíno does not reach the erudite. He has popular appeal. He is really very citified. So that we are obliged to see him as what he claims to be, a cultured painter; and in this context he is cultured without tradition behind him, cultured without having learned enough, cultured without culture.

Padre Jesuíno's contribution is slight if viewed against the splendid religious baroque of Salvador or the lyrical creole-baroque sculpture by "Aleijadinho" in Minas Gerais. Yet his painting showed, albeit incidentally, a vitality and relevance to local life that artists of the later metropolis have been at pains to recapture.

Theater was confined to the cramped stage of the *Casa da Opera*, a narrow one-story structure whose décor was less showy than that of some private residences. Actors were colored and the actresses women of doubtful virtue whose talent, wrote Saint-Hilaire, "was in perfect harmony with their morality; one would have called them marionettes moved by wires." Martius, however, reported that a barber who appeared as the leading character in the French operetta *Le déserteur* "deeply affected his fellow-citizens," despite a musical accompaniment resembling "a chaos of elementary sounds." Here as with painting it was not the European formula which appealed but the popular native spirit which infused and transfigured it:

> [It] is impossible not to smile at the effect produced by white and red make-up on these more or less dark-complexioned faces. The costumes are no less grotesque, and fealty to local color is certainly what least concerns these extempore artists.
> There is more charm and at the same time more originality in the purely national divertissements.

In the late 1820's, and as a consequence of national independence, certain catalysts were introduced into the somnolent, isolated town. Important among them were the crown-appointed presidents of the province who brought to its capital the citified concerns and pretensions of the court at Rio de Janeiro. There came also the city's first printed newspaper, through whose columns ideas and rallying-cries of the outer world were gradually to reach the townsmen. Finally, an imperial law of 1827 established in São Paulo and in Olinda Brazil's first two law academies. For the next sixty years, until the era of metropolitan growth, São Paulo was to be a university town.

During its early years the Law Academy remained without roots. Enrollment, after an initial rise, declined sharply, and the students appeared disoriented in their social as well as intellectual life. An anonymous "Memorandum Offered to the Most Illustrious and Excellent Counselor Lomonosoff, Minister Plenipotentiary of His Majesty, the Emperor of Russia, to the Imperial Court of Brazil" (c. 1840) recommended that the Academy be transferred to Rio de Janeiro because, as current books were almost unavailable in São Paulo, professors and their lecture notes soon became antiquated. "There are professors of great merit who, placed elsewhere, would certainly achieve fame in the Republic of Letters." Literary circles were "contraband," while student discipline was minimal and in 1835 approached anarchy when a youth who had struck his professor in public continued his course with impunity and received his *bacharel* degree.

By mid-century, however, students began to measure up to the prestige accorded to literary and forensic careers in a nation whose life-center was swinging from the rural and patriarchal into the urban domain. Their hedonism, mental lethargy and acts of violence gave way to a zealous pursuit of letters, journalism, and theater that made São Paulo an intellectual springhead for the whole empire. They, like their professors, came from throughout Brazil and from abroad, bringing attitudes and needs that stirred the introverted community into ferment: a chiding scepticism, ever ready to disjoint the narrow patterns of provincial life; political ideas and passions that transcended local issues; and a demand for theaters, reviews, newspapers, bookstores, dances and informal gathering-places such as cafés and restaurants.

The years from, roughly, 1845 to 1855 witnessed the first flowering of the student mind. These were the years of romanticism, and the tenor of city life which they represent can conveniently be appraised through the writings of the most precocious student of the period, the poet Manuel Antônio Alvares de Azevedo.

Alvares de Azevedo entered the Academy in 1848 at the age of seventeen and, like a story-book romantic, died four years later. His mixed sentiments toward São Paulo suggest the underlying complexity of his literary personality. "[Lacking] any place to go," he wrote in a letter, "and seeing no pleasure in wandering around the streets, I find myself in the greatest insipidity possible, eager to leave this tedious life of badly paved São Paulo." Yet this same locale—which had none of the overpowering qualities of the Amazon jungle, the drought-land of Ceará, Rio de Janeiro's extravagant bay, the wide plains of Rio Grande do Sul or even the contorted hills and red soil of Minas Gerais—held a subtle, insistent fascination. One evening the poet was returning from a leave-taking outside São Paulo:

And there in the distance arose the black city; and its lamps, swayed by the wind, seemed like those ephemeral meteors that rise from the marshes and were deemed in the traditions of northern Europe to be spirits destined for distracting wayfarers . . . or stars of fire, sparks of some furnace of hell sown over the black field.

A few years ago I talked with Lasar Segall, one of São Paulo's foremost modern painters. Segall told me he finds that the gray and brown and ocher "tonalities" of the city's environment allow the artist eclecticism and freedom for subjective expression. Though the remark may have been a private sentiment or rationalization, it calls to mind Henry James's observations about the compelling beauty and traditions of Venice which distracted him from "the fruitless fidget of composition." In Venice, James wrote, one works "less congruously, after all, so far as the surrounding picture is concerned, than in the presence of the moderate and the neutral, to which we may lend something of the light of vision."

Just as São Paulo's traditions do not boast the wealth and panoply of colonial Bahia or an exotic Indian or African popular culture, so the city's physical setting is "moderate" and "neutral." The soil is neither rich nor sterile, the land neither flat nor mountainous, the climate neither frigid nor tropical. At the same time the natural elements which do exist fail to blend in the "homeyness" of many settlements in a temperate clime. They are unresolved, one might say, or pitched in a minor key, in a way that is haunting to some, lackluster to others. One of the city's distinctive features, for example, is its celebrated *garôa*, a heavy fog verging on precipitation borne in from the southwest by Pacific air masses; romanticists saw in it the mystery and melancholy of Byron's London.

Returning to mid-century literature—São Paulo did not conspicuously yield the tried and true themes of romanticism, such as the northern poet Antônio Gonçalves Dias (1823–1864), himself part Indian, found among surviving folkways of the "noble savage" in Maranhão. In São Paulo the themes were more latent and diffuse; to elicit them required the "tonal" sensitivity to which Lasar Segall refers. Unlike Alvares de Azevedo, however, many of his colleagues assumed exclusive attitudes. A case in point was the students' *Sociedade Epicuréia*, whose members wrote, talked and lived in the Byronic manner, so much so that they caricatured their prototype and fell into orgiastic degeneracy and a morbid worship of death and its sepulchral emblems. Although Alvares de Azevedo attended sessions of the *Sociedade*, his extensive literary production and high academic attainment prove him not to have been a debauchee. His verse shows that he found in Byron something more elevated than a bacchanal appeal; and he once affirmed that the "immoral can be beautiful" but that "from the immoral to the vile" is only a step and (showing perhaps excessive charity) that Byron's verse, though immoral, never trespasses over the "abyss."

The distinctive complexity of Alvares de Azevedo's outlook is further illustrated if one compares him with a fellow law student, Francisco de Paula Ferreira de Rezende. The latter recalled in a memoir of 1887 that at the Academy "[I began] to experience the first attacks of my hypochondria; and since then I have almost never ceased being a mere bearer of life's burden." In 1853 he contributed a piece entitled "Ignorance and Happiness" to a student magazine, which held that only the ignorant are happy and that science and felicity are incompatible—a view he maintained throughout his life.

This strain of alienation runs through much of Alvares de Azevedo's poetry and correspondence. In 1850 he wrote: "There is but one thing that could today give me strength: that I should die." The poet's "solitary existence, closed up alone in my room, most of the time *reading without reading*, writing without seeing what I write, contemplating without knowing what I am thinking," seems in retrospect to forebode the denial of the artist and his creative spirit in the materialistic era that was to follow. Yet with his melancholia the poet embodied a strenuous will-to-do, an urge to smash discreet idols and to look to a far horizon. In a speech of the same year he denounced servility to foreign models and urged his fellow students to build a vigorous and progressive nation by creating a genuinely Brazilian literature and philosophy and by fighting for universal education of the masses. The poet subsequently emphasized that his speech had been concerned with realities and not with rhetorical theorizing, that he entertained "no idea of exaggerated liberalism, and much less of republicanism" and that he wanted less liberal fanfare and more liberal institutions.

Alvares de Azevedo's most significant work for the present study is his play "Macário," which roots his ambivalences directly in the city itself. The play is a dialogue between Macário—a yearning student, arriving in São Paulo to study at the Academy, who is in love with the romantic ideal of love—and a mocking, irreverent Satan. The poet is as closely identified with one as with the other. The duality of the play, consisting in half-toned echoes of Hispano-Moorish romance and mordant realities of a small creole town, was the mainspring of São Paulo's romanticism. Because Alvares de Azevedo so precisely specified it the critic Sílvio Romero called him, above all others of the generation, "a local, indigenous product, son of an intellectual milieu, of a Brazilian academy."

The tensions in "Macário" call to mind a reference by the historian Buarque de Holanda to the "voracious, subterranean crisis" wrought in mid-century Brazilian writers by the "transition from life next to the elemental things of nature to the more regular and abstract existence of the cities." Their romanticism "was artificial and insincere only in certain formal aspects." "The best men, the most sensitive ones, set about frankly to detest life—the 'prison of life,' to use the phrase of the time."

In spite of his flashes of faith in the invigorative powers of education, Alvares de Azevedo wrote in an elegy at the end of his life that:

> . . . nós somos condemnados
> A' noite da amargura: o vento norte
> Nossos pharóis apaga . . .
> Iremos todos, pobres naufragados,
> Frios rolar no litoral—da morte,
> Repellidos da vaga!

The critic Allen Tate points out that certain romanticist poets met frustration because, "under the illusion that all order is scientific order," they forfeited use of poetic imagination. Poetry tried to compete with science but lacked any "systematic method of asserting the will." The inflated style of such poets signifies a "rhetorical escape" that endowed their "will with the illusion of power." Defying "the cruel and naturalistic world" and lacking means to comprehend and cope with it, they were inevitably broken by it. Alvares de Azevedo was a victim of this "romantic irony." He stands not only for what there was of mid-century fulfilment but also for prescience of the "naturalistic world" to follow.

The most explicit misgivings about the currents of mid-century *paulista* life that I have found are in a letter written by Ricardo Gumbleton Daunt in 1856. Daunt, born an Irishman but become a staunchly Catholic and conservative Brazilian, writes from the stolid, traditional little city of Itu and inveighs in the manner of a Tocqueville or John Calhoun against the new tenor of life in São Paulo:

> There are many who wish to see São Paulo grow in wealth and make outstanding progress, but little are they concerned if it occurs with the loss of traits of *paulista* character. . . . I, however, though I do not wish to yield to them in my love for the Province, do not hope for so rapid a transformation. . . . In my opinion uniformity of thought, custom, taste and character presages the decadence of any great Empire, for being in itself a forced and unnatural thing, it can emanate only from the undue influence of the Court or some other center and is always an index of a lack of spirit, of virility, in people thus uniformalized, who are in this fashion prepared for Despotism.

The innovations that appeared ominous to Ricardo Daunt were occasioned by the widening acceptance in Brazil of the rationalistic thesis that a people's welfare and achievement are primarily contingent upon such factors as public literacy, material progress and economic productive efficiency. Significantly, this acceptance coincided with the entry into high office of the first generation of law graduates, with the dethronement, that is, of the rural patriarch by the city-bred *bacharel*. In São Paulo the new outlook was reflected in school reforms, in material embellishments for the city and in public and private plans for economic advancement. Furthermore, since coffee-planting was then invading the rich heartland of the *paulista* plateau, the outlook was served by a fast-increasing source of wealth.

By mid-century, then, although São Paulo's size and physical appearance were not yet much changed, city life was evincing a certain stress and ferment. The old and the new, the regional and the national, the parochial and the cosmopolitan hung in the balance—as is suggested in the writings of Alvares de Azevedo. And the apprehensions of the poet, like those of Ricardo Daunt, seemed to herald a subversion of the time-honored patriarchal order.

Gradually the Byronic star dropped from the ascendant, and the sign of the one to replace it was the word "science," which appeared in the titles of no less than five student journals between 1859 and 1866. The successors of Alvares de Azevedo's generation became impatient with the obstinacies of regional tradition and with the discursive yearnings of romanticism. The 1860's imbued students with the nationalism of the Paraguayan War and turned their attention to programmatic campaigns for abolition of slavery and for republican government. As Joaquim Nabuco, who entered the Academy in 1866, recalled decades later, "escapades and Bohemian living were out of style, and elegance and intellectual prestige were highly respected." His classmate Rui Barbosa recollected that student abolitionists did away with the masonic rituals and occultism that had fascinated the romanticists. "Our whole plan was to react in the open; every object of our activity was public; all our instincts conduced toward the light."

The poet and ardent abolitionist Antônio de Castro Alves, for six months a classmate of Nabuco and Rui, was as symptomatic of his era as Alvares de Azevedo had been of his. The earlier poet was introverted, chary of notoriety, diligent and in love only with women of his dreams. Castro Alves was impetuous, self-assertive, neglectful of classes, given to public declamation and to incessant amours. If, returning to Mr. Tate's analysis of romanticism, Alvares de Azevedo is the Shelley who becomes spiritually impotent before a scientific world and "falls upon the thorns of life," then Castro Alves leans toward an alternative solution. With the "crude, physical imagination" of a Tennyson he "enjoys something like the efficient optimism of science; he asks us to believe that a rearrangement of the external relations of man will not alone make him a little more comfortable, but will remove the whole problem of evil, and usher in perfection."

The following letter written by Castro Alves from São Paulo in 1868 shows how the city's romantic mystery had become the mere backdrop for a salvational crusade:

You find me in São Paulo, land of Azevedo, beautiful city of mists and mantillas, the soil that weds Heidelberg to Andalusia.

We sons of the north . . . dream of São Paulo as the oasis of liberty and of poetry. . . . If poetry lies in smoking up the room with the classic cigar while outside the wind smokes up space . . . with a still more classic *garôa;* if poetry lies in black eyes peeping through the balcony blinds or through the lace of the mantilla . . . then São Paulo is the land of poetry.

. . . As for liberty . . . I tend to prefer São Paulo to Recife. . . .

I should tell you that my *Slaves* are nearly ready. Do you know how the poem ends? (I owe São Paulo this inspiration.) It ends at the crest of the *serra de Cubatão,* as dawn breaks over America, while the morning star (Christ's tear for the captives) dies gradually out in the west. It is a song of the future. The song of hope.

One day in 1868 while Castro Alves was hunting near the city, an accidental discharge of his rifle caused a wound that within three years claimed his life. It seemed almost as if the little agrarian town had made, as it passed into history, a final gesture of protest against this northern "condor," as he has been called, and his apocalyptic vision of social justice.

By 1870, then, the city appeared to harbor only certain romanticist ideals and to have forfeited the broad (if somewhat ill-defined) eclecticism that had been counseled by Alvares de Azevedo. Refinement—as purveyed by French coiffeurs and hotelkeepers—and progress—as represented by the English railroad which in 1868 linked São Paulo and Santos—seemed simpler and more readily attainable commodities than the romanticists had imagined. Social and political issues were resolved into the formulae of campaign oratory. The achievement, within the next twenty years, of two of the liberals' principal ideals—abolition of slavery and of monarchical government—was to leave an ideological vacuum rather than directing attention to more complex concerns. Intellectual apathy, however, went unnoticed by *paulistas* owing to the stir and clamor which attended the fulfilment of material progress.

The surge of city growth began in the 1880's. Between 1886 and 1893 the population increased three fold, from 44,030 to 129,409. Railways, fanning out from São Paulo, gave it dominion over a farflung coffee frontier. Coffee wealth subsidized the advent of tens of thousands of European immigrants, many of whom were drawn to the *paulista* capital, where nascent industries and rapid urbanization offered livelier promises than did the *fazendas.* In short, the city now exhibited a complex of energies which guaranteed it the hallmarks of a metropolis: industry, commerce, public utilities, banking, ornamental parks and buildings, cultural diversions and a fast-expanding populace. Little demand existed for the political and philosophic speculation of earlier decades—except perhaps when fragments of federalist theory were exhumed to chide the government for siphoning off *paulista* wealth. So confident was the city of the rewards and inevitability of its progress that, in contrast to Rio de Janeiro, it scarcely offered a foothold to the formal cult of positivism.

When, after a thirty-year absence, the former law student "Junius" returned to São Paulo in 1882, he was struck by its quick, noisy tempo of life. Earlier, at mid-century, upper-class families had entered the streets only to attend church or to make formal visits, and were always escorted by the paterfamilias. Cafés did not exist, and if a youth went to a restaurant for beer or even "agua com assucar," he was held as extravagant and perhaps immoral. So few were the carriages that citizens hurried to their windows to identify the owner of any that passed. Now, however, in 1882, there were countless pedestrians, including unescorted ladies, and the streets reverberated with the constant passage of streetcars. Junius was amazed by the profusion of shops and the luxury of their wares; by the availability of toys and musical instruments, foreign wines and tobacco, foreign books and journals; by the ease with which man or woman could acquire a complete Parisian wardrobe or grooming; by the resplendent Grande Hotel, which had no equal in Brazil and was reminiscent of Europe's best. He was impressed by the new suburbs, railways, public buildings and the illumination and activity of streets after dark.

The change which had come over the city is further pointed up in the comments of two travelers, made some fifty years apart. In 1855 the American J. C. Fletcher ascribed "a more intellectual and a less commercial air" to São Paulo, where "you do not hear the word *dinheiro* constantly ringing in your ear, as at Rio de Janeiro." In 1909 the Frenchman Denis remarked that: "The society of São Paulo is less given to literature, diction and eloquence than that of Rio; though one feels it to be more active, São Paulo is not the capital of Brazilian letters. It is impassioned over economic questions."

With the passage of urban Brazil into the republican era Gilberto Freyre associates a denial of the humanistic and intimately experienced Afro-Portuguese heritage. Family heirlooms of silver and jacarandá were auctioned off to foreigners and replaced by more modish acquisitions from Europe. "The bad Portuguese habits of picking the teeth in public and of spitting noisily on the floor" were outlawed by a new Frenchified élite. Classics and humanities yielded to practical, technical disciplines. Children were baptized Newton, Jefferson and Edison instead of Ulysses, Demosthenes and Cicero. Harsh English words like "trust," "funding-loan" and "deficit" were injected into vocabulary. One spoke of the abstract complexities of coffee valorization, but no longer of the "valorization of the Brazilian man—of the man and of the people."

In such an atmosphere cultural pursuits were subordinated to the order of material progress, becoming an adjunct rather than a dimension of city life. Practitioners of the arts were often professional virtuosi from Europe, who, as dramatic and operatic performers for example, left students and townspeople in only a spectator's rôle. To patronize the arts was an emblem of social distinction or, at best, a sentimental indulgence. In 1887 dilettantes were reported to have arrived at a concert of chamber music in São Paulo "with plenty of strong coffee in their stomachs to resist the temptations of Morpheus [*sic!*], God of classical music." They were "deeply versed in dissonant harmonies; all of them perform a duet with the players, for if the latter play some Hungarian hodgepodge in Ti, the former with falsetto voices snore in Sol."

Art served to advertise wealth, as did the palatial but hybrid styles of the new residences (*palacetes*) along aristocratic Avenida Paulista. By the 1870's the time-honored *taipa* construction was looked upon as drab and rustic, and use of the once-romantic *rótula* was officially banned. By the next decade, as the architect Ricardo Severo later recalled, immigrant Italian stuccoers were introducing:

. . . sculptured ornament applied to completely smooth façades without dis-cretion, architectural composition or minimal esthetic sense. . . .
   The thread of tradition was wholly lost in the eclectic labyrinth of foreign influences. . . . Heed was no longer paid to the physical milieu and the oro-graphic conformation of its terrain and local countryside, to the social scene with its uses and customs, its habits of family and collective life; and the structural forms inherent in the materials of the country were not forthrightly developed.

The tycoon of this new architecture was Francisco de Paula Ramos de Azevedo (1851–1928). More engineer than architect, more entrepreneur than engineer, Ramos de Azevedo, with his associates, set up a dictatorship over the city's taste that has only recently begun to crumble; his "style" was pinchbeck, derivative and best described as promiscuous eclecticism with leanings toward the Renaissance. The ostentatious way of life for which the *palacete* stood is depicted in the daydreams of Lenita, the sen-sual heroine of Júlio Ribeiro's *A carne* (1887); the novel itself, a social-Darwinian jeremiad lacking art or compassion, is indicative of the times.

The burgeoning metropolis which has been described soon engulfed the once-prominent student body of the Law Academy. The *bacharel* degree, now a mere entrée to a niche in the bureaucratic urban order, no longer entailed pioneer responsibilities for marking out horizons of na-tional life. As one professor remarked in 1888, most students hoped only for "legal admission into certain careers," some going so far as to yield all faith in their own abilities and place all hope in "nepotism and political protection."

Student writers of the 1880's formed beer-drinking cliques, displayed studied eccentricities and produced languid poetry of an escapist or orna-mental nature. Until well into the twentieth century their literary circles were characterized by bohemian affectation. Such a group was that of Ricardo Mendes Gonçalves of the class of 1905, who lived in a yellow chalet called *O Minarete* with the future writer and publicist José Bento Monteiro Lobato, the future anthropologist Arthur Ramos and other young literati. They were known as "a cainçalha," Gonçalves was "o cão que ladra à lua," and none—in their student days at least—showed traces of the *modernismo* which is now to be discussed.

It was, according to Mário de Andrade, in about 1916 that "the conviction of a new art" came to "a little group of *paulista* intellectuals." Perhaps the single most stimulating influence was the exhibit in that year of the bold expressionist paintings of the young artist Anita Malfatti, who had just returned from Europe and from studies in the United States. It was not long before another painter, Emiliano di Cavalcanti, the poet Guilherme de Almeida and the novelist Oswald de Andrade were holding daily conversations in the bookstore *O Livro*. Soon others joined them. Authors read new poems and books; more exhibits were held; musicians played new compositions. And the idea of the public sessions that were organized in February, 1922, as the *Semana de Arte Moderna* gradually took shape.

The *Semana* represented the efforts of a group of young men and women who, with diverse media and outlooks, had found a common enterprise in trying to penetrate and render into form the flux of modern life. Most or all of them had been born since 1890 and were thus the first generation to have experienced São Paulo as a metropolis from their earliest years. Although certain of them eventually defined the artist's social mission with uncompromising rigidity, one of the *modernistas'* primary services was to reincorporate art and society. Art, as indicated above, had come to mean virtuosity; the virtuoso was isolated from his milieu by a routinized vision of it and from fellow artists by the competitiveness of their interchangeable talents. The *modernistas* were once again, like the romanticists of 1850, artists-in-community. During the early years "we were really pure and free, disinterested," Mário de Andrade later wrote. "No one thought of sacrifice, no one treasured the unintelligible, no one imagined himself precursor or martyr."

The *Semana* was celebrated in the Municipal Theater, an imitation of the Parisian *Opéra* which stood for the very cultural attitudes that *modernismo* sought to explode. A few offerings, such as the piano-playing of Guiomar de Novaes and the music of the young composer Heitor Vila Lôbos, were appreciatively received by the public. Writers and painters, however, elicited a furore reminiscent of New York's Armory Show of 1913. Scandalous gossip about them was invented and circulated. Canvases by Lasar Segall—a young Russian-born, German-trained expressionist who had first exhibited in São Paulo in 1913—and by Anita Malfatti were attacked with canes. Readings by poets and novelists were rendered inaudible by hoots and catcalls. *O Estado de São Paulo* suggested that the *modernistas* had planted claques to aggravate the uproar, and, certainly, the poet Menotti del Picchia went out of his way to provoke tumult in a speech that began:

The automobiles of the planets career dizzily along the highway of the Milky Way. . . . The constellations play in a jazzband of light, syncopating the harmonic dance of the spheres. The sky seems a huge electric billboard that God set up on high to advertise for eternity His omnipotence and glory.

... This is the style that traditionalists expect of us. ... What an error! Nothing more orderly and peaceful than this vanguard group, freed of traditional totemism, alive to the policed, American life of today.

What was striking about the young *modernistas* was not, however, their insolence and iconoclasm but their self-consciousness and missionary dedication. This was reflected in their first literary review, which referred to the *Semana* as a medical necessity: "Damp, chilled, rheumatic with a tradition of artistic tears, we made up our minds. Surgical operation. Excision of the lachrymal glands."

That the 1922 group had not been doctrinally or stylistically unified was evident after 1924, when manifestoes and magazines of such cliques as *Pau Brasil*, *Verdamarelismo* and *Antropofagia* began to counteract European currents with nativist and nationalist appeals. As 1930 drew near and political restlessness increased, artistic programs were infiltrated by political credos. Novels by such writers as the self-styled "mural" novelist Oswald de Andrade and fascist-oriented Plínio Salgado challenged the supremacy initially enjoyed by poetry, since they were better vehicles for social concern.

After 1930 it is hard to speak of *modernismo* as a single phenomenon. Even among the non-political, the ramification of interest and emphasis became extreme. There were nativists, Europeanizers, Americanizers. Some continued to shock the bourgeois; others courted the underprivileged; others created worlds of private symbolism. There was increasing exchange with other cultural regions of Brazil. There was interplay between the arts and research disciplines. For many, *modernismo* became social anthropology; recovery of neglected folklore; study of Brazil's social, economic and political institutions; ethnology and philology; or literary criticism. The philosophically inclined were attracted to the less schematic, less deterministic systems (notably the Germanic thought diffused by Ortega y Gasset) and to an eclectic, historically oriented quest for a Brazilian "ontology." Still another *modernista* concern was with rehabilitating and preserving documents, art works and architecture of the past, a task in large part assumed by the local branch of the Serviço do Patrimônio Histórico e Artístico Nacional.

Those who kept to artistic creativity displayed similar diversity. Of one salon of painters in the 1930's the critic Sérgio Milliet said that it represented "a state of spirit" rather than "a school." "And that state of spirit," he pointed out, "is that of our contradictory century, pained and joyful, troubled and mystical, disillusionsed but nonetheless constructive." Likewise the literary reviews assumed an attitude of serious, pluralistic inquiry. In 1941 *Clima* announced its title to signify a " 'climate' of curiosity, interest and intellectual ventilation." The editors had multifarious interests but looked beyond the encyclopedism of positivists and evolutionists; they hoped to mediate among the realms of the modern mind and to avoid facile systematizing. This exploratory, self-critical phase of *modernismo* was in some measure a response to an atmosphere of world crisis and to the disillusion engendered by the inadequate leadership and ideals of the *paulista* Revolution of 1932.

Though virtually unrepresented at the *Semana de Arte Moderna*, architecture has in recent years come to be the clearest manifestation of the urban, social dimensions of *modernismo*. By the 1930's, following the example of Rino Levi and Austrian-born Bernardo Rudofsky, architects began to discriminate among modern techniques and solutions from abroad with an eye to the particular needs of São Paulo. Cinemas, hospitals and workers' communities were boldly designed for the comfort and movement of large concentrations of people. Attention was paid to the seasonal cold which distinguishes the climate from that of Rio de Janeiro, and buildings were faced to catch the afternoon rather than the morning sun. Office and apartment skyscrapers were stripped of stuccoed embellishment, and the structures made possible by the lightness and flexibility of reinforced concrete were increasingly explored. Walls came to be thought of not as unwieldy supports of brick but as ductile partitions, or as an epidermis mediating between living-space and outer environment.

Levi and Rudofsky have designed private residences that are as striking as the public buildings—with their sliding partitions that allow house and garden to interpenetrate; their modulations of contour, volume and light; their accentuation of regional building materials; and their plain walls, set off by the shifting outlines of semi-tropical foliage. It might almost be said that the handsome country *chácara* of a century ago has been recreated in the idiom of the modern age.

The *modernista* movement, becoming ever more labyrinthine, may be said to have lasted some twenty-five years; its terminus was perhaps marked by the death of Mário de Andrade in 1945, or perhaps by the appearance of a group of young poets whose skilled, hermetic verse has been advertised as *neo-modernista*. One cannot say, however, that *modernismo* has been "superseded." Like romanticism, it was a "state of spirit," not a body of dogma, and therefore an open, not a closed system. And, it may be surmised, the roots of *modernismo* are more deeply struck than were those of romanticism; its ramifications have been more diverse and conscientiously explored. It appears to be a threshold to cultural maturity, and to an era of organic, less spasmodic cultural change.

Although São Paulo was not exclusively the cradle of *modernismo*, the city and its *Semana* imparted a spirit and impetus to the movement. The critic Alceu Amoroso Lima explains this, first, by pointing out that *modernismo*—with its "esthetics of noise, color, light, movement, raucous impression, protest, scandal, rupture with the obsolete and established"— reintegrates art into modern life. He then identifies São Paulo as the Brazilian city in which artists were most fully dominated by components of this life:

. . . motor, asphalt, radio, tumult, rumor, open-air life, great masses, big effects, the cinema carried into the other realms of art and stamping them with its esthetics of splintered reality, imagistic illusion, superposition and distortion of forms, primacy of technique over nature and of rational or irrational effect over nostalgic and lyrical inclination.

Rio de Janeiro was inhibited from sudden renovation by the leisurely, self-satisfied internationalism of its élite and by the forkloric "ruralism" of its common people. São Paulo had international affinities which were not inherited and official, which shared the immediacy of its trade and industry. The city, moreover, was oriented by tradition and economy to a broad hinterland, rather than to a colorful, circumscribed region. The *paulista* mind, as was earlier suggested, is less preconditioned, more free to select and to sympathize. It is a paradox, though not a puzzling one, that São Paulo, perhaps the country's least "picturesque" city, should sponsor the most urgent inquiries into Brazilian culture.

Social factors are also to be considered. Commercial, materialist, fast-moving São Paulo had produced the cautious, literal-minded subject of Mário de Andrade's "Ode ao burguês" (1920):

> Eu insulto o burguês! o burguês-níquel,
> O burguês-burguês!
> A digestão bem feita de São Paulo!
> O homem-curva! o homem-nádegas!

This creature, living with no margin of culture, confidence or humor, cannot risk being a loser and becomes the ideal, the inevitable target of the revolutionary. "Now in malicious Rio," wrote Mário, "an exhibit like that of Anita Malfatti might have caused a public stir but no one would have been carried away. In ingenuous São Paulo, it created a religion."

Along with the bourgeoisie and parvenus, moreover, São Paulo could boast a small aristocracy having the cultural self-assurance to patronize *modernismo*. Paulo Prado, himself an author and famous for his sardonic *Retrato do Brasil*, held Sunday gatherings of *modernistas* in his mansion on Avenida Higienópolis, and in 1924 he subsidized the magazine *Knock-out*, successor of *Klaxon*. Another aristocrat, Dona Olívia Guedes Penteado, maintained a similar salon, and a member of her family was the first to buy a painting from di Cavalcanti.

As long as the movement was supported solely by the indulgent rich, however, and until it found ways to strike roots in the lives of the people at large, *modernismo* could be little more than a cultural incrustation. Although official subsidies were available to a few modern artists soon after the *Semana*, the municipal government was in no way prepared, during the 1920's, to carry out an integrated cultural program. The city's contract with an Italian musical and dramatic company in 1926 made clear that bureaucrats still judged culture in terms of quantity, spectacle and

European affiliation. Mário de Andrade remonstrated that this troupe performed only worn-out *Toscas* and *Traviatas*, that it engaged incompetent
artists and that in any case the high admission charge turned away students
and the general public. "Let us cease that absurd pretension, the display
of luxury of the mere few and not of the city, simply because in its present
economic, intellectual and moral situation the city has no reason or wherewithal for showing off."

It was under the private auspices of publisher Monteiro Lobato,
rather than under official ones, that new cultural horizons were opened
to the public. Although Monteiro Lobato was not himself a full-fledged
modernista—as his caustic review of Anita Malfatti's early canvases, entitled "Paranoia or Cynicism," clearly revealed—he commanded a pungent,
ironic style for laying bare neglected problems of contemporary Brazil.
He first caught the public eye during World War I with a letter on page
one of *O Estado de São Paulo* which decried the effects of slash-and-burn
agriculture; his anemic, prototypical *caboclo* Jeca Tatu, created shortly
thereafter, was soon a household word. In 1920 he founded Monteiro Lobato
& Cia. and set about to develop a reading public and to disseminate books
by Brazilians. Within three years he had edited such younger, experimental
authors as Oswald de Andrade, Ribeiro Couto, Lima Barreto, Menotti del
Picchia, Guilherme de Almeida and Oliveira Vianna. The house failed
financially in 1925, but only after having created an audience for the new
generation of writers and given São Paulo's publishing industry an impetus
which was to bring it into rivalry with that of Rio de Janeiro. Book production in São Paulo state rose from 173,000 copies in 1926 to 2,300,000
in 1937; and by 1946 it had reached 6,700,000, in which year the state was
buying 40% of the volumes printed in Brazil.

Only after 1930 did public authorities begin to create institutions
which effectively answered both the cultural needs of the populace and
the outlook of the younger intelligentsia. One obvious task confronting
the state government was to provide a center for disciplined humanistic
and scientific studies that would take over functions abandoned by the
Faculty of Law. Although the Faculty itself had graduated a few *modernistas*, such as Guilherme de Almeida and Oswald de Andrade, it continued
to be censured during the first three decades of the century for having a
demoralized student body and for its rôle as an antechamber to the sordid
arena of political factionalism. In 1934 a *decreto estadual* created the University of São Paulo by uniting the law school and several other faculties.
Among them was a new Faculty of Philosophy, Sciences and Letters which,
with a distinguished staff of Brazilian and foreign professors, has become
one of Latin America's liveliest intellectual centers, and a source of well
qualified secondary-school teachers for the state. In 1946 a Faculty of
Economic and Administrative Sciences was established, largely designed
to redress the glaring deficiencies of public administration in Brazil. More
recently, São Paulo's well known School of Sociology and Politics, founded

in 1933 by a group of private firms and persons, has been made an "instituição complementar" of the University.

Another institution created in 1934 was the Departamento Municipal de Cultura, whose first director was Mário de Andrade. Among the many functions that the Departamento undertook were:

. . . holding contests for works in the fields of history, theater, folklore and music; organizing a municipal orchestra; developing educational cinema; installing a Brazilian record library and a *museu da palavra;* organizing popular orchestras and traditional *festas;* restoring and publishing São Paulo's historical documentation; and conducting commercial, economic, industrial and agricultural life of the people and, through playgrounds and "bibliotecas infantis," encouraging tourism.

Of particular interest to scholars are the Departamento's books and periodicals relating to *paulista* history, and the facilities of the modern, twenty-four-story Municipal Library, which is one of its dependencies. Mário de Andrade was himself primarily dedicated, however, to enriching the cultural life of the people and, through playgrounds and "bibliotecas infantis," that of their children. Although political pressures curtailed his plans, Mário's three years in office sufficed for him to prove that *modernismo* could be at home with the common man, and ably to develop new areas of municipal service in his behalf.

In his life and writings Mário de Andrade was the incarnation of *modernismo,* as Alvares de Azevedo had been of romanticism. He embodied its introspection and its social consciousness; its brooding narcissism and its carefree iconoclasm; its intellectual preciosity and its sidewalk slang and familiarity; its lyricism and its raucous barbarity; its nostalgia and its anti-traditionalism. Prose fiction, poetry, musicology, research into folkloric or scholarly themes, sociology, criticism of all the arts were each within his province. Mário was responsive to the cultures of Europe, the Americas, the regions of Brazil and to their interplay. His was preeminently a city mind, attuned to imperatives of the outer world, and free to range across and to interpret the things of Brazil. This city mind, moreover, gave a fixed center to his imagination: São Paulo. Milliet calls him: "Above all an urban poet, without a single rural landscape, without bucolic images, but immersed in city coal-smoke, pointing out factories and skyscrapers among the mists of his Piratininga." His poetry, Milliet continues, expresses a love grounded in psychological ambivalences and poignantly sublimated in the city which is still "adolescent, assuming form, hesitant between the feminine tenderness of certain cities like Paris and the masculine strength of others like Chicago."

The *modernista,* like the romanticist of a century ago, finds São Paulo to lack the salient traits of a Rio de Janeiro or Salvador. What conspicuously characterizes São Paulo—movement, speed, lights, traffic, skyscrapers, factories, money—is universal, with no explicit voice or design. To encounter the city's *genius loci* demands a particular sensitivity. Sometimes it is discovered in a small restaurant where students and *petits fonction-naires* chatter over a fragrant *feijoada* and coffee; or perhaps in the foreign *bairros*—among Japanese and Hungarians, Germans and Jews, Baltics and Spaniards, Portuguese and Turks—where laughter and rhythms of other lands, not yet wholly absorbed, lend the city an accent of mystery; perhaps in secular fragments of ancient beliefs, heterogeneously pooled in the common man's corpus of magical acts and phrases; perhaps in the ageless ditties (*trocinhas*) of children at play, perhaps in the impromptu *samba*, beaten out by bootblacks on their shoeboxes, bottles and tins; or perhaps in the anonymous ballad (*modinha*), slangy, unromantic, factual, journal-istic, rudely versifying the sensational crime or disaster—so different from the deftly satirical, politically conscious balladry of Rio de Janeiro.

Writers and artists appear to find that São Paulo offers an idiom con-genial to the elusive and many-dimensioned, partly bitter and partly yearn-ing quality of the modern world itself. One finds this idiom in the images of Mário de Andrade's verse: the city's winds and *garôa*, its April after-noons, its "millions of roses," its little seamstresses, its bulky streetcars, its never-finished "horrible cathedral made of pretty stones." One also finds it in the intense yet delicate "tonalities" of Segall's canvases which, accord-ing to the novelist Jorge Amado, reflect a mystery hidden in the city's bars, in the twilight of its Praça da República, in its quiet family suburbs with tree-lined streets. One finds it in the quick, allusive, catalectic Italo-Brazilian dialogue of Alcântara Machado's tales and sketches; in the wist-ful but vibrant lyricism, the shifting rhythms, the subtle polyphony of the music of Camargo Guarnieri—which contrast with the more telluric, sym-phonic mode of Rio's Vila Lôbos.

The folklorist Amadeu Amaral once made a distinction between the popular music of the *paulista* countrymen and that of urban balladeers. The former "lives in tradition and of tradition. It is simple, monotonous, plaintive." Its rhythm falls naturally in with the "ageless measure of seven-(or less commonly five-) syllable verses, arranged most of the time in regular strophes." The music of the city balladeer, however, is of the moment. It draws unpredictably on a host of traditions, and exhibits the diversity, freshness and early obsolescence of a world of flux and fashion. It is "complex, capricious, melodic, with a great variety of rhythms, compris-ing verses of every measure and strophes of every type."

Persons of an older generation had been unable to discern the vigor and relevance of the city's daily vernacular. Predisposed to a classical con-cept of "culture," one scholar, over thirty years ago, accused the city's com-mon man of "intentional, calculated and selfish disdain" for failing to com-memorate the exploits of the colonial *bandeiras* in popular Homeric epics. The work of the *modernistas* has been to reveal that, when man lives with a curtain between himself and the world of immediate experience, symbols and idiom for expression, and for coherent thought itself, will elude his grasp.

The degree of cultural awareness that has been achieved in modern São Paulo city is attested by the manner in which the fourth centenary of its founding in 1554 is being commemorated. Although there are those who criticized the extravagant and occasionally factitious nature of the festivities, one cannot fail to be impressed by the extent to which they center in the cultural order. The buildings for the four-hundred-acre fairgrounds were designed by such leading architects as Oscar Niemeyer and Eduardo Kneese de Mello. A film festival and a modern art show have been held in connection with the celebrations. A symphony orchestra and theater and ballet companies have been formed. Prizes have been offered for achievements in music, literature, history and science. A series of old and new works pertaining to the city's history is appearing as the *Biblioteca do IV Centenario*. Some twenty international cultural and scientific congresses are being held in the city during 1954.

Much has been written about the "decadence" of metropolitan life and, with particular relevance to Latin America, about the political and socio-economic disruption created by large cities in agrarian societies. São Paulo's quadricentennial celebrations are a reminder, however, that only through cities are the highest forms of cultural expression attained, and that only with the knowledge and vision acquired through urban institutions may the insistent problems of agrarian Latin America be effectively addressed.

Recent Articles on Historiography

Arnade, Charles W. "The Historiography of Colonial and Modern Bolivia." XLII (1962), 333-384.

Barager, Joseph R. "The Historiography of the Río de la Plata Area Since 1830." XXXIX (1959), 588-642.

Bishko, Charles Julian. "The Iberian Background of Latin American History: Recent Progress and Continuing Problems." XXXVI (1956), 50-80.

Corbitt, Duvon C. "Cuban Revisionist Interpretations of Cuba's Struggle for Independence." XLIII (1963), 395-404.

Griffin, Charles C. "Francisco Encina and Revisionism in Chilean History." XXXVII (1957), 1-28.

Griffith, William J. "The Historiography of Central America since 1830." XL (1960), 548-569.

Hoffmann, Fritz L. "Perón and After." XXXVI (1956), 510-528; XXXIX (1959), 212-233.

Humphreys, R. A. "The Historiography of Spanish American Revolutions." XXXVI (1956), 81-93.

Lavretskii, I. R. "A Survey of the Hispanic American Historical Review, 1956-1958." XL (1960), 340-360.

Oswald, J. Gregory. "A Soviet Criticism of the Hispanic American Historical Review." XL (1960), 337-339.

Potash, Robert A. "The Historiography of Mexico Since 1821." XL (1960), 383-424.

Ross, Stanley Robert. "Bibliography of Sources for Contemporary Mexican History." XXXIX (1959), 234-238.

Stein, Stanley J. "The Historiography of Brazil, 1808-1889." XL (1960), 234-278.

———. "The Tasks Ahead for Latin American Historians." XLI (1961), 424-433.

Smith, Robert Freeman. "Twentieth-Century Cuban Historiography." XLIV (1964), 44-73.

Szászdi, Adam. "The Historiography of the Republic of Ecuador." XLIV (1964), 503-550.

Walne, Peter. "Guide to Sources for the History of Latin America, British Volume." XLIV (1964), 375-276.

The Staff of the *Hispanic American Historical Review*

Managing Editors

James Alexander Robertson	1918–1939
John Tate Lanning	1939–1944
James F. King	1945–1949
Charles C. Griffin	1949–1954
Lewis Hanke	1954–1960
Donald C. Worcester	1960–1965
Robert E. Quirk	1966–

Board of Editors *(August 1965)*

C. J. Bishko	University of Virginia
Fritz L. Hoffmann	University of Colorado
John J. Johnson	Stanford University
Edwin Lieuwen	University of New Mexico
Lyle N. McAlister	University of Florida
Richard M. Morse	Yale University
John H. Parry	University College of Swansea, Wales
James J. Parsons	University of California, Berkeley
John L. Phelan	University of Wisconsin
Robert A. Potash	University of Massachusetts
Stanley R. Ross	State University of New York

Advisory Editors *(August 1965)*

Charles C. Griffin	Vassar College
George P. Hammond	University of California, Berkeley
Lewis Hanke	Columbia University
John Tate Lanning	Duke University
Irving A. Leonard	University of Michigan

Dana G. Munro	Princeton University
J. Fred Rippy	Durham, North Carolina
France V. Scholes	University of New Mexico
Lesley B. Simpson	University of California, Berkeley
Arthur P. Whitaker	University of Pennsylvania